SELF AND INNER GROWTH

About the Authors

Dr. Salma Seth is a Professor of Psychology in the Department of Applied Psychology of Vivekananda College, University of Delhi (India). She has been taking innovative initiatives in the teaching-learning process with the students for more than three decades now. She is, also, using her acumenship in supervising Ph.D. scholars in their research in psychology. Dr. Seth being a prolific writer has co-edited the book, *The Psychological Realm: An Introduction* and is the author of the books, *Counselling Skills: Knowing Self and Others* and *Qualitative Methods: A Practical Journey into Research*. She has written a few book chapters, book reviews, and research papers which have been published in both national and international journals. Dr. Seth is making a humble attempt and is passionate about extending her services to counselling students and is sensitive towards the students' deep and manifold needs as they struggle to fulfil their Self.

Professor Emeritus N.K. Chadha is the former Head, Department of Psychology,University of Delhi (India); former Director and Head, Department of Adult, Continuing Education and Extension; and Chairman, Board of Research Studies in Humanities and Social Sciences, University of Delhi (India). For five consecutive years, he was on the Panel of Judge for PM's Trophy for the Steel Industries and the Cabinet Secretariat, Government of India. He was the senior consultant to UNDP on career development.

Professor Chadha had been teaching in the Department of Psychology, University of Delhi since 1982. He has authored several books which are referred as textbooks in many universities in India and abroad at undergraduate, postgraduate level, and for research. He has also co-authored the book with John Van Willigen,University of Kentucky, USA entitled, *Social Aging in a Delhi Neighbourhood*. He has been conducting many ongoing research projects with foreign universities and has carried out a number of major interdisciplinary and collaborative projects. He has published more than 120 articles in various scientific national and international journals which are often quoted by other researchers. He is on the management bodies of many institutes in India and abroad. He was invited by the UN to attend expert's group meeting in UN headquarter on family issues.

He has travelled extensively and delivered lectures in UK, USA, Spain, Hungary, Sweden, Malta, Germany, France, Canada, New Zealand, Hong Kong, Australia, Singapore, Taipei, Japan, UAE, China, Columbia, South Africa, Philippines, and Vietnam. He is involved in the development of standardized psychological test for many Multinational Companies and Public Sector Companies for the purpose of recruitment and selection of middle and higher management levels. He is one of the leading psychometricians in India and his book on *Applied Psychometry* (Sage) is widely used by the students and practitioners of psychological assessment.

Professor Chadha is the President of the India Career Development Association and also of the Indian Association of Positive Psychology. He is the former President of the Asia Pacific Career Development Association, Maryland, USA.

Professor Chadha was awarded the National Career Development Association (USA) presidential award on 28 June 2017 at Orlando, USA and Global Practitioner of the Year 2015 on 30 June 2015 during the annual conference held at Denver, USA. He has received the Lifetime Achievement Award by the Asia Pacific Career Development Association during its annual meeting held on 22 May 2019 in Vietnam.

Recently, has taken the responsibility of President, International Career Coach Association, USA, and advisor at SGT University, India.

SELF AND INNER GROWTH
Eastern Perspectives and Traditions

Salma Seth
N.K. Chadha

CONCEPT PUBLISHING COMPANY PVT. LTD.
NEW DELHI - 110 059

ISBN: 978-93-6344-505-5

First Published 2025

Published and Printed by

Since 1974

Concept Publishing Company Pvt. Ltd.
A/15-16, Commercial Block, Mohan Garden
New Delhi-110059 (India)
T: +91-11-41101460
E: publishing@conceptpub.com, *W*: www.conceptpub.com

Cataloging in Publication--Courtesy: D.K. Agencies (P) Ltd. <docinfo@dkagencies.com>

Seth, Salma, author.
Self and inner growth : eastern perspectives and traditions / Salma Seth, N.K. Chadha.
pages cm
Includes bibliographical references and index.
ISBN 9789363445055

1. Self-perception. 2. Self. 3. Spiritual life. 4. Philosophy--Psychological aspects. 5. Psychology--India. I. Chadha, N. K., author. II. Title.

LCC | DDC

ETERNAL UNIVERSITY
(WORLD PEACE THROUGH VALUE BASED EDUCATION)
Established under the Himachal Pradesh Government Act No. 3 of 2009. Recognized by UGC, ICAR, AICTE, INC, NCTE, DSIR, DRDO and NAAC Accredited

Foreword

The academic scenario is changing in India. The scientific community is better prepared now than in the past to accept psychology rooted in native wisdom and philosophical traditions. Psychologists in India and the East are increasingly aware of the gap between their academic pursuits and the real-life problems of people. Eastern psychologists want to break free from the theoretical and methodological constraints of the discipline to grapple with the real issues of development and to act as social catalysts in the change process.

Eastern perspectives and traditions have been derived from indigenous thought systems and are best suited to address specific psychological issues and problems. Researchers have focused on the contemporary relevance of cultural heritage and native theories.

Eastern psychology has developed around the existential quest to overcome human suffering and in the process to raise the person to higher levels of awareness, achievement, and collective evolution. Also, to explore the methods and means of transforming the person in pursuit of perfection in being, certainty in knowing, and happiness in feeling. Indian Psychology, or more appropriately "psychology of Indian origin" focuses on the inner self, which is accessible through subjective methods of self-verification. It has its distinct identity, that is, it can be deemed as universal, spiritual in its orientation, and is applied. With India emerging as a major economic power in the world, there is a renewed interest in Indian values, philosophies and practices, as well as in the strength and resilience of Indian society.

Against this backdrop, this book on *Self and Inner Growth: Eastern Perspectives and Traditions* would engage its readers and provide the academia with exciting possibilities.

A significant attempt is made to embrace Hindu practices, Integral psychology, Zen and Buddhist traditions, Islamic way of life, and Sufism, etc. in viewing the Self and its evolution. These Eastern Systems have been derived from careful observations of human experience. They are built on centuries of empirical observations of the psychological, physiological, and spiritual effects of a variety of ideas, attitudes, behaviours, and experiential exercises. These centuries-old systems are still relevant, still changing, and developing. The concluding chapter is, also, very engaging and resonates with my views of the convergence of Eastern with Western psychologies.

The authors' efforts are praiseworthy, and I am sure readers will benefit immensely from the new insights gained from this endeavour.

Prof. Jaswinder Singh
Vice-Chancellor, Eternal University
HP

BARU SAHIB, VIA RAJGARH, DISTT. SIRMOUR,
HIMACHAL PRADESH-173101 (INDIA)
Tele: 01799-276012, Fax: 01799-276006, Mob: +91-9805098724
E-mail: contact@eternaluniversity.edu.in Website: www. eternaluniversity.edu.in

Preface

Apart from its other achievements, the ancient Indian civilization undertook the most profound examination of the Self and inner growth that has ever been attempted anywhere. The entire process of *yoga*, particularly the system based on Patanjali's *Yogasutra*, developed a methodology for stilling the modifications of the mind. The *Bhagavad Gita* also contains specific instructions for stilling the mind, and thereby accessing the deeper reaches of our psyche. Psychology of Indian origin therefore has a firm base and a profound underlying philosophy.

Due largely to centuries of Western domination, we have tended to be unduly influenced by the West, even in the area of psychology. This is not in any way to denigrate the great breakthroughs of Western psychology, particularly those of Sigmund Freud and Carl Gustav Jung. Indeed, post-Jungian psychology, especially Transpersonal Psychology, which has developed in recent years in California and around the world, are welcome efforts to delve deeper into the self. What is really needed is a creative fusion between the Eastern traditions and the newer Western methodologies.

As they do in so many other areas, Sri Aurobindo's writings throw a flood of light upon various elements connected with the quest for the inner light. He has used Vedic symbolism to postulate a highly original interpretation, which places Indian thought at the heart of the entire study. It is important that Indian insights become part of mainstream psychology around the world, and not be treated merely as an esoteric phenomenon.

An attempt is being made in this book on *Self and Inner Growth: Eastern Perspectives and Traditions* to bring together a broad and rich spectrum of knowledge, practices and dealing with various aspects of psychology. I hope this book will be of great value to students and scholars.

Recent research on the brain and the mind-brain relationship has thrown fascinating light upon how the human mind functions. Indian psychology, of course, goes beyond the mind into what we would call the spiritual centre of our being. The co-relation of these various elements and dimensions represent a fascinating field of study.

Living as we are in age of great stress and tension, the psychological aspects of human welfare and individual happiness, more so post-COVID-19 globally, can no longer be neglected. I take great pleasure in writing this book, also, for the general reader interested in delving deeper into the marvels and transformations of self and inner growth.

Salma Seth

Acknowledgments

With immense faith in the Divine, I pursued working on this book as a "seeker" – as the one who acknowledges that one knows very little, as the one who was always willing to know, one who made attempts at being non-judgmental and open-minded, one who was totally committed to the path, and one who had an abundance of patience and perseverance. During this journey of seeking, the significance of those who are a part of my life dawned on me and as I proceeded many more became a part. I refer to all of them as *guru* who took me beyond the intellect to the realm of being. It was a journey from the head to the heart. They illuminated my intellect, touched my heart, and provided practical guidance and brought love and laughter. How can I adequately thank them all, because to thank them implies separation? When you say "thank you" you complete something. You are finishing a transaction, a relationship, a process. Deep within there is no need to thank because there is Oneness. Does one hand thank the other? There is no "other" to be thanked. These *guru* made me realise that knowledge is a burden if it robs you of your innocence, if it makes you feel you are special, if it gives you an idea that you are wise, if it is not integrated into life, if it does not bring you joy, and knowledge is a burden if it does not set you free.

Vandeham sacchidanadam bhedatitam jagadgurum
Nityam purnam nirakaram
Nirgunam svatmasrva sasthitam

Asato ma sadgamaya
Tamso ma jyotirgamaya
Mrityor ma Amritamgamaya
OM
Shanti Shanti Shantihi

I bow down to the Universal Teacher
Who is Absolute Truth, Pure Consciousness, and Bliss
Who is beyond all differences
Who is ever Full, without attributes, formless
Who is all-pervading and ever centred in the Self.
Lead me from unreality to reality
Lead me from darkness to light
Lead me from death to immortality

I humbly dedicate this endeavour to my beloved parents.

Salma Seth

Contents

1

Self, Culture, Gender and Inner Growth

The self is first and foremost the collection of beliefs that we hold about ourselves. What are our important characteristics? What are we good at? What do we do poorly? What kinds of situations do we prefer or avoid? One person may think of herself as a black women who plans to become a sociology professor. Another might think of himself as not academically inclined but good at most sports. A third person may think of herself primarily in terms of a future goal, such as the desire to become the biggest real-estate Mogul in the Midwest. The set of beliefs we hold about who we are is called the self-concept.

Often we have a clear idea of who we are, whereas at other times we hold self doubts and confusion and feel we are buffeted by external pressures and evaluations by others. This distinction refers to self-concept clarity and a sense of self that is clearly and confidently defined, providing a coherent sense of direction (Campbell, 1990; Kernis, Paradise, Whitaker, Whe*ātman*, and Goldman, 2000).

Self-esteem is the evaluation we make of ourselves. That is, we are concerned not only with what we are like but also with how we value these qualities.

People with high self-esteem have a clear sense of what their personal qualities are. They think well of themselves, set appropriate goals, use feedback in a self-enhancing manner, savour their positive experiences (Wood, Heimpel, and Michela, 2003), and cope successfully with difficult situations. For example, when people with high self-esteem receive feedback implying that they have been rejected by others, they are more likely than those with low self-esteem to respond by reminding themselves of their positive qualities or by persisting at an alternative goal (Sommer and Baumeister, 2002). And conveniently, people with high self-esteem remember their daily experiences more favourably—a memory bias that may itself strengthen high self-esteem (Christensen, Wood, and Barrett, 2003).

In addition to our overall sense of self-esteem, we hold specific evaluations of our abilities in particular areas. Pooja may think well of herself generally but may know that she is not very diplomatic and not very talented artistically. Dinesh may generally think poorly of himself but know that he is organised and a good pianist. Two dimentions that are central to self-esteem are self-competence and self-liking, that is, evalautions of ourselves as capable and personal fondness for the self (Tafarodi, Marshall, and Milne, 2003). The importance and value we attach to these more specific self-views also influence global feelings of self-worth. That is, people are selective about the domains on which they base their self-worth. For one person, being attractive might be important; for another person, being smart might be more important (Crocker and Luhtanen, 2003).

For the most part, researchers have studied people's explicit self-esteem, that is, the concrete positive or negative evaluations they make of themselves. But more research suggests the importance of implicit self-esteem as well (Greenwald and Banaji, 1995; Greenwald and Farnham, 2000). Implicit self-esteem refers to the less conscious evaluations we make of ourselves. Studies of implicit self-esteem sometimes reveal things that studies of explicit self-esteem do not (Egloff and Schmukle, 2002; Woike, Mcleod, and Goggin, 2003). For example, implicit self-esteem seems to be more sensitive than explicit self-esteem to the specific situation a person is in (Bosson, Swann and Pennebaker, 2000; Dijksterhuis, 2004).

As we will see, one strong cultural difference is that Asians, especially the Japanese, are much less likely to answer explicit self-esteem scales in a self-enhancing manner. Instead, they report relatively modest self-esteem. However, in a test of implicit self-esteem (Kitayama and Karasawa, 1997), Japanese students were found to hold a preference for alphabetical letters contained in their own names over letters that were not in their names. They were also found to prefer numbers that corresponded to the month or the day of their birthdays over numbers that did not appear in their birthdays. These measures of implicit self-esteem, then suggested a self-enhancing quality that the students did not acknowledge more directly.

How does a sense of self develop? One of the most influential theories of how the self develops was put forth by Erik Erikson (1963), who argued for a stage theory of ego development.He maintained that although identity formation is a lifelong task (Whitborne, Zuschlag, Elliot, and Waterman, 1992), it is of critical importance during adolescence and young adulthood. This time, when identity begins to come together, marks the transition between childhood and adulthood. Erikson (1963) believed that the goal of this process is "the ability to experience one's self as something that has continuity and sameness, and to act accordingly". Once the young adult has acquired a firm sense of identity, s/he has a basis for making job or career plans and for establishing intimate relationships.

Although Erikson was no doubt correct in his assessment of adolescence and young adulthood as pivotal times for developing a sense of self, it would be false to claim that the sense develops and is maintained only or primarily during this time. The sense of self begins in infancy with the recognition that one is a separate individual (Butterworth, 1992; Pervin, 1992). Very young children have fairly clear concepts of their personal qualities and what they do or don't do well. Moreover, many changes occur in middle and late adulthood that may influence the self-conceptions that people hold. Thus, although psychologists continue to believe that Erikson was essentially right when he argued that issues of identity are especially important in adolescence and young adulthood, it is also clearly the case that the development of a personal sense of self is a lifelong process that begins in childhood and never truly ends.

Self and Culture

Cross-cultural research suggests that concepts of the self vary greatly, depending on one's culture (Rhee, Uleman, Lee and Roman, 1995; Triandis, McCusker, and Hui, 1990). In an investigation of this point, Markus and Kitayama (1991) explicitly contrasted American culture with Japanese culture to illustrate the substantial differences in self-conceptions that may exist between Western and Eastern cultures.

In America, there is a strong emphasis on individuality and how one can best distinguish one self from others by discovering and making use of one's unique talents. This independent self "a bounded, unique, more or less integrated motivational and cognitive universe, a dynamic centre of awareness, emotion, judgement, action, organised into a distinctive whole and set in contrast, both against other such wholes and against a social and natural background" (Geertz, 1974). Not only do Westerners construe the self as an independently functioning unit, but also they actually define independence as a fundamental task of socialisation. Westerners teach their children how to be independent (Kitayama, 1992).

The interdependent self of many Eastern, southern European, and Latin cultures consists of seeing oneself as part of an encompassing social relationship and realizing that one's behaviour is determined and dependent on what one perceives to be thoughts, feelings, and actions of others in the relationship (Markus and Kitayama, 1991). The self becomes meaningful and complete largely within the context of a social relationship, rather than through independent, autonomous action. Although the interdependent self is regarded as possessing a set of internal qualities, such as abilities or opinions, these attributes are thought to be situation specific and unstable, rather than defining characteristics of the self (Bochner, 1994; Cousins, 1989). Thus the interdependent self is not a bounded whole but changes its structure with the nature of the social context (Kanagawa, Cross, and Markus, 2001). In interdependent cultures, so fundamental is the emphasis on blending in that those attributes that uniquely differentiate one person from another are not regarded as particularly representative of the self. So, for example, although people from the United States would regard great musical talent in a child as a distinctive quality of that particular child, the Japanese might not.

The Western viewpoint regards the self as composed of individual attributes, such as ambition, good humour, or extraversion (Trafimow, Triandis, and Goto, 1991). These attributes are considered to be distinctively one's own, even when they are shared with others. A student, for example, may regard herself as creative, but this judgement is unrelated to judgements she might make about her roommate's creativity. Even if she regards both herself and her roommate as creative, her creativity is independent other roommate's, not shared. In contrast, the collectivist view of the interdependent self regards the individual not in terms of distinctive qualities, but in terms of those that are shared. Because people are regarded as fundamentally connected to each other, they are thought to have attributes in common rather attributes that they uniquely possess (Bochner, 1994;Trafimow *et al.*, 1991). Thus, two students might be creative interdependently and not independently. These different culture-based views of the self are illustrated in Fig. 1.1.

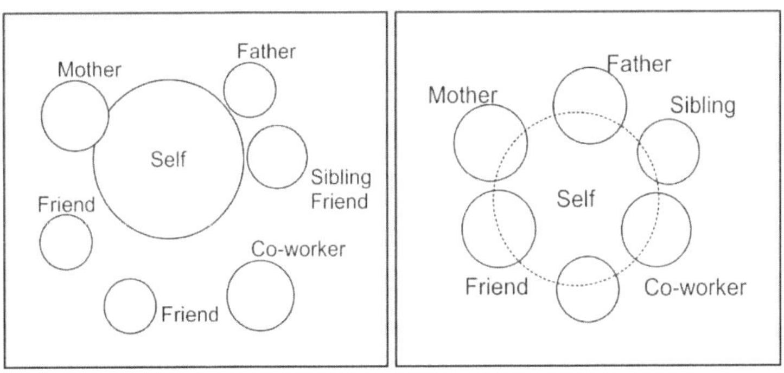

A. Independent Self B. Interdependent Self

Fig. 1.1: Modes of the self

Markus and Kitayama (1991, 1994) suggest that this conception of self as independent *vs.* interdependent is a fundamentally important aspect of an individual's self-system. It influences how people think about their own personal characteristics, how people relate to others, what emotions are experienced in different situations, and what motivates people to engage in action. Moreover, this cultural conception of the self becomes rooted in the ideas, value, and social scripts of a culture, further shaping individual experience and the expression of the self (Han and Shavitt, 1994; Markus and Kitayama, 1994). Table 1.1 shows items from a scale that assesses independence and interdependence. Which are you?

Table 1.1: The Measurement of Independent and Interdependent Self Construals

Indicate the extent to which you agree or disagree with each of the items below based on the following scale:

1	2	3	4	5	6	7
strongly disagree						strongly agree

1. I have respect for authority figures with whom I interact.
2. I am comfortable with being singled out for praise or rewards.
3. My happiness depends on the happiness of those around me.
4. Speaking up in class is not a problem for me.
5. I should take into consideration my parent's advice when making education and career plans.
6. My personal identity independent of others is very important to me.

If you answered "agree" on items 1, 3, and 5, you scored high in interdependence, whereas if you answered "agree" on items 2, 4, and 6, you scored high in independence. Note that the entire scale is longer than the excerpt above.

Source: T.M. Singelsis, *Personality and Social Psychology Bulletin*, 20(5): 580-91, copyright(C) 1994 by Sage Publications, Inc. Reprinted by permission of Sage Publication, Inc.

Independent and interdependent modes of self closely correspond to the individualism/collectivism syndrome. People in individualist cultures often give priority to their personal goals even when they conflict with the goals of important in-groups. Individualism is very high in the United States and is generally high in English-speaking countries (Hofstede, 1980). In collectivist culture, the self is defined in terms of membership in in-group, which influences a wide range of social behaviours. Collectivists are usually organised hierarchically and tend to be concerned about the results of their actions on members of their in-group. They share resources with in-group members, and feel interdependent and involved in their lives. A relationship orientation is very common. They tend to follow social norms and maintain normative or obligatory relationships (Sinha,1990; Sinha and Kanungo, 1997; Sinha and Verma, 1987).

The interdependent mode of self-construal questions the decontextualised individualistic view of self and locates self in the social-spiritual/divine context. Such a model is prevalent in Japan, Korea, China and India (Chao, 1995; Cousins, 1989; Kapur *et al.*, 2005; Mascolo and Bhatia, 2002; Misra, 2001; Roland, 1988; Singelis and Sharkey, 1995). It is held that self is inseparable from the surrounding context and people. The goal of self-development is not individuation but dissolving the self/other boundary. Such models assume that an individual is an open system who communicates with other selves.

To realise oneself is not to express the internal attributes but to become part of a group, community, and of divinity. Its strategies invite self-control and self-discipline. As *Yogasutra* proclaim, *yoga* (union) is the goal and controlling the mental functioning is its means (*yogaschittavrittinirodhah*).

The Indian self appears to be continuous with others, shares their space and is in immediate relation with them. The individual develops through participation in the unity of all things and it requires emphasis on diverse goals, which include engagement as well as dissociation and detainment. Interpersonal behaviour depends on the factors of role, place and relationship. Kakar (1978) has noted that the basic of relationship is mutual caring, involvement, and emotional affinity. Empirical studies of self-construal in the Indian context indicate greater prevalence of social identity (Dhawan *et al.*, 1995) and contextually in self-descriptions (Lalljee and Angelova, 1995). Misra and Giri (1995) observed that both interdependent as well as independent kinds of self-construal were present among Indians. In a study, Srivastava and Misra (1997) reported that the descriptions involving social identity were predominant over autonomous self-descriptions. It was also noted that independent and interdependent life goals were moderately positively related.

A number of researchers have noticed that there is a considerable degree of tolerance for dissonance and coexistence of disparate elements in the Indian world view and experience of self (Marriott, 1990; Ramanujan, 1990; Sinha *et al.*, 2001; Sinha and Pandey, 2007; Sinha and Tripathi, 1994; Tripathi and Leviatan, 2003; Varma, 2004). Shweder *et al.* (1997) have shown that the moral discourse in the Indian context is situated in the context of autonomy, community and divinity. Mascolo *et al.* (2004) found that individual and relational concepts of self were present both in Indian and American samples. The cultural differences arose in the specific ways the two nations were constructed. We, therefore, need to look within as well as between cultures. The indigenous Indian perspective on self goes beyond the dichotomies and presents an alternative model which would unfold in the subsequent chapter.

Culture, Cognition, Emotion, and Motivation

Different construals of the self have potentially important cognitive consequences. For example, those with an independent sense of self see themselves as distinctive. Although they may regard other people as like them, they do not regard themselves as similar to other people. In contrast, among those with interdependent selves, the self and others are considered part of a specific social context in which both are embedded. Thus, both self and others are construed as quite similar.

The factors underlying personal motivation to achieve may be different as well. For example, Americans tend to strive for personal achievement, whereas the Japanese tend to strive for the achievement of group goals. Personal choice of tasks or activities enhances motivation for those in the United States, whereas it has a lesser effect on Asian students' intrinsic motivation (Iyengar and Lepper, 1999). For example, European Americans are more likely to select a task if they think they will do well on it or have done well on it in the past, whereas Asians' choice of task is not based on such expectations or prior performance (Oishi and Diener, 2003).

Individualistic (or agentic) motives *vs.* interdependent (or communal) ones are even used to recognise information about the social world in memory (Woike, Gershkovich, Piorkowski, and Polo, 1999). People with independent self-construals are more likely to ignore the context in the inferences they draw about the social environment, whereas those with interdependent self-construals process social stimuli by paying attention to their relation to the context (Kuhnen, Hannover, and Schubert, 2001). For example, whereas North Americans often describe events in terms of the specific actors involved and their personal qualities, those with collectivist orientations are more likely to refer to the social groups to which those others belong (Menon, Morris, Chiu, and Hong, 1999).

People with independent *vs.* interdependent selves may experience fundamentally different kinds of emotions. Those with an independent sense of self, as found in U.S. culture, frequently experience ego-focused emotions, such as the experience of pride ("I did well") or frustration ("I was treated unfairly"). In contrast, cultures with interdependent conceptions of self tend to experience other-focused emotions. As an example, Markus and Kitayama (1991) use *amae* the Japanese word for the sense of being lovingly cared for and dependent on another's indulgence. *Amae* is the formation and maintenance of a mutually reciprocal interdependent relationship with another person. There is no equivalent for *amae* in the English language. The differences between independent and interdependent self-conceptions are summarised in Table 1.2.

Table 1.2: Summary of Key Differences Between an Independent and an Interdependent Perception of Self

Feature Compared	Independent	Interdependent
Definition	Separate from social context	Connected with social context
Structure	Bounded, unitary, stable	Flexible, variable
Important features	Internal, private (abilities, thoughts, feelings)	External, public (statuses, roles, relationships)
Tasks	Be unique Express self Realise internal attributes Promote own goals Be direct: Say what's on your mind	Belong, fit in Occupy one's proper place Engage in appropriate action Promote others' goals Be indirect: read other's mind

(*Contd.*)

Feature Compared	Independent	Interdependent
Role of others	Self—evaluation: others important for social comparison, reflected appraisal	Self—definition: self defined by relationships with others in specific contexts
Basis of self- esteem	Ability to express self; validate internal attributes	Ability to adjust, restrain self, maintain harmony with social context

Esteeming the self may be primarily a Western phenomenon, and the concept of self-esteem should perhaps be replaced by "self-satisfaction", or by a term that reflects the realisation that one is fulfilling the culturally mandated task.

Source: H.R. Markus and S. Kitayama (1991), "Culture and the Self: Implications for Cognition, Emotion, and Motivation". *Psychological Review*, *98*: 224-53. Copyright ©1991 by the American Psychological Association. Reprinted with permission.

Similarly, self-esteem is likely to vary, depending on the sense of self that a person holds (Crocker, Luhtanen, Blaine, and Broadnax, 1994). The kinds of items that assess self-esteem, such as "I feel I am a person of worth". Members of cultures with an independent sense of self are more likely to endorse these items than are members of cultures where the self is viewed interdependently (Markus and Kitayama, 1991; Yik, Bond, and Paulhus, 1998). More generally, the importance one attaches to self-esteem and its implications for life satisfaction vary between independent and interdependent countries. Evidence for this assertion was reported by Diener and Diener (1995). They found that the relation between self-esteem and life satisfaction was lower in interdependent or collectivist countries, whereas in independent countries, individuals with high self-esteem reported high life satisfaction as well (Diener and Diener, 1995). In collectivist cultures, social norms (such as social approval) are better predictors of life satisfaction, whereas individual emotions are stronger predictors of life satisfaction in individualistic cultures (Suh, Dirner, Oishi, and Triandis, 1998). So different are these patterns that some have questioned how psychologists should measure self-esteem, arguing that important components of self-esteem in interdependent cultures are missing from traditional Western definitions. Nonetheless, people are capable of thinking of themselves in more than one culture simultaneously. How does biculturalism affect self-perceptions?

In an ingenious study, Ross, Xun, and Wilson (2002) gave several questionnaires to Chinese-born students, who were randomly assigned to participate in either Chinese or English; Canadian-born participants served as a control group and participated in English. Chinese-born participants who responded in Chinese endorsed more collective self-statements in their self-descriptions, scored lower on self-esteem, and expressed more agreement with Chinese cultural views than did their Chinese-born counterparts responding in English. The results suggest that these Chinese-born students had both East Asian and Western identities, with each being correspondingly activated by its associated language.

Despite differences between independent and interdependent cultures in willingness to endorse items on self-esteem scales, people in interdependent cultures who score high in self-esteem show many of the same effects as those from independent cultures who score high in self-esteem. For example, even in interdependent cultures, those who see themselves especially positively have higher levels of self-esteem (Yik *et al.*, 1998). Members of interdependent cultures who have more independent self-construals appear similar to those from independent cultures. Moreover, as already noted, measures of implicit self-esteem suggest that even in interdependent cultures, there is some tendency to self-enhance indirectly, as by overvaluing the letters in one's name (Kitayama and Karasawa, 1997).

Relatedly, although Westerners are more likely to express the independent sense of self just described, there is much variability in the degree to which this is true. Members of some Western ethnic and religious groups think of themselves in interdependent or relational terms, despite living in a Western culture. Women are more likely than men to have an interdependent sense of self and to think of themselves in terms of their relationships with others rather than primarily as independent others (Cross, Bacon, and Morris, 2000; Cross and Vick, 2001). Thus, although there are culture differences in self-construals, there is also considerable variability in whether members of a particular culture will think of themselves in independent or interdependent terms.

The salience of motives also appears to vary culturally. People from Western cultures, such as the United States, are more likely to self-enhance, whereas those from interdependent cultures, such as the Japanese, may be more concerned with self-improvement and therefore more likely to engage in self-criticism (Kitayama, Markus, Matsumoto, and Norasakkunkit, 1997).

The phenomenon of self-enhancement may represent an insight about the self that is culturally bounded. Japanese people are far more self-critical than are their Western counterparts, for example (Heine and Renshaw, 2002). The self-serving bias is another example. People tend to see themselves as the origin of actions that have good, not bad, consequences. Such attributions are thought to have self-enhancing qualities. We would expect to find that the self-serving bias is greatly lessened or even non-existent in cultures such as that of Japan that have an interdependent sense of self. Indeed, some research suggests that this is the case. Takata (1987) found no self-enhancing bias among Japanese students, but the opposite: a bias in a self-effacing direction. When Japanese students outperformed another person, they tended to regard their success as situationally caused, whereas when they were outperformed by another, they were more likely to see that other person's qualities as responsible for her or his success. The more modest self-attributions and self-perceptions of the Japanese and others with an interdependent sense of self appear to be consistent findings (Heine, Takata, and Lehman, 2000; Oishi, Wyer, and Colcome, 2000).

Nonetheless, one may ask the question, might people from interdependent cultures self-enhance on communal traits? That is, it may be that self-enhancement is not absent from Eastern cultures but merely assumes a different form, namely, enhancing the group and one's standing with respect to thegroup rather than to individual autonomous qualities. Kurman (2001) examined this possibility in collectivistic (i.e., Singapore, China) and individualistic (Israeli-Jews) cultures and found that self-enhancement of traits reflecting personal agency was associated with an independent self-construal, but self-enhancement of communal traits was associated with an interdependent self-construal. These findings imply that self-enhancement may not be absent in some cultures and present in others, but may assume different forms depending on the values of the culture in which it is explored.

Self and Gender Differences

Many important gender differences may also be linked to divergent construals of the self. Traditional theories of development have emphasised the growth of an autonomous self with firm boundaries, separated from context and moving toward greater use of abstract logic and self-sufficiency. Miller (1976), Gilligan (1982), and Jordan *et al.* (1991) have posited a contextual, relational paradigm for the study of what has traditionally been called self-experience. Rather than focus on the "bounded" and contained self, these approaches emphasise the connected and relationally emergent nature of human experience. The movement of relating, of mutual initiative and responsiveness, is the ongoing, centrally organising dynamic in women's lives. Because of this shift in paradigm, the independent self is no longer the primary target of centre of the examination (Jordan, 1989).

Mutual empathy and mutual empowerment are at the core of growth-enhancing relationships. Empathy involves a motivational component (the desire to know the other), a perceptual component (the ability to perceive verbal and non-verbal signals), an affective component (the capacity to resonate with another person's feelings), and a cognitive component (the ability to make sense of this joining resonance). Mutuality, another characteristic of "good" connection, involves openness to change and growth in both people. Each person remains respectful of the other's experience (Jordan, 1986). The focus of interest of feminist approaches is not just the development of self but equally the movement of relationship.

The relationship approach has been found helpful in understanding broader cultural contexts. The reframing of the concept of dependency have suggested a different explanation of certain characteristics of the Japanese culture (Kobayashi, 1989). Turner (1987) explored the ways in which the relational approach reflects and validates African American women's experience. It also illuminates some of the specifics of lesbian development. For instance, the relational model offers a new perspective on the concept of fusion when applied to lesbian women as well as other issues in lesbians' lives. In lesbian relationships fusion has been pathologised and viewed pejoratively, in models of human development that emphasise the separation of the individual; however the intense intimacy, sense of equality, value placed on communication, and emotional support by both partners—which have been seen as indications of fusion—seem to contribute to high levels of satisfaction in such relationships (Mencher,1990). Mencher suggests that these indications of fusion point to intense relational engagement, a sign of health and growth.

Miller acknowledges women's relational qualities and activities as potential strengths that provide pathways to healthy growth and development. Gilligan notes that women's sense of self and morality revolves around issues of responsibility for, and care of, other people. It is embedded in a compelling appreciation of context.

More recently, feminists theorists have begun to explore the ways in which traditional theories of development also misinterpret men's experience. Bergman (1991) observes that society pressurises boys to move away from a more connected and empathic relational context into one of competition, power, and disconnection.

The process of psychological growth requires the participants to respond empathically to each other. Because each feels this empathic response, each can "take off" from this empathic base and add thoughts and feelings as they arise. These additions create the interplay, the flow. This mutually empathic interplay is created by both people and builds new psychological experience—that is, growth for both.

The result of this process is that both people develop psychologically in at least five important ways (Miller, 1986):

- Both feel a connection with the other that gives a sense of increased zest, or energy.
- Both are active in the immediate relationship, and they feel more empowered to act beyond the relationship.
- Each person has some more self-knowledge as well as knowledge of the other person; more is learned about feelings and thoughts and how they are for each person.
- Because these processes have occurred, both people feel a greater sense of self-worth.
- As a result, both desire more connections in the future.

Self and Identity in Modern Psychology

In contemporary psychological discourse, the formulations related to psychological functioning in almost all domains are ego centred. For example, psychodynamic theory uses a language that is replete with terms such as "ego-strength", "ego-weakness", "ego-boundary", "ego-loss", "strengthening of ego" and "ego-functions". Similarly, Piaget, in his theory of cognitive development, identified "egocentrism" as one of the characteristics of the stage of pre-operational thinking. Egocentrism is difficulty in seeing the world from another's outlook. "Ego resilience" is another concept recently used in life span developmental context, which refers to "powerful personality resource that enables people to handle midlife changes" (Kail & Cavanaugh, 2004, p. 514).

Similarly, the goals of psychotherapy are conceptualised as "promoting autonomy", "enhancing self-esteem", "increasing self-regulation", "achieving self-efficacy", "facilitating self-actualisation", and so on. It is observed that in general, the Western conception of the self is of an individual who is separate, autonomous and atomised (that is, made up of a set of discrete traits, abilities, values and motives), seeking separateness and independence from others (Markus & Kitayama, 1991).

Prevalence of ego related constructs in modern psychology can be understood, both as a cultural phenomenon and as a matter of the range and depth of human consciousness studied. As a cultural phenomenon, these constructs gain importance because the psychological theories and methods developed in the West in general, and in the United States in particular, adopted the *individual* as the basic unit of analysis, affirming the individualistic bias of Western culture (Kim & Berry, 1993). Berry *et al.* (1992) observe that the notion that a person is a bounded individual has been central to the discipline of psychology in general, and to personality psychology in particular (Much, 1995). Since psychodynamic and other theories are rooted in Western culture, the formulations of psychopathology and therapy as well as the mental health profession per se, are guided by the Western ethos.

The Western view of the relation between ego and consciousness is spelt out clearly by Carl Jung, who does not admit consciousness without ego at its centre (Jung, 1971). The Indian tradition agrees that in the ordinary waking state the ego seems to be the centre of one's consciousness, but it does not limit consciousness to the ordinary waking state. It considers the ego too limited a construct to encompass the entire range of consciousness and human identity, and asserts that there also exists a type of pure consciousness, beyond all the dualities, called *cetanā* in its awareness aspect, and *caitanya* in its energy aspect. It is in this pure consciousness that it locates the real/true identity of a person, his *puruṣa*. From this perspective, the altered states of consciousness can be considered more appropriately as altered states of mind, pure consciousness being the substratum which remains changeless (Salagame, 1988). The distinction between pure consciousness and mind is crucial in the Indian tradition and has far-reaching implications for understanding human self and identity.

It is only in the last four decades, with the emergence of transpersonal psychology, that Western researchers have paid attention to the distinction between pure consciousness and mind, and the corresponding identity sense. In Eastern cultures the conception of a transcendental "Self" is more prevalent than in Western cultures. It should be noted that Abraham Maslow In his last days recognised that human beings have a "need for transcendence" and spoke of "Being-Needs" (or "B-Needs" for short), "Meta-Needs" and "meta-motivations" (Maslow, 1971). He was responsible for the establishment of Transpersonal Psychology.

Transpersonal psychology emphasises the spiritual dimension of human nature. It considers man as divine and spiritual in addition to being an animal and uniquely human. Sigmund Freud, a physician by profession, boldly postulated a theory of unconscious mental process out of necessity to account for certain disorders. In a similar way, some Western psychologists and psychiatrists took the bold step of establishing Transpersonal Psychology (Sutich, 1969; Tart, 1975) and Transpersonal Psychiatry and Psychotherapy (Cortright, 1997; Scotton, Chinen & Battista, 1996) when they encountered "peak experiences" and altered state phenomena. Within the discipline of psychology, psychoanalysis and transpersonal perspectives may be considered as marking a distinct shift from body to mind, and from mind to spirit. They have turned towards Eastern traditions, such as Buddhism and Hinduism, in their attempt to formulate new theories and models. Thus psychology has completed a full circle, recovering the soul/spirit that was lost on its way (Salagame, 2006).

Identity and Self in Indian Thought

The Indian perspective views human beings as bio-psycho-social-spiritual organisms. Hence, there are many concepts related to identity and self, referring to different aspects. Among them are: *atman*, *puruṣa*, *jīva*, *dehī*, *kṣetrajña*, *ahaṁkāra*, *ahambhāva*, *asmitā*, *jñātā*, *bhoktā*, and *kartā*, which are used in different contexts with specific meaning and significance. They represent transcendental, empirical (physical), and psychosocial dimensions of human nature.

On the transcendental level, identity refers to *ātman* in Vedānta and *puruṣa* in Sāṁkhya. Since the Upaniṣads declare that the transcendent Self, *ātman*, is identical with the highest principle of the universe, *Brahmana* (*ayam ātmā brahma*), the Upaniṣads also declare that this self is *Brahman* (I am *Brahman*) (*aham brahmāsmi*). The notion of a transcendent Self, *ātman*, requires further elaboration because it is said to be beyond the distinction of subject object. Viewed in this context, transcendence is really not an "experience" in the ordinary sense because, transcendence implies no experiencer or experienced. The transcendent state of consciousness, if it can be called a state at all, is itself called Self, *ātman*. Hence, the idea of self here is not the same as the idea of self-sense on the empirical level or its psychological referent, and it is cogently articulated in *Māṇḍūkya Upaniṣad* as follows:

> The Fourth (*turīya*), the wise say, is not inwardly cognitive, nor outwardly cognitive, nor cognitive both-wise; neither is it an indefinite mass of cognition, nor collective cognition, nor non-cognition. It is unseen, unrelated, inconceivable, un-inferable, unimaginable, indescribable. It is the essence of

> the one self-cognition common to all states of consciousness. All phenomena cease in it. It is peace. It is bliss, it is non-duality. This is the Self, and it is to be realised. (*MU*, 7, Trans. Swami Sarvananda, 1976)

Thus *turīya* or the so-called fourth state of consciousness, vis-à-vis the other three—*jāgrat* (waking), *svapna* (dream) and *suṣupti* (deep sleep)—is the substratum of all phenomenal experience, irrespective of the state. Hence, as one follower of Vedānta put it (personal communication), *turīya* is the original condition and the real state; and all other phenomenal states of consciousness, including waking, are altered states from the Upaniṣadic point of view (Salagame, 1988). Thus, *turīya* is the "ground" of awareness, on which waking, dream, deep sleep, and other experiences happen with a "subject-object/self-other" duality as "figure". Therefore, *turīya* was considered as the essence of the one self-cognition common to all the other states, and was regarded as the Self to be realised—*sa ātmā sa vijñeyaḥ*.

This "subject/self" of phenomenal experience is termed as *jīva* or *dehin* in the Indian tradition, and they are incorporated into the linguistic structures of many regions. The person who undergoes the cycle of birth and death is *jīva* and it is at empirical plane. It is also referred to as *dehī* in the *Bhagavad Gītā* (II.22).

vāsāmi jirṇāni yathā vihāya navāni gṛhṇāti naroparāni ı
tathā śarirāṇi vihāya jīrṇānyanyāni samyāti navāni dehī ıı

> Just as a human being casts off worn-out clothes and takes on a new one, similarly, the owner of this body (*dehī*) gives up worn-out bodies and takes on new ones. (Author's translation)

The term *puruṣa* is also used in a pluralistic sense to refer to *jīva*. Thus the concept of person or individual or self or subject is represented by three terms—*jīva*, *dehin*, and *puruṣa*—in the Indian tradition. Padmapāda, the foremost disciple of Śaṅkara, gives a definition of *jīva* as follows:

> And that *jīva*—of the nature of "not this", conditioned as ego in the waking and dream state, and conditioned in sleep by *avidyā* which has within it traces of the

> impressions (that the inner sense has left behind) which is the opposition of *jñāna* and which obstructs the light (of *ātmā*)—keeps going forwards and backwards and as such is termed in Sruti, Smṛti in common parlance as *saṁsārī* (the worldly person), *jīva, vijñānaghana, vijñānātmā, prajñā, śarīrī, śarīraḥ, ātmā, samprasāda, puruṣa, pratyagātmā, kartā, bhoktā,* and *kṣetrajña.*
> (*Pañcapādikā of Padmapāda*, XXXIV.135, pp. 100-101, quoted in safaya, 1976, p. 213)

In the preceding definition, we find that different terms have been used to represent the different aspects of the self in conditioned existence. Their connotations are as follows:

- *Saṁsārin*—involved in worldly enjoyment and activity;
- *Jīva*—soul;
- *Vijñānaghana*—embodiment of discriminatory knowledge with a spiritual dimension;
- *Vijñānātman*—prime mover of discriminatory knowledge;
- *Prajnā*—self as cogniser;
- *śarīrī* one who is embodied;
- *śarīra*—the equipment which enables the *jīva* to function in the phenomenal world;
- *Samprasāda*—the self-sense present in dream;
- *Puruṣa*—human being;
- *Pratyagatman*—self as *Brahman*;
- *Kartā*—self as agent;
- *Bhoktā*—self as experience/enjoye different;
- *Kṣetrajña*—knower of the field.

It is the identification with the *jīva* that is called *avidyā* (ignorance of one's true nature) or *ajñāna* (lack of transcendental Self-knowledge). Therefore, the tradition emphasises on delinking the self-sense from *jīva*. All phenomenal experiences are attributed to *jīva* or *dehin*, while *ātman* is "experience-less" as the term experience understood with reference to an empirical subject.

Ahaṁkāra is derived from the word *aham*. *Aham* simply means a feeling of "I" as in the question "who am I?" (*ko 'ham*). The Sanskrit term *aham* is a nominative singular of the term *asmad*, a pronominal base from which several cases of the first personal pronoun are derived. *Asmad* refers to individual soul or embodied soul (Apte, 1988). *Ahaṁkāra* represents the sense of doership and ownership, thus serving as a generic term representing the cognition and the feelings associated with me and mine. In the Vedānta tradition, *ahaṁkāra* along with *buddhi*, *citta* and *manas* constitute what is called the *ahaṁkāra catuṣṭaya*, the quartet of the internal organ. In its technical sense *ahaṁkāra* refers to that aspect of the *antaḥkaraṇa* which provides a subjective frame of reference to experience (Rao, 1962). Rama *et al.* (1976, p. 70) illustrate it thus: "... when a sensory-motor mind functions, a rose is seen. But when *ahaṁkāra* adds its influence, I see a rose". Thus *ahaṁkāra* appropriates the experience to itself, leading to an affirmation of the sense of an objective world as perceived by the subject—resulting in increasing differentiation between subject and object serving as the principle of individuation. *Ahaṁkāra* also refers to the feeling of individuality/uniqueness, one's identifications and the sense of differentiation of oneself from the other, the "I" from the "not-I". Thus, the term *ahaṁkāra* refers to the subject in the subject-object duality in the realm of mind/psyche, and therefore it is more appropriate to translate it as "self-sense". On the other hand, scholars often translate the term *ahaṁkāra* in English as "ego", "egoism", "egotism", etc. (Salagame and Raj, 1999).

In the ontological sense, *aham* represents "being". Hence, when the question is asked as to who this being is, in the first person as "who am I?" (*ko 'ham*), it has different referents, depending on the level at which it is understood—transcendental, empirical and psychological. For example, one may say *ahaṁ ātmā* (I am *ātman*), *ahaṁ puruṣaḥ* (I am *puruṣa*), *ahaṁ jīvaḥ* (I am the embodied soul), *ahaṁ bhoktā* (I am the experiencer) and *ahaṁ kartā* (I am the doer). A layperson's understanding from his/her dally experiences is that whoever is that "experiencer" or the "subject"—who participates in all experiences during *jāgrat* (waking state) is the real self. This includes our body, our mental states and our social relationships. So we incorporate most experiences of *jāgrat* as part of our identity or self-sense, and deny some of them into our self-structure, which constitutes the Freudian unconscious. Hence, a layperson's identity is largely biopsychosocial (Salagame *et al.*, 2005).

A layperson also usually treats experiences that occur during *svapna* (dream state) as not part of reality (exceptions being certain tribal people—Tart, 1969), though at the time of dreaming their reality is no less than those of the *jāgrat* experience. Similarly, many other types of experiences that may happen to people are rejected as figments of the imagination, dreams, hallucinations, delusions, far-fetched ideas and so on. In other words, they are treated as non-real. Thus, whatever one tends to identify with, becomes part of reality; and whatever one denies, becomes unreal. Hence a vast domain of possible human experiencing is declared unreal.

In the Indian tradition, all experiential phenomena which involve a subject-object (*vyakti-viṣaya*) duality, like the experiencer (*bhoktā*) and the experienced (*bhogya*), the observer (*dṛk*) and the observed (*dṛśya*), the knower (*jñātā*) and the known (*jñeya*), are considered to be in the realm of *manas* (mind) in its broadest sense. From the Indian perspective, all types of human experiences involving subject-object duality—be it normal, abnormal, pathological, paranormal, religious or mystical—are all mental phenomena (*manovyāpāra*), however extraordinary they may be. There is a vast domain of possible human experiences which we now call paranormal and mystical, and Indian texts provided detailed descriptions of such experiences. They also discussed dreams, illusions, hallucinations and delusions (Sinha, 1985). However, they went a step ahead of the modern psychologists in their analysis of the real and unreal. They declared that even the commonly understood self of *jāgrat* is actually non-real and declared that the only true self is that "ground awareness", or *ātman*. This is the unique contribution of the Veda and the Upaniṣads.

Thus, the difference between most modern psychologists and the Indian view can be summarised as follows. The former affirm a narrow range of human experience as real and self, and they deny a vast domain as unreal. The latter declare all human experiences involving a subject-object/self-other dichotomy as not more than relatively real and as only "figures" against the backdrop of a "ground awareness" that is the only fully true reality; and the only real Self while the rest is seen as non-real and non-self. Hence, for them *jīva* (soul) or *dehin* (owner of the body) is also non-self and it is a wrong understanding to treat non-self as Self. This is *ajñāna* (lack of transcendental Self-knowledge), and leads to wrong identification with the non-self-*jīva* or *dehin* instead of Self-*ātman*, and this is seen as the root of all human problems and suffering. The solution lies in first obtaining the right understanding of the distinction between the non-self and the Self, called *viveka* (discrimination), through the process of listening (*śravaṇa*) (in modern times includes other means of acquiring information) and reflection (*manana*). The next step involves making a conscious attempt to overcome the wrong identification through a process of meditation (*nididhyāsana*). It is only then that a person becomes *jñānī* (Self-realised). Therefore, in the Indian scheme of understanding the self and identity, two processes play a crucial role. One is *viveka* or discrimination, and the other is *vairāgya*, or the process of dis-identification or detachment.

The question is who identifies with the non-self, who has to make the discrimination between the non-self and the Self, and who has to make the conscious attempt to dis-identify with the non-self? *Ahaṁkāra* is regarded as one of the *antaḥkaraṇa* ("inner instrument", mind) as the one involved in this process. Safaya (1976, pp. 221-22) observes that different schools have used different terminologies to refer to what is called the Mind, "Sāṁkhya named it *antaḥkaraṇa*, *Yoga* named it *citta* and Nyāya named it *manas* (*buddhi*, etc., included in the same). Vedānta calls it *antaḥkaraṇa*, but enumerates distinctly the four aspects, viz., *buddhi*, *manas*, *citta* and *ahaṁkāra*". However, it is debatable whether the term *antaḥkaraṇa* as used in Sāṁkhya and Vedānta is generic in its meaning, or refers exclusively to the cognitive aspect, requiring further research. On the other hand, *citta* of Yoga and *manas* of Nyāya are more generic in nature.

As Rao (1966) has clarified, according to Sāṁkhya the *buddhi* is only the *adhyavasāya* or discriminating principle in general. It does not have any "individual" or "egoistic" touch about it. So at this level the *puruṣa* does not even feel that he is the enjoyer or sufferer. It happens to be the function or contribution of *ahaṁkāra* to make the *puruṣa* strictly "personal". Further, Rao (1966) notes that self-consciousness or a feeling of personal identity cannot arise if the mental organ does not present something determinate to it. Though it is generally believed that it is a Sāṁkhya concept, references to *ahaṁkāra* are also found in the *Chāndogya* and *Praśna Upaniṣad*. In the *Praśna Upaniṣad* (IV.8, Trans. Subramanya Sharma, 1947), *ahaṁkāra* is listed along with *buddhi*, *manas*, and *citta*. *Chāndogya Upaniṣad* (VII.25.1 & 2, Trans. Sachhidananda Saraswati Swami, 1956) speaks about *ahaṁkāra* as self-sense, and points out that those who fail to discriminate between *ātman* and body will confound the self-sense with the body.

Elucidation of the nature and function of *ahaṁkāra* can be found in the *śloka*s related to *antaḥkaraṇa, aham-padārtha-nirūpaṇa*, and *ahaṁkāra nindā* in the *Viveka-Cūḍāmaṇi* of Śaṇkarācārya. In *śloka* 103, *Śaṅkara* defines *ahaṁkāra* by stating that the *antaḥkaraṇa* dwells in the sensory and motor organs and in the body as *aham* with *abhimāna* (*ahamityabhimānena*) in the reflected brightness of *ātman*. In *śloka* 104, he states that it is to be understood as *ahaṁkāra*, which due to *abhimāna* (identification) becomes *kartā* (doer) and *bhoktā* (enjoyer), and also due to its association with *sattva* and other *guṇa*s, will have *avasthātraya* (three states—waking, dream, and sleep). It is made clear that *ahaṁkāra* experiences happiness and sadness in relation to favourable and unfavourable circumstances, and therefore *sukha* (happiness) and *duḥkha* (sorrow) are its *dharma*, and not the *dharma* of the *ātman* which is *sadānanda* (forever blissful).

Śaṅkara further makes a distinction between *ahaṁkāra* and *ahaṁ-padārtha* (*Viveka-Cūḍāmaṇi, śloka*s: 292-96). He equates *ahaṁ-padārtha* with *ātman* and elucidates it as the self-sense which remains even in deep sleep, and which is the witness even for *ahaṁkāra* and other functions. Therefore, he exhorts giving up *abhimāna* (identification) with *māṁsapiṇḍa* (body made of flesh), as well as with that *ahaṁkāra* which has *dehābhimāna* (bodily identification), and is fashioned out of *mūḍha buddhi* (dull intellect). Further, *Śaṅkara* exhorts giving up *abhimāna* (identification) with *kula* (caste), *gotra* (clan), *nāma* (name), *rūpa* (form) and *āśrama* (stage of life), which are dependent on the "living corpse" (*ardhaśava aśriteṣu*). He also exhorts giving up *abhimāna* with the doer and enjoyer of the *liṅga śarīra* (subtle body). Thus, in modern terms, *Śaṅkara* is exhorting one to give up one's sense of identity with biopsychosocial and even psychical aspects of human nature—all of which constitutes *ahaṁkāra* in order to realise the *ātman*, attain *śānti* and to realise *akhaṇḍa ānanda*—inseparable bliss, itself.

Thus, it appears that *abhimāna* is the essence of *ahaṁkāra*. Apte (1988) has listed different meanings of the term *abhimāna*, one of which is "referring all objects to self, the act of *ahaṁkāra*, personality". As mentioned earlier, Swami Rama illustrates this with a very lucid example—when sensory-motor mind functions, a "rose is seen". But when *ahaṁkāra* adds its influence, this becomes "I see a rose" (Rama *et al.*, 1976, p. 70). To see a rose, therefore, an "I" is not essential. Similarly, to experience life, a sense of self is not essential.

According to the Upaniṣads and Vedānta, all problems start when this non-essential factor adds its influence in our lives. Therefore, *ahaṁkāra* is considered negative, and we find many *śloka*s denigrating *ahaṁkāra* (*ahaṁkāra nindā*) (14 as against 3 describing its nature) in the *Viveka-Cūḍāmaṇi*. *Ahaṁkāra* is looked down upon with the following metaphors and descriptions (*śloka*s 297-310). It is *vikāra, duḥkha, rāhu*, powerful wild serpent, residue of poison in the body even after it is purged from a body, a thorn in the throat of a person taking food, an enemy to be slain with the sword of *vijñāna*, and fashioned out of *mūḍha buddhi* (dull intellect). Even after it is completely rooted out, if its thought is left for a while, it sprouts hundreds of *vṛtti*s (mental modes, movements, and disturbances). Even after it is completely controlled, it should not be given scope through sense objects. If it is given any such leeway, it is like watering a withering lemon plant that will come into life.

Some Indian psychologists and philosophers have described the nature of *ahaṁkāra* in modern terms. Rao states:

> "The general consciousness which is undifferen-tiated and rudimentary in course of time gets individuated.

> It acquires a subjective frame of reference and the process of individuation is afoot. This state, a further development of the capacity to be conscious of objects may be designated as self-consciousness. The Sāṁkhya theory has brought into currency the expression "ahaṁkāra" to denote this. This is a word which superficially signifies "I making"' (1962, p. 41).

Srinivasan (1967, p. 199), interpreting the views of the Viśiṣṭādvaita Vedānta of Rāmānuja, states thus,

> "*Ahaṁkāra* is characterised by the contracted consciousness of the individual whereby he imposes on himself artificial and ego-centric "separative" limitation, conceives himself as divided from "God" and opposed to other individuals and lands himself in a state of struggle and suffering in the pursuit of selfish desires. This is the state of human bondage or inauthentic existence. Only by transcending this state of *ahaṁkāra* can the true status of the individual soul be realised".

Śafaya (1976) notes that according to Sāṁkhya, with the development of *ahaṁkāra*, the subject-object differentiation in living beings takes place. Joshi (1979) observes that through this process a false centre is created, around which one moves, and becomes a subject of constant friction and irritation. Rama *et al.* (1976, p. 70) observe that the I-ness inherent in *ahaṁkāra* "provides a sense of separateness from the rest of the world, a feeling of distinction and uniqueness. It is the agency, which defines what of the sensory data and memories is 'I'. It is the property of subjectivity". Ajaya (1983, p. 128) notes that as the distinction between "not-I" and "I" rigidify, the human being comes increasingly under the illusion that this distinction is real rather than an artificial creation of the mind. This illusion limits the human being from experiencing the "holistic substratum of existence".

Self and Inner Growth

As mentioned earlier, subjects from Asian cultural backgrounds (presumably those with predominantly interdependent selves) often provide extremely global self-descriptions, that is, one's relationship to the cosmic system and inner growth. Most of what is today called "personal growth" aimed at by various psychotherapeutic approaches (such as Gestalt Therapy, Rational Emotive Behaviour Therapy. Cognitive-Behaviour Therapy, etc.) and by the various techniques associated with the Human-Potential Movement (such as Encounter Group, Sensitivity Training, Assertiveness Training, etc.) pertains to what is referred to as the development of the ego and uniqueness. On the other hand, "inner growth" aimed at by Eastern spiritual approaches (such as Yoga, Zen, Sufism, etc.), consists of "transpersonal" development beyond the ego-state and represents, in varying degrees, a reversal of the normal, ego-bound state of consciousness. Jung (Analytical Psychology) and Assagioli (Psychosynthesis) are among the few psychotherapists who distinguish between the ego and the self, however, unlike Eastern spiritual disciplines, they do not conceive of the dissolution of the ego in the transpersonal state. Hence, personal growth consists in the development of the individual as human being, whereas, inner growth lies in transforming and transcending the human state of consciousness. Inner growth, thus represents a new dimension of evolution—that which lies in the transcendence of the ego, liberation from the ignorant identification with one's superficial nature, and the discovery of the true self (efforts towards higher perfection by the expression and experiences of the potentialities latent in the being). Numerous are the paths that have been discovered for achieving inner growth. The various psychological paths may be classified into three broad types: the Path of Knowledge, corresponding to the cognitive aspect; the Path of Devotion, related to the affective or emotional side of human nature; and the Path of Action, based on man's conative aspect which has to do with striving and willing. Whatever the path followed, the process of inner growth involves a transformation of the normal state of consciousness, a progressive awakening of inner and higher states of being, culminating in a total reversal of consciousness, a new birth. One feature of the reversal of consciousness—which gives it the appearance of a sudden revolution rather than a gradual change—is that it involves a process similar to what has been called "unconscious incubation". It is a sudden happening, preceded by a more or less long period of preparation which takes place behind the veil of the surface consciousness and of which the seeker is therefore unaware. In this backdrop, inner growth would be dealt with as an experiential process throughout the chapters.

There is growing recognition that Western psychologists may have underestimated the psychologies and therapies of other cultures. Certain Asian disciplines contain sophisticated therapies and experimental studies have demonstrated their ability to induce psychological, physiological, and psychotherapeutic effects. An increasing number of Westerners, including mental-health professionals, now use Asian therapies. Benefits include new perspectives on psychological functioning, potential, and pathology as well as new approaches and techniques. In addition, the study of other cultures and practices often has the healthy effect of revealing unsuspected ethnocentric and limiting beliefs, thus leading to a broader view of human nature and therapy.

Asian perspectives focus primarily on existential transpersonal levels and little on the pathological. They contain detailed maps of states of consciousness, developmental levels, and stages of enlightenment that extend beyond traditional Western psychological maps. Moreover, they claim to possess techniques for inducing these states and conditions. These systems do differ from most Western perspectives in their greater concern with values, moral considerations, and psycho-spiritual development. Each of these Eastern traditions stresses the futility and foolishness of valuing external form over inner function. These psychologies like their Western counterparts, are derived from careful observations of the psychological, physiological, and spiritual effects of a variety of ideas, attitudes, behaviours, and exercise.

The vitality and importance of these Eastern psychologies, however, rest on the continual testing, reworking, and modifying of their initial insights to fit new settings and interpersonal situations as well as different cultural conditions. In other words, these centuries-old psychologies are still relevant, still changing, and developing.

In this chapter, an attempt is being made to highlight some of the Western perspectives on self and growth. Whereas, the Eastern perspectives on self and inner growth would unfold in the later chapters.

Western Perspetives on Self and Growth: An Overview

1. *Psychodynamic Perspectives*

According to **Sigmund Freud (1856-1939)** the self is the total being—the body and the instincts, as well as the conscious and unconscious parts of the mind. A self not limited by the body or detached from it had no place in Freud's biological beliefs. When confronted with such a metaphysical (or spiritual) image of humankind, Freud asserted that this was not within his province as a scientist. Psychoanalysts have since moved past Freud's position and have written extensively about the self.

According to **Carl Gustav Jung (1875-1961)** the self is a central archetype responsible for psychological order, integration and wholeness of personality, and a deep, inner guiding factor. Its functions also include reconciliation of polarities and maintaining dynamic equilibrium of the psyche. Like ego is the centre of consciousness, similarly the self is the centre of the conscious and the unconscious. The development of self does not mean that the ego dissolves; the ego become linked to the self. The ego receives the light from the self as a result of long, hard work of understanding and accepting the unconscious processes. Jung believed that every individual has an innate urge toward individuation or self-development or self-realisation.

Individuation is a process of moving toward greater freedom. The process includes development of a dynamic relationship between the ego and the self, along with integration of the various parts of the psyche: the ego, persona, shadow, anima or animus, and other archetypes. As people become more individuated, these archetypes may be seen as expressing themselves in more subtle and complex ways.

Through self-knowledge we become more conscious of ourselves and act accordingly. The personal unconscious superimposed on the collective unconscious diminishes. This results in the widening of the consciousness which is no longer egotistical, bringing the individual into an indissoluble communion with the world.

Individuation might be represented as a spiral in which we keep confronting the same basic questions, each time in a more refined form. This concept relates closely to the Zen Buddhist conception of enlightenment, in which an individual never solves a personal koan, or spiritual problem, and the searching is seen as a goal in itself.

In Adlerian **(Alfred Adler, 1870-1937)** psychology, the self is the individual's style of life. Adler considered the self a dynamic, unitary principle rather than a structure to be found within the psyche. The self is not considered as an entity. There is literally no self to actualise but through transactions with its world. Adler's position concerning the self strongly resembles the concept of selflessness in Buddhist psychology.

Psychological growth is primarily a matter of moving from the self-centred goal of personal superiority to an attitude of constructive mastery of the environment and socially useful development.

Neo-analysts focused on identity and sense of self. **Karen Horney (1885-1952)**, in analysing neurotics, described different aspects of self. First, there is the Real Self, the inner core of personality that we perceive about ourselves, including our potential for self-realisation; this core is damaged by parental neglect and indifference. This parental neglect can produce the Despised Self, consisting of perceptions of inferiority and shortcomings, often based on others' negative evaluations of us and our resulting feelings of helplessness. Perhaps most important, Horney identified the Ideal Self—what one views as perfection and hopes to achieve, as moulded by perceived inadequacies. For Horney, the goal of psychoanalysis was not to help someone achieve his or her Ideal Self, but rather to enable the person to accept his or her Real Self. Someone who is alienated from his or her Real Self becomes neurotic and develops an interpersonal coping strategy to "solve" the conflict.

The first of these approaches she referred to as "Moving Toward" people—that is, always attempting to make others happy, to gain love, and to secure the approval and affection of others. Horney believed that individuals employing this coping strategy are overidentifying with a Despised Self and are therefore seeing themselves as unworthy of love. Their actions to gain love are attempts, on the one hand to disguise what they believe to be true of themselves, and, on the other hand, to make others believe that they are worthy of affection.

Horney called the second approach "Moving Against" people—that is, striving for power, recognition, and the admiration of others. Horney believed that these individuals, instead of overidentifying with the Despised Self, are overidentifying with the Ideal Self. They have come to believe that all the things that they wished they were are true, and their strivings for recognition and power are an effect to reaffirm for themselves the truth of this illusion.

A third approach was called "Moving Away" from people—that is, the withdrawal of any emotional investment from interpersonal relationships, in an effort to avoid being hurt in those relationships. Horney believed that these individuals want to overcome the Despised Self, and yet they feel incapable of ever becoming the Ideal Self. They see themselves, in their present state, as unworthy of the love and attention of others, and yet they feel unable to achieve anything greater. Thus, to avoid the unpleasant contrast—the gap between these two aspects of self, they hide behind independence and solitude.

Heinz Kohut (1913-81), like other object relations theorists, was also instrumental in creating new notions of the self. A psychoanalyst, Kohut argued that a key problem for many anxious people is the fear of the loss of an important love object (most often the parent). He worked with patients who had a narcissistic personality disorder, meaning that they felt powerless and dependent yet projected bravado and self-aggrandisement. He believed that the problems of these patients stemmed from a lack of acceptance on the part of their parents, which resulted in an inability on the part of the patients to fully accept themselves. He found that by playing the part of the therapist—parent he could often reverse this process and enable his patients to develop a healthy self-concept.

In brief, it is important to recognise that some brilliant thinkers took Freudian theory and developed it so that it could deal with emerging insights into what it means to have a social self—an identity in a social world.

For the post-Freudian, **Erik Erikson (1902-97)** a sense of identity includes both the development of ego identity and the flowering of a sense of self. Self-identity results from the integration of our past and present social roles and self-images.

The focus on positive growth and positive characteristics developed at each stage distinguishes Erikson's schema from Freud's and from those of many other theorists. Erikson views basic strengths, or virtues, as more than psychological defences against mental illness or negativity and more than simply as attitudes of nobility or morality. These virtues are inherent strengths and are characterised by a sense of potency and positive development. Hope is the virtue of the first stage, trust *vs.* mistrust. Will is the strength that arises from the crisis of initiative *vs.* shame and doubt. Purpose is rooted in the initiative *vs.* guilt stage. Competence is the strength resulting from the stage of industry *vs.* inferiority. Fidelity comes from identity *vs.* identity confusion. Love is the virtue that develops from intimacy. Care originates in generativity. Wisdom is derived from the crisis of integrity *vs.* despair.

2. *William James' Psychology of Consciousness*

William James (1842-1910) viewed self as that personal continuity that we all recognise each time we awaken. It is more than personal identity; it is the place from which all our mental processes originate and through which all our experiences are filtered. James described several layers of the self, like consciousness, he saw, paradoxically, as simultaneously continuous and discrete.

The biological self is our physical, corporal being. It is our hereditary make up, our physical features, our physiological processes. It is everything to do with our biological functions. It is the vehicle that transports us physically from birth to death, that exists in the physical world. It is this unique heart that is mine, this unique brain, just this hand, just this foot, just this tongue—the physicalness of personal identity that is me and no other person. It can be taken as a subset of the material self.

In addition to the biological self, the material self includes those specific items in the physical world with which we personally identify. It is the total world of objects that we own. The material self encompasses the sum total of our home, possessions, family, and friends. To the extent that a person identifies with an external person or objects, it is part of her or his self. Teenagers in gangs, for example, will even kill one another to protect a piece of clothing or a street corner that they see as part of themselves.

We willingly or unwillingly accept any and all roles. A person may have few or many social selves. These may be consistent or inconsistent. But whatever they are, we identify with each in a proper setting. We have, in fact, as many different selves as we have individual relationships. James suggests that the proper course of action is to pick a self that seems admirable and to act like that self in as many situations as possible. All other selves thereupon become unreal, but the fortunes of this self are real. Its failures are real failures, its triumphs real triumphs. This phenomenon James called the **selective industry of the mind**. Some researchers have reduced this idea to the distinction between private and public selves. The social self constitutes patterns of personal habits that form the mainstay of our relationships. James viewed it as the shifting malleable surface of personality, often little more than a set of masks, changed to suit different audiences. James argued that social habits are necessary; they make life orderly. Habit is a cushion; it renders relationships safe and predictable. To James, the constant interplay between cultural conformity and individual expression was both beneficial.

The spiritual self is the individual's inner and subjective being. It is an active element in all consciousness. According to James, it is most enduring and intimate part of the self. It is not where we experience pleasure or pain but that part of us that pleasure and pain affect. It is the source of effort, attention, and the will. Our expression of this self is exemplified in religious experiences, which James saw as coming from a region more central than the area of ideas or intellect. James remained undecided on the reality of a personal soul; however, he was convinced that there is something greater than individual identity. He also said that while all of our various selves could be unified in the experience of mystical awakening, this unification is never complete. We may be permitted to see the possibility of unity, but its actualisation remains the great task of living.

James was convinced that there is an underlying drive in human beings to increase their own well-being. Running through his lectures and papers is the notion that awareness can lead to self-control and that controlled awareness will almost always improve the quality of a person's life.

3. *Behavioural Perspective*

B.F. Skinner (1904-90) considers the term self an explanatory fiction. "There is no place in the scientific position for a self as a true originator or initiator of action" (1974: 225). Growth for skinner means the ability to minimise adverse conditions and to increase the beneficial control of our environment. By clarifying our thinking, we can make better use of the available tools for predicting, maintaining, and controlling our own behaviour.

4. *Humanistic and Existential Perspectives*

Carl Rogers (1902-87) wrote that within the field of experience is the self. The self is ever changing. At any given moment, it appears firm and predictable. The self is an organised, consistent gestalt, constantly forming and reforming as situations change.

According to Rogers, self is a process, a system. From the notion of fluidity, Rogers formulated the belief that not only are people capable of growth and personal development but this positive change is a natural phenomena, an expected progression. A person's self or self-concept, then, is an understanding of oneself as a result of past and present experiences, and future expectations.

The ideal self is a model toward which a person can strive. Like the self, it is a shifting structure, constantly undergoing redefinition. The ideal self can become an obstacle to personal health when it differs greatly from the real self. However, based on his own clinical experience, Rogers concluded that individuals have the potential to experience and be aware of their maladjustments. That is, an individual can experience the incongruence between the ideal self and one's actual experiences.

This capacity is coupled with the ability to modify one's ideal self or one's self-concept so that it becomes congruent with the reality. Thus, Rogers postulates a natural movement away from conflict and toward resolution. He sees adjustment as process in which new learning and new experiences are accurately assimilated. Individuals have within them numerous resources for understanding one's self and modifying one's self-concept, attitudes, and self-directed behaviours.

Rogers is convinced that these tendencies toward health and growth are facilitated by social relationships in which at least one individual is in touch with his or her own self-correcting centre. Self-acceptance is another prerequisite to a genuine acceptance of others. In turn, being accepted by others leads to an easy and greater willing acceptance of oneself. The last necessary element is empathic understanding, the ability to accurately sense the feelings of others. This cycle of self-correction and self-enhancement helps people overcome obstacles and facilitates psychological growth.

This self-actualisation tendency is a part of human condition. It is not only limited to humans but is a process of all living things: it is an urge evident in all to expand, extend, to become autonomous, to develop, and mature. It is the tendency to manifest and activate all the capacities of an organism such that activation enhances the self or the organism. Rogers concludes that in everyone lies an innate motive to become as competent and capable as we can biologically be.

Abraham Maslow (1908-70) describes eight ways in which individuals self-actualise: through concentration, growth choices, self-awareness, honesty, judgement, self-development, peak experiences, and lack of ego defences.

Rogers did not include any religious or spiritual dimensions in his formulations; others have expanded these theories to include transcendental experiences.

According to **existentialism**, the world changes as people's ideas about it change. Simply put, the self cannot exist without a world and the world cannot exist without a person (a being) to perceive it. Existential theories suggest that attempts to focus exclusively on self-concepts and cognitive structures, or exclusively on environmental contingencies, must ultimately fail. Instead, we also must examine people striving to make sense of their worlds. Rollo May (1969, 1977) focuses on the anxiety that must accompany any attempts to live to its fullest. May sees the human journey as a noble and dignifying one. In this sense, his view is consist with much religious philosophy about the inherent worth of humankind: there must be struggle for there to be dignity. Victor Frankl (1962) emphasise the benefits of personal choice. If people choose to grow and develop, the challenge of the unknown produces anxiety; but this anxiety can lead to triumph and self-fulfilment.

5. *Cognitive Perspective*

Albert Bandura (1925-) sees the self as a set of cognitive processes and structures "for perceiving, evaluating, and regulating behaviour, not a psychic agent that controls action" (Bandura, 1978, p. 344).One aspect of the self is self-efficacy, and another is self-regulation. We receive reinforcement for our behaviour from others and from the environment, we also set personal standards for our behaviour and reward ourselves when we meet those standards.

Self-efficacy is defined as "people's beliefs in their capabilities to produce desired effects by their own actions". "By sticking it out through tough times, people emerge from adversity with a stronger sense of efficacy" (Bandura, 1997). Self-efficacy develops from five sources—successful performance, vicarious experiences of success, internal success images, verbal persuasion, and physiological and emotional arousal.

Bandura found that the sense of self-efficacy can be enhanced by the following practical methods:

- Provide people with success experiences by setting for them difficult but achievable goals.
- Observe models performing successfully.
- Supply verbal encouragement that the person can perform successfully.
- Use diet, stress reduction, and exercise to control physiological arousal and thus increase stamina, strength, and relaxation under pressure.

Modern theories agree that we imagine ourselves in different roles as states, but this is seen as a more rational, cognitive process rather than rooted in deeper emotional conflicts. The psychologist Tory Higgins writes about tha actual self (the current self-concept), an ideal self (hopes, wishes, or aspirations), and the ought self (beliefs about one's duties). Discrepancies between one's actual and ideal selves result in chronic disappointment and dissatisfaction. Discrepancies between one's actual and ought selves lead to guilt and anxiety over failure in one's responsibilities. For Higgins, emotion and motivation come from these discrepancies.

Roy Baumeister is another contemporary researcher who is trying to more fully explain what we mean by "self". But he believes that much of human preoccupation with "finding oneself" is really a disguised search for a meaningful life. Therefore, to Baumeister, self might best be defined by our abilities: to find purpose, to make a difference, to justify actions, and to feel self-esteem.

Self-Management and Inner Growth: An Experiential Approach

Exercises for Growth and Mastery

Exercise 1—Stepping Back

Most of you live on the surface of your being, exposed to the touch of external influences. You live almost projected, as it were, outside your own body, and when you meet some unpleasant being similarly projected you get upset. The whole trouble arises out of your not being accustomed to stepping back.

You must always step back into yourself—learn to go deep within—step back and you will be safe. Do not lend yourself to the superficial forces which move in the outside world. Even if you are in a hurry to do something, step back for a while and you will discover to your surprise how much sooner and with what great success your work can be done.

If someone is angry with you, do not be caught in his/her vibrations but simply step back and his/her anger, finding no support or response, will vanish. Always keep your peace, resist all temptation to lose it. Never decide anything without stepping back, never speak a word without stepping back, never throw yourself into action without stepping back. All that belongs to the ordinary world is impermanent, so there is nothing in it worth getting upset about. What is lasting, eternal, immortal and infinite—that indeed is worth having, worth conquering and worth possessing. When you get the sense of the relativity of things, then whatever happens you can step back and look; you can remain quiet and call on the Divine Force and wait for an answer. Then you will know exactly what to do. Remember, therefore, that you cannot receive the answer before you are very peaceful. Practice that inner peace, make at least a small beginning and go on in your practice until it becomes a habit with you.

Source: Collected Works of the Mother-Centenary Education (*CWMCE*), Vol. 3 (Questions and Answers), p. 160.

Exercise 2—Becoming Aware of "Oneself"

It is one of the most indispensable things to do if one wants to succeed in having self-control and even a limited self-knowledge: to be able to localise one's consciousness and move it about in the different parts of one's being, in such a way as to distinguish between one's consciousness and one's thought, feeling, impulses, become aware of what the consciousness is in itself.

And in this way one can learn how to shift it; one can put one's consciousness in the body; one can put one's consciousness in the mind, can raise it above the mind, and with one's consciousness one can go into all the regions of the universe. But first of all one must know what one's consciousness is, that is, become conscious of one's consciousness, localise it. And for this there are many exercises. But one of them is very well known, it is to observe oneself and watch oneself living, and then see whether it is really the body which is the consciousness of the being, what one calls "myself", and then when one has realised that it is not at all the body, that the body expresses something else; then one searches in his/her impulses, emotions, to see whether it is that, and again onc finds out that it is not that; and then one seeks in his/her thoughts, whether the thought is truly himself/herself, what he/she calls "myself", and at the end of a very short time one becomes aware "No, I am thinking, therefore myself is different from my thought". And so, by progressive eliminations one succeeds in entering into contact with something, something which gives you the impression of being

> "Yes, that is "myself". And this something I can move around, I can move it from my body to my mind. I can move it into other people, and it is in this way that I can identify myself with things and people.
>
> I can with the help of my aspiration make it come out of my human form, rise above towards regions which are no longer this little body at all and what it contains".

And so one begins to understand what one's consciousness is; and it is after that one can say, "Good, I shall unite my consciousness with my psychic being and shall leave it there, so that it may be in harmony with the Divine and be able to surrender entirely to the Divine." Or else, "If by this exercise of rising above my faculties of thinking and my intellect I can enter a region of pure light, pure knowledge ... " then one can put his/her consciousness there and live like that, in a luminous splendour which is above the physical form.

But first this consciousness must be mobile, and one must know how to distinguish it from the other parts of the being which in fact are its instruments, its modes of expression. The consciousness must make use of these things, and not you mistake these things for the consciousness. You put the consciousness in these things, so you become conscious of your body, conscious of your mind, conscious of all your activities through your will for identification, but for this, first your consciousness must not be completely entangled, mingled, joined, so to say, with all these things, it must not take then for itself, must not be mistaken.

When one thinks of herself/himself (obviously out of millions of humans perhaps there are not ten who do otherwise) s/he thinks "Myself... that is my body, that is what I call myself, what is like this. And so, I am like that; and then my neighbour, s/he also is the body. When I speak of another person, I speak of her/his body." And so, as long as one is in this state s/he is the plaything of all possible movements and has no self-control.

The body is the last instrument and yet it is this which one calls "myself" most of the time, unless onehas begun to reflect.

Source: Collected Works of the Mother-Centenary Education (*CWMCE*), Vol. 7 (Questions and Answer 1955), pp. 254-55.

Exercise 3—Self-observation and Self-organisation

One must be clearly aware of the origin of one's movements because there are contradictory velleities in the being—some pushing you here, others pushing you there, and that obviously creates a chaos in life. If you observe yourself, you will see that as soon as you do something which disturbs you a little, the mind immediately gives you a favourable reason to justify yourself—this mind is capable of gilding everything. In these conditions it is difficult to know oneself.

One must be absolutely sincere to be able to do it and to see clearly into all the little falsehoods of the mental being. If in your mind you go over the various movements and reactions of the day like one repeating indefinitely the same thing, you will not progress. If this reviewing is to make you progress, you must find something within you in whose light you can be yourself your own judge, something which represents for you the best part of yourself, which has some light, some goodwill and which precisely is in love with progress.

Place that before you and first pass across it as in a cinema all that you have done, all that you have felt, your impulses, your thought, etc. then try to coordinate them, that is, find out why this has followed that. And look at the luminous screen that is before you: certain things pass by well, without throwing a shadow; others, on the contrary, throw a little shadow; others yet cast a shadow altogether black and disagreeable.

You must do this very sincerely, as though you were playing a game: under such circumstances I did such and such a thing, feeling like this and thinking in this way; I have before me my ideal of knowledge and self-mastery, well, was this act in keeping with my ideal or not? If it was, it would not leave any shadow on the screen, which would remain transparent, and one would not have to worry about it. If it is not in conformity, it casts a shadow. Why has it left this shadow? What was there in this act that was contrary to the will to self-knowledge and self-mastery? Most often you will find that it corresponds to unconsciousness—then you file it among unconscious things and resolve that next time you will try to be conscious before doing anything.

But in other cases you will see that it was a nasty little egoism, quite black, which had come to distort your action or your thought. Then you place this egoism before your "light" and ask yourself: "Why has it the right to make me act like that, think like that?" And instead of accepting any odd explanation you must search and you will find in a corner of your being something which thinks and says, "Ah, no, I shall accept everything but that". You will see that it is a petty vanity, a movement of self-love, an egoistic feeling hidden somewhere, a hundred things. Then you take a good look at these things in the light of your ideal: Is cherishing this movement in conformity with my seeking and the realisation of my ideal or not? I put this little dark corner in front of the light until the light enters into it and it disappears. Then the comedy is over. But the comedy of your whole day is not finished yet, you know, for there are many things which have to pass thus before the light. But if you continue this game for truly it is a game, if you do this sincerely—I assure you that in six months you will not recognise yourself, you will say to yourself, "What? was like that! It is impossible!"

You may be five years old or twenty, fifty or sixty and yet transform yourself in this way by putting everything before this inner light. You will see that the elements which do not conform with your ideal are not generally elements which you have to throw wholly out of yourself (there are very few of this kind); they are simply things not in their place. If you organise everything—your feelings, your thoughts, your impulses, etc.—around the psychic centre which is the inner light, you will see that all inner discord will change into a luminous order.

It is quite evident that if a similar procedure were adopted by a nation or by the earth, most of the things which make humans unhappy would disappear, for the major part of the world's misery comes from the fact that things are not in their place.

As an old sage has said:

"There is no evil. There is only a lack of balance."

"There is nothing bad. Only things are not in their place."

If everything were in its place, in nations, in the material world, in the actions and thoughts and feelings of individuals, the greater part of human suffering would disappear.

Source: Collected Works of the Mother-Centenary Education (*CWMCE*), Vol. 4 (Questions and Answers 1950-51), pp. 38-40.

References

Ajaya, Swami (1983). *Psychotherapy East and West: A Unifying Paradigm*. Honesdale, PA: Himalayan Institute.

Apte, V.S. (1988). *The Student's Sanskrit-English Dictionary*. Delhi: Motilal Banarsidass.

Au, T.K. (1983). "Chinese and English Counterfactuals: The Sapir-Whorf Hypothesis Revisited". *Cognition, 15*: 162-63.

Au, T.K. (1984). "Counterfactuals: In Reply to Alfred Bloom". *Cognition, 17*: 289-302.

Belenky, M.F., Clinchy, B.M., Goldberger, N.R. and Tarule, J.M. (1986). *Women's Ways of Knowing: The Development of Self, Voice, and Mind*. New York: Basic Books.

Berry, J.W., Poortinga, Y.H., Segal, M. and Dasen, P.R. (1992). *Cross-cultural Psychology: Research and Applications*. Cambridge, UK: Cambridge University Press.

Bloom, A. (1981). *The Linguistic Shaping of Thought*. Hillsdale, NJ: Erlbaum.

Bloom, A. (1984). "Caution—The Worlds You Use May Effect What You Say: A Response to Au". *Cognition, 17*: 281.

Bond, M.H. (1986). *The Psychology of the Chinese People*. New York: Oxford University Press

Briggs, J. (1970). *Never in Anger*. Cambridge, MA: Harvard University Press.

Bruner, J. (1986). *Actual Minds, Possible Worlds*. New York: Plenum Press.

Buck, R. (1988). *Human Motivation and Emotion* (2nd edn.) New York: Wiley.

Chao, R.K. (1995). "Chinese and European American Cultural Models of the Self-reflected in Mother's Child-rearing Beliefs". *Ethos, 23*: 328-54.

Chiu, L.H. (1972). "A Ccross-cultural Comparison of Cognitive Styles in Chinese and American Children." *International Journal of Psychology*, 7: 235-42.

Chodorow, N. (1978). *The Reproduction of Mothering: Psychoanalysis and the Sociology of Gender*. Berkeley, CA: University of California Press.

Cortright, B. (1997). *Psychotherapy and Spirit: Theory and Practice in Transpersonal Psychotherapy*. Albany, NY: State University of New York Press.

Cousins, S. (1989). "Culture and Selfhood in Japan and the US." *Journal of Personality and Social Psychology*, *56*: 124-31.

Dalal, A.K., Sharma, R. and Bisht, S. (1983). "Causal Attributions of Ex-criminal Tribal and Urban Children in India". *Journal of Social Psychology*, *119*: 163-71.

D'Andrade, R. (1981). "The Cultural Part of Cognition." *Cognitive Science*, *5*: 179-85.

Darwin, C.R. (1896). *The Expression of Emotions in Man and Animals*. New York: Philosophical Library.

Davis, M.H. and Stephen, W.G. (1980). "Attributions for Exam Performance." *Journal of Applied Social Psychology*, *10*: 235-48.

De Riviera, J. (1984). "The Structure of Emotional Relationships". In P. Shaver (Ed.), *Review of Personality and Social Psychology: Emotions, Relationships, and Health* (pp. 116-45). Beverly Hills, CA: Sage.

Dhawan, N., Roseman, L.J., Naidu, R.K., Thapa, K. and S.I. Rettek (1995). "Self-concepts Across Two Cultures: India and United States." *Journal of Cross Cultural Psychology*, *26*: 606-21.

Doi, L.T. (1973). *The Anatomy of Dependence*. Tokyo: Kodansha.

Doi, T. (1986). *The Anatomy of Self: The Individual vs. Society*. Tokyo: Kodansha.

Ekman, P. (1972). "Universals and Cultural Differences in Facial Expression of Emotion." In J.K. Cole (Ed.), *Nebraska Symposium on Motivation* (pp. 207-83). Lincoln: University of Nebraska Press.

Festinger, L. and J.M. Carlsmith (1959). "Cognitive Consequences of Forced Compliance. *Journal of Abnormal and Social Psychology*, *58*: 203-10.

Fiedler, F.E. (1978). "Recent Development in Research on the Contingency Model." In L. Berkowitz (Ed.), *Group Processes*, (pp. 209-25). New York: Academic Press.

Frijda, N.H., Kuipers, P. and ter Schure, E. (1989). "Relations Among Emotion Appraisal and Emotional Action Readiness." *Journal of Personality and Social Psychology*, *57*: 212-28.

Gilligan, C. (1982). *In a Different Voice: Psychology Theory and Women's Development*. Cambridge, MA: Harvard University Press.

Gilligan, C. (1986). "Remapping the Moral Domain: New Images of the Self in Relationship." In T.C. Heller, M. Sosna, and D.E. Wellbery (Eds.), *Reconstructing Individualism: Autonomy, Individuality, and the Self in Western Thought* (pp. 2237-52). Stanford, CA: Stanford University Press.

Gilmor, T.M. and D.W. Reid (1979). "Locus of Control and Causal Attribution for Positive and Negative Outcomes on University Examinations." *Journal of Research in Personality*, *13*: 154-60.

Gilovich, T. (1983). "Biased Evaluations and Persistence in Gambling." *Journal of Personality and Social Psychology*, *40*: 797-808.

Goethals, A. (1989, April). Studies of False Uniqueness. Paper presented at the Research Centre for Group Dynamics Seminar, Institute for Social Research, University.

Greenberg, J., Pyszczynski, T. and S. Solomon (1982). "The Self-serving Attributional Bias: Beyond Self-presentation." *Journal of Experimental Social Psychology, 18*: 56-67.

Greenwald, A.G. (1980). "The Totalitarian Ego: Fabrication and Revision of Personal History." *American Psychologist, 35*: 603-18.

Greenwald, A.G., and Pratkanis, A.R. (1984). "The Self." In R.S. Wyer and T.K. Shrull (Eds.), *Handbook of Social Cognition* (*3*: 129-78), Hillsdale, NJ: Erlbaum.

Harter, S. (1990). "Causes, Correlates and the Functional Role of Global Self-worth: A Lifespan Perspective." In R.J. Sternberg and J. Kolligian, Jr. (Eds.), *Competence Considered* (pp. 67-97). New Haven, CT: Yale University Press.

Hayashi, C. (1988). *National Character of the Japanese.* Tokyo: Statistical Bureau, Japan.

Hess, R., Azuma, H., Kashiwagi, K., Dickson, W.P., Nagano, S., Holloway, S., Miyake, K. Price, G. Hatano, G. and T. McDevitt (1986). "Family Influences on School Readiness and Achievement in Japan and the United States: An Overview of a Longitudinal Study." In H. Stevenson, H. Azuma, and K. Hakuta (Eds.), *Child Development and Education in Japan* (pp. 147-66). New York: Freeman.

Hilgard, E.R. (1987). *Psychology in America: A Historical Survey.* New York: Harcourt Brace Jovanovich.

Hofstede, G. (1980). *Culture's Consequences: International Differences in Work-related Values.* Beverly Hills, CA: Sage.

Hollander, E.P. (1985). "Leadership and Power." In G. Lindzey and E. Aronson (Eds.). *Handbook of Social Psychology* (*2*: 485-537), New York: Random House.

James, W. (1890). *Principles of Psychology*. New York: Holt.

Johnson-Laird, P.N. (1983). *Mental Models: Towards a Cognitive Science of Language, Inference, and Consciousness.* Cambridge, MA: Harvard University Press.

Jordan, J.V. and Surrey, J.L. (1986). "The Self-in-relation: Empathy and the Mother-daughter Relationship." In T. Bernay and D.W. Cantor (Eds.), *The Psychology of Today's Women* (pp. 81-104). Cambridge, MA: Harvard University Press.

Joshi, R.V. (1979). *Studies in Indian Logic and Metaphysics.* Delhi: Bharatiya Vidya Prakashan.

Jung, C.G. (1971). *The Portable Jung.* New York: The Viking Press (Penguin Paperback, 1977).

Kail, R. and Cavanaugh, J.C. (2004). *Human Development: A Lifespan View* (3rd edn.). Belmont, CA: Wadsworth/Thomson Learning.

Kakar, S. (1978). *The Inner World: A Psychoanalytic Study of Childhood and Society in India.* Delhi: Oxford University Press.

Kapur, P. and G. Misra (2005). "Image of Self in the Sikh Community: Continuity of the Core and Global Presence." *Psychology and Developing Societies, 15*: 103-16.

Kashima, Y., Kim, U., Gelfand, M.J., Yamaguchi, S., Choi, S. and M. Yuki (1995). "Culture, Gender, and Self: A Perspective from Individualism Collectivism Research." *Journal of Personality and Social Psychology, 69*(5): 925-37.

Kim, U. and Berry, J.W. (1993). *Indigenous Psychologies*. New Delhi: Sage.

Kitayama, S., and H. Markus (1990, August). Culture and Emotion: The Role of Other Focused Emotions. Paper presented at the 98th Annual Convention of the American Psychological Association, Boston.

Kitayama, S., Markus, H., Tummala, P., Kurokawa, M. and K. Kato (1990). *Culture and Self-cognition.* Unpublished manuscript.

Lalljee, M. and R. Angelova (1995). "Person Descriptions in India, Britain, and Bulgaria." *Journal of Cross Cultural Psychology*, *26*: 645-57.

Lau, R.R. (1984). "Dynamics of the Attribution Process." *Journal of Personality and Social Psychology, 46*: 1017-28.

Lebra, T.S. (1976). *Japanese Patterns of Behaviour*. Honolulu: University of Hawaii Press.

LeDoux, J.E. (1987). "Emotion." In V. Mount Castle (Ed.), *Handbook of Physiology:* Vol. 1. *The Nervous System* (pp. 419-59). Bethesda, MD: American Physiological Society.

Levy, R. (1973). *The Tahitians*. Chicago: University of Chicago Press.

Liu, I. (1986). "Chinese Cognition. In M.H. Bond (Ed.), *The Psychology of the Chinese People* (pp. 73-105). New York: Oxford University Press.

Liu, T.Y. and M. Hsu (1974). "Measuring Creative Thinking in Taiwan by the Torrance Test. *Testing and Guidance*, *2*: 108-09.

Lutz, C. (1988). *Unnatural Emotions: Everyday Sentiments on a Micronesian a Toll and their Challenge to Western Theory.* Chicago: University of Chicago Press.

Marks, G. (1984). "Thinking One's Abilities are Unique and One's Opinions are Common." *Personality and Social Psychology Bulletin*, *10*: 203-08.

Markus, H.R. and S. Kitayama (1991). "Culture and the Self: Implications for Cognition, Emotion, and Motivation." *Psychological Review*, *98*(2): 224-53.

Markus, H., and D. Oyserman (1988). "Gender and Thought: The Role of the Self-concept." In M. Crawford and M. Hamilton (Eds.), *Gender and Thought* (pp. 100-127), New York: Springer Verlag.

Marriott, K. (1990). *India Thought Hindu Categories.* New Delhi: Sage.

Mascolo, A.H., Misra, G. and C. Rapisardi (2004). "Individual and Relational Conceptions of Self in India and the United States." *Culture and Developing Selves: Beyond Dichotomization*, *104*: 9-26.

Mascolo, M. F. and S. Bhatia (2002). "The Dynamic Construction of Culture, Self, and Social Relations." *Culture and Developing Societies, 14*: 55-92.

Maslow, A.H. (1954). *Motivation and Personality*. New York: Harper.

Maslow, A.H. (1971). *Farther Reaches of Human Nature*. New York: Penguin Books.

Matsumoto, D. (1989). "Cultural Influences on the Perception of Emotion." *Journal of Cross Cultural Psychology, 20*: 92-105.

Matsumoto, D., Kudoh, T., Scherer, K. and H. Wallbott (1988). "Antecedent of and Reactions to Emotions in the United States and Japan." *Journal of Cross Cultural Psychology, 19*: 267-86.

Miller, J.B. (1986). *Toward a New Psychology of Women* (2nd edn.). Boston: Beacon Press.

Miller, J.G. (1984). "Culture and the Development of Everyday Social Explanation." *Journal of Personality and Social Psychology, 46*: 961-78.

Misra, G. (2001). "Culture and Self: Implications for Psychological Inquiry." *Journal of Indian Psychology, 19*: 1-20.

Misra, G., and R. Giri (1995). "Is Indian Self Predominantly Interdependent?" *Journal of Indian Psychology, 11*: 15-19.

Misumi, J. (1985). *The Behavioural Science of Leadership: An Interdisciplinary Japanese Research Programme*. Ann Arbor, MI: University of Michigan Press.

Moser, D. (1989). *If This Paper were in Chinese: Would Chinese People Understand the Title*? Unpublished manuscript, Indiana University.

Much, N. (1995). "Cultural Psychology." In J.A. Smith, R. Harre, and L.V. Langenhove (Eds.), *Rethinking Psychology*. New Delhi: Sage.

Murray, H.A. (1938). *Explorations in Personality*. New York: Oxford University Press.

Myers, D. (1989). *Social Psychology* (3rd edn.). New York: McGraw Hill.

Pennebaker, J.W. (1982). *The Psychology of Physical Symptoms*. New York: Springer Verlag.

Rama, Swami., Ballentine, R. and Ajaya, Swami (1976). *Yoga and Psychotherapy*. Honesdale, PA: Himalayan Institute.

Ramachandra Rao, S.K. (1962). *Development of Indian Psychological Thought*. Mysore, India: Kavyalaya Publishers.

Ramakrishna Rao, K.B. (1966). *Theism of Pre-classical Sāṁkhya*. Mysore, India: Prasaranga, University of Mysore.

Ramanujan, A.K. (1990). "Is There an Indian Way of Thinking?: An Informal Essay." In M. Marriott (Ed.), *India Through Hindu Categories*. New Delhi: Sage.

Roland, A. (1988). *In Search of Self in India and Japan: Toward a Cross-cultural Psychology*. Princeton, NJ: Princeton University Press.

Rosaldo, M.Z. (1984). "Toward an Anthropology of Self and Feeling." In R.A. Shweder, and R.A. LeVine (Eds.), *Culture Theory: Essays on Mind, Self, and Emotion* (pp. 137-57). Cambridge University Press.

Roseman, I.J. (1984). "Cognitive Determinants of Emotion: A Structural Theory." In P. Shaver (Ed.), *Review of Personality in Social Psychology* (5: 11-36). Beverly Hills, CA: Sage.

Ross, M. and G.J.O. Fletcher (1985). "Attribution and Social Perception." In G. Lindzey, and E. Aronson (Eds.), *The Handbook of Social Psychology*, *2*(3): 73-122, New York: Random House.

Sachhidananda Saraswathi, Swami (1956). *Chhandogya Upanishad.* Kannada translation with commentary of Sri Śaṅkaracharya. Holenarshipura, Karnataka, India: Adhyātmā Prakasha Karyalaya.

Safaya, R. (1976). *Indian Psychology: A Critical and Historical Analysis of the Psychological Speculations in Indian Philosophical Literature.* Delhi: Munshiram Manoharlal Publishers Private Limited.

Salagame, K.K.K. (1988). "States of Consciousness: Perspectives from Modern Psychology." In M.A.S. Rajan (Ed.), *Consciousness: Proceedings of the Workshop.* Melkote, India: The Academy of Sanskrit Research.

Salagame, K.K.K. (2006). *Concepts of Self and Identity in Indian Thought and their Implications for Mental Health Profession.* Psycho award oration delivered at the 32nd Annual Conference of the Indian Association of Clinical Psychologists, Jaipur.

Salagame, K.K.K., and Raj, A. (1999). "Ahamkara and Ego Functions Among Meditators and Normals." *Journal of Indian Psychology, 17*(1): 46-55.

Salagame, K.K.K., Raj, A., Murthy, K.P., Parimala, N., Rekha, K. and S. Gaur (2005). "Concept Ahamkara: Theoretical and Empirical Analysis." In K.R. Rao (Ed.), *Towards a Spiritual Psychology: Essays in Indian Psychology.* New Delhi: Samveda Publishers.

Sampson, E.E. (1989). "The Challenge of Social Change for Psychology: Globalization and Psychology's Theory of the Person." *American Psychologist, 44*: 914-21.

Sarvananda, Swami (1976). *Mandukya Upanishad.* English translation with a summary of Gaudapada's Karika. Madras: Sri Ramakrishna Math.

Scherer, K.R. (1984). "Emotions as a Multi-component Process: A Model and Some Cross-cultural Data." In P. Shaver (Ed.), *Review of Personality and Social Psychology: Emotions, Relationships, and Health* (pp. 37-63). Beverly Hills, CA: Sage.

Schwartz, J.M. and W.P. Smith (1976). "Social Comparison and the Inference of Ability Difference." *Journal of Personality and Social Psychology, 34:* 1268-75.

Scotton, B.W., Chinen, A.B., and Battista, J.R. (1996). *Textbook of Transpersonal Psychiatry and Psychology.* New York: Basic books.

Sharma, Subramanya (1947). *Prasna Upanishad.* Kannada translation with commentary of Sri Śaṅkaracharya. Holenarsipura, Karnataka, India: Adhyātmā Prakasha Karyalaya.

Shaver, P., Schwartz, J., Kirson, D. and O'Connor, C. (1987). "Emotion Knowledge: Further Exploration of a Prototype Approach." *Journal of Personality and Social Psychology, 52*: 1061-86.

Shikanai, K. (1978). "Effects of Self-esteem on Attribution of Success-failure." *Japanese Journal of Experimental Social Psychology, 18*: 47-55.

Shweder, R.A. and E.J. Bourne (1984). "Does the Concept of the Person Vary Cross-culturally? In R.A. Shweder, and R.A. LeVine (Eds.),

Culture Theory: Essays on Mind, Self, and Emotion (pp. 158-99), Cambridge, England: Cambridge University Press.

Shweder, R.A., Much, N.C., Mahapatra, M. and L. Park (1997). "The Big Three of Morality (Autonomy, Community, Divinity) and the Big Three Explanations of Suffering." In A. Brandt and P. Rozin (Eds.), *Morality and Health.* New York: Routledge and Kegan Paul.

Singelis, T.M. and W.F. Sharkey (1995), "Culture, Self-construal, and Embar-Assability." *Journal of Cross Cultural Psychology, 26*: 622-44.

Sinha, D. and R.C. Tripathi (1994). "Individualism in a Collectivist Culture: A Case of Co-existence of Opposites." In U. Kim, H.C. Triandis, C. Kagitcibasi, S. Choi, and G. Yoon (Eds.), *Individualism and Collectivism: Theory, Method, and Applications* (pp. 123-36). California: Sage Publication.

Sinha, J.B.P. (1990). "The Salient Indian Values and their Socio-ecological Roots. *Indian Journal of Social Sciences, 3*: 477-88.

Sinha, J.B.P. and R.N. Kanungo (1997). "Context Sensitivity and Balancing in Organisational Behaviour. *International Journal of Psychology, 32*: 93-105.

Sinha, J.B.P. and A. Pandey (2007). "Indian's Mindsets and the Conditions that Evoke Them." *Psychological Studies, 52*: 1-11.

Sinha, J.B.P., Sinha, T.N., Verma, J., and R.B.N. Sinha (2001). "Collectivism Coexisting with Individualism: An Indian Scenario." *Asian Journal of Social Psychology, 4*: 133-45.

Sinha, J.B.P. and J. Verma (1987). "Structure of Collectivism." In C. Kagitcibasi (Ed.), *Growth and Progress in Cross-cultural Psychology* (pp. 123-29). Lisse: Swets and Zeitlinger.

Smith, C. and Ellsworth, P.C. (1987). "Patterns of Appraisal and Emotion Related to Taking an Exam. *Journal of Personality and Social Psychology, 52*: 475-88.

Solomon, R.C. (1984). "Getting Angry: The Jamesian Theory of Emotion in Anthropology." In R.A. Shweder and R.A. LeVine (Eds.), *Culture Theory: Essays on Mind, Self and Emotion* (pp. 238-54). Cambridge, England: Cambridge University Press.

Srinivasan, G. (1967). *The Existential Concepts and the Hindu Philosophical Systems.* Allahabad, India: Udayana Publishing.

Srivastava, R. and G. Misra (1997). *Self-construal, Control and Eastern Orientation.* Unpublished manuscript, Department of Psychology, University of Delhi, New Delhi.

Steele, C. (1988). "The Psychology of Self-affirmation: Sustaining the Integrity of the Self." In L. Berkowitz (Ed.), *Advances in Experimental Social Psychology, 21*: 181-227, San Diago, CA: Academic Press.

Stevenson, H., Azuma, H. and K. Hakuta (1986). *Child Development and Education in Japan.* New York: Freeman.

Stewart, A.J. and M.B. Lykes (eds.) (1985). "Conceptualising Gender in Personality Theory and Research." In *Gender and Personality: Current Perspectives on Theory and Research* (pp. 2-13). Durham, NC: Duke University Press.

Stipek, D., Weiner, B. and Li, K. (1989). "Testing Some Attribution-emotion Relations in the People's Republic of China." *Journal of Personality and Social Psychology*, *56*: 109-16.

Sutich, A.J. (1969). "Some Considerations Regarding Transpersonal Psychology." *Journal of Transpersonal Psychology*, *1*(1): 15-16.

Swann, W.B. Jr. and S.J. Read (1981). "Self-verification Processes: How We Sustain our Self-conceptions." *Journal of Experimental Social Psychology*, *17*: 351-72.

Takata, T. (1987). "Self-deprecative Tendencies in Self-evaluations Through Social Comparison." *Japanese Journal of Experimental Social Psychology*, *27*: 27-36.

Tart, C.T. (1969). *Altered States of Consciousness: Book of Readings.* New York: John Wiley & Sons.

Tart, C.T. (1975). *Transpersonal Psychologies: Perspectives on the Mind from Seven Great Spiritual Traditions.* San Francisco: Harper Collins.

Taylor, S.E. and J.D. Brown (1988). "Illusion and Well-being: A Social Psychological Perspective on Mental Health." *Psychological Bulletin*, *103*: 193-210.

Tesser, A. (1986). "Some Effects of Self-evaluations Maintenance on Cognition and Action." In R.M. Sorrentino and E.T. Higgins (Eds.), *Handbook of Motivation and Cognition: Foundations of Social Behaviour* (pp. 435-64). New York: Guilford Press.

Triandis, H.C. (1989). "The Self and Social Behaviour in Differing Cultural Contexts." *Psychological Review*, *96*: 506-20.

Tripathi, R.C. and Leviatan, U. (2003). "Individualism and Collectivism: In Search of a Product or Process." *Culture and Psychology*, *9*: 79-88.

Varma, P. K. (2004). *Being Indian: The Truth about Why the 21st Century will be India's.* New Delhi: Viking.

Wada, M. (1988). "Information Seeking in Self-evaluations of Ability (Abstract)." *In Proceedings of Japanese Psychological Association Meeting*, *52*: 222.

Weiner, B. (1986). *An Attributional Theory of Emotion and Motivation.* New York: Springer Verlag.

Weisz, J.R., Rothbaum, F.M. and Blackburn, T.C. (1984). "Standing Out and Standing in: The Psychology of Control in America and Japan." *American Psychologist*, *39*: 955-69.

Whitley, B.E., Jr. and I.H. Frieze (1985). "Children's Causal Attributions for Success and Failure in Achievement Settings: A Meta-analysis." *Journal of Educational Psychology, 77*: 608-16.

Wylie, R.C. (1979). *The Self-concept:* Vol. 2. *Theory and Research on Selected Topics*. Lincoln: University of Nebraska Press.

Yang, K.S. (1982). "Causal Attributions of Academic Success and Failure and Their Affective Consequences." *Acta Psychologica Taiwanica, 24*: 65-83 (From Psychological Abstracts, 1985, 72, Abstract No. 13126)

Yang, K.S. and W.H. Liang (1973). "Some Correlates of Achievement Motivation Among Chinese High School Boys (In Chinese)." *Acta Psychologica Taiwanica, 15*: 59-67.

Zuckerman, M. (1979). "Attribution of Success and Failure Revisited, or: The Motivational Bias is Alive and well in Attribution Theory." *Journal of Personality, 47*: 245-87.

2

The Journey from the Ego to the Self

When we study the psychologies that exist today and classify them according to differences in their fundamental assumptions, four major paradigms emerge:

(1) the reductionist paradigm, in which all complex psychological phenomena are understood in terms of something more elemental. For example, psychoanalysis and behaviourism are both reductive psychologies;
(2) the humanistic paradigm, which emphasises and values those qualities which are unique to human beings;
(3) the dualistic paradigm, which interprets experience as an interaction between two complementary principles. For example, Carl Gustav Jung's psychology, writings of Pierre Teilard de Chardin, General Systems Theory, Sāṁkhya Philosophy; and
(4) the monistic paradigm, which considers all phenomena to be the illusory manifestation of one unified consciousness. For example in Vedānta philosophy and psychology, especially as it is interpreted by the Advaita school established by Śaṅkara in India in the eighth century A.D. The word *advaita* literally means "no-division" or "no two". Unitary consciousness is all that exists.

The Origin and Limitations of Ego-Consciousness

The newborn baby has little or no sense of identity and self-definition as a distinct being separate from his/her surroundings. The baby is born into a society that functions by way of the distinctions it makes. In the view of the adults who look after the infant, there are those who are good and those who are bad, there are insiders and outsiders, parents and children, and so on. The infant adopts the distinctions of those who are taking care of her or him, and s/he makes other distinctions, such as pleasure and pain, as a result of her or his contact with the physical environment. One of the most fundamental polar distinctions made by the growing child is *I*/not-I. The child begins to draw a boundary around what s/he defines as herself or himself and thereby considers what is outside that boundary as not herself or himself, as separate, different, or alien. That aspect of the mind concerned with drawing the boundary between I and not-I has been termed the ego by modern psychology.

The ego enables consciousness to reflect upon itself and to give definition to itself. It also establishes self-responsibility in the individual. The child in the pre-ego state cannot manage himself or herself in his or her environment because he/she has no clear sense of being a distinct entity. But the child gradually establishes and elaborates the duality *I*/not-I and thereby creates an artificial distinction between a subject who experiences and the objects that are experienced. This construction enables the child to circumscribe a limited territory (*I*) that s/he is able to manage. Those who do not establish a relatively clear distinction between *I* and not-I (subject and object) do not become responsible members of society.

There is a common belief in modern psychology that ego-consciousness represents the most advanced stage in the unfolding of consciousness and is therefore the most accurate and objective perspective possible for experiencing oneself and the world. Modern psychology, in this respect, is expressing the self-glorifying position of ego-consciousness. From this position, every other form of consciousness is regarded as inferior, for when ego-consciousness comes into power, like certain totalitarian governments it tries to maintain its dominant position by creating a closed one-party system that suppresses the recognition of alternative means of governing the human being.

Psychoanalytic psychology regards the ego as the centre of consciousness; it has established the ego as the monarch of the psyche. According to psychoanalytic theory, all other structures and processes in the mature person, including the id, superego, regression, and primary process functioning, are subservient to the regulation of the ego. In the reductive model, there is no conception of a centre of integration that is more comprehensive than the ego and to which the ego may itself be subservient.

In contrast to this, those who take the dualistic or monistic perspective recognise inherent limitations in ego-consciousness. Jung wrote: "All ego-consciousness is isolated; because it separates and discriminates, it knows only particulars ... Its essence is limitation." One who identifies with a limited *I*, with its artificial boundaries and distinctions, will inevitably experience a sense of isolation, of loneliness, and a longing for all that has been defined as outside. The ego seeks to complete itself. This *I* seeks out and becomes dependent on, or addicted to, those "external" objects and conditions it has artificially separated from itself, but completion and unity cannot be attained in this way because by definition the ego remains distinct from the object. Furthermore, however many objects the ego acquires, these are few in comparison to all that continue to remain outside its grasp. Though the ego seeks to extend itself, it remains a limited system within the individual, with a limited perspective. It is inevitably constricted by preoccupations, fears, and biases created by identifying with certain qualities and excluding others. It is inherently limited because it can experience only through others. It is inherently limited because it can experience only through the subject-object mode of consciousness.

The developed ego operates through formal operations thinking and through what psychoanalysts have called "secondary process". According to psychoanalytic theory, there is a more primitive, primary mode of functioning that disregards space and time constrictions and ordinary logic. But secondary process functioning, the functioning by which the ego operates, is bound by the constrictions of space, time, classical logic, and linear causality. This mode of functioning allows the ego to achieve a great deal, but also imposes severe restrictions on one's experiences. Formal operations functioning represents the culmination of egoistic reasoning; if consciousness is to comprehend paradox, synchronicity, and monistic conceptions, formal operations must be transcended. There must come into the foreground new modes of awareness that are not bound by the limitations of secondary process reasoning and yet are not a regression to a more primitive mode of experience. Psychoanalysis has not envisioned the possibility of a more evolved mode of cognition but has insisted on interpreting all no secondary process functioning as primary process functioning, a more primitive level of being.

Ego-consciousness is not able to reach the dualistic mode of awareness precisely because its experience is centred, or egocentric. It does not give equal weight to both sides of a polarity, including the fundamental polarity *I*/not-*I* on which it is established. And it cannot reach the monistic mode of awareness because it cannot transcend polarised thinking. Its perspective, though certainly more objective than primitive thinking, is nevertheless considerably biased. In egoistic thinking, there is a greater degree of detachment and objectivity than in primitive thinking, but one remains in the *I* who is perceiving, with all the inevitable attendant biases and insecurities. The ego is never as objective as it purports to be.

Although ego-consciousness is a necessary and very important step in the evolution of consciousness for it establishes self-consciousness and prepares the way for another more evolved mode of consciousness the potential aroused through ego-consciousness is not fulfilled until the egoistic stage is transcended.

Humanistic psychology helps one make the transition from the egoistic mode of consciousness to consciousness based on a larger and more integrative centre. Fromm speaks of a "new man", whose distinguishing qualities and characteristics include a joy comes from giving and sharing, a love and respect for life, an ever-developing capacity for love, a shedding of narcissism, and a sense of oneness with all life. Other humanistic psychologists have stressed the development of creativity, dichotomy-transcendence, playfulness, and various other qualities that lead to ego-transcendence.

While modern psychology believes that the ego is the centre of consciousness, *yoga* psychology does not regard the ego as the real centre of consciousness but as the subject-object mode of consciousness. According to this view, the ego is a provisional centre created to achieve a particular purpose, in much the same way that a scaffolding is erected to construct a building. If one becomes enamored of the scaffolding and spends her or his time decorating and admiring it, s/he may never complete the building. Many people have such a relationship with their egos.

Modern depth psychology conceives of consciousness as an attribute of the ego. *Yoga* psychology, on the other hand, regards the ego as a useful instrument of consciousness. Through the creation of the subject-object mode of consciousness, with the ego as the subjective pole, a person is able to relate to the world in a way that can be useful for certain purposes. But any instrument has limitations, and when those limitations are not understood and taken into account, a distorted perspective results. An analogy may be helpful to clarify the yogic conception. The microscope is an extremely valuable instrument in helping one to become aware of minute aspects of the environment and even in uncovering fundamental processes in the natural world that could not otherwise be observed. However, try to imagine the preposterous situation of someone who has accidentally and without awareness spilled glue over the eyepiece of her or his microscope, so that when one uses this instrument, s/he becomes bonded to it. Now s/he can see only through the limited perspective of the microscope. What was formerly an aid to enlarge her/his view and understanding of the phenomenal world has become an encumbrance from which s/he is eager to separate herself or himself. Now imagine a large group of such people who have shared this predicament for so long that they have forgotten their original state and who now assume that the way they are presently perceiving is the only way, that what they are seeing is the only reality that exists. According to the yogic conception, this is the situation most people are in.

The ego, like the microscope, is an instrument for knowing in a particular way. But there is a strong tendency for the consciousness of a person to become bonded to or identified with the ego, to experience the world primarily through the ego, and furthermore to forget that any bonding ever occurred. Since most people are in a similar situation, one thinks that the world one experiences through the ego is the whole of reality rather than merely a mode of experience brought into focus by her or his instrument. S/he forgets that there was ever any distinction between consciousness and the instrument called the ego, and one identifies with the ego as the subject of all modes of consciousness. Western depth psychologies, of both the reductive and dualistic schools, adhere to this egocentric view of consciousness.

Yoga psychology offers an alternative and more comprehensive perspective for understanding human development. It recognises and values the subject-object mode of consciousness and gives the ego its due, but it does not build an entire psychology around the ego as if it were the central aspect of the human being. Through the practice of *yoga*, one can become aware of the limitations of ego-consciousness, learn to loosen the hold of this mode of consciousness, and come in touch with a more unifying and comprehensive centre of organisation within. From the limited perspective of the threatened ego, such a development may result in regression, annihilation, or, at the very least, loss of the ego's control and supremacy. Indeed, the ego eventually does come to occupy a subsidiary role; it becomes a subsystem within a larger framework.

Ego-consciousness need not be abandoned when a more comprehensive centre of organisation is established; both organisations may continue to exist and work together. Instead of conceptualising the experience of the newly won state as a regression in the service of the ego, as is done in psychoanalysis, it is more accurate to conceive of the retreat to ego-consciousness as a regression in the service of unitary consciousness. Such regression enables the individual to maintain an organisation for functioning in the world; however, in this case, the person remains identified with the more comprehensive centre rather than with the ego. One recognises that the boundaries established by the ego are merely useful and temporary constructions rather than the reality of "who I am" and "who and what I am not".

Although the conception of a more comprehensive level of conscious organisation than the ego has not yet gained acceptance in contemporary schools of psychotherapy, precedence for such a model can be found in other areas of modern psychology. For example, it is generally believed that the evolution of the human brain took place in successive stages or layers. With the evolution of the hindbrain, the rudimentary integrative functions of the spinal cord were superseded. This new centre integrated sensory-motor reflexes and stimulation from various sensory receptors and helped maintain posture, balance, and movement. This centre of organisation in turn was superseded by the midbrain, then by the old forebrain, and finally by the new forebrain. While the more primitive structures integrated reflexive functions, the more evolved structures regulated affective and cognitive functioning. With each development of a new and more comprehensive centre of organisation, the less evolved structure did not atrophy or disappear. It continued to do its job, but was now subject to the regulation of the more evolved structure.In a normal person, if a higher order of integration beyond the ego has not evolved one remains under the sway of doubts, fears, addictions, anxieties, and other limitations of ego functioning.

Yoga psychology uses the metaphor of a chauffeur and his employer to clarify the hierarchical relationship between the ego as a centre of integration and a more comprehensive centre. A chauffeur is able to drive a limousine and to respond to traffic lights and other external conditions; he performs an important function. But imagine that the chauffeur closes the window between the front and back seat and turns off the intercom, forgetting that the owner of the car is seated at the back. The chauffeur might than take the car wherever he desires rather than doing his work, which is attending to the business and needs of the owner. Sooner or later the chauffeur will run into severe difficulties. He does not have the resources to maintain the car, to refuel it, or to use it for a higher purpose than his own satisfaction. This is exactly the situation one is in when her or his ego tries to assert its sovereignty.

The Self in Jungian Psychology and in Vedānta

Carl Gustav Jung was greatly attracted to and influenced by the teachings of the East even in early childhood. He stated in his autobiography:

> "I remember a time when I could not yet read, but pestered my mother to read aloud to me out of... an old, richly illustrated children's book, which contained an account of exotic relations, especially that of the Hindus. There were illustrations of Brahmā, Viṣṇu, and Shiva which I found an inexhaustible source of interest."

During his formative years Jung put aside his fascination with Eastern thought, yet he later seemed to incorporate more of an Eastern than a Western perspective in his own developing theories:

> "When I began my career as a psychiatrist and psychotherapist, I was completely ignorant of Chinese philosophy, and only later did my professional experience show me that in my technique I had been unconsciously following that secret way which for centuries had been the preoccupation of the best minds of the East."

During a particularly trying period of his life Jung actively practised *yoga*, and he studied Eastern philosophy and psychology intently. Of the *Tibetan Book of the Dead*, he said:

> "For years, ever since it was first published, the *Bardo Thodol* has been my constant companion, and to it I owe not only many stimulating ideas and discoveries, but also many fundamental insights."

Jung believed that *yoga* and other meditative traditions had evolved a psychology far more advanced than the psychologies of the West: "What we have to show in the way of spiritual insight and psychological technique must seem, when compared with *yoga*... backward..." Jung also believed that those who grew up in Western cultures had not yet evolved enough to incorporate the wisdom of the East: "The philosophy of the East, although so vastly different from the West, could be an inestimable treasure for us too: but, in order to possess it, we must first earn it." Jung felt that Eastern teachings were too often misunderstood; he observed his fellow Europeans adopting the trappings of Eastern spiritual traditions without truly appreciating the insights of those traditions. Some used *yoga* as physical and mental culture to suppress the unconscious rather than to bring it forward to be integrated; others adopted the philosophy and trappings with uncritical and untested belief; some pedantically accumulated knowledge about *yoga* philosophy and methods rather applying the philosophy and methods to lead them inward toward a more unified consciousness.

Jung stood at a point halfway between the psychologies of the West and the East. He acknowledged the superiority of Eastern psychology but did not believe that Westerners could really assimilate the philosophy and practises of *yoga*. He felt that it was necessary for the West to develop a *yoga* of its own, one better suited to the extraverted mind of Western man, and he regarded his own psychology as just such a development.

Although Jung relied heavily on *yoga* philosophy and psychology in developing his own theories, he differed from the monistic viewpoint on one fundamental assumption, and as a result his psychology remains within the dualistic framework. Jung followed a path toward self-understanding that in many respects was parallel to *yoga*, but he stopped short, unable to reach the more encompassing perspective of monistic psychology. *Yoga* psychology goes on to a greater purview, leaving Jung behind to take in a more limited survey of the landscape below, albeit one that is far more encompassing than that of other modern psychologies.

The point at which Jung parts company with *yoga* is clear. It can be seen in the way in which he practiced hatha *yoga* exercise:

> "I was frequently so wrought up that I had to do certain *Yoga* exercises in order to hold my emotions in check. But since it was my purpose to know what was going on within myself, I would do these exercise

> only until I had calmed myself enough to resume my work with the unconscious. As soon as I had the feeling that I was myself again, I abandoned this restraint upon the emotions and allowed the images and inner voices to speak afresh. The Indian, on the other hand, does *yoga* exercises in order to obliterate completely the multitude of psychic contents and images".

It is evident that Jung sought to travel beyond ordinary awareness to experience the world of archetypal forms. He was primarily interested in experiencing and studying the underlying forms of psychic life, much as the atomic physicist is interested in studying the underlying forms of the physical universe. In contrast to the *yogī*, Jung was not interested in exploring further, in going beyond these forms to arrive at a consciousness that is prior to, and underlies, the archetypes. Jung stated that

> "the Indian's goal is... the condition of *nirdvandva*. He wishes to free himself from nature; in keeping with this aim, he seeks in meditation the condition of imagelessness and emptiness. I, on the other hand, wish to persist in the state of lively contemplation of nature and of the psychic images. I want to be freed neither from human beings, nor from myself, nor from nature; for all these appear to me the greatest of miracles. Nature, the psyche, and life appear to me like divinity unfolded and what more could I wish for?"

Jung doubted that a state of unitary consciousness is attainable, and, even if it could be experienced, whether it would be of any worth. He firmly believed that the only form of consciousness is ego-consciousness, or the subject-object mode of consciousness. According to Jung, consciousness requires that one must have the experiences of being a subject who experiences the objects of thought.

> "To us, consciousness is inconceivable without an ego.... If there is no ego there is nobody to be

> conscious of anything.... The Eastern mind, however, has no difficulty in conceiving of a consciousness without an ego. Consciousness is deemed capable of transcending its ego condition; indeed, in its "higher" forms, the ego disappears altogether. The realisation of the One Mind... creates the at-one-ment. But we are unable to imagine how such a realisation could ever be complete in any human individual.... One cannot know something that is not distinct from oneself."

Jung believed that one could let go of the ego but that such a state inevitably consisted of falling back into unconsciousness rather, as the *yogīs* believe, transcending the limitations of the ego to reach a superconscious state. It is precisely on this point that Jung parts company with *yoga* and remains within the framework of dualistic psychology.

The dualistic models bring forth the possibility of a more comprehensive centre than the individual ego. In the older dualistic psychologies, this centre was thought of as outside the ego and was called God. The goal of the developmental process was to bring the ego into harmony with that more comprehensive centre by making it subservient to that centre. In the Jungian model, there is a similar conception, except that this more comprehensive centre is understood as existing within the individual.

Jung viewed the unconscious as stratified. He believed that the first layer below the level of the conscious mind comprises all the qualities that are opposed (opposite) to those qualities with which the ego identifies. Jung called this layer the shadow, one's dark side. Its contents are considered by the conscious mind to be negative and undesirable. For example, if the individual believes himself to be efficient and logical, his shadow may express itself in irrational outbursts and lead him to be at once both fascinated and repelled by irrationality in others. At a deeper layer of the psyche, one's ideal is found in the form of the anima and animus, the archetypes of soul and spirit that, upon being projected onto others, create the transference.

Jung believed that there is an even deeper level in the psyche beyond the anima and animus, a centre of integration, understanding, and guidance within the individual that transcends the ego, for it embraces the ego, for it embraces both the conscious and the unconscious mind. He considered this to be the archetype of wholeness or unity and called this centre the self, acknowledging the similarity of this conception to the Self or *Ātman* of Indian philosophy:

> "The union of the conscious mind or ego-personality with the unconscious... produces a new personality compounded of... both together. Since it transcends consciousness it can no longer be called "ego" but must be given the name of 'self'. Reference must be made here to the Indian idea of the *ātman*, whose personal and cosmic modes of being form an exact parallel to the psychological idea of the self.... The self... is the "uniting symbol" which epitomises the total union of opposites".

Jung also compared the process of attaining realization of the Self in *yoga* to the transformative process of analytic therapy:

> "To experience and realise this self is the ultimate aim of Indian *yoga*, and in considering the psychology of the self we would do well to have recourse to the treasures of Indian wisdom. In India, as with us, the experience of the self is a vital happening which brings about a fundamental transformation of personality."

In contrast to the psychoanalytic tradition, in which the ego is considered to be centre of integration for the personality, Jung believed that the ego is only the circumscribed centre of the conscious mind and that the self is the more comprehensive centre that takes into account the unconscious as well. In this respect, Jung's perspective appears similar to that of *yoga* psychology, for both psychologies help to make the individual aware of the distinction between the ego and self as centres of determination and both lead the individual away from identification with the limited perspective of the ego to become increasingly guided by the Self. It should not be assumed that the Self is a more comprehensive form of subjective consciousness. The Self is neither subject nor object. Subject-object is a distinction created by ego-consciousness and is not relevant to the Self. The Self is unified consciousness devoid of any such polarisations.

Despite these apparent similarities, there is a striking and crucial difference between Jung's conception of the self as an archetype and the yogic conception of the Self as the centre of consciousness. According to *yoga* psychology, the ego is the centre of a limited and circumscribed type of consciousness (the subject-object mode of consciousness), whereas the Self is the very centre of consciousness that comprehends all modes of awareness. Jung, however, took the ego to be the centre of all consciousness and the self to symbolise the integration of the conscious and the unconscious. He believed that the self, though comprehensive, lies beyond consciousness. According to Jung, one can never be fully conscious of the self because the self as a centre of integration for the individual includes unconscious contents, and these unconscious contents can never be made fully conscious. Jung asserted that

> "a complete "emptying" of the unconscious is out of the question... Consciousness, no matter how extensive it may be, must always remain the smaller circle within the greater circle of the unconscious, an island surrounded by the sea; and, like the sea itself, the unconscious yields an endless and self-replenishing abundance of living creatures, a wealth beyond our fathoming."

Jung concluded that

> "there is little hope of our ever being able to reach even approximate consciousness of the self, since however much we may make conscious there will always exist an indeterminate and indeterminable amount of unconscious material which belongs to the totality of the self".

Thus, according to Jung, full self-realisation is an ideal never to be attained. Consequently, human suffering can never be fully eliminated. Jung believed one could only become conscious of the self-partially and indirectly through the symbols it produces. To the extent that these symbols can be grasped be ego-consciousness, one can make use of these treasures in achieving a more complete integration. However, to turn away from the ego and toward the self was considered by Jung to be dangerous. In fact, he went so far as to assert that "it must be reckoned a psychic catastrophe when the *ego is assimilated by the self.*" In taking this position, Jung resurrected the dualistic religious dogma that the individual can never merge with the transcendent. Throughout history the Western mind has consistently viewed such a possibility as a threat of annihilation of the individual consciousness and has opted to remain identified with the subject-object mode of consciousness, seemingly keeping the transcendent consciousness at a distance, as an object.

Jung risked more than most in confronting the archetypes of the collective unconscious, but he preferred to enjoy the majestic splendour that he uncovered rather than to explore further to find it indeed there might be a more comprehensive mode of consciousness transcending the subject-object distinction. In this respect he was similar to Sri Ramakrishna, who upon encountering the Divine Mother became transfixed by his experience of the divine form. Even though he knew of the more comprehensive unitary consciousness, for a long time Ramakrishna could not let go of his attachment to this divine form in order to attain that greater height. Only the continued insistence of his mentor finally enabled Ramakrishna to make such a transition.

> "When I sat for meditation I could by no means make my mind go beyond the bounds of name and form.... The mind withdrew itself easily from all other things but, as soon as it did so, the intimately familiar form of the universal Mother... appeared before it as living and moving and made me quite oblivious of the renunciation of names and forms of all descriptions... this happened over and over again. Almost despairing of the attainment of the *nirvikalpa samādhi*, I then

> opened my eyes said, ..."No, it cannot be done; I cannot make the mind free from functioning and force it to dive into the Self". Scolding me severely, the naked one (Ramakrishna's mentor) said very excitedly, "What, it can't be done!"... "Collect the mind here to this point". With a firm determination I sat for meditation again and, as soon as the holy form of the divine Mother appeared now before the mind as previously, I looked upon knowledge as a sword and cut it mentally in two with that sword of knowledge.... The mind... transcended quickly the realm of names and forms, making me merge in *samādhi*".

Vedānta psychology clearly disagrees with Jung's belief that the Self can never be known directly. The very aim of Vedānta is to fully experience the Self, which is the centre of pure consciousness. According to Vedānta, the assimilation of the ego by Self, rather than being a psychic catastrophe, result in a state of illumination. In striking contrast to the dualistic position of Jung, Śaṅkara, the most respected exponent of the nondual philosophical position, unequivocally asserted:

> "You are pure consciousness, the witness of all experiences.... Cease this very moment to identify yourself with the ego, the doer.... Its intelligence is only apparent, a reflection of the *Ātman*, which is pure consciousness. It robs you of peace and joy in the *Ātman*. By identifying yourself with it, you have fallen into the snare of the world the miseries of birth, decay and death".

The difference between Śaṅkara's non-dualism and Jung's dualism is resolved when one takes into account the relative viewpoint of each position. Jung experienced the world through the waking state of ego-consciousness, and from that perspective all other modes of experience seem to be unconscious. Each night we go to sleep and pass through the cycles of dreaming and deep sleep, but most individuals do not remember much of their dream experience upon wakening, and practically no one recalls any experiences from deep sleep. So to the person who is awake, these appear to be unconscious states. In terms of the waking state, experiences from the other two states become conscious only if they can be brought over and integrated into waking consciousness.

Vedānta psychology regards the dreaming state and state of deep sleep as modes of consciousness that are just as valid or invalid, real or unreal, as the waking state. In fact, according to the *Māṇḍūkya Upaniṣad*, the other two states are in certain respects superior to the waking state.

The ordinary person cannot correlate these states. However, there are yogic methods for achieving a correlation between these states, and one who has attained such a correlation realises that each is a state of consciousness and that the ability to observe all three states leads to a fourth state of consciousness that is comprehensive and is identical with the Self.

Those rare individuals who have evolved their consciousness to the degree that they can remain aware in the stage of deep sleep have described that state as devoid of all objects, a seeming void, the obscrve of the waking state. In the Buddhist tradition, this state has been referred to as *nirvāṇa*. When one enters this state, he cuts himself off from awareness of objects. He remains still and is completely withdrawn within. To the external observer, he may appear to be unconscious:

> "Objectively viewed, the individual appear to enter a complete state of ecstatic trance, in which there is a suspension of vital and conscious... process.... This is all that the physical scientist qua physical scientist can observe. And if the observer holds to the theory that the sāṁgsāric type of consciousness is the only possible consciousness, then he would say the trance involved the total extinction of consciousness in every sense. Some psychologists take this position, but since they are unable to trace what they cannot see, they are quite unqualified to pass judgement upon the state in question."

Franklin Merrell-Wolff, a contemporary of Jung who successfully followed the Vedāntic path to achieve a correlation between these states, agrees with Jung to a certain degree. He acknowledges that, for some, the experience of this state can be a kind of regression:

> "Some writers conceive *nirvāṇa* as being like the state of the newly born infant, wherein there is little or no self-consciousness.... In this view there is a part truth and a great error. Without full self-consciousness, this state may be likened to a sort of original nascent consciousness, such as must precede the development of organised consciousness. It is entirely of organised consciousness to sink back into such a nascent stage. Therefore, *nirvāṇa* is not the immediate goal for immature men and women. In fact, the immature entering of the state is a sort of failure."

Wolff acknowledges that giving up the subject-object mode of consciousness may indeed be a return to unconsciousness, but he attests that this is not inevitable:

> "For most individuals the centre of consciousness in the Spatial Void is a state like dreamless sleep, in other words, a psychical state that analytic psychology has called the "unconscious"... It is possible, however, to transfer the principle of self-consciousness into the Spatial Void, in which case it is no longer a state like dreamless sleep."

This state of *nirvāṇa* may be conceived of as the opposite or complement of the waking state. One who is able to remain self-conscious in this spatial void experiences a state of ongoing ecstasy far in excess of any pleasure experienced through the waking mode of consciousness. Though this is a state of mystic bliss devoid of all the pain and suffering experienced in the waking state, it is not the highest state of consciousness. The most transcendent state of conscious is that which transcends all polarities, including the primary polarity between *nirvāṇa* and the world of names and forms. This is a state that comprehends and encompasses the waking state and the nirvāṇic state along with the dreaming state of consciousness. According to the Upaniṣads, this is the fourth state of consciousness, the nondual state, in which all limitations of form are transcended. It cannot be defined except perhaps by paradox or by negating any form that may be attributed to it.

Jung was able to make the correlation between waking consciousness and dream-consciousness a great and rare achievement but he was not able to correlate the state of deep sleep with the other two states of consciousness. This in a nutshell explains why and how his position differs from other psychologists and how it differs from non-dual psychology. Jung's entire life was devoted to exploring the dream state in its own right and translating his experiences into waking consciousness. This led to a great deal of struggle in certain phases of his life as he tried to maintain the correlation between the dream state and egoistic consciousness. He was more than amply rewarded for his struggle, for he explored majestic and heavenly realms whose doors remain closed to all but a few. But Jung was not able to integrate into his awareness the state of deep sleep nor to reach that state of consciousness that comprehends both the world of form and its polar opposite, the world of *nirvāṇa*. He thus was not able to experience the Self directly, and as a result he posited as part of his psychology that the Self could not be directly known.

Ordinary human consciousness does not have the capacity to comprehend the transcendent unified state of consciousness any more than a being who lived in a two-dimensional world could imagine the experience of someone living in three dimensions. The mind can create maps and metaphors to give one clues to the nature of this transcendent state, but all these necessarily remain within the framework of the subject-object mode of experience and therefore are distorted and far from complete. Furthermore, looking at a map is far different from experiencing that which the map is designating. The seer-philosophers who have experienced this unified consciousness have attempted as best they could to describe it to those who are functioning in the subject-object mode of consciousness. In some they have done so by negating any conceptions or distinctions that one might apply to nondual consciousness from within subject-object framework. The *Bṛhadāraṇyaka Upaniṣad* explains it thus:

> The Self described *as not this, not that.* It is incomprehensible, for it cannot be comprehended; undecaying, for it never decays; unattached, for it never attaches itself; unbound, for it is never bounds.

> ...the changeless Reality... is neither gross nor fine, neither short nor long, neither hot nor cold, neither light nor dark, neither of the nature of air, nor of the nature of ether... without relations... without measure... without inside or outside.

Other sages have also described this state in terms of the transcendence of all polarities. Śaṅkara, for example, said: "The absolute Reality is beyond good and evil, pleasure and pain, success and disaster." "All sense of duality is obliterated. There is pure, unified consciousness." Merrell-Wolff has asserted that this state is "neutral with respect to every polarity and thus in principle gives command over all polarities". He has written:

> "In it are blended, at once, all dualities... It is the Desire and the desire fulfilled, at this moment and forever.... Here is the utter Fullness, beyond the highest reach of the imagination."

Since this undifferentiated consciousness from which the world of appearance is projected transcends all polarities, he who experiences the Self will likewise be free from identification with the pairs of opposites that comprise the phenomenal world. In describing the awakened, sage Śaṅkara said:

> "Sometimes he appears to be a fool, sometimes a wise man. Sometimes he seems splendid as a king, sometimes feeble-minded. Sometimes he is calm and silen... Sometimes people honour him greatly, sometimes they insult him. Sometimes they ignore him....

> He has no riches, yet he is always contended. He is helpless, yet of mighty power. He enjoys nothing, yet he is continually rejoicing. He has no equal, yet he sees all men as his equals.... He appears to be an individual, yet he is present in all things, everywhere...."

If a man identifies himself with the gross and subtle coverings within which he dwells, he will experience pleasure and pain, good or evil. But nothing is either good or evil to the contemplative sage, because he has realised the *Ātman* and his bonds have fallen from him.

Like the proponents of Vedānta psychology, Jung conceived of a universal centre or self within. However, he believed that the self can never be experienced directly, that it always remains in the unconscious and can be known only through symbols. In other words, the duality that formerly existed in Western thought between man/woman and God now existed within the psyche as the duality between the ego as the seat of consciousness and the self as the comprehensive centre of the psyche. Monistic psychology posits a centre within each being that is a centre of universal consciousness. The final phase of a person's evolutionary process consists of recognising her/his true identity as the Self or unitary consciousness. Monistic psychology describes the means for becoming aware of one's essential nature and the practice of *yoga* leads toward this awakening.

Exercises for Growth and Mastery

Exercise 1: Visualisation for Discovering One's Being

As when one goes on the discovery of one's inner being, of all the different parts of one's being, one very often has the feeling that one is entering deep into a hall or room, and according to the colour, the atmosphere, the things it contains, one has very clear perception of the part of the being one is visiting. And then, one can go from one room to another, open doors and go into deeper rooms each of which has its own character. And often, these inner visits can be made during the night. Then it takes a still more concrete form, like a dream, and one feels that s/he is entering a house, and that this house is very familiar to her/him. And according to the time, the periods, it is internally different, and sometimes it may be in a state of very great discorder, very great confusion, where everything is mixed up, sometimes there are even broken things; it is quite a chaos. At other times these things are organised, put in their place; it is as though one had arranged the household, one cleans up, puts it in order, and it is always the same house. This house is the image, a kind of objective image, of your inner being. And in accordance with what you see there or do there, you have a symbolic representation of your psychological work.

To sit in meditation before a closed door, as though it were a heavy door of bronze—and one sits in front of it with the will that it may open—and to pass to the other side; and so the whole concentration, the whole aspiration is gathered into a beam and pushes, pushes, pushes against this door, and pushes more and more with an increasing energy until all of a sudden it bursts open, and one enters. It makes a very powerful impression. And so one is as though plunged into the light and then one has the full enjoyment of a sudden and radical change of consciousness, with an illumination that captures one entirely, and the feeling that one is becoming another person. And this is a very concrete and very powerful way of entering into contact with one's psychic being.

...when I ask you to go deep down within yourselves, some of you will concentrate on a sensation, but others may just as well have the impression of going down into a deep well, and they clearly see the picture of steps going down into a dark and deep well, and they go down farther and farther, deeper and deeper, and sometimes reach precisely a door; they sit down before the door with the will to enter, and sometimes the door opens, and then they go in and see a kind of hall or a room or a cave or something, and from there, if they go on they may come to another door and again stop, and with an effort the door opens and they go farther.

And if this is done with enough persistence and one can continue the experience, there comes a time when one finds oneself in front of a door which has... a special kind of solidity or solemnity, and with a great effort of concentration the door opens and suddenly enters a hall of clarity, of light; and then, one has the experience, you see, of contact with one's soul....

Sources: [(i) *Collected Works of the Mother—Centenary Education* (*CWMCE*), Vol. 7 (Questions and Answers 1955) pp. 271-72. (ii) *Collected Works of the Mother—Centenary Education* (*CWMCE*), Vol. 9 (Questions and Answers 1957-58) p. 379.]

References

Fromm, E. (1976). *To Have or To Be*? New York: Harper and Row.

Jung, C.G. (1963). *Memories, Dreams, Reflections*. New York: Random House, Vintage Books.

Masterton, R.B. (1980). The Nervous System and Behaviour. In Gregory A. Kimble, Norman Garmezy, and Edward Zigler (5th Ed.), *Principles of General Psychology*. New York: Wiley and Sons.

Merrell, Wolff, F. (1973). *The Philosophy Through to Space*: *A Personal Record of Transformation in Consciousness*. New York: Julian Press.

Prabhavananda, S. and F. Manchester (1969). *The Upanishads*: *Breath of the Eternal*. New York: New American Library, Mentor Books.

Rama, S. (1982). *Enlightenment Without God*: *Mandukya Upanishad*, Honesdale, PA: Himalayan Institute.

Rama, S. and Ajaya, S. (1976). *Emotion to Enlightenment*. Honesdale, PA. Himalayan Institute.

Read, H., Fordham, M. and G. Adler (1953-80). *The Collected Works of C.G. Jung* (Translated by R.F.C. Hull, Bollingen Series, No. 20, 18 volumes). Princeton, N.J.: Princeton University Press; London: Routledge and Kegan Paul.

Shankara (1978). *Crest-jewel of Discrimination*. (Translated by Swami Prabhavananda and Christopher Isherwood). Hollywood, California: Vedānta Press.

Srimat Swami Saradanandaji Maharaj (1952). *Sri Ramakrishna: The Great Master*. (Translated by Swami Jagadananda). Mylapore, India: Sri Ramakrishna Math.

3

Indian Knowledge System

The mere effort of writing about the Vedas and the Upaniṣads, which are regarded as the source of the highest knowledge there is, is vast injustice to the profoundness and the sheer superiority of these two ultimate sources of knowledge. Therefore, not only this brief explanation about Vedas and the Upaniṣads is outside the scope of this book; it is an utter underestimation of their significance in our lives. Nevertheless, an attempt has been made to help readers to broadly relate the teachings of the Vedas, Upaniṣads, and Vedānta and Sāṁkhya philosophy, to understand the contribution of the Indian knowledge systems in perceiving self and inner growth.

Vedas

The word *veda* comes from its Sanskrit root called *vid*, which indicates the *activity of knowing*. Therefore, the Vedas are considered to be the book of knowledge, to say the least. Vedas are known to contain the highest knowledge. It is the product of the minds of some greatest human beings that have ever walked this earth. These people who lived during the times when human languages were still being developed, these people with their intellectual as well as spiritual brilliance, meditated and underwent immense effort, known as *tapasyā*, to attain the Supreme knowledge. The result of their incredible effort is what constitutes the Vedas.

Sri Aurobindo has called the Vedas and the other sources as the ancient Indian spiritual knowledge. The Vedas, the Upaniṣads, Purāṇas, Tantra, the Gītā—all are scriptures but also books of knowledge for what they reveal is not made for all times, it is the knowledge that can be tested, experimented with, and verified over and over. It is like scientific knowledge that can be expanded upon, one can surpass it, add a new revelation, a new knowledge.

The text of Vedas in itself is humongous. It consists of four books: (1) *Ṛgveda*; (2) *Yajurveda*; (3) *Sāmaveda*; and; (4) *Atharvaveda.* Among these, *Ṛgveda* is the biggest with ten chapters and around ten thousand verses. *Atharvaveda* is around half of the *Ṛgveda*, *Yajurveda* is more than one-fourth of the *Ṛgveda*, and *Atharvaveda* is the shortest of the four.

Basically, *Ṛgveda* is regarded as the "The Veda" and Sri Aurobindo had studied it in depth. The word *ṛg* means hymn. It signifies a hymn of praise, a hymn of call which emerges out of a human being in extreme ecstasy, or mystery, or wonder, or victory. Western philosophers, on the other hand, did not find the knowledge of the Veda valuable. According to them it just reflected the thinking of the ancient times who were naive in their imagination, were superstitious and materialist. They believed that the knowledge given in the Vedas was only good for historical purposes for it will show how the primitive people of the ancient times thought, reasoned, and imagined. In fact, seeing such interpretations by the Westerners, the Indian philosophers at that time dared not deviate. This pointed out the difficulty of understanding the Vedas. Western philosophers" interpretations seemed to have emerged from the interpretations of a great Indian scholar of the fourteenth century A.D., Sāyaṇa, a ritualist himself. Sāyaṇa's interpretations of the Veda reflected it as more ritualistic. Sāyaṇa's own claims that Vedas contain knowledge and the greatness of the Vedic ṛṣis appeared to be fictional. The interpretation, in itself, does not give the reader sufficient proof that the Vedas are the source of some profound knowledge. This could be due to the fact that Sāyaṇa himself was a ritualist and he conceived the Vedas to be written for ritualistic purposes.

However, having said that, unlike the Western philosophers, Sāyaṇa revered the Vedas. For him, Vedas was a book of rituals whose *mantra*s had magical effects and properly chanting these *mantra*s may produce results like materialistic gains. However, the Western philosophers went a step ahead, ignoring the reverence or the importance for the Vedas in Sāyaṇa's interpretative texts, tried to prove that Vedas were important only as a reflection of the primitive history.

Sri Aurobindo, nonetheless, accessed the depths of the Vedic texts starting from the Upaniṣads. Given how the significance of the Vedas had been controversial, Upaniṣads, that claim that they are nothing but the reaffirmation of the Vedic knowledge, are considered as being of "tremendous importance" and full of light by scholars all over the world. As a matter of fact, *Bhagavad Gītā*, Purāṇas, Tantra—all regard Vedas as a book of Knowledge. In fact, Indian schools of philosophy consider Vedas as the authority, and it is a tradition in Indian schools of philosophy that if one's conclusions are not in agreement with that of the Vedas, they are wrong.

In the early stages of Sri Aurobindo's life, without really having studied the Vedas, he thought may be the modern interpretations of the Vedas were quite meaningful. One of the last interpretations of the Vedas was by the great scholar of the nineteenth century, Maharṣi Dayananda Saraswati. He had also criticised Sāyaṇa's interpretation and had declared Vedas to be a book of great Knowledge. Sri Aurobindo paid a tribute to Dayananda Saraswati by dedicating an illuminating article and essay on him, even though, Sri Aurobindo's own interpretation was different from Dayananda Saraswati's.

By the time Sri Aurobindo started studying the Vedas seriously for the first time after coming to Pondicherry, he had had three realisations of his *yoga*: (1) Brāhmic *nirvāṇa*; (2) Universal Vāsudeva-Kṛṣṇa; and (3) the Knowledge of the planes between the mind and the supermind. Following which, he had the experience of what are called the four female energies in the Vedas—Ilā, Saraswatī, Saramā, and Dakṣa. However, at the time of the experience, Sri Aurobindo did not have a clue about what they were or what they meant. So, when he read the Vedas having experienced all this, he found meaning and confirmation of his experiences in the Vedas. Therefore, Sri Aurobindo found a clue to understanding his own experiences of the highest powers of the consciousness in the *Ṛgveda*. According to Joshi (n.d.), "it is said in the Vedas that only a seer can understand the words of a seer."

> *ninya vacāṁsi kavaye nivacanāmi*
> (Secret words are revealed only to the *kavi*, to the poet, to the seer.)

The Upaniṣads or the *Bhagavad* Gītā also cannot be understood without fully understanding the Vedas. The Vedas are not only of significance for our own country but is the only remaining text of the ancient times that is available to the whole of humanity. That is, from the conception of mankind, Vedas are the earliest known as well as the only remaining text of humanity. Vedas represent the only written text of the earliest thought of mankind, the only proof of the earliest document of mankind. Whether one understands it or not, there is no denying that these are the most ancient texts available to and of mankind.

These Vedic texts were, however, known to have preceded by a great civilization of which the current known Vedic knowledge is only a fragment. A ṛṣi called Vyāsa knew the Vedas in its wholeness and totality. He made an anthology of the then known Vedic knowledge. The currently known four Vedas are not the full Vedic texts that were available at that time, rather these are just a selection of the whole.

Based on what Sri Aurobindo has said about the Vedas, Joshi posits that there are three important points to consider:

First, Vedic poetry is mantric poetry. Sri Aurobindo has talked about the meaning of *mantra* and the significance of the Vedas in his book called, *The Future Poetry*. He has stated that *mantra*, a word which does not have an accurate English counterpart, is a rhythmic expression which produces a physical effect upon its recitation. For instance, if one says *tathātsu* that is, "let it be so" in mantric form, then that is it will be so physically. Sri Aurobindo postulated three criteria for a poetry to be considered mantric poetry:

(a) It must have the highest intensity of rhythm. Having rhythmic words, but just that is also not enough. The rhythmic words should be of the highest intensity.

(b) It must have the highest intensity of style. This means that there should be a "perfect congruence between the mode of expression and the meaning of expression".

(c) It must contain within it the highest version of the highest truth. This means that all poetry is basically a perception. A perception so deep that it takes the form of an image. When your poetry captures the vision and the experience of the Highest Truth, the deepest of the most comprehensive Truth, and not just a beautiful worldly phenomenon, that is *mantra*. And Sri Aurobindo says that the entire Vedas are composed of mantric poetry.

Second, the Vedas have been written in symbolic language, a disguised form, that is, their external meaning is different from what they actually convey. The reason for doing that was to protcct the knowledge from reaching the wrong hands, therefore, a secret code was developed. Sri Aurobindo, nonetheless, was able to crack this code because of the insight he had gained as a result of his own experiences.

Third, the final point to consider is that the Vedas contain a very deep knowledge of reality, of the world, and of the Self. It is a triple knowledge: God-knowledge, world-knowledge, and soul-knowledge.

God knowledge answers the questions to What is God? What is the Ultimate Reality? According to the first few statements of the Ṛgveda, a *mantra* says:

na nunam asti no shvaḥ kastadveda yadadbhutam anyasya ।
cittamabhi samcareṇyamutadhitam vinaśyati ।।

> "The Ultimate Reality is neither today nor tomorrow. Who knows that reality, which is wonderful? Why is it wonderful? It has motion, it is alone, there is no other but it has motion in another, it is *adbhutam*. It has motion in another. If you try to approach it through your intellectual thought, where you always distinguish one and another, and divide the two, and

don't understand the mystery of one being another, if you apply that intellect on it, it vanishes". (Joshi, n.d.)

In other words, if one tries to approach the Ultimate Reality, understand it intellectually, one may never grasp it simply because it is "wonderful". The logic of the finite does not work here. Sri Aurobindo says the Ultimate Reality is both simple and complex, it is one but many, and it is the static which is dynamic. Isha Upaniṣad has also said the same thing—*tadejāti tannaijāti.*

World Knowledge

In the Vedas, it has been said that the physical world is just the outer periphery of the whole world. And even this world that we see consists of three earths, not one—the world of the physical, the world of the vital, and the world of the mental. These three worlds are the first three to which we have the normal access. But later the Vedic Seers found out *turīyam svid*, meaning "the fourth one". The three worlds represent the body, life, and mind. However, the fourth world discovered by the Vedic *ṛṣi*s—the fourth reality—*saptadhi*, meaning the seven-headed thought. This fourth reality was later interpreted by Sri Aurobindo as representing the Supermind. And beyond this Supermind, Vedic Seers discovered the triple reality which later came to be known as—*sat cit ānanda* (Existence, Consciousness, and Bliss). According to Joshi (n.d.), this simple, naive explanation does not do justice to the profoundness of the Vedic Knowledge, however, it does incorporate its basic formula.

Soul Knowledge

The knowledge of the soul, the inner self, is considered to be the most sacred knowledge according to the *Ṛgveda*. This inner soul or inner self is what Sri Aurobindo has called the "psychic being" in his own study of psychology. It took a long time and search to know or understand about this inner soul. This is regarded as the most important discovery made by the Vedic seers and our most precious knowledge today. The self-knowledge is the most profound secret of the Vedic knowledge according to the Vedas; because without the knowledge of the self, one cannot go into the realms of the Vedic knowledge. One must know about themselves deeply enough to understand the world and only by knowing about oneself, the world can rise to know the Supreme and discover this wonderful reality that has motion in another. The word used in the Vedas for the innermost soul or inner self is *agni*. *Agni* is the mystic fire. This mystic fire has been described differently in the Vedas itself. In fact, upon a closer examination of the Veda, we discover that Agni is not just a physical fire principle; rather, it represents the psychological principle of Will-Force, of which physical fire is merely one external manifestation. This can be used as a symbol to try and bring the physical mind closer to a sense and feeling for something that is profoundly present and dynamic in the universe.

Agni is also the force of evolution, pushing ahead constantly, shattering the dark layers of Matter (*annam*) and Inconscience (*tamas*) to release the throbbing life-force. It is that which generates growth, amplifies power, creates and seals relationships between vegetations, plants, and herbs, propels the greater forces of intelligence, forms and build complex organisations in which the mind can be enabled to vibrate efficaciously, thereby permeating the material form with consciousness and even self-awareness.

In his book, *The Life Divine*, Sri Aurobindo has described as the flame burning in our hearts—inextinguishable. It can be related to Socrates "daemon", which always turns itself to the truth, beauty and goodness, which detects the truth from falsehood, without a mistake. That is our true Soul within us and without knowing this fire burning within us, we cannot possible know and understand the knowledge imparted by the Vedas. This is the reason why it is considered the most important discovery of the Vedic *ṛṣis*; it marks the beginning of the quest of the Ultimate Knowledge. What we are from the inside is this fire.

Sri Aurobindo posits that Vedas is a great book of *yoga*. It is not something to attain materialistic outcomes from, it is a knowledge of the battle of life. It is a revelation of the real nature of Life; when in harmony, disharmony comes about.

One of the most chanted verses of the Vedas is the following Gāyatrī Mantra which says:

oṁ bhūr bhuvaḥ svaḥ
tat savitur vareṇyam bhargo devasya dhīmahi
dhiyo yo naḥ pracodayāt

> "We are meditating upon the most blessed lustre of that light, of that God, who is known as sun, so that our intellect may be directed by it". (Joshi, n.d.).

This particular *mantra* talks about the three worlds in the first line—*bhūr* signifying the physical world, *bhuvaḥ*—the intermediate world which is beyond the physical world, and *svaḥ*—the higher world which is further beyond the intermediate world. *Svaḥ* represents the world of Light.

Thus, the Vedic *ṛṣi*s have provided us with a roadmap for achieving human destiny. It is the result of the victory of the Vedic seers over the heart and mind that the story of Indian culture is one of continuity and change, of quest and knowledge unfolding, free from dogma and all constrictive ideas of life. Today, the Indian heritage is one of and with continuous knowledge discovery, and the people most respected in our society are those who discover new things. It is true that the Vedas are infinite, *vedāḥ anantāḥ*.

Upaniṣads

Upaniṣads provide us with the resurgence of the Vedic *yoga*; and the synthesis of this Vedic *yoga* opens up the gates to a high spiritual knowledge. The Upaniṣads offer an integrated account of all that was seen and experienced by the inspired and liberated seekers of the Eternal reality throughout the valuable period of yogic seeking. If Vedas are considered as the world's first existing account of *yoga*, then Upaniṣads are the first yogic interpretation, explication, and emergence of the *yoga* contained in the Veda.

In the Upaniṣads, the intuitive and the innermost psychological experiences of the Vedic Seers lead us to the most superior culmination in which the Spirit, uncovers its own body and divulges the very word of its self-manifestation.

The number of Upaniṣads has increased over a very long period of time, and there are books that have 250 Upaniṣads. However, there are just twelve principal Upaniṣads. These Upaniṣads are—the *Bṛhadāraṇyaka Upaniṣad*, the *Chāndogya*

Upaniṣad, the *Taittirīya Upaniṣad*, the *Aitareya Upaniṣad*, the *Kauṣītaki Upaniṣad*, the *Kena Upaniṣad*, the *Kaṭha Upaniṣad*, the *Īśa Upaniṣad*, the *Muṇḍaka Upaniṣad*, the *Praśna Upaniṣad*, the *Māṇḍūkya Upaniṣad*, and the *Śvetāśvatara Upaniṣad*. The *Upaniṣads* are the most revered because they represented more accurately the *yoga* of the Veda.

The primary goal of the *Upaniṣad* is the same for all the principal Upaniṣads: to attain the state of immortality. However, it focuses more on the relationship between the Divine, the all-powerful and all-possessing *Brahman*, and the world as well as human consciousness. It also addresses passing from our current state of suffering, ignorance, and divided self to oneness, the truth, true knowledge, integral knowledge, and divine beatitude. The *Upaniṣad* concludes with the desire for ultimate happiness.

It is, however, interesting to note that there is no period in the history of the rest of the world that parallels the Upaniṣadic period in India. Sri Aurobindo has claimed that Upaniṣads is what that has given India its soul, its temperament. India cannot be understood without understanding the Vedas and the Upaniṣads. Upaniṣads was born out of a quest, a stir of a kind, that was a gift to each and everyone in the Indian soil.

Upaniṣads have no parallel in the history of the world, unlike Vedas which had its counterparts in different parts of the world, for instance, orphism, an ancient movement in Greece. This could be one of the reasons why Upaniṣads, and not Vedas are regarded by the entire world as the source of profound knowledge. Upaniṣads have been the key in marking the Indian temperament, Indian *dharma*, and Indian consciousness. There are three characteristics of this quest of the Upaniṣads which indicate its value and significance.

The Vedas were written in a symbolic language, a secret language that could not be understood by merely anyone who knows the Sanskrit language. Only those who could understand its symbolism, could really understand the meaning and teachings of this great book of the Highest Knowledge. In due course of time, the meanings of symbols were lost and thus started a strenuous yet incredible effort to uncover and recover the lost symbolic knowledge of the Vedas. There was an abundance of knowledge present, hidden behind the symbolism of language. The knowledge had become buried and curtained by the veil of language, by the veil of words. Just like a speaker of one language cannot understand what is said or written in another language until s/he learns that language, it was difficult to understand the true meaning behind the external words written in the Vedas. In addition, it was even harder to understand the Vedic language as it was composed symbolically. Therefore, the Upaniṣads reflected a tremendous effort, a marvelous quest to unveil this symbolic language to discover its ultimate Knowledge. This was the first characteristic of the quest of the Upaniṣads. It is important to note that this quest for unmasking the Vedic Knowledge was no ordinary effort. It was a striving that had never taken place in the history of the world. Eleusinian mysteries were similar to the Vedas, however, when the knowledge of the Eleusinian mysteries was lost, there was no effort to recover it. It was permanently lost. The Upaniṣadic *ṛṣi*s could have interpreted the knowledge in their own ways, but they chose not to do it ordinarily. Therefore, emphasis is given on how significant and magnificent feat it was to even attempt to recover the lost knowledge of the Vedas, and even more to successfully do so.

The second characteristic of the quest focuses on the intensity of the quest. The intensity of the quest for knowledge was quite extraordinary in the Upaniṣads. People were ready to sacrifice anything and everything to attain this knowledge—that was the intensity of the quest, the mark of the *Upaniṣad*. The courage to leave everything behind, give up everything, in pursuit of true knowledge was the tradition set up by the Upaniṣads. If the object of one's knowledge that they believe is the most supreme, then to attain it, one must be willing to detach oneself from everything and sacrifice everything. The Upaniṣadic *ṛṣi*s were ready for this kind of abandonment and renunciation to seek the Highest Knowledge.

This quest for knowledge was not limited to a handful of people, in fact it had spread over to all the sections of society. That is why the Upaniṣads reflect a story of the people which is unprecedented. This was the third characteristic.

In order to go beyond the symbolism in the Vedic text, the Upaniṣadic *ṛṣi*s found a method. This method is discussed at great lengths by Sri Aurobindo in a chapter titled, "The Methods of Vedāntic Knowledge" in his book *The Life Divine*. The word *vedānta* is made up two words *veda* plus *anta*, literally meaning the end of the Veda. Upaniṣads are considered as Vedānta because they came after the Vedas and signify their end. Upaniṣadic effort is therefore, Vedāntic effort. The chapter in Sri Aurobindo's book that discussed about the methods that were used by the Upaniṣadic *ṛṣi*s to uncover and recover the Vedic knowledge was divided into three parts.

The first part dealt with the knowledge attained through the senses. The knowledge that we gain from our five senses is crucial, however it is important to go beyond these senses to arrive at the sixth sense, which is the real sense. This sixth sense is called *manas* in Sanskrit. *Manas* is the mind that senses, it is the sense that is attached to our other senses, which can detach itself from the senses. You see, but if your mind is not attached to your eyes, you wouldn't really see what your eyes saw. This was long discovered by the Vedic *ṛṣi*s that there exists a sixth sense beyond our five senses that has incredible capacities—it can see without seeing and hear without hearing, and it cannot see while seeing and not hear while hearing. This method, which was the initial discovery of the Vedic *ṛṣi*s, was later recovered by the Upaniṣadic seers.

The second part dealt with the knowledge gained through reason. There is a faculty in us—the faculty of reason that goes even beyond the sixth sense. According to Sri Aurobindo, Vedic *ṛṣi*s and later the Upaniṣadic seers had discovered that reason is a function of ideas, and not just words. This means that unless your words take you to the ideas, your reasoning will not function. Merely thinking with words is not enough, one should begin thinking with ideas and this is the real proper exercise of reason. Reason arrives only when one starts to think with ideas.

The third part focused on intuition. After knowing through the sixth sense and through thinking with ideas, one has to grasp by experience, called intuition. Intuition that takes place through experience—not just any experience, but an experience that happens when you widen yourself and heighten yourself to the utmost. When that happens, that is the real experience called intuition.

Therefore, by breaking free from the boundaries of the senses, the boundaries of reason, and entering into the experience of widening yourself to the utmost, using intuition did the Upaniṣadic Seers recover the lost and buried symbolic Vedic knowledge.

In conclusion, the ultimate goal of yogic knowledge, *Brahman*, or *brahma-vidyā*, is the common subject of all these Upaniṣads. However, each Upaniṣad approaches it differently, entering the kingdom of *brahma-vidyā* through their own gate, taking their own path, and having their own point of arrival.

Vedānta

The word Vedānta is composed of two words—*veda* and *anta* (end). Thus, the literal meaning of Vedānta is the end of the Vedas. In this sense, Vedānta can be regarded as the last teachings or the final teachings of the Vedas.

Vedānta is a philosophy that has its roots in the oldest Indian scriptures, the Vedas. Its central teaching is that we are inherently divine. God is the fundamental reality that permeates all beings and is our deepest Self. According to Swami Vivekananda, Vedānta is simply the core of the entire philosophy of Hinduism.

The fundamental teachings of the Vedānta include:

(1) the impersonality and universality of Supreme Truth;
(2) the divinity of the soul;
(3) the unity of existence, or the oneness of matter and energy, or the ultimate oneness of God, man and nature;
(4) the harmony of religions;
(5) the immanence and transcendence of God who is both the material and the efficient cause of the universe; and
(6) *Mukti* or total freedom from bondage, that is, spiritual union with the Divine during one's lifetime.

These are the eternal teachings of Vedānta, that is why Vedānta is also referred to as the "Eternal Religion" or Sanātana Dharma (Swami Tathagatananda, n.d.).

In Hinduism, the Reality is referred to as *Brahman*, an infinitely powerful and expansive entity that cannot be measured (Swami Tathagatananda, n.d.).

Śaṅkara says:

> "That omniscient and omnipotent source must be *Brahman* from which occur the birth, continuance and dissolution of this universe that is manifested through name and form, that is associated with diverse agents and experiences, that provides the support for actions and results, having well-regulated space, time and causation, and that defies all thoughts about the real nature of its creation." (*Brahmasūtra*, I.1-2)

Brahman is characterised by Satcidānanda—*sat*, *cit*, and *ānanda*, that is, self-Existence, self-Awareness, and inherent Bliss.

In Vedānta, one of the mainstreams of thought is represented by Śaṅkara's Advaita school of Vedānta. The search for what is really real is ingrained with the idea of *Brahman* in the Śaṅkara's Advaita. Śaṅkara believes that the ultimate real must be permanent and changeless. It is argued that since being real entails being enduring and permanent, the very fact of change and becoming implies that whatever changes cannot be the true being. Therefore, in their search for the permanent amidst ever-changing phenomena, Advaita scholars ultimately recognise *Brahman* as the sole everlasting, all-encompassing, self-revealing, and unchanging reality. In brief, the Self (*Ātman*) and *Brahman* are the same at the individual level. The Supreme Self, the *Brahman*, is the undifferentiated subjectivity (consciousness) that underlies all reality. The Self is the basis of all conscious states and is also the same as the Supreme Self. However, because of the self's identification with the body and mind, the products of *avidyā* and primordial ignorance, the self appears confined at the individual level. The Upaniṣhadic statement "Thou art that" (*tat tvam asi*) is interpreted by Śaṅkara as an unqualified affirmation of identity between the *Brahman*, the Supreme Self, and the self (*ātman*) in an individual.

Advaita holds that the self is self-revealing. It cannot be questioned since it is the very essence of the one who questions. Śaṅkara says that as the Self is the antithesis of qualities that are perceived and provided by the senses, the only way to understand it is to strip it of all the contents and objective judgements we encounter through a process of elimination. It is stated that as a result of the process of denying all characteristics, the Self is "not this and not this" (*neti neti*). All types of relationship with the outside world, the gross physical components of the body, the interior states produced by the senses and the mind, and all of the essential bodily activities are among the traits that are denied to the Self. Therefore, the body, senses, and mind are not the Self.

Even though *Brahman* is the one ultimate principle that underlies all reality, nondual and undifferentiated, the human state presents reality as distinct, with subjects and things situated in space and time. This is because, in the existential scenario, the individual consciousness of the *Ātman*, the Supreme Being, rests in the abode of *jīva*. The embodied self, or *jīva*, is Consciousness (*Ātman*) constrained by the senses, body, mind, and intellect.

It is crucial to understand that under Advaita, the individual is neither a component of the supreme awareness nor a different entity from it. The *Ātman* is veiled in *avidyā*, or ignorance, itself. The mental processes known as *upādhis* constrain our comprehension of the *Ātman*. Śaṅkara makes the observation that just as the sun and moon's reflections on water are merely appearances, so too are our individual selves, or our personal consciousness. These are distinct representations of the same reality that *Ātman* in *avidyā* experiences. They're not really real. Once *avidyā* is overcome, reflections end and only the true consciousness remains.

Sāṁkhya Philosophy

Sāṁkhya school of philosophy is one of the six orthodox (Āstika) schools of Indian philosophical thought. The Āstika school of thought believes in the authority of the Vedas as the book of Ultimate, highest knowledge, as opposed to the *Nāstika* school of thought. The Sāṁkhya philosophy has its roots in the teachings of the Vedas and the Upaniṣads. Despite being one of the orthodox or Āstika schools of Indian philosophy, Sāṁkhya school of Indian philosophical thought holds some distinctive features that makes it unique as compared to the other Āstika philosophical traditions. It posits the dualism between *Puruṣa* (consciousness or the eternal self) and *Prakṛti* (nature or matter). *Puruṣa* symbolises the unchanging, pure consciousness whereas *prakṛti* represents the physical, material world, marked by change and plurality.

Sāṁkhya also specifies the principles or *tattva*s that constitute this universe, which are, the *Puruṣa*, *Prakṛti*, the three *guṇa*s or qualities (*Sattva*, *rajas*, and *tamas*), the mind, the senses, and different features of the material world. Moreover, according to the Sāṁkhya school of Indian philosophy, liberation or *kaivalya* can be attained through discriminative knowledge (*jñāna*) and the realisation of the distinction between *Puruṣa* and *Prakṛti*. In this respect, Sāṁkhya philosophy is different from the other schools that encourage different paths to liberation, for example, devotion (*bhakti*) in Vedānta or meditation in Yoga.

As mentioned above, *Prakṛti* is one of the most fundamental aspects of Sāṁkhya philosophy. It means "nature" or "primordial matter", however, it goes beyond the conventional understanding of matter. It represents that foundational substance from which this whole material universe emerged. It is known to be that dynamic force that is responsible for the manifestation and the diversity of this entire cosmos.

Prakṛti is inherently characterised by the interaction of three primary qualities or *guṇa*s—*sattva*, *tama*s, and *raja*s. These qualities are the driving forces behind the evolution and the diversity of the world.

Sattva (purity, harmony) symbolises the qualities of balance, harmony, and purity. It is linked to attributes like clarity, tranquillity, wisdom, and understanding. When *sattva* predominates in *Prakṛti*, it gives rise to the higher and more refined parts of the material universe, and people with enhanced consciousness.

Rajas (activity, passion) symbolises the qualities of activity, restlessness, and desire. Motion, change, and ambition are fuelled by it. When *raja*s is strong in *Prakṛti*, it leads to more energetic and dynamic forces in the material world as well as people motivated by aspirations and worldly goals.

*Tama*s (gloom, lethargy) symbolises delusion, gloom, and lethargy. It is linked to inertia, ignorance, and bewilderment. When *tamas* rules *Prakṛti*, it creates more inert, thick, and unconscious elements of the material universe, as well as people who might display apathy, ignorance, and a lack of awareness.

Prakṛti is a dynamic, constantly-evolving force rather than a static, fixed entity. Within *Prakṛti*, the *guṇa*s are always shifting, with one *guṇa* dominating at any given point in time.

The material universe is continuously changing and diversifying as a result of the dynamic interaction of the *guṇa*s. Due to the constantly changing fractions of the *guṇa*s and their interconnection with each other, various shapes and sensations in the universe are formed.

Puruṣa, on the other hand, represents pure consciousness. It is important to understand the role of *Puruṣa* to grasp the perspective of Sāṁkhya philosophy on the self, consciousness, and the process of creation. *Puruṣa*, often described as the "seer", "witness", or "observer", symbolises the aspects of reality that are entirely different from *Prakṛti*. It is neither susceptible to the processes of evolution and change that regulate *Prakṛti*, nor is it influenced by the characteristics of the *guṇa*s—*sattva*, *rajas*, and *tamas*. *Puruṣa* is unchanged, unaffected, and untouched by the material world. It represents the nature of a pure, absolute consciousness.

Puruṣa does not actively participate in the formation or evolution of the universe. It is neither affected by nor acts upon. *Puruṣa* is detached and indifferent to all of the dynamic processes, changes, and manifestations that occur in the material universe that the *Prakṛti* is responsible for. It doesn't feel happiness or sorrow or interact in any way with the physical world. Having said that, the interaction between the *Puruṣa* and *Prakṛti* is of utmost importance in Sāṁkhya philosophy. In fact, without the presence of the *Puruṣa*, the *Prakṛti* is inert and inactive. *Puruṣa* is regarded as the "illuminator" or "light of consciousness" that lets *Prakṛti* to create and evolve. The existence of *Puruṣa* is responsible for making the material world accessible to individual consciousness.

One of the primary aims of Sāṁkhya philosophy is to help an individual realise their true nature as *Puruṣa* and detach themselves from the association with the *Prakṛti*. Once you realise that your self (*Puruṣa*) is distinct and separate from the mind, body, and other shackles of the material world, you attain liberation or *kaivalya*. By achieving this, you can break free from the cycle of birth and death and from the bonds of *Prakṛti*.

The ideas of evolution and involution are used in Sāṁkhya philosophy to explain the cyclical and transformational nature of the universe. These processes offer a framework for comprehending the origins of the material world and its ultimate return to *Prakṛti*. They also provide a comprehensive understanding of the path that each person takes to achieve spiritual emancipation. It highlights how crucial self-realisation is to achieving ultimate liberation (*kaivalya*), as well as how *Puruṣa* must be isolated from *Prakṛti* in order to transcend the physical universe. Thus, this philosophical system provides significant teachings of the nature of reality and the route to enlightenment.

References

Joshi, K. (2002, September 16). *Isha Upanishad—Super School—Auroville—Session 1: The West and the East; The Upanishadic Quest with Transcript*. [Speech audio recording]. Kireetjoshiarchives. https://www.kireetjoshiarchives.com/audio-video/session/144.html

Joshi, K. (2002, September 17). *Isha Upanishad—Super School—Auroville—Session 2: Three Characteristics; The Methods of Vedantic Knowledge with Transcript*. [Speech audio recording]. Kireetjoshiarchives. https://www.kireetjoshiarchives. com/audio-video/session/145.html

Joshi, K. (n.d.). *Vedic Knowledge and Supermind in the Light of Sri Aurobindo*. Kireetjoshiarchives.https://www.kireetjoshiarchives.com/philosophy/philosophy-and-yoga-of-sri-aurobindo-and-other-essays/vedic-knowledge-and-supermind-in-the-light-of-sri-aurobindo/&page=43

Rao, K.R. and A.C. Paranjpe (2016). *Psychology in the Indian Tradition*. Springer.

Swargiary, K. (2023, October 18). Sāṁkhya Philosophy. *Research Gate*. https://www. researchgate.net/publication/374582107

Tathagatananda, S. (n.d.). *Fundamental Principles of Vedānta*. Vedānta Society of New York. https://www.vedāntany.org/articles/blog-post-title-two-6txr3

4

Indian Approaches to Self and Identity

Paranjpe (1998) has pointed out three meanings of identity:

(a) the standard of being similar in significance, inherent characteristics, or in particular qualities under complete and necessary similarity or oneness,
(b) the prerequisite that a person or a thing itself, and
(c) the prerequisite of being recognised in emotions, interest and the like.

The first point is related to the philosophical understandings of identity. The second deals with the personhood. The third meaning of identity is usually identified and understood in psychology where the person himself identifies with various dimensions of his personal and social being (Mishra, Akoijam and Misra, 2009).

The indigenous perspectives of self are gaining voice and are now recognised as legitimate academic endeavours. Traditionally there are two radically opposite views of self. The ancient Upaniṣads conceived of *ātman*, or the self, as the fundamental principle of unity and permanence that manifests in human experience. The *Māṇḍūkya Upaniṣad* called it as the fourth state of consciousness that is an extraordinary state. Gautama Buddha was opposed to the several ideas and practices of the Upaniṣads.

Following Buddha several schools of thought developed in Asia, and of these the Sāṁkhya, *yoga* and the Advaita schools developed varying perspective on the nature of self. The term *Puruṣa* is used in Sāṁkhya and Yoga and *ātman* in the Advaita for the self-sameness. Other schools of Buddhism developed a different view of the no- self (*anatta*) or denial of the self. His focus of this kind of thought is that an assumption of the permanence of body and possessions often leads to increase in craving for adoring the body and amassing possessions, while at the same time ignoring the need to change oneself in morally desirable ways. This would help persons recognise the folly in presuming the perceptual continuation of the "material Me" and help them try change oneself in morally desirable ways (Paranjpe, 2011).

Self in Tradition of Upaniṣad

The ancient *Upaniṣad, Bṛadāraṇyaka, was the first to discuss self in a systematic manner.* It mentions sage Yājñavalkya talking to his two wives that essential quest in ones" life should be one's love for oneself. It is the reason for all the love one has towards one's attachments and belongings such as property, children, home, etc. by introspecting one's thoughts about oneself, person can realise the true nature of self.

This led to a more polished theory of self in the Advaita Vedānta system. The *Kaṭha Upaniṣad* describes a story of teenage boy called Naciketā who was thrown outside the gates of Yama's (God of death) kingdom by his angry father. Yama is unable to welcome his unexpected guest, he offers three wishes to Naciketā. His first wish was to reunite with his angry father. As a fulfilment of his second wish, he asks for knowledge of how to secure place in the heaven. As a third wish, he asks Yama to explain to him the cycle of birth and death. Unable to fulfil his third wish Yama offers him rebirth on earth with innumerable powers. Naciketā refused to accept this award as he believes that this can be gained only through good deeds. He wanted a permanent bliss. The Indian culture also focuses on ways to eliminate suffering and achieve a never-ending happiness. It focuses on finding unlimited bliss and inner peace which is unaltered by the happenings of the world outside.

In *Taittirīya Upaniṣad* the idea of *pañckośa* or five sheaths is developed, which considers the *jīva* as a multilayered hierarchical structure. There are five layers or sheaths nested in one another. The gross physical body is said to be the product of food (*ānnamaya kośa*). Different from one within it is the self that consists of life (*prāṇamaya kośa*), which involves breathing and other metabolic processes that activate the organs and keep them functioning. Within it and different from it is the third layer called *manomaya kośa*, which involves the sense organs. It is considered as the seat of the ego strivings and manifests itself in the form of personal involvement. Next is the sheath of intellect or cognition (*vijñānamaya kośa*) that involves ideas, constructs, and concepts used in knowing world. The innermost core of the self is the *ānandmaya kośa* or joyous sheath. It reflects bliss. The inner layers get progressively subtler than the outer layers and the duality between self and non-self is minimised.

Self in the Advaitic Method

The medieval text, *Dṛg-dṛśya-viveka* (1931) mentions the Advaitic method to know about self. Herein Śaṅkarācārya explores the common manifestations of self. He talks about aspects of self which are open to change and which are changeless. The self as seer is the aspect of self that remains unchanged. The Sāṁkhya philosophy describes two basic principles of reality, *Puruṣa* and *Prakṛti*. *Puruṣa* implies pure consciousness or awareness. *Prakṛti* implies to the material aspects. Any material/objective manifestations cannot help one attain understanding of true self. One needs to realise and become aware of pure consciousness or true self. Meditation is one of the key methods to achieve this.

There is a difference between self as a subject and self as an object. A demarcation is made between the self—as-subject and as-object. The self that is object is visible such as the body features, roles in social life, other aspects open to observation by others, thoughts, dreams, etc. The self which is seen as object characterises itself with certain features such as body, social roles, thoughts, and dreams. A form of meditation called as *nirvikalpa samādhi* is a means to absolve the subject-object distinction. Another path to self-realisation is *jñāana-yoga*. It is difficult to practice. A self-realised person exhibits absence of ego. Maharṣi Ramaṇa is one of the successful practitioners (Paranjpe, 2008).

Self in Sāṁkhya Yoga System

According to Sāṁkhya-Yoga system, it is *Puruṣa* or the true self, which provides the unchanging backdrop on which varied images of the self—keep appearing and disappearing. The ego as identified with passing thoughts, stops functioning for a moment and gives the meditator the experience of "no ego". This state is called *samādhi.* After returning to normal day-to-day life and its stresses, the *yogi* does not feel easily bowed down with successes and failures or stress and has developed an inner peace. A person who successfully practices *yoga* becomes grounded in an "I" beyond "Me" and its egoistic attachments. When the mind is emptied of all its contents brings moments of self-realisation and its effects can be seen in the changes in one's personality. Pātañjali Yoga is a method of restraining the flow of thoughts in the mind so as to ultimately bring it to a halt through a detailed method. Vyāsa, the earliest and most important commentator of Patañjali's teachings, claims that true self is directly experienced when the flow of thoughts stop.

Sri Aurobindo experiences following his successful practice of *yoga*:

> "It threw me suddenly into a condition above and without thought, unstained by any mental or vital movement; there was no ego, no real world, there was no One or Many even, only just absolutely. That featureless, relationless, sheer indescribable, unthinkable, absolute, yet supremely real and solely real". (Sri Aurobindo, 1971: 101)

The modern scientists have conducted innumerable research on the benefits of *yoga* on human mind and body. Some of the benefits are mentioned below:

Yoga not only benefits the body but also the soul. The journey through life is calmer, happier and more fulfilling, when one is in harmony.

1. Fitness of the Mind and Body—It helps achieve physical, emotional, mental and spiritual fitness and not just freedom from disease.
2. Reducing Weight—Regularly practice of *yoga āsanas* can lead to weight loss. *Āsanas* such as sun salutations and *kapālabhāti prāṇāyāma*.
3. Relief from Stress—Yogic practices and meditation can help one get relief from stresses.
4. Inner Peace—Mediation and healthy mind help calm one's mind.
5. Increase Immunity—As the body and mind becomes fit it increases ones immunity to fight off diseases. It can be improved through breathing techniques and mediation.
6. Living a Fuller Life—The wanderings of the mind can be brought under control and help one relax and live in the moment. This helps one become calm, stay happy and focused.
7. Improved Relationships—The mediation techniques help one become de-stressed and content, thus becoming sensitive to relationships. This helps to strengthen social bonds.
8. Increased Energy—Overall increase in body strength is experienced. Also, one feels rejuvenated after guided mediation for a short time.
9. Increased Flexibility and Better Posture—Through regular performance of *yoga* and meditation one's body is strengthened, muscles get toned and pain is relieved.
10. Better Intuition—Those who regularly do *yoga* and meditation believe that intuitive ability is increased.

Self in Vedāntic View

In the Vedāntic view, there is a clear recognition of "I" as a doer or an agent of action (*kartā*) as well as enjoyer of pleasure and suffering of pain (*bhoktā*). It is contended that the consequences of a life of *karma* result in pleasure and pain, prosperity, and adversity while liberation from the cycle of births and deaths can be achieved when there is no more *karma*. To attain this end, all desires (*vāsanās*) must come to an end and a sense of complete detachment from the worldly objects leading to a stance of witness (sākṣī) be developed. (Mishra, Akoijam, and Misra, 2009).

Towards the end of the Vedic period (1500 B.C.) the doctrine of *karma* was written. The Ṛgveda states the Universe has a certain order to it and not at the mercy of whims and fancies of the universal gods. The principle of the cosmos states that all persons in the end would have to face the consequences of one's good and bad *karma*s done in this life and previous life. In addition, each person is responsible for one's own prosperity and misfortunes. The problems faced by a person in the present life are attributed to his past *karma*s in his present life or past life. This principle of *karma* cannot be judged as cruel. It also gives hope to people to do good deeds in present life to have a good life in future. Lord Kṛṣṇa in the *Bhagavad Gītā* states that one should always perform the duties he has in a given role and never back off from these duties and never expect or desire anything from his *karma*s.

*Saṁskāra*s are also actions. These actions leave imprints which each person carries forward in the next birth. It is believed that suffering is "good" and it should be gone through as it is deserved from the past deeds. The new action or *karma* then leaves imprints for the next life and thus the cycle continues. Thus one has to undergo the cycle of life, death, and rebirth. The Vedas also suggest various ways to escape this suffering and attain mokṣa.

Vedas and Contemporary Psychology

The key ideas and ideals are contained in the four *veda mantra* collections *(saṁhitā)*, which are known as *Ṛgveda*, *Yajurveda, Sāmaveda* and *Atharvaveda.* The *Yajurveda* contains verses with metrical structures as well as short rhythmic prose passages called *Yajur mantra*s. The remaining three have only verses (or *mantra*s) with metrical structures. The metres in these verses have names such as *gāyatrī* and *anuṣṭup,* characterised by the number of syllables. The four books have substantial overlaps and together they comprise about 26,000 *mantra*s, including repetitions. In the early days, all these *mantras* comprised a single collection as noted in the *Viṣnu Purāṇa.* The *Ṛgveda* itself has about 10,500 metrical verses, divided into ten books, known as *maṇḍala*s. Each *maṇḍala* is made up of hymns or *sūkta*s, each *sūkta* having about ten *mantra*s or verses. Many of the *mantra*s of the *veda* deal with the concept of an all-sided perfection of human life and modes of its realisation.

The ideal of an all-sided perfection has been mentioned in several so-called "New Age" and self-help books. Achieving perfection in a particular activity that is more or less under one's control is straightforward. If someone is serious about learning music, she may approach the best music teacher in the neighbourhood for learning. However, achieving harmony and beauty in all of one's own activities, and especially in those involving others, is a different matter. Perhaps the only way to do this is "to completely spiritualise one's everyday life" (The Mother, 1978: 517), that is, to recognise the existence of a Supreme Spirit which pervades and energises every aspect of existence and invoke. That in every activity.

In the Indian tradition, the meaning of the word "spiritual" is quite different from religion as commonly understood. Spirituality is free from any dogma or creed. Spiritual experience is an experience of the spirit or spiritual consciousness, which pervades the entire cosmos including all human activities. For instance, from the point of view of our ordinary consciousness, each being is different from every other being, human or non-human. But from the point of view of spiritual consciousness, each one of us is but a point in the ocean of consciousness. Thoughts, desires, and emotions appear as waves in the ocean of the spirit; each wave waxes and wanes through each point of the cosmos, each point corresponding to a being. The movement of a particular wave of desire through a particular point gives the impression to the experience that that particular wave of desire originated in him. Further, the power of a person depends on the cosmic forces over which he has conscious or unconscious control. Consequently, there is no hard barrier between individual human beings and the cosmic powers called *deva*s, or even the Supreme One. Only when we understand the unity of the universe, we can answer the question:

> "How to introduce beauty and harmony in every aspect of our life, that is, harmony and beauty in

thoughts and feelings, harmony and beauty in every outward action and movement, harmony and beauty in our surroundings?"

Another important aspect of life is that everyone is engaged in some form of work. The work may be cooking, reading, listening to or making music, doing athletics, or whatever else that occupies us. However, do we understand why we work? Some people claim that they work for enjoyment. Others complain that the work they have undertaken, does not give them any joy. They seek their enjoyment by some other means utilising the monetary resources obtained through their work. But what is the source of enjoyment?

It appears that the *Ṛgveda Samhitā* has answers to all the above questions—the nature of work, the forces behind activity, the relationship between work and enjoyment, and between work and progress—by relating to life as a unique journey.

Life as a Unique Journey

According to the Vedic sages, everyone should regard his or her life as a journey from one peak of perfection to another peak. They have indicated that help is always available for those who embark on such exciting journeys. I shall quote here one *mantra* from the *Ṛgveda* (1.10.2, that is *mantra* 2 in *sūkta* 10 of *maṇḍala* 1 of the *Ṛgveda*) Because of its metre, each *mantra* is naturally divisible into three or four parts whose meanings are relatively self-contained. This particular *mantra* has four parts whose translation is given below. The corresponding Sanskrit text is given as an endnote.

When the worshipper climbs from peak to peak (1),
He (she) realises the progress that is yet to be achieved (2).
Then (the cosmic-power) Indra awakens in the seeker the purpose of the journey (3),
And manifests with his troop to aid (the devotee in his journey) (4). (*ṚV*, 1.10.2)[1]

This verse or *mantra* is straightforward in its meaning and the symbolism is transparent. The phrase, "climbing from peak to peak" indicates the life-journey of an individual, attaining one level of perfection after another.

The second line indicates the deep psychological insight that only a person who starts on a journey can understand how much is still to be done.

The third phrase makes an important statement that the person undertaking the journey is not alone or helpless. The cosmic force (or the god) Indra himself awakens in him the purpose of his journey and indicates within him or her, the next peak to be pursued. The God Indra literally comes in a subtle manner to give the help.

This verse is not unique in the *Ṛgveda*. There are many others which deal with the life-journey and the ascent. Some translators hold that the *Ṛgveda* is ritualistic and is devoid of any reference to higher mental operations. They should notice here the use of the word "awakens" (*cetati*). The *Ṛgveda* has at least thirty-six different words dealing with mental operations (Purani, 1963: 43). It is a sign of incompetence to regard all these words as synonyms. Sri Aurobindo (1914/1998: 295) makes the difference between them explicit. For instance, the two words *vicetas* and *pracetas* mean, respectively, "one wide in consciousness" and "one who has the perceptive knowledge".

Further, one may wonder whether the climbing refers only to meditative activities or to the activities of everyday life, involving the life-energy (*prāṇa*) and the mind. It should be borne in mind that the Veda does not indulge in a rigid separation of the realm of activities into "worldly" and "spiritual". Its aim is that all activities, including those of daily life, must be made spiritual. In support I quote this verse or *mantra* (*ṚV*, 5.7.5).

When in his service (*veṣaṇe*) (1),
Men cast down their sweat (as an offering) on the paths (2),
They ascend to a self-born (self-joyous, *svajenyam*) ground (3),
As if to wide levels (4).

In other words, the ascent to the peaks is possible by physical and mental activities.

The *Ṛgveda* is the earliest book which deals with the topics of work, enjoyment and progress from a "cosmo-psychological" angle. What I have presented here is based on the insights of Sri Aurobindo and Sri Kapali Sastry. The recognition of psychological powers behind deities like Agni and Varuṇa is credited to Sri Aurobindo. The idea of invoking the spirit all the time, as part of a spiritual attitude towards life is mentioned in the Upaniṣad, and by medieval saints such as Sri Madhvācārya, and others. Sri Aurobindo's great contribution is to show us that by invoking the great *mantra*s of the Vedas we can still develop the powers of intuition, inspiration, will within us.

Note

1. The original Sanskrit text is:
   yat sānoḥ sānum āruhat (1),
   bhūri aspaṣṭa kartvanm (2),
   tad indro artham cetati (awakens) (3),
   yūtheṇa vrṣṇir ejati (4). (*ṚV*, 1.10.2)

References

Aurobindo, Sri (1914/1998). *The Secret of the Veda.* Pondicherry: Sri Aurobindo Ashram Publication Department.

Bhaktivedānta, A.C.S. Prabhupada. *Bhagavad Gītā* as It Is Bombay: The Bhaktivedānta Book Trust.

Bhawuk, D.P.S. (2008). "Anchoring Cognition, Emotion, and Behaviour in Desire: A Model from the Bhagavad-Gītā". In K.R. Rao, A.C. Paranjpe and A.K. Dalal (Eds), *Handbook of Indian Psychology* (pp. 390-413). New Delhi, India: Cambridge University Press.

Dasgupta, S.N. (1975). *A History of Indian Philosophy* (Indian edn. Vols. 1-5). Delhi: Motilal Banarsidass. (Originally published 1922).

Datta. D.M. (1972). *The Six Ways of Knowing: A Critical Study of the Advaita Theory of Knowledge.* Calcutta: University of Calcutta. (Original work published 1932).

Dṛgdṛśya Viveka. (1931). (Ed. and Trans. S. Nikhilananda). Mysore, India: Sri Ramakrishna Asrama (The date of the original work unknown).

James, W.T. (1975). *A History of Western Philosophy* (2nd and Rev edn., Vols. 1-5). New York: Harcourt, Brace and World.

Kuppuswamy, B. (1985). *Elements of Ancient Indian Psychology.* Delhi: Konark.

Manu (1971). *The Laws of Manu* (Trans. G. Bühler). Delhi: Motilal Banarsidass. (Translation first published 1886, date of original work Manu Smrti unknown).

Paranjpe, A.C. (1998). *Self and Identity in Modem Psychology and Indian Thought*. New York: Plenum.

Paranjpe, A.C. (2008). "Sri Ramana Maharshi: A Case Study in Self-realisation". In K. Ramakrishna Rao, A.C. Paranjpe and A.K. Dalal (Eds), *Handbook of Indian Psychology* (pp. 564-576). New Delhi: Cambridge University Press, India.

Paranjpe, A.C. (2010). "Theories of Self and Cognition: Indian Psychological Perspectives". *Psychology of Developing Societies, 22*(5).

Purani, A.B. (1963). *Studies in Vedic Interpretation*. Varanasi: Chowkambha Sanskrit Series.

Sinha, Jadunath (1961). *Indian Psychology* Vol. 2: *Emotions and Will*. Delhi: Motilal Banarsidass.

The Mother (1978/1999). *On Education*. Pondicherry: Sri Aurobindo Ashram Publication Department.

5

Self in the Indian Thought

An Integral Perspective

One of the deepest needs we have as human beings is to know and understand our own self and others. The questions about our origin, dimensions of our human nature and their potential continuously haunt us. This quest for self-knowledge is reflected in almost all the fields of human enquiry and more so in the discipline of psychology.

Sri Aurobindo made several observations about the nature and scope of Western Psychology as it was in the earlier part of the twentieth century. The psychologists of that time according to Sri Aurobindo make three major initial errors that have hampered the study of the human phenomena and the achievement of profound knowledge. These are:

- The error whereby psychologists identify the study of mental processes and behaviour with biological and physical sciences.
- The sceptical error which hinders investigation of the nuances of human existence.
- The objective mistake made by the psychologist to study others as passive observers or from outside instead of viewing knowledge and experimentation within herself or himself.

Sri Aurobindo too believed that psychology ought to be a science. However, according to him it ought to be a science of consciousness and its operations, with a methodology that is significantly different from the natural sciences. According to him, we must proceed from knowledge of oneself to the knowledge of others because psychology is essentially a subjective science. The main method of psychology therefore has to be primarily introspective and experiential in nature.

Our surface personality, according to Sri Aurobindo, is a tiny part of the being and does not encompass the depths of our character, mental processes, and behaviours. Sri Aurobindo considered psychology as it was in the half of this century as an infant science, which was rash and fumbling in its approach. With specific reference to Psychoanalysis, he stated:

> "This new psychology looks to me very much like children learning some summary and not very adequate alphabet, exulting in putting their a-b-c-d of the subconscient and the mysterious underground super-ego together and imagining that their first book of obscure beginnings (c-a-t-cat, t-r-e-e tree) is the very heart of the real knowledge. They look from down up and explain the higher lights by the lower obscurities; but the foundation of these things is above and not below. The superconscient, not the subconscient, is the true foundation of things. The significance of the lotus is not to be found by analysing the secrets of the mud from which it grows here; its secret is to found in the heavenly archetype of the lotus that blooms forever in the Light. The self-chosen field of these psychologists is besides poor, dark and limited, you must know the whole before you can know the part and the highest before you can truly understand the lowest. That is the promise of the greater psychology awaiting its hour before which these poor groupings will disappear and come to nothing." (Sri Aurobindo, 1970)

Thus according to Sri Aurobindo, a complete psychology must be able to map the full complexity of the human consciousness—its inner depths, its width and its heights. To fully understand this complexity, the psychologists need to refer to the metaphysical basis of the psychological phenomena.

Sri Aurobindo's Perspective of Self

From the viewpoint of Sri Aurobindo's thought, the human being is not separated from but is one with the universal being. There are two systems—a concentric system and a vertical system—which are simultaneously active in the organisation of the being and its parts.

The concentric system is a series of rings, comprising of the outer being, the inner being, and the inmost being. The outer being and the inner being form our phenomenal or instrumental being, belonging to Nature or *Prakṛti*. Physical, vital, and mental are its three corresponding parts. The *Puruṣa*, the true being, is the inmost being. The *Puruṣa* comprises of an inmost mental, an inmost vital and an inmost physical. At the very core is the psychic being or soul. The psychic being is usually referred to as the inmost being (Fig. 5.1).

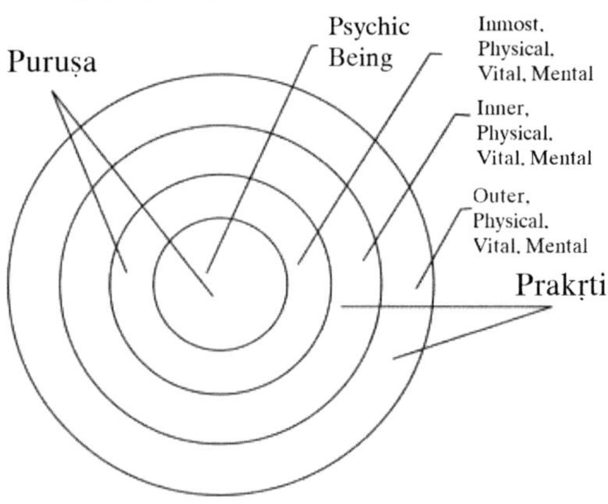

Fig. 5.1: The Concentric System

The vertical system resembles a staircase, comprising of different levels, planes or gradations of consciousness. It ranges from the lowest—thc Inconscicnt—to thc highcst, Saccidānanda (Fig. 5.2)

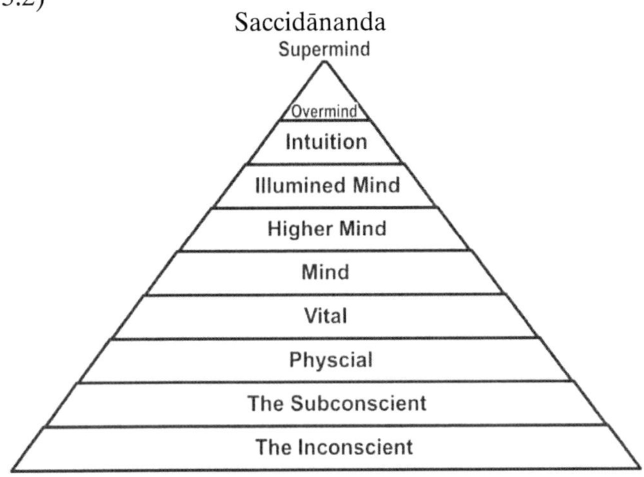

Fig. 5.2: The Vertical System: Levels of Consciousness

Ancient Indian wisdom divided the human being, the microcosm, as well as the world-being, the macrocosm, into a higher hemisphere, *parārdha*, and a lower hemisphere, apara parārdha. The higher hemisphere is where the Spirit reigns perfectly and eternally; in the lower hemisphere, the Spirit is veiled by mind, life, and body. Overmind is the intermediary plane dividing the two hemispheres.

The main parts and planes of the being as described by Sri Aurobindo are explained below.

The Outer Being

The outer or surface being has three main parts: the mind (the mental), the life-nature (the vital), and the body (the physical). Though in our ordinary awareness we are unable to distinguish among these parts, each has its own distinct type of consciousness. We tend to regard the mental, vital, and physical constituents of our consciousness, and all these diverse elements simply as our "mind". In *yoga* psychology, "mind" refers to the part of the being which has to do with cognition and intelligence. Desires, feelings, instincts, and impulses constitute the vital being or life nature. The body (*prāṇa*) is animated by the life-energy which is an aspect of the vital. The body's own distinct consciousness operates in the involuntary functions of the different physiological systems. Body-consciousness is one part of the physical consciousness. It, also, includes the physical mind and the physical vital which will be presently explained.

Though separate and distinct, the three main divisions of the outer being just mentioned are intertwined, giving rise to clear subdivisions in the main parts of the being. Thus, besides the mind proper, there is a vital mind, which is the part of the mind that is intermixed with the vital. The vital mind, unlike the thinking mind, is not governed by reason but is dominated by impulses and desires of the vital, and seeks to rationalise actions resulting from the desires of the vital. Another subdivision is the physical mind, which is the part of the mind that is intermixed with the physical, and takes up the characteristics of the physical consciousness such as inertia, obscurity, and mechanical repetitiveness, doubt, and obsessive thoughts. The part of the mind which is closest to the physical is called the mechanical mind; its characteristic is that of a machine that goes on turning round and round whenever thoughts occur in it. Another subdivision which is important for self-understanding is the physical vital; it is the part of the vital which is turned entirely upon physical things, and is fullof desires and seekings for pleasure on the physical plane. Closely connected with it is vital physical, the part of the vital force which constitutes the nervous being, it is the vehicle of the nervous responses and is related to the reactions, desires, and sensations of the body.

The Inner Being

Behind the surface or frontal consciousness of the outer being there is an inner or subliminal consciousness of all the three levels—physical, vital, mental. Thus, there is an inner mind, an inner vital, and an inner physical. The inner physical is in touch with the universal physical forces around us, the inner vital with the universal life-forces, and the inner mind with the universal mind. Thus, whereas the outer being knows only indirectly as perceived through the senses and the outer mind, the inner being is directly aware of the surroundings (universal forces) that act through us.

The inner or subliminal being, through the circum-conscient, projects itself beyond the body.

The Inmost Being: The Psychic Being

Sri Aurobindo uses the term "psychic being' (from Greek *psukhe*, meaning the soul) for the inmost being. The psychic being is a portion of the Divine or a spark present in all things and creations. In the course of evolution the psyche grows into an individual psychic personality in the human being and is then called the psychic being.

The psychic being is the evolving soul which goes though the cycles of physical birth and death, growing from life to life. Whereas, the *Ātman*, the universal Self, is unborn and is above the evolutionary process.

The Inconscient

The Inconscient is sometimes known as the Non-Being or *asat* and is characterised by darkness, inertia, insensibility, disharmony and disintegration. It harbours forces that maintain the negativity, the unconsciousness, pain, suffering, illness, death, disharmony and evil. It also includes all that is Divine and striving to evolve into Light, Consciousness, Power, Perfection, Beauty and Love.

The Subconscient

This is the half-conscious part in us. "Sub" means "below" the consciousness. In the subconscient there is an obscure mind full of obstinate *saṁskāraa*s, impressions, associations, fixed notions, habitual reactions formed by our past, an obscure vital full of the seeds of habitual desires, sensations, nervous reactions, a most obscure material that governs much that has to do with the conditions of the body. It is largely responsible for our illnesses; chronic or repeated illnesses are indeed mainly due to the subconscient and its obstinate memory and habit of repetition of whatever has impressed itself on body consciousness. The Subconscient is the cause why people say that character cannot be changed, the cause also of constant return of things one hoped to have got rid off forever. All that is suppressed without being wholly got rid of sinks down there and remains as a seed ready to surge up or sprout at any moment.

The Superconscient

The superconscient consists of higher levels of consciousness above the ordinary mind from which the higher consciousness comes down into the lower planes of the being.

> "The role of the superconscient has been to evolve slowly the spiritual man out of the mental half-animal. The superconscient includes the higher planes of mind—Higher Mind, Illumined, Intuition and Overmind as well as what is beyond mind, namely Supermind and the Supreme Reality called Sachchidananda (Existence—Consciousness—Bliss)"(Dalal, 2001).

The traditional Path of Knowledge (*jñānayoga*) in India aims at eliminating successively the body, the life and the mind and taking a straight plunge by merging into the supracosmic Reality of Saccidānanda. However, for an integral self-knowledge, says Sri Aurobindo, it is necessary to ascend through each of the superconscient planes including the supermind in the passage to Saccidānanda.

The Pyschic Being and Transformation

In spiritual experience there exists one sole Being, one sole Existence which embraces all beings and existing things in the universe, and which in spiritual realisation is experienced as the One Self of all things and creatures. But in our ordinary experience we perceive the world as inhabitated by a plurality of beings and things existing outside what we felt to be our self. This is because our true self, described previously as the *Puruṣa*, who is one with the Self of all things and beings, has identified itself through ignorance with *Prakṛti*, its outer instrumental nature made up of body, life, and mind. This identification of *Puruṣa* with *Prakṛti* has led to the formation in us of an ego—physical, vital, and mental—which gives us the sense of a self that is separate from the rest of the universe. Thus, it is the ego that gives rise to the distinction ingrained in our ordinary consciousness between what we feel to be our self and the rest of the universe which is perceived as the not-self. Also, it is the ego—physical, vital, and mental—which, due to its complexity and heterogeneity, leads to the formation of multiple selves causing division, conflict, disharmony, and disorganisation in our outer being. Harmonisation and unification of the outer being can be brought about only by discovering our inmost being—*Caitya Puruṣa* or the psychic being—and organising the outer being around the psychic as its centre and governing principle.

The aim of spiritual quest in the past has generally been to obtain liberation from the bondage to suffering caused by the illusory sense of a separate self, the ego, and thereby escape from the perpetual cycle of birth and death. According to Sri Aurobindo, the farthest goal of evolution of spiritual being goes beyond emancipation and tranformation of different constructs of the spirit which are phsical body, mind and life as a whole, so that the empire of the spirit on mother earth could be set up. It is when the outer being is unified and governed by the psychic being that the transformation of mind, life, and body becomes possible transformation of mind, life, and body becomes possible through *sādhanā*.

Integral Yoga Psychology

Sri Aurobindo's Integral *Yoga* is psychology in action, aimed at bringing about the transformation of individual consciousness. The main objective of Sri Aurobindo's Integral *Yoga* is not just a transmutation of consciousness to progressively higher spiritual levels but its radical transformation with an aim of manifesting the supramental consciousness which is an evolutionary principle that transcends the human mind altogether.

The study of the processes of achieving this trans-formation can be called the Integral *Yoga* psychology.

This process of transformation requires the individual to progressively psychicise, spiritualise and supramentalise her/his consciousness. In this process there is not only an ascent to the highest Divine consciousness by the human aspirant but also a descent of the Divine consciousness into the lower mental, vital and physical being which transforms the whole individual radically. The aim of Integral *Yoga* is thus to bring about evolution towards a supramental principle beyond the mind which requires the conscious collaboration of the human with the Divine.

The Psychology of Inner Development

According to Sri Aurobindo, it is fundamentally an evolution of consciousness that has been taking place in Nature. The inner growth of the human being is simply a continuation of the evolution of consciousness which has hitherto resulted successively in the emergence of Life out of Matter and of Mind out of Life. In other words, consciousness has developed ever higher forms of its manifestation on earth—from the mineral to the plant, to the animal, to man the mental being. What is called inner growth refers to the evolution of consciousness beyond mind.

Prior to the appearance of the human or mental being, evolution has been a slow, subconscious process. The emergence of mind marks the beginning of *a new process of evolution* by which the human being, through a conscious will and aspiration for inner growth, becomes a conscious participant and collaborator in the evolution of consciousness. Thus inner growth is a process of *conscious evolution*. A system of proven methods for achieving inner growth is through *yoga*; for *yoga* is a methodised effort towards self-perfection by the expression of the potentialities latent in the being.

Even after the emergence of mind, the growth of consciousness in the human being continues to be a more or less unconscious process, because the roots of matter, life and mind lie in the inconscient out of which they have evolved. The first step for emerging out of the primeval unconsciousness is to develop a conscious ego—a separate and independent individuality. So long as an individuality has not been formed, the human being remains an amorphous entity. More or less fused with the unconscious totality of existence. It is by the development of a conscious ego—individualisation of being in becoming—that a person becomes an individual. Ego is the identification of our being with the superficial, outer self made up of the body, the vital nature and the mind. Due to the ego, a certain formation of physical, vital and mental experience is distinguished from the rest of the being and is regarded as the "self". Thus, the ego serves to bring about the emergence from unconsciousness through a progressive consciousness (awareness) of the physical, vital and mental aspects of the being.

Once the separative ego has been adequately developed, evolution of consciousness can be accelerated through growth in a different dimension—that which lies in the transcendence of the ego, liberation from the ignorant identification with one's superficial nature, and the discovery of the true Self. Inner growth, thus, represents *a new dimension of evolution.*

The divergence among the presently normal state of consciousness and the more evolved state of consciousness at which inner growth aims is reflected in their contrasting characteristics, some of which are indicated below:

(a) The normal state of consciousness is more or less submerged in unconsciousness: in the normal state, a person is totally unconscious of the deeper and higher levels of the being, and largely unconscious of even the superficial being made up of the body-consciousness, thoughts and feelings. With the inner growth of one's being, there comes an increasing consciousness, for consciousness is the very nature and essence of being.

(b) One of the chief characteristics of the normal state of consciousness is distractibility. The changing impressions and sensations from the outside and the flux of thoughts and feelings from within produce a state of constant distraction. On the other hand, the inner consciousness is centred or concentrated. As the consciousness grows, and one learns to live more and more in the deeper consciousness, one experiences a state of centredness or concentration.

(c) Associated with distraction is another characteristic of the normal state of consciousness, namely, dispersion. In the normal state, consciousness is scattered, so to speak, in the superficial parts and movements of the being—physical, vital and mental. The dispersed nature of the normally prevailing consciousness stand in sharp contrast to the in-gathered and collected nature of the deeper consciousness.

(d) The normal state of consciousness is a state of continual disquiet and agitation due to its constant distractibility and dispersion. As the consciousness grows, one becomes more and more aware of a deeper consciousness which is felt as a substratum of quiet and peace.

(e) In the normal state, consciousness is involved and identified with its instruments—the body. The vital nature and the mind; one feels oneself to be the body, thoughts and feelings. As consciousness evolves, it experiences itself more and more as detached and separate from the outer physical, vital and mental nature. Instead of being identified with the movements of the outer nature, it observes them as a detached witness—*sākṣī*, to use a term of the *Gītā*.

(f) Because of the identification with its instrumental nature, the ordinary consciousness is afflicted by the "pairs of contraries"—heat and cold, pleasure and pain, attraction and repulsion, etc.—which are an inherent characteristic of physical, vital, and mental nature. Ordinarily, therefore, consciousness is in a more or less constant state of disturbance and disequilibrium. Contrastingly, the higher consciousness is unmoved, mixed or steady—*sthira*, to use another term of the *Gītā*. Associated with this quality is *samatā*—equanimity born of an equal response to the pairs of contraries.

(g) A fundamental characteristic of the normal consciousness is its sense of being a separate self or ego, that is, of being an individual who exists apart from the rest of the universe. On the other hand, the greater consciousness, as described by those who have attained it permanently or experienced it momentarily, is unitary, universal and transpersonal, devoid of separation and division.

The difference, from the viewpoint of *yoga*, between personal growth and inner growth may be restated in somewhat different words thus: personal growth consists in the development of the individual as a human being, whereas inner growth, which is the aim of *yoga*, lies in transforming and transcending the human state of consciousness.

An important point to note is the even moral development—which is often confused with spirituality—is part of growth that belong to the human state; it does not constitute inner growth which aims at a state of the being beyond the human ego-bound state.

However, just as the development of the ego is indispensable for emerging out of unconsciousness, so too moral development, which is one of the highest aspects of human growth, is a necessary step towards a state of consciousness beyond the human.

Inner growth needs to be distinguished also from what is commonly called the growth of awareness, sought to be fostered by various modern psychological methods and techniques. The term "awareness", as used in modern psychology, has acquired a wide range of meanings and connotations, ranging from the detection of a very weak sensory stimulus, such as a dim light, to the acquisition of insight into the unconscious dynamics which motivate one's actions. From the viewpoint of *yoga* psychology, what is called awareness in Gestalt therapy and other similar approaches of psychological growth refers to awareness of the outer or surface being, consisting of physical, vital, and mental parts of the human make-up; growth of such awareness lies in becoming more and more aware of one's body, feelings, emotions and thoughts. Inner growth, on the other hand, pertains to the progressive awakening and awareness of the inner and higher parts of the being.

In the normal state of consciousness, in which we are identified with the outer being—the body, impulses and feelings, and the mind—we are almost totally unconscious of the inner being and of its constant action on the surface consciousness. We sometimes awaken into the consciousness of the inner being during the sleep of the body, and occasionally bring back to the normal waking consciousness some of our experiences of the inner consciousness during sleep in the form of lucid, symbolic or premonitory dreams, though most of our dreams, which are confused and incoherent, pertain not to the inner consciousness but to the subconscient.

We also get glimpses of the inner consciousness through certain images, perceived either spontaneously or during the practice of visualisation, and, in rare cases, through visions or inner voices. In the state of meditation, too, we sometimes become aware of the inner being as a detached, calm and observing consciousness. Apart from these occasional, momentary and fragmentary experiences, the inner being is shut out from the outer by the thick wall or veil of the normal, surface consciousness. The process of inner growth consists in the gradual breaking down of the wall or the lifting of the veil, and awakening to the consciousness of the inner being.

A salient aspect of Sri Aurobindo's *yoga* pertaining to the psychology of inner growth is its view of the inner and higher planes of consciousness as dynamic forces. Though hidden from the outer surface consciousness, the inner and higher parts of the being exercise on the surface parts of the being a constant influence and pressure, pushing towards the evolution and growth of consciousness.

To sum up, the inner growth of the individual, like the evolution of the universe, is the process by which the Supreme Consciousness—the Truth of Existence or the Reality of Being, immersed in the Inconscience of Matter through a prior process of involution, manifests itself in progressively higher states of its being due to the evolutionary thrust inherent in it.

In Sri Aurobindo's *yoga*, the Supreme Consciousness, Truth or Reality is spoken of as the Divine, the Supreme Being from whom all have come and in whom all are. The portion of the Divine Consciousness which develops in the process of evolution is called the soul or the psychic essence. It grows and becomes a distinct individuality, referred to as the psychic being. It is through the psychic being that the evolutionary dynamism inherent in the Supreme Consciousness brings about the inner growth of the individual.

Numerous are the paths that have been discovered for achieving inner growth and realising the Truth. The various psychological paths may be classified into three broad types, corresponding to the three basic psychological aspects of the human make-up: the Path of Knowledge, corresponding to the cognitive or thinking aspect, the Path of Devotion, related to the affective or emotional side of human nature, and the Path of Works or Action, based on man's conative aspect which has to do with striving and willing. Almost all paths contain elements of each of the three broad types just mentioned, though one particular type element—Knowledge, Devotion, or Works—may predominate. The seeker is drawn to one path or another depending on what predominates in one's psychological make-up.

Though the different paths vary greatly in their methods and processes, certain elements are common to them all. One such universal element is a certain preliminary cleansing or purification of the outer nature, consisting of the physical, vital, and mental consciousness. An attempt to enter into the inner consciousness without adequately ridding the outer consciousness of its turbidity is apt to fail, if at all one succeeds in some measure, one is most likely to be confused, misled or overwhelmed by the experiences of the inner consciousness without a sufficient foundation of a calm purity in the outer being.

A second element common to all paths of inner growth consists in developing an in-gathered attitude, a state of inner concentration which progressively replaces the state of outer dispersion characteristic of the normal consciousness. The in-gathered state is most often sought to be inculcated through the practice of meditation. That is why, to many people, the spiritual life is almost synonymous with the practice of meditation.

Such an attitude tends to lead to a false compart-mentalisation of life, a division and antagonism between the spiritual life and the ordinary life. However, true spirituality lies, not in any form of practice, but in living in a certain *state of consciousness* pervading *all* life and activities. Meditation—in the sense of a set practice—is not indispensable for cultivating such a spiritual state of inner concentration, action and work done with the right consciousness also produce a state of meditation.

The form in which one experiences and realises the Truth depends on the nature of the path one follows. Thus the paths of the Advaitin and the Buddhist lead to the experience of *nirvāṇa* and the realisation of the Truth as an impersonal Principle—an Impersonal Absolute Existence (Advaita) or an Impersonal

Absolute Non-Existence (Buddhism). On the other hand, the paths based on self-consecration through works and action, such as the path of the *Gītā*, and the paths of devotion and prayer, such as that of the Christian mystics, lead to the experiences of the Truth as Personal Being, *Īśvara*, the Lord. An integral approach, states Sri Aurobindo, leads to the realisation of the Truth as both personal and impersonal.

Whatever the path followed, the process of inner growth involves a transformation of the normal state of consciousness, a progressive awakening of inner and higher states of being, culminating in a total reversal of consciousness, a new birth.

References

Anand, K.C. (2000). *What is Consciousness? Know Thyself Series*-3. All India Magazine Booklet, Sri Aurobindo Society, Pondicherry, India.

Cornelissen, M. (2001). *Cornelissen, Mconsciousness and Its Transformation: Papers presented at the Second International Conference on Integral Psychology*. Sri Aurobindo International Centre of Education, Sri Aurobindo Ashram, Pondicherry, India.

Dalal, A.S. (1987). *Living within: The Yoga Approach to Psychological Growth and Health.* Sri Aurobindo Ashram, Pondicherry, India.

Dalal, A.S. (1990). *Growing Within: The Psychology of Inner Development.* Sri Aurobindo Ashram, Pondicherry, India.

Dalal, A.S. (1990). *The Hidden Forces of Life.* Sri Aurobindo Ashram, Pondicherry, India.

Dalal, A.S. (1998). *Power Within.* Sri Aurobindo Ashram, Pondicherry, India.

Dalal, A.S. (2001). *A Greater Psychology: An Introduction to the Psychological Thought of Sri Aurobindo.* Sri Aurobindo International Centre for Education, Sri Aurobindo Ashram, Pondicherry, India.

Joshi, K. and M. Cornelissen (2004). *Consciousness, Indian Psychology and Yoga*, Vol. 11, Part-3. Project on History of Science, Philosophy, and Culture, Centre for Study in Civilisations, New Delhi, India.

Paranjpe, A. (1998). *Self and Identity in Modern Psychology and Indian Thought.* New York: Plenum Press.

Sen, I. (1998). *Integral Psychology: The Psychological System of Sri Aurobindo.* Sri Aurobindo International Centre for Education, Pondicherry, India.

Sri Aurobindo (1994). *Essays Divine and Human.* Sri Aurobindo Ashram, Pondicherry, India.

6

Hindu Traditions and Practices

Hinduism is one of the oldest religions, not only of India, but also of the world. It is also the religion with largest number of followers, following Christianity and Islam. It is one of the most predominant religions found and followed in India. Under the larger umbrella of Hinduism, diverse traditions such as Śaivism, *Śāktism* and *Vaiṣṇavism* have existed. Nonetheless, with the passage of time, several traditions have faded away. Only two schools, Vedānta and Yoga have survived in current times.

Hinduism cannot be attributed to a founder, rather has diverse beginnings. Some also view it as a fusion of different Indian cultures, and traditions such as the Vedic traditions, Indus Valley civilization, popular or local traditions. Hinduism posits existence of one Supreme Being and numerous Divine Beings subordinate to Him. It also prescribes a wide range of laws and behaviours based on *karma* and *dharma*. Hinduism is also a firm supporter of "belief in Reincarnation".

Modern Hinduism

With the advent of British rule in India, a profound change in understanding of Hinduism followed, which reverberated both in India and outside India. The Hindu Renaissance in the nineteenth century is evident from origin of Academic Discipline called Indology, which subjected Indian culture to

European perspective. The scriptures like Vedas and Upaniṣads were subject of enquiry as scholars searched for the essence of Indian religions. The "Hindu Modernism" was propagated by Vivekananda, Aurobindo and Radhakrishanan. Hinduism was reformulated as its foundational texts were translated and abridged by influential twentieth century Hindus like Prabhupada (Founder of ISKCON), Sri Chinmoy, BKS Iyengar, Paramhans Yogananda. These new thoughts gave Hinduism prominence both in India and other countries.

In freedom struggle, Hinduism gained attention as a Political Force. Hindutva ideology came forward as a national ideology once the Rashtriya Swayamsevak Sangh (RSS) came into existence in 1925. Hindu Religiosity thus played an important role in the National Movement. As a religion, Hinduism has suffered much scrutiny from Indians as well as foreigners, especially after it was brought into the political arena, nonetheless, Hindu religion continues to be ardently followed and revered even today.

Hindu Texts

The Hindu text mainly consists of philosophy, mythology, theology, Vedic *yajña*, temple building, etc. It is classified into two categories: "Śruti"—the revealed and "Smṛti"—remembered. The major scriptures that are in Śruti are Vedas and Upaniṣads. The major scriptures that are in Smṛti are *Mahābhārata*, *Rāmāyaṇa*, *Bhagavad Gītā*, etc.

Smṛti is generally seen as secondary in authority to Śruti as Śruti is believed to be direct revelation of "Cosmic sound of Truth" heard by holy saints. Smṛti on the other hand, portrays many traditions of the time it was written in, reflecting characteristics of virtuous persons.

Śruti is the body of sacred texts that has main philosophy of Hinduism and a source of *dharma*. It is believed that Śruti was the cosmic truth heard by the *ṛṣi*s and translated in simple form for better understanding by humans such that it can be a source of guide. These works were written after the Vedas around 500 B.C. Smṛti shows the path of *dharma*, of law, and good human virtues. Such as the path followed by Lord Rāma or Lord Kṛṣṇa guides people to take decisions and follow moksha and not to accumulate the pain from bad deeds.

Hindu Rituals

In Hinduism, ever since its inception, certain rituals are characteristic of a Hindu *pūjā* (deity worship) and *bhajana*s (holy song recitation), pilgrimages and *vrata*s (fasts) are commonly seen in Hindu households.

Yajña—Hindu religion as other religions have elaborate rituals written in their texts. One of the important ritual is performing "*yajña*". Typically a "*yajña*" is a ritual involving showering offerings to the deities to worship them, praise their creation and prosperity giving to us and to sacrifice something to please them. Its procedures are prescribed in the Vedas. It signifies worshipping the deities and being unified with them. It also signifies giving alms in charity to please the deities. In a typical *yajña*, a holy fire is lit in the centre as it is believed to be the purestand a direct path to gods. Various herbs of significant values are poured in the fire along with ghee, milk, grains, spices, etc. It may be done in private or in elaborate ceremonies like marriage or funeral with the presence of large number of people.

Vedic (Śrauta) *yajña*s are typically performed by four Vedic priests, the Hotṛ, the Adhvaryu, the Udgātṛ and the Brahman. Rituals associated with each of the priests are detailed in dialogue between Aśvala and Yājñavalkya in the *Bṛhadāraṇyaka Upaniṣad*. The right to perform a *yajña* or *homa* is received by an initiation ceremony known as *yajñopavīta*. In this ceremony, a "sacred cord" is vested to the initiate, symbolising this right.

The functions associated with the priests are:

- The Hotṛ (priest), recites invocations and litanies drawn from the *Ṛgveda*. The verses recited by the Hotṛ are of three kinds—introductory verses, verses pertaining to *yajña* and eulogistic verses. The Hotṛ is also supposed to contemplate on and identify with the deity of speech—Fire or Agni.
- The Adhvaryu is the priest's assistant and is in-charge of the physical details of the ritual like measuring the ground, building the altar, etc. mentioned in the *Yajurveda*. The Adhvaryu offers three kinds of oblations, those that blaze up, those that make great noise and those

that sink. The Adhvaryu is supposed to contemplate on and identify with the deity of the eye—Sun or Sūrya.

- The Udgātṛ is the chanter of hymns set to melodies (*sāman*) drawn from the *Sāmaveda*. The Udgātṛ, like the Hotṛ, chants the introductory, *yajña*, and eulogistic verses. These three types of hymns are identified with the three kinds of vital breath *prāṇa*, *apāna* and *vyāna* in the body and the Udgātṛ himself contemplates on the vital breath.
- The *Brahman* is the superintendent of the entire performance, and is responsible for correcting mistakes by means of supplementary verses invoking the Viśvedevas (pantheon of celestials or *deva*s). In the *Bṛhadāraṇyaka*, the pantheon of Viśvedevas are held to be a creation of an infinite mind assuming infinite forms. Therefore, the only God that protects the *yajña* and with which the *Brahman* has to identify himself with is the deity of the mind—Moon or Candra.

Āgamic rituals involve temple worship. Vedic rituals involve *mantra*s to communicate with deities or Divine gods through fire. The rituals are described in Vedas called as *karma-kāṇḍa.*

Types of Yajñas: Four hundred *yajña*s are described in the Vedas, of which 21 are deemed compulsory and are called as *nitya-karma*. The optional ones are called as *kāmya-karma* and are usually for wishes and benefits. The *nitya-karma*s called as Agnihotra and Upāsanā need to be performed at dawn and dusk daily. The complex ones are less frequently performed. The first seven *yajña*s involve cooked items as sacrifices and are called as *pāka-yajña*s. The next seven require burnt offerings and called as *haviryajña*s. The last seven are called as *soma-yajña*s.

Sixteen *yajña*s are one time *saṁskāra*s as conducted to mark different milestones in life. They are *garbhādhāna, puṁsavana, simanta, jātakarma, nāmakaraṇa, annaprāśana, cūḍākarma, niṣkramaṇa, karṇavedha, vidyārambha, upanayana, keśānta, snātaka* and *vivāha, niṣeka, antyeṣṭi*. These are specified by the Gṛhyasūtras.

Pūjā

The word *pūjā* is derived from Sanskrit, meaning worship and adoration. It is a symbol of reverence for holy deity, or sometimes done to celebrate any special occasion, like advent into a new home (*graha praveś*) or marriage (*vivā*).

Pūjā is done with the aim of establishing a metaphorical link with God, with result being consciousness of God through homage to Him. The worshipper experience oneness with deities and their spiritual essence. *Pūjā* helps the devotee communicate desires and appeals, such as money, freedom from illness and prosperity, power and long age of self and loved ones. *Pūjā* is done with varied frequency, for varied duration, in varied settings. For example, in some homes daily worship is done, others may do it only at special occasions, like beginning a new venture. Though not mandatory, periodic *pūjā* is prescribed. *Pūjā* can be done at any hour of the day, in home, office, temple or any other location. Some people can do *pūjā* for hours while others may infrequently just light incense sticks. *Pūjā* may also vary by region, occasion, deity worshipped and intentions of worshipper. In some ceremonies, deity may be present while in some, it may not be the case. For example, in Nigama ceremonies, a fire is lit to show respect for deity Agni, however, no idol is necessarily present. In temple, priest assists *pūjā* sometimes. A dīpaka (candle), dhūpa (incense stick) is lit. *Āratī* or a *bhajana* is sung. Towards the end of the *pūjā*, food, fruits or sweets are offered to the deity, which is then distributed among all as blessed prasāda.

Significance of Pūjā

The *pūjā*s help one to connect with the supreme force and experience oneness with it. Paying respect to God through spiritual meditation is its aim. It is also a form of communication of one's desires and wishes to God for their fulfilment such as good luck, wealth, freedom from illness, recovery, etc. The role of rituals is to help a devotee to concentrate on the spiritual task of connecting with God. It also helps purify one's consciousness. It helps in liberating one's soul from this life to attain *mokṣa*. God can be worshipped in various forms such as rivers like Gaṅgā, Yamunā and Sarasvatī. And by connecting with even these can help one have a spiritual oneness with God.

Why do We do Āratī?

Towards the end of every ritualistic worship (*pūjā* or *bhajana*) of the God or to welcome an honoured guest or saint, we perform the *āratī*. This is always accompanied by the ringing of the bell and sometimes by singing, playing of musical instruments and clapping.

It is one of the sixteen steps (*ṣoḍaśa upacāra*) of the *pūjā* ritual. It is referred to as the lighted lamp in the right hand, which we wave in a clockwise circling movement to light the entire form of God.

Each part is revealed individually and also the entire form of God. As the light is waved we either do mental or loud chanting of prayers or simply behold the beautiful form of God illumined by the lamp.

At the end of *āratī* we place our hands over the flame and then gently touch our eyes and the top of the head.

We have seen and participated in this ritual from our childhood. Let us find out why we do the *āratī*?

Having worshipped the God of love—performing *abhiṣeka*, decorating the image and offering fruits and delicacies, we see the beauty of God in all His glory. Our minds are focused on each limb of the Lord as the lamp lights it up. It is akin to silent open-eyed meditation on His beauty. The singing, clapping, ringing of the bell, etc. denote the joy and auspiciousness, which accompanies the vision of God.

Āratī is often performed with camphor. This holds a telling spiritual significance. Camphor when lit, burns itself out completely without leaving a trace of it. It represents our inherent tendencies (*vāsanā*s). When lit by the fire of knowledge which illumines the God (Truth), our *vāsanā*s thereafter burn themselves out completely, not leaving a trace of ego which creates in us a sense of individuality that keeps us separate from God.

Also while camphor burns to reveal the glory of God, it emits a pleasant perfume even while it sacrifices itself. In our spiritual progress, even as we serve the *guru* and society, we should willingly sacrifice ourselves and all we have, to spread the "perfume" of love to all. We often wait a long while to see the illumined God but when the *āratī* is actually performed, our eyes close automatically as if to look within. This is to signify that each of us is a temple of God.

Just as the priest reveals the form of God clearly with the *āratī* flame, so too the *guru* reveals to us the divinity within each of us with the help of the "flame" of knowledge (or the light of spiritual knowledge). At the end of the *āratī*, we place our hands over the flame and then touch our eyes and the top of the head. It means—may the light that illuminated God light up my vision; may my vision be divine and my thoughts noble and beautiful.

The philosophical meaning of *āratī* extends further. The sun, moon, stars, lightning, and fire are the natural sources of light. God is the source of this wonderous phenomenon of the universe. It is due to Him alone that all else exist and shine. As we light up God with the flame of the *āratī*, we turn our attention to the very source of all light, which symbolises knowledge and life.

Also the sun is the presiding deity of the intellect, the moon, that of the mind, and fire, that of speech. The God is the supreme consciousness that illuminates all of them. Without Him, the intellect cannot think, nor can the mind feel nor the tongue speaks. The God is beyond the mind, intellect, and speech. How can this finite equipment illuminate the God? Therefore, as we perform the aarti we chant:

na tatra sūryo bhāti, na candra tārakam ।
nemma vidyuto bhānti kutoyamagnib ।
tameva bhāntam anubhāti sarvam ।
tasya bhāṣā sarvam idam vibhāti ।

> He is there where the sun does not shine, not the moon, stars and lightning. Then what to talk of this small flame (in my hand), everything (in the universe) shines only after God. And by His light alone are we all illumined.

Why do We Chant Oṁ?

Oṁ is one of the most chanted sound symbols in India. It has a profound effect on the body and mind of the one who chants and also on the surroundings. Most *mantra*s and Vedic prayers start with *oṁ*.

All auspicious actions begin with *oṁ*. It is even used as a greetingo *oṁ*, *hari oṁ* etc. It is repeated as a *mantra* or meditated upon. Its form is worshipped, contemplated upon or used as an auspicious sign.

Oṁ is the universal name of God. It is made up of the letters *a* (phonetically as in "around"), *u* (phonetically as in "put") and *m* (phonetically as in "mum"). The sound emerging from the vocal chords starts from the base of the throat as *a*. With the coming together of the lips, *u* is formed and when the lips are closed, all sounds end in *m*. The three letters symbolises the three states (waking, dream and deep sleep), the three deities (Brahmā, Viṣṇu and Śiva), the three Vedas (*Ṛg*, *Yajur* and *Sāma*) the three worlds (bhuḥ, bhuvaḥ, suvaḥ), etc. The Lord is all these and beyond.

The formless, attribute less God (*Brahman*) is represented by the silence between two *oṁ* chants. *Oṁ* is also called *praṅava* that means, "that(symbol or sound) by which the Lord is praised". The entire essence of the Vedas is enshrined in the word *oṁ*. It is said that God started creating the world after chanting *oṁ* and *atha*. Hence its sound is considered to create an auspicious beginning for any task that we undertake. The *oṁ* chant should have the resounding sound of a bell (*aaooommm*).

Oṁ is written in different ways in different places. The most common form symbolises Lord Gaṇeśa's. The upper curve is the head; the lower large one, the stomach; the side one, the trunk; and the semi-circular mark with the dot, the sweetmeat ball (*modaka*) in Lord Gaṇeśa's hand. Thus *oṁ* symbolises everything—the means and the goal of life, the world and the Truth behind it, the material and the Sacred, all form and the Formless.

Source: sanskritdocuments.org/articles/Hindu_Rituals.pdf

Hymns

Hindu music is as old as the Sanskrit literature itself. A *bhajana* is a lyrical song, praising God and expressing heartfelt Love and Devotion towards God. As a religion, Hinduism has ample anecdotes and episodes from scriptures, the teachings of saints and descriptions of gods, tales of holy men and women. These have been mostly the topics of *bhajana*s. Some of the notable composers of their times are Nānak, Mīrā, Narottama Dās, Tulsīdās, Sūrdās, etc. *Bhajana*s like—*mere to girdara gopāla, dūsarā nā koi* by Mīrā and *maṅgala bhavana amaṅgala hārī* by Tulsīdās have been sung and passed through generations. In fact, the musical tradition of Hinduism is amongst the oldest in the entire world.

Pilgrimage

Pilgrimages are voyages taken by Hindus to their deities' temple which have historic significance in their scriptures. Mostly these are hard to reach places, and require great physical and mental strength to accomplish the pilgrimage. However, with the availability of modern transport, they can now be easily reached. For example, Vaiṣṇo-Devī, a pilgrimage of Hindu Goddess by the same name was a difficult journey, which can now be done by helicopter easily. Similarly, Amarnāth and Kedarnāth, the holy places dedicated to Lord Śiva are easily accessible by trains and car rides.

Some of the famous pilgrimage sites are Haridwar-Rishikesh, Ayodhya-Chitrakoot, Vrindavan-Gokul-Mathura. The Char-Dham Yātrā includes Purī, Badrīnāth, Dwārkā and Rāmeśvaram spread out in entire India in four directions. Allahabad, which is also the location of famous Kumbh Mela that is held in every 12 years is also a famous pilgrimage site. Pilgrimage is not mandatory in Hinduism, yet many Hindus go there with firm belief that they will attain salvation and find a place in heaven.

Hindu Symbolism

Hinduism has an ancient system of symbolism and iconography. These symbols gained their meaning from the scriptures, cultural traditions, and mythology. The sign of *svastika* which stand for auspiciousness and the syllable *oṁ* which represents God have grown to represent Hinduism itself, while other markings such as *tilaka*s identify a follower of the faith. There are in fact, many types of *tilaka*s in Hinduism representing different sects. Hinduism also associate many symbols with particular deities like snakes and tiger skin with Lord Śiva, lotus and *cakra* with Lord Viṣṇu, *vīṇā* with Goddess Sarasvatī, Money with Goddess Lakṣmī.

Rituals and Self-realisation

All rituals performed in the Hindu tradition are aimed at becoming one with the Supreme God. Through various forms of worship, *yajña*s, *pūjā*s, singing, *bhajana*s, people try different means to achieve the Bliss of Oneness. All paths lead to one goal attainment of true and pure bliss.

Self-realisation can only occur when the mind is calm and concentrated, reflecting the qualities of Self within. As the Self is infinite, illumination is not a static or final stage. Illumination includes a variety of states of consciousness. The contents in the field of consciousness become more and more subtle as meditation deepens. Eventually there exists consciousness of deep joy or peace and finally all that remains is the consciousness of Self.

The four types of spiritual practices through which self-realisation can be achieved are *karma-yoga, rāja-yoga, bhakti-yoga* and *jñāna-yoga*.

Karma-yoga: It pronounces the path of action without the desire for fruits/benefits of action. The actions done should fulfil all aspects of the present moment, leaving one in a state of fulfilment until the next impulse arises. All actions should be devoid of personal component which is unavoidable, be it pleasant, neutral or unpleasant and should be performed as the situation demands and these will lead to self-realisation.

Rāja-yoga: Patañjali's *rāja-yoga* is *yoga* of mind meditation and controlling one's thoughts is simultaneously brought about.

Bhakti-yoga is the *yoga* of love and ode to Supreme God and other beings be it animal or humans.

Jñāna-yoga is the meditation in the form of *samādhi* to discover oneself and connect with Supreme God.

The Hindu tradition prescribes sacraments, practices, sacrifices, and rituals which marks a person's movement from one stage (*āśrama*) of life to another. The Vedas prescribe a set of sacrifices with oblations for deities and ancestors. These rituals serve to purify a person and bestow him with good qualities. These qualities are termed as *guṇa*s. A person may practice rituals without having deep spiritual knowledge or may have religious and spiritual knowledge and may not perform rituals.

Vedic rituals comprise of a *havana/homa*. A *havana* is a sacrificial fire in which oblations are offered to deities and ancestors along with recitation of *mantra*s from Vedas by priests. In addition the gifts to be given in charity are distributed in the presence of elders for blessings. Every human milestone is celebrated in the Hindu tradition in the form of a particular *saṁskāra*. The whole life of a Hindu is covered in the *saṁskāra*. It starts from conception in the womb until his/her death-involving funeral ceremonies for movement to the next world. *Saṁskāra*s are considered as purification ceremonies to get the best form out from the person, whether it is physical, psychical, or spiritual. The main goal of *saṁskāra*s is to invoke the beneficence from one's deities and to keep away the effect bad omen and evil forces at different stages of life.

People seek material gain from the *saṁskāra*s and wish for good health, healthy children, intellect, and prosperity. These are also dignified ways to express one's joys and sorrows, hopes and desires. These are celebrated with feasts for all, decorations, music, and gifts. For example, a sorrowful event like the death ceremony also has *saṁskāra*s and rituals associated with it to conduct the funeral in an appropriate mood.

These also serve the purpose of making people aware of one's social status and privileges. For example, when a child undergoes the janeū ceremony he earns the right to study the Vedas. Also after the ceremonies done in marriage a man can now perform his dhārmic duties.

A child is considered impure at the pre-natal stage. To make the human body sacred and fit for the gods to reside, one needs to perform the *saṁskāra*s. These help remove the impurities from the human body.

Purpose of Saṁskāras

(1) Cultural: It is believed that the *saṁskāra*s help in the development and transformation of one's personality. Hence, the Hindu tradition believes in guiding the individuals and moulding their character to become strong and face the hardships of life.

(2) Spiritual: A higher and purer sanctity to human life. The impurities are removed from human body and made fit for the *ātmā* to reside. The *Atri Smṛti* talks about how a person born in the lower *Śūdra* caste can be born again (*dvija*) by performing the *upanayana saṁskāra*, by learning the Vedas he becomes a *vipra*, and one can become a Brāhmaṇa by realising God (*Brahman*). It is a form of *sādhanā*, that is, a spiritual endeavour from external discipline towards internal spiritual edification. The final goal of *saṁskāra* is to escape the bondage of life and *karma*s and cross the ocean of death to attain *Paramātmā*. Hence, the aim of *saṁskāra*s is to become spiritual, practical, dignified for human welfare.

Ṛgveda has the earliest mentions of the *saṁskāra*s. Along with the rituals, hymns are sung in conception, marriage, and funeral. Some of these are recited in all rituals. The *Yajurveda* mentions the tonsure ceremony. Several *mantra*s to be recited in marriage, funeral and commencement of Vedic studies are mentioned in the *Atharvaveda*.

In the Brāhmaṇa period, *Gopatha Brāhmaṇa*, the thread ceremony is found mentioned. The *Satapatha Brāhmaṇa* mentions the word *brahmacarya*.

The *mantra*s for cremation are mentioned in the *Taittirīya Āraṇyaka*. The initiation in the *gurukula* is written in the *Chāndogya Upaniṣad*. Bṛhadāraṇyaka and other Upaniṣads mention the Gāyatrī *mantra*. With the start of civilization, the *saṁskāra*s were developed, elaborated, and coded in a manner that ordinary person could understand and it was given an institutional basis. These help bring discipline in society.

Relation between Karmas and Guṇas

The literal meaning of *karma* is action or work. The rituals performed throughout lifetime to purify her/him both inwardly and outwardly. Her/his task is to realise the *ātman*. The *karma*s performed for this purpose are known as *saṁskāra*. A *saṁskāra* removes the impurities from a person and instills in good qualities in the person.

The Vedas mention forty *saṁskāra*s and the eight *Ātmaguṇa*s for this purpose *Ātmaguṇa* is rendered pure and devoid of impurities. The Hindus believe in the theory of dualism of self (Dvaitins). This means that there are two selves. One is the individual self which is different from the Param*ātman*. However, the reality is that there is only one self called as the *ātman*. It also means that *jīvātman* or individual self and the *Para-Brahman* are one. The self is pure in itself and cannot be purified by *saṁskāra*s. It does not have any qualities.

However, in our daily living owing to the lure of *māyā* people fail to recognise that we are the pure *ātman* without qualities. When we speak of *saṁskāra*s we refer to the dualistic thought of impure self to be purified. The bad qualities called the *durguṇa* can be removed by the developing eight good qualities. Once we succeed, we will transcend to the highest *guṇa* called *sattava guṇa*.

Finally, self will merge with the *Paramātman* devoid of any *guṇa* or *karma*. This can be achieved by observing these rules in our daily routine, how we should perform our self in real world. This can help us control our mind's wanderings, subduing our passions and ego and our feelings of anger, hatred, fear and sorrow will gradually wither away. These *saṁskāra*s and *ātmaguṇa*s help acquire noble qualities of the Purāṇic characters mentioned in the stories.

Guṇas and Saṁskāras

The qualities of *dayā, kṣānti, anasūyā, śauca, anayaśa, maṅgala, akārpaṇya, asprhiā* are the eight *guṇa*s mentioned in the Hindu philosophy. *Dayā* connotes love, care, compassion, and empathy for all creatures. The happiness and sense of fulfilment derived from such love is boundless. It is the basis of all qualities. *Kṣānti* implies being patient and peaceful. One meaning of *śānti* is patiently suffering disease, poverty, misfortune, and so on. The other meaning is forgiving people for their misdoings.

The third *guṇa* gets its name from Sage Atri's wife Anasūyā who did not experience jealousy. The feeling of jealousy may be caused by other person's success, wealth, or status. We must learn not to envy people even though they may be less deserving as it is attributed to the rewards of *karmas* done in the previous life.

Śauca means cleanliness. Cleanliness is emphasised in all activities such as clothes, bathing, food and home. It is believed that being clean makes a person happy and content. Looking at a neat and hygenic person makes us feel clean too. The list of *dharmas* prescribed by Manu to be followed by all are non-violence, truthfulness, *asteya* (non-covetousness; non-stealing), *śauca* (cleanliness) and *indriya-nigraha* (subduing the senses or even obliterating them).

Anayaśa is the fifth *ātmaguṇa*. The opposite of this is *ayaśa* which denotes effort, exertion, etc. *Anayaśa* means to have a feeling of lightness, to take things easy. One must not keep a long face, wear a scowl or keep lamenting one's hardships. *Anayaśa* is a great virtue. This practice helps one to keep free from mental stress and not to be put down by hindrances at work or in life.

Maṅgala is the sixth *guṇa*. It implies having an auspicious air characterised by dignity and purity. It suggests one to always have a cheerful disposition and not snap at people on little things. Being cheerful helps one radiate positive energy, happiness, and auspiciousness. Loving what you do and doing it with a feeling of lightness, creates joy wherever we go. This is *maṅgala*. We must spread happiness wherever we go.

The next *guṇa* is *akārpaṇya*. It is the opposite of *kṛpaṇa* that is miserliness. It implies that we must donate generously. In the battlefield of *Kurukṣetra* when Arjuna refused to fight with his own kin, he was subdued by *kārpaṇya doṣa*." It implied that he put himself in a miserly state and became weak. *Akārpaṇya* is the quality of a courageous and zestful person who can face problems determinedly.

The last *guṇa* is *aspṛhā*. It is the opposite of *spṛhā* which means desire. Since desires are believed to be the cause of all suffering, evil, and misfortunes,it is very difficult to remove desires from mind. By constantly practicing the rites to acquire the *guṇas* or ātmic qualities one can become free from desires. Gautam Buddha called desires as thirst. One of his main teaching is to conquer the desires. Many of the other religions also have similar qualities prescribed to be followed by people.

The Pre-natal Saṁskāras

In the Gṛhasūtras, the major *saṁskāra*s prescribed fluctuates between 12-18. However 16 *saṁskāra*s are commonly followed and called as *Ṣoḍaśa saṁskāra*s." Many complex *saṁskāra*s such as those related to marriage, pregnancy, childbirth, education and death are followed by most Brāhmaṇa communities.

(i) *Garbhādhāna*

Garbhādhāna literally means gifting the womb. It is the act of conception. After the matrimonial union this is the first *saṁskāra*. Before a woman conceives, certain rites are to be performed. *Niṣekam* is the act of first sexual intercourse. According to the astrological condition an auspicious day and time is chosen for doing the rituals for *garbhādhāna*. The *mantra*s recited are essentially prayers offered to God to help the successful conception of a good and healthy son. The *mantra*s make use of occasional metaphors of joint action. Extending one's family is one of the ways to repay the debts to the ancestors. It is an essential duty except when either or both the partners are functionally unfit.

(ii) *Puṁsavana*

Puṁsavana means engendering a male child. It is a ritual conducted in the third or the fourth month of pregnancy. As part of the rituals the pregnant woman eats one bead of barley and two beads of black grain, along with a little curd. The religious chanting of *mantra*s is done along with this. It may sometimes be done in the eighth month also.

Since the male child is more celebrated in Hindu tradition, the purpose of the ceremony is to help pray and conceive a male child. The male *nakṣatra* day is chosen for this ritual. It is believed that the banyan tree has medicinal properties and help relive problems in pregnancy. Hence, few drops of the juice of the banyan stem are put into the right nostril of the pregnant lady to inhale it along with a prayer for the birth of a son or a worthy child.

For protection from evil forces a *rolī* or sanctified thread is tied to the left wrist of the lady. The *mantra*s, freely rendered, pray:

> "May God Īśāna fulfil our wishes; Dhātā bless the world with children and wealth. May He bless this household, too, with children. May the immortals live in this house. May Agni bless me with sons. May Indra bless me with children. May I have handsome children."

Strict discipline for diet and movement is prescribed for the pregnant lady. For example, a medicinal herb called giloy and dry ginger should be consumed with milk by the woman. Other restrictions include sleeping for long hours, talking too much, food with high salt, sour, pungent, bitter things and purgatives like *harītaki*, papaya, etc. She should keep away from negative emotions such as anger, aversion, greed, etc. and should always keep her mind calm, peaceful, and happy. She is also suggested to follow a life of good conduct.

(iii) *Sīmantonnayana*

Sīmantonnayana means parting the hair. It is a ritual conducted in the fourth or fifth month of pregnancy. *Sīmantonnayana* is performed to protect the mother-to-be in the pregnancy. This *saṁskāra* protects the mother and child within from demons and spirits that might want to cause harm to them. It also helps ensure good health, success, and prosperity for the child.

First of all the woman's hair is oiled. Then using three stalks of *kuśa* grass it is parted three times from the forehead upwards. The *praṇava mantram auṁ, bhūr, bhuvaḥ, svaḥ* are chanted during each partition.

The materials used are the quill of a porcupine, an ear of ripe paddy and some *udumbara* leaves. Rākā is the deity of full moon who is invoked in this ceremony. These materials signify that pregnancy shall bear fruitful results, child should be gifted with sharp intellect (like the sharp quill of the porcupine) and be beautiful like the full-moon.

It is believed that music help increase the mother's suckling power besides conferring having a positive psychological impact. Hence, some music especially on *vīṇā* is played. The ceremony ends with the mother to be touching a male calf, symbolising a son.

Childhood Saṁskāra

I. *Jātakarma*

As the name suggests, the *jātakarma* ritual is performed at the birth of a child. According to the Hindu astrology, the sun, the moon, planets, and celestial stars have deep and lasting impact on the new born baby. They determine important aspects of a child's life, like spouse, education, parental and sibling relationship, source of income, longevity, etc. The placement will indicate if the childbirth has happened at an auspicious time or not. If the case be latter, then *jātakarma* can be performed to ensure that no evil can harm the child.

The celebration of *childbirth* is not restricted to family and friends. Holy men called *paṇḍit*s" are called upon to chant *mantra*s and bless the expecting mother by sprinkling water on her. In fact, even prior to childbirth, a proper ceremony is held before cutting the umbilical cord. However, if there has been a death in the family recently, then the ceremony is not performed.

After the baby is born and blessed by Holy men, the father looks at the face of the baby and through this action, he is supposed to have paid back his debt to his ancestors. Then he takes a gold ring and dips it into honey, which he puts briefly into the infant's mouth. The symbolic significance of this action is that it is believed that this action endows the child with superior intelligence.

When the infant is born, his immunity is so low that he cannot defend himself to the evil of the world and highly prone to black magic. To ward it off, the father writes *AUṀ*" on the baby's tongue and whispers *vedoasiti* (that is, your name is Veda) in the right ear of the child and make the child lick a mixture of honey and ghee while reciting *mantra*s. This ceremony also has symbolic significance. The underlying principle is emphasis on the intellect in a human. According to Suśruta, ghee has the power to remove hysteria, increases digestion, memory, luster, semen, talent and life, and also imparts beauty. The ceremony also increases the life of the child. In the ceremony, the child is placed at mother's side and father places water by the mother's side as it symbolically wards off demons.

II. *Nāmakaraṇa (Name Giving)*

According to the caste in which the child is born and the position of stars and constellations at the time of birth, a day is fixed for naming the child. It is normally performed on the tenth or twelfth day after the birth. Prior to that, the child does not have a formal, distinct name. In the Hindu tradition, there is a pattern to name the child after holy names like that of gods and demi-gods, sacred places, goddesses. Usually the name of boys should have even syllables and girls have odd syllables and end with *i* and *ā*. The name should be simple, pleasing to hear and easy to pronounce by others. Also, unlike other cultures, in which children are not named after a dead person, there is a widespread practice to name the child after their ancestors. Sometimes, the names are chosen depending upon the location of stars. The practice of allocating a particular name has its own symbolic significance.

Naming a child after God imparts God-like qualities to her or him. It also gives the opportunity to parents to utter the name of God every time they refer to their child.

On the day of *nāmakaraṇa*, a havana is organised in which sages, priests and elders are invited to commence the ceremony along with recitation of *mantra*s and prayers. The mother bathes the child, dresses him/her up with new clothes and sits at the right side of her husband with the baby on her lap, his/her head directed at north direction near the *yajñakuṇḍa*. Herein a holy fire is lit in the *yajñakuṇḍa* where father along with holy sages offer *havana sāmagrī*. The *yajña* is performed with father offering one oblation with spoonful of ghee reciting the *mantra—oṁ prajāpataya swāhā* amongst many other *mantra*s. Thereafter, the father feels the breadth of the child being exhaled which symbolises that the baby's consciousness has awakened. The father utters—"your name is..." Then, everyone attending the ceremony refers to the child with that name only and blesses him/her.

III. *Niṣkramaṇa (First Outing)*

In the first two months, the child is usually confined to the safety of home. In the third month, the child goes out to see the moon and, also, the fire. The child also has his/her first official outing in the fourth month, and is taken by any male of the family, either father or uncle, to the temple. Preferably, the child goes out only when weather conditions are favourable, so as to avoid him/her from getting sick. It is usually the third full moon night after the birth.

The procedure for *niṣkramaṇa* ceremony is that in the early morning, the infant is bathed and dressed in new clothes. Thereafter, the mother takes the child to *yajñaśāla* and gives him/her to her husband. The ceremony is very similar to *jātakarma* ceremony in terms of incantation of *mantra*s. Afterwards, the infant is taken out into sunlight and fresh air. When she/he is taken back, the people bless the baby with the following sentence:

> *tvam jīva śaradaḥ śatam vardhamānaḥ*"
> May you be endowed with health and strength and live a life of hundred years).

In the night, both the parents take the child out to expose him/her to moonlight and thereafter, take the infant back into the safety of home.

IV. *Annaprāśana (First Feeding)*

Up until now, the child is only breastfed by the mother. Feeding solid food for the first time to the baby is the next ceremony, called *annaprāśana*. For a son, it is usually done in even months, and for daughters, it is usually done in odd months symbolically their ceremony signifies an important milestone in the baby's life. The time has come for the child to wean away from the mother and for the mother to reduce breastfeeding to the child. It is thus, no surprise, that this ceremony must be performed only when the child is grown up enough to digest solid food. The food usually offered is cooked rice and ghee. This food is given to the child only after some portion of it is given to the *purohita*s (holy priests) and *ṛtvij* accompanied with chanting of *mantra*s. The small portion for the baby is mixed with small quantities of curd and honey. It is then given to the child.

As with other *saṁskāra*s, prayers are offered to gods and goddesses to bless the child with healthy and long life. Special prayers are offered to Goddess of speech. According to the Hindu *dharma*, this ceremony must be ideally performed when the child is of six months of age. The following *mantra* from the *Yajurveda* is chanted while feeding solid food to the child for the first time:

> *oṁ annapate annasya no dehya namivasya suṣminaḥ pra pra datāram tāriśa ūrjvam no dhehi dvipade catuṣpade*"
> O Lord of plenty, vouchshare us a share of food that strengthens us, and brings no illness,
> O Lord, our leader, grant us nourishment both for bipeds and quadrupeds.

Thereafter, the child is blessed by everyone in the congregation, including the parents, the elders, and priests.

V. *Cūḍākarma (Shaving of Head)*

The *cūḍākarma saṁskāra* mainly refers to the shaving of the head in the first, second, third or fifth year of the child. An auspicious day is selected for the ceremony and a barber is invited. The hair on the child's head is cut, but a tuft of hair is left at the top of the head. The famous Caraka also agreed on this. According to the *Suśruta Purāṇa*, that area is the joint of artery and critical juncture. In the tuft of hair, there is a sensitive spot called Adhipati and any damage to this portion can be fatal. In earlier times, the Hindu proponents used to keep *śikhā* (the tuft of hair) and removing it was considered a cardinal sin.

In the ceremony, four earthen pots are also brought and filled with rice, barley, *mūṅga* and sesamum. They are placed in the northern side of *havana kuṇḍa* of *yajñaśālā*. Thereafter, a *havana* is performed. The following *mantra* from Āyurveda is recited:

> *oṁ āyamagāntsavitā kṣurenoṣnena vāya udakenehi āditya rudrā vasava undantu sa cetasaḥ somasya rājño vapata pracetasaḥ.*

The barber cuts the hair by a razor or scissors and all the cut hair assembled on the floor are collected in a container containing *kuśa* grass and *mimosa* leaves. The barber is given the four pots along with some clothes and money and then he takes the cut hair to bury them in some hard to reach place like forest or riverside, where he may or may not be accompanied by some family member. Meanwhile, the child is blessed by her/his father and other family members.

Once the barber has left, the father rubs some butter or curd on the child's head and then he is taken to be bathed. The child is then dressed in new clothes and sits with the father facing east as he chants Mahādeva Gaṇa. The guests bless the child with strength, long life, and vigour before leaving.

VI. *Karṇavedha (Piercing the Earlobes)*

The child's earlobes are pierced on some auspicious day, usually the sixth or seventh month. According to Suśruta, the reason for the same is that pierced ears protect the child from diseases like hernia. Although, for boys, the right earlobe is supposed to be pierced first, but nowadays, this practice has drastically reduced and lost its religious significance. In girls, the left earlobe is to be pierced first. For girls, this ceremony is held more often than boys for the purpose of enabling them to wear earrings. Either a goldsmith or a surgeon pierces the ears.

The procedure for *karṇavedha saṁskāra* begins in the morning, whcn the mother bathes the child and dresses him/her in new clothes and ornaments, and brings the child to *yajñaśālā*. A *havana* follows, in which holy *mantra*s are chanted from *sāmānya prakāśana*.

The physician then pierces the earlobe and inserts a thin wire into the holes to prevent it from closing. To prevent bleeding or any subsequent damage, a healing ointment is applied.

Educational Saṁskāras

Educational *saṁskāra*s are the *saṁskāra*s related to the life of a person after the age of six when s/he is believed to be ready for formal education. These are the ones to facilitate education, values, and respect of authority and *guru* in life. These prepare the child to a future life with respect to career, family, and community. Traditionally the Vedas were taught as part of education. Hence these are significant for a holistic development of the individual.

Types of Educational Samskaras

1. Vidyārambha (Learning the Alphabet)

The first of the educational *saṁskāras* is *vidyārambha*. This *saṁskāra* is also known as *akṣarārambha, akṣaralekhana, akṣaravikaraṇa* and *akṣaraviṣkaraṇa*. Before the child starts formal education or vedic study (called *vedārambha*), this *saṁskāra* is performed at the age of five. The child is bathed and made to sit with the face towards the west. The teacher or *ācārya* of the child sits facing the child. On a silver plate rice and saffron are placed. Using a pen made of gold or silver the child is made to write letters on the rice. Salutation to Gaṇeśa and Sarasvatī Goddess of knowledge, salutation to family deities and salutation to Nārāyaṇa and Lakṣmī are given. The symbol auṁ is written by the child. The teacher is honored with gifts such as Pagh and Safi. The child is then blessed by the teacher.

Around six years of age a child starts going to school entering into a formal phase of learning. In this phase of middle childhood a child can attain mastery through knowledge and successfully achieving the learning tasks would bring a sense of competency in the child. As the child competes with her/his peers such as in class, sports, etc. she would experience success and failure.

2. Upanayana (Yajñopavīta): Sacred Thread Initiation

The *upanayana* is considered the most supreme of all *saṁskāras*. The word *upa* means "near" and *nayana* means "to take (him) to", that is, to take the son to the teacher. A sacred thread called *janeū* or *yajñopavīta* is used to start the ceremony. It is considered as the beginning of a new life called as *dvija*. Here the child starts his formal education and a life of strict discipline involving *bhramacarya* or celibacy. The *ācārya* brings the child under his guardianship. The castes that follow this *saṁskāra* are *Brāhmaṇa*s, *Kṣatriya*s and Vaiśyas. It is conducted for both boys and girls. Traditionally hence both girls and boys were given training in discipline, living a truthful life, and *sevā* or physical service. However, over time this *saṁskāra* has been ceased for girls. This has led to stopping of their being formally educated.

The *ācārya* stands on the pedestal next to parents. The child lives in a traditional *gurukula* which is the house of the teacher. He is given the child to mould him with love and patience into a person with a strong character. The teacher will provide him the vast knowledge of the Vedas. As compared to various other cultural systems, Hindu system prescribes stringent measures for an ideal student. This is the path to become a successful student. His personality developed during this period will help him in his life as a household man/woman. However, it is now not possible to reside with the teacher. Nowadays there are facilities of boarding school in which the student lives in close proximity with the teacher.

Janeū is made up of three *khādī* cotton strings. These signify the three *guṇas*—*sattva* (reality), *raja*s (passion), and *tama*s (darkness). It is also a reminder about the debt a person owes to seers, ancestors, and gods. A knot called as *brahmagranthi* ties the three strings together. It symbolises Brahmā (creator), Viṣṇu (sustainer) and Śiva (leveller). It reminds the wearer of these three deities. He would always be aware of his actions and not do anything against the path of *dharma*.

3. Vedārambha (Commencing Vedic Study)

The earlier list of *dharmaśāstras* did not mention this *saṁskāra*. It however listed the four Vedic vows—Veda *vrata*s. It seemed that though *upanayana* marked the beginning of education, it did not coincide with Vedic study. Therefore a separate *saṁskāra* was felt necessary to initiate Vedic study. In this *saṁskāra*, each student, according to his lineage, masters his own branch of the Vedas.

4. Keśānta (Godāna): Shaving the Beard

Keśānta is listed in one of the four Veda *vrata*s. The word Keśa" implies hair and *anta* implies end. It is marked by first time shaving of the beard by the student when he turns sixteen. A cow is gifted to the *ācārya*, called as *godāna* and other gifts to the barber.

It is the beginning of manhood and now he should become more vigilant of his impulses of youth and exert control over them. He renews his vow of *bhramacarya*. He also begins to live in strict discipline over a period of one year.

During adolescence there are dramatic changes in all aspects of development. The word "adolescence" meaning "to grow into—adulthood", thus adolescence is a transitional phase in human life cycle that is a transition from childhood to adulthood. As the child attains puberty, it signals achieving sexual maturation and in many traditional societies it is celebrated as the "puberty rites function".

Erikson termed this stage as a conflict of identity vs. identity diffusion. The developmental task during adolescence is to choose an identity for oneslf. He or she needs to integrate earlier childhood identities with the current, biological, and social changes. The conflict an adolescent faces is to make a commitment to a role, after choosing from one's multiple roles. This specific chosen role would be his/her identity. Adolescence is the phase of exploration that is why there is going to be some diffusion.

5. Samavartana (Termination of Studentship)

The end of *bhramacarya* phase also signifies end of studentship. The word *samavartana* meant "returning home from the house of *ācārya*". A sacred ritual, sacrificial bath, known as *avabhṛt snāna* is performed. The observance of *bhramacarya* is terminated with this ritualistic bath. It symbolises the crossing of the ocean of knowledge and learning by the student. Hence is also known as *vidyāsnātaka*.

The *ācārya* decides the time when the student has acquired knowledge and is ready to end studentship. It certifies the person as learned, possessing good qualities and character for a healthy and happy married life. The student returns gifts to the *ācārya* with *guru-dakṣiṇā*. It is also believed that one can never repay the debts of a *guru*/teacher. The *guru* blesses the child and praises him and says impressive statements, known as *dikṣānta pravacana*, as mentioned in the *Taittirīya Upaniṣad*.

Marriage/Vivāha Saṁskāras

The fifteenth *saṁskāra*, *vivāha*—the sacred institution of marriage—is described in detail.

As a lot of significance is given to married couples and their roles in Indian society, marriage or *vivāha saṁskāra*, is believed to be of foremost importance for the individual (Harman, 1989). Life has been ideally differentiated into four stages of development according to the Vedic vision, these are called as *āśrama*s. The first, which begins with the initiation ceremony, is known as the stage of *brahmacarya* or an age devoted to learning spiritual and moral principles. After that comes the other stages like the householder (*gṛhastha*), the retiree (*vānaprastha*) and finally the renunciate (*saṁnyāsa*). Manu prescribes,

> "Having spent the first quarter of one's life in the *guru*'s house, the second quarter in one's own house with the wife, and the third quarter in the forest, one should take *saṁnyāsa* in the fourth, casting away every worldly tie" (*Manusmṛti* IV.1).

Vivāha or "marriage" means taking over and embracing specific responsibilities. It is a progression of the couple. It is considered as the most significant of all the Hindu *saṁskāra*s. It corresponds to the advocating and upholding of sense of duty which the householder imbibed during his initial years in the *brahmacarya āśrama*. The householder was the most honoured stage in Indian society as the householder constitutes the backbone of the social order. The Smṛtis praise the *gṛhastha* (householder) *āśrama* as the supreme, as it is the main support of and provide assistance to the other three *āśrama*s. The greater good of the society as well as the environment is guided by the proper management of resources by the householders. It is believed that by marriage an individual is capable to actualise the four *puruṣārtha*s (endeavours) of life: *dharma* (righteousness), *artha* (wealth), *kāma* (desire) and *mokṣa* (salvation). The other important purpose of marriage is procreation for children. It is postulated that a human being is able to repay the ancestral obligations by having children. The householder thus seems to act in the banal world the role of Lord Viṣṇu—the Preserver of the Hindu Tri gods. Interestingly in the Hindu marriage tradition, during the nuptial rituals, the bridegroom is beheld as Lord Viṣṇu and the bride is treated as Goddess Lakṣmī. Hindu marriage emphasises carrying out and committing to one's duties. The married person has a duty (*dharma*) to exercise himself to legitimately attaining material pursuits in order to happily lead his life, to practice *sva-dharma* and to provide support to dependents like retired persons, renuciates, and students.

Marriage is recognised to be of near equal importance for men. With few exceptions, males cannot perform religious sacrificial offerings without their spouse and marriage is perceived to be necessary to live one's life according to *dharma* (Harman, 1984; Sharma, 1985). This salience is likewise depicted within Hindu religious mythology wherein unmarried gods may be portayed as powerless. For example, in one of the representations, Lord Śiva is a corpse until his marriage to Śakti gave life to him.

Marriage has been regarded as an essential element in all civilizations of the world for developing a stable and ideal society. History reveals that a society without loyalty in marital ties tends to degrade. One of the reasons for the downfall of the Romans has been attributed to promiscuity. Marriage is an alliance in which individuals and society as a whole, while following the moral norms, can advance together. At the same time, it does not cause harm to others nor intrude upon one's freedom. This *saṁskāra* helps to expand and improve cultural values and *dharma*. It maintains and promotes good character, righteousness, and self-restraint.

(i) *Types of Marriage*

In the Hindu sacred texts eight types of marriage are recognised. In the *Manusmṛti* (iii.21) they are partitioned into two groups: (i) the morally approved (*praśasta*) and (ii) the disapproved (*apraśasta*).

(i) *Praśasta*

(a) Brāhma: This is acknowledged as the most legitimate and virtuous kind. It was termed so, as it was considered to be appropriate for Brāhmaṇas. In this type of marriage the daughter is given by the father with ornaments (that he can afford) to a righteous, learned and man of character, whom he has approached himself and greeted with respect, without accepting anything in return (*Manusmṛti*, iii.17). The Smṛtis regard this type as the supreme type, as it is devoid of physical force, erotic passion, insistence of conditions and greed for monetary assets. Societal correctness and religious commitment are duly taken into account.

(b) Daiva: Daiva is the another type of marriage but considered subordinate to *brāhma*. In this, the girl is adorned and handed over by the father to a priest who presides at a *yajña* (sacrifice). It is named *daiva* as the offering is made at the time of a *daiva yajña*. This practice was popular among the first three Hindu classes. This kind has declined for it is thought not right to offer the daughter to a priest.

(c) Ārṣa: In this type the bride's father gets a pair or two bovines—a cow and an ox or two cows and two oxen—from the groom for the objective of a *yajña* that constitutes a religious sacrament. It is important to note here that the pair of kine was not the bride's price. This system was called as *ārṣa* because it was common among the clerical and priestly households. No matter what is the aim behind this custom, from the perspective of the *Manusmṛti* (iii.53)welcoming a gift no matter small or large, amounts to a sale.

(d) Prājāpatya: This entails the father giving away his daughter to a suitable candidate with the cognisance that they will carry out their societal and religious duties together. The name *prājāpatya* indicates that the newly-weds enters the marriage bond for carrying out their duties towards *prājāpatya*, that is, for producing and raising children. From the Western perspective this kind of wedding may be deemed satisfactory because the interests and power of the husband and wife are equally well taken care of. But from the point of view of the Hindu scriptures, it is subordinate to the first three as the daughter is given subject to wordly conditions. Thereby the "gift" cannot in a true sense be regarded as free. Interestingly, Kauṭilya in his *Arthaśāstra* forbade dissolution of marriage (divorce) for the four *praśasta* marriages.

(ii) *Apraśasta*

(a) Āsura: The *Manusmṛti* (iii.31) defines this as, "When the husband pays money to the bride and the relatives of the bride and accepts her out of his free will". This type of marriage in reality is a purchase, where the main consideration is money. Manu denounced it, he says

> "The wise father of the bride should not accept any amount of money. The learned father of the girl should not accept even the least amount of price. Accepting the price out of greed, he becomes the seller of children."(*Manusmṛti*, iii.51).

The *Aitareya Brāhmaṇa* (I.16) terms this type as *paśuvivāha*—animal marriage. In the contemporary period this from of marriage is still prevailing in certain sections of Hindu society in the form of dowry where monetary and other material objects are demanded by the groom's family fromthe bride's family. In contemporary times there has been a rising public opinion against dowry. Many religious leaders and social activists have criticised it and are working to oppose it.

(b) Gāndharva: According to Manu, "Where the boy and girl meet each other on their own and the marriage is consummated in passion, that form is called *gāndharva*". (*Manusmṛti*, iii.32) The name *gāndharva* is acquired from a tribe of that name living in Himalayas, in which this form was prevalent. It was more common among the Kṣatriyas as they exemplified the most liberal community in society. However, majority of the lawmakers deprecated it on religious and moral grounds. It was considered as lower to the first five forms as it was carried out without sacred rites and it has its origin in passionate love, an aspect which appear to be ethereal and frivolous.

(c) Rākṣasa: The word *rākṣasa* denotes demonic. *Rākṣasa vivāha*, according to *Manu* is, "Getting hold of a girl by force while she is resisting after having killed, banished or injured her family members". (*Manusmṛti*, iii.21). This type of marriage usually occurred during war or political disruptions. It was practiced more by the Kṣatriyas since they engaged in wars and acquired women as war loots.

(d) Paiśāca: Amongst all, this is the most unacceptable and despised. *Manu* (iii. 34) defines this as, "conjugating with a girl when she is lonely, sleepy, mad or intoxicated". Undeniably, this was the most condemned and beastly method. *Paiśāca* denotes "of witches".

Hindu Marriage: Beliefs and Emotions

The Hindu marriage system is delineated as a religious and social institution. It is not only a union of two bodies or individuals, but a union of two spirits. Looking at it metaphysically, a person is a combination of three bodies: physical—made up of matter (*sthūla*), subtle—comprising mind (*sūkṣma*) and causal—consisting of the *jīva* (*kāraṇa*). The Vedic marriage is a confluence between all the three—body with body, mind with mind and *jīva* with *jīva*.

Through the sacramental pledges, the married couple begin on the life course together to attain the four *puruṣārtha*s (goals) of life. During this journey the husband and wife fulfil their basic aspirations and duties—to earn, to procreate children, and to contribute to society. In addition to this, they can progress together in the path of *bhakti* (devotion) and come closer to the divinity within. This is symbolised in one of the ceremonial rites where *mantra*s are chanted to invoke Lord Viṣṇu in the bridegroom and Goddess Lakṣmī in the bride. All others present at that time-the parents, relatives, and acquaintance then bow down to them symbolising reverence. Thus the union is seen to be between God and Goddess, not two physical bodies. The underlying direction to the newly weds is, "You are not the material body, but *ātman*". To regard one another as the *ātman* or the higher self is the essential premise of a Hindu marriage. It is a unique feature amongst the entire world's civilization's—which largely follow the *gāndharva* system based on passion. This Vedic thought plays all the more important role in material turmoil. It can be seen that at the root of any material discord lies in couple's low tolerance for each other due to identification with body and one's ego—the "I" "me" and "mine". If both the partners identify themselves as *ātman*, and are connected as *ātman* for a shared, ultimate aim of *mokṣa*, then "I" and "you" will not exist. This is so because the seemingly different "I" and "you" are inherently *ātman*. And when "I" and "you" are believed to be *ātman*, there is less scope of conflicts that has its origin in self-centered motives and yearnings. Therefore, in a Hindu marriage whenever differences, conflicts and frictions arise, they can be resolved comfortably and promptly. There is a need for the married couple to consider each other as the *ātman*, because the *ātman* is pure, beyond the gender, age and class differences, and intrinsically divine. The word *vivāha* itself connotes "to lift, to uphold, to support, to sustain". Undisputedly, both the spouses have to make sacrifices and work towards to inculcate this commanding philosophy. To live this philosophy is not easy, and certainly not a short-term process, but more a sustained, long-term, sacred engagement. It is this ideology which has sustained the Vedic marriage for such a long period and made it a grand success. Rise in materialism in the recent years, primarily for the fulfilment of man's greed, desires and superficial fanfare, having its roots in body consciousness, are the primary factors that have begun to weakened and damaged today's Hindu marriages. The above-mentioned sentiments, and others, are symptomatically denoted and emphasised orally by various *mantras* chanted during the *vivāha* ceremony, the steps of which are discussed next.

Hindu Marriage: Ceremonies and Associated Rituals

There are considerable variations in the actual wedding ceremony in different places in India (based on region, castes, community, etc.). However, Sharma (1985) outlines six common rites that are practised across India. The first is *madhuparka*—in this the bridegroom arrives at the bride's house, traditionally on a horseback, with his gathering of people. They are greeted with affection and respected by the bride's family and the groom is treated equivalent to a deity. The second ceremony is that of *kanyādāna*. In this the father entrusts his daughter to the groom and the couple follows marriage rites around a fire in the sacrificial pit. During *pāṇigrahaṇa*, the groom takes the hand of the bride in his hand and ties *maṅgalasūtra*, or a pendant around her neck, symbolising their marriage.

The bride steps on the north stone by the sacrificial fire, following the ritual of *pāṇigrahaṇa*, this is called as *asmarohaṇa* and is symbolic of the couple's firmness and resolute against their adversaries. The bride also gives three offerings of rice into the fire (*lājāhoma*) during *asmarohaṇa*. One of the last rites during the wedding ceremony which legally seals marriage, and is regarded the most important, is referred to as *saptapadī*. During this the bride and groom go around the sacred fire seven times with a part of their apparels fastened together with a piece of cloth. Known as the *sāta phere* or the seven steps, each round around fire signifies a different facet of the marriage such as friendship, prosperity, and fertility. The marriage is made official by the priest after taking the seventh and final step. The completion of the ceremonies is typically followed or preceded by celebration that include singing, dancing and feasting. The last ceremony is the *varagṛhaprasthāna* which is marked by bride leaving her family's home to her husband's home under her in-laws care, where she will stay for the remaining life post her marriage. In many families culmination of marriage does not occur until three days after the marriage ceremony and is termed as *caturthīkarma* (Sharma, 1985).

As India has a rich and diverse cultural heritage the actual ceremonies and rituals vary from one subculture to another. At some places in India, particularly, the southern India the ceremonies are:

1. *Haridralepana*
2. *Varaprekṣana* (Welcoming the bridegroom)
3. *Madhuparka* (Offering honey)
4. *Pāṇigrahaṇa* (Proffering of the bride's hand)
5. *Vaivāhika homa* (Invoking the sacred fire)
6. *Śilārohana* (Stepping on the stone)
7. *Lājā homa* (Offering parched rice into sacred fire)
8. *Saptapadī* (The seven steps)
9. *Agni parikramā* (Circumambulation of sacred fire)
10. *Saubhāgya cinha* (Blessing the bride)

11. *Sūrya darśana* (Looking at the sun)
12. *Hṛdaya-sparsa* (Touching the hearts)
13. *Annaprāṣana* (Feeding the bridegroom)
14. *Pūrṇāhuti* (Completion of ceremony)

In most families, completion of the ceremonies is followed by a celebration that includes dancing, singing, and feasting. The ceremony of *varagṛhaprasthāna* characterises the bride's departure from her parent's home to her husband's, where she is expected to stay during the course of her marriage.

In the next section, the sixteenth *saṁskāra* is described, that is death *saṁskāra*s—the various beliefs related to death and the death rites.

Conception of Death in Hinduism

In Hinduism, death is not perceived as a formidable inevitability but as the most important recourse for freeing an individual from this world or the chain of birth and death. According to Sage Baudhāyana, "the rites or *saṁskāra*s carried out while one is living helps one to control the earth while that done at the time of death helps one gain ground in heaven". The cycle of life and death forms a continual mechanism—this concept of reincarnation or rebirth is the principal element of Hinduism. Life is not perceived to be a linear progression but cyclical process, thereby death is not appraised as an end point but just another phase in the journey of self-realisation and oneness with the Divinity. The physical body here is conceptualised nothing more than a vehicle to carry the consciousness.

The sages, rishis and Dharmasūtras all had a shared conception about the ultimate aim of life, which they prescribed in the four *āśrama*s—stages of life.

> "One undertakes to seek knowledge during childhood years (*bramacarya āśrama*), works to fulfil his aspirations during youth (*gṛhastha āśrama*), abandon earthly-profane activities for silent introspection during the later/last part of life (*vānaprastha āśrama*) and then strives for realisation of divinity or self, following which he gets free from his body."

Death and cremation are the processes that allow the spirit from the dead body to leave this world and enter the ancestral realm.

Knipe, as quoted in Richard Davis (1988) "Cremation and Liberation: The Revision of a Hindu Ritual" states,

> "Other than few exceptions, there are almost no or little differences throughout the regions of India in terms of the Hindu *saṁskāra*s at the time of dying and the practices for cremation (*antyeṣṭi*). ... This congruity and consistency in rituals across different time periods: Vedic, epic, Purāṇic, Āgamic and on into modern practice, is exceptional."

Death Saṁskāras: From Dying Stage to Śrāddha

oṁ kṛtvā tu puṣkaram karma janata vapyajānatam ।
mṛtyuḥ kalavasam prāpya naram pañcatvamāgatan ।।
dharmādharma saṁyuktam lobhamohasamavṛtam ।
deheyam sarvagotrāṇi divyān lokān sa gacchatu ।।

> "After having carried out known and unknown actions for attaining respectability; after getting timely death and dissolved the physical body into the five elements; having completed a life of desires and done actions corresponding to righteousness (*dharma*) and against it (*adharma*), may you travel to your next dwelling."

Rituals at the Time of Dying

When an individual becomes certain that s/he is about to die the priests are called and the family performs prayers to the family deity or to Lord Viṣṇu through the *śālagrāma* stone. The one dying offers prayers to God asking for grace and mercy for all the sins committed knowingly or unknowingly by him/her during the life-time. In the cases where the dying person is unable to do it himself/herself due to poor health or any other reasons then, the eldest son undertakes the rite of absolution on behalf of dying person and offerings are made to the needy and destitute. The person on the verge of death is then shifted from the cot to the ground. The reasons cited for this are:

1. It helps in the practice of chanting *mantra*s and carrying out the rituals since the Brāhmaṇas/Priests are seated on the floor. These *mantra*s and the rites assist the dying person to leave this abode smoothly and with awareness.
2. Another reason is if a person is allowed to die on the bed, in that case, the bed has to be discarded.

In most cases, all weeping and wailing is discouraged as this may affect the consciousness of the dying person and result in feelings of guilt and difficulties for the dying person in detaching from the family. In one of the initial rituals, the sacred water (in most cases its of holy River Gaṅgā) and *tulsī* leaves are placed in the mouth of dying person with chanting of the hymns of a thousand names of Lord Viṣṇu (*Viṣṇu Sahasranāma Stotram*) by the priest and family members. The belief behind this is that the thoughts and feelings which the person experience at the time of death influences the next birth/life—it is easier for one to obtain liberation if one leaves his body with the thoughts of divinity or Supreme Lord. In many houses after the death of the individual, during the period of mourning, it is customary to read *Garuḍa Purāṇa*, which talks about the topic of death, rebirth, and experiences in the life after death.

Antyeṣṭi (Death Rites)

Antyeṣṭi or cremation is the primary ritual for disposing of the dead body in Hindu Religion (Davis, 1988), and the ultimate *saṁskāra* in a life of a Hindu. In Hindu ideology cremation of the dead is considered a *saṁskāra* because it involves changing the state of the person from one realm to another; it is seen as a medium between this life and the ancestral realm (*pitṛloka*). *Antyeṣṭi* is regarded as sixteenth *saṁskāra* in *Ṛgveda* while *Yajurveda* regards *vivāha* as the sixteenth *saṁskāra*. The ritual of *Antyeṣṭi*, although carried out by the relatives of the dead person, is of great significance because in Hinduism value placed on the next birth is greater than that of the present. Thereby the last rites are carried out with painstaking effort under the guidance of Brāhmaṇa priests. As basil leaf is considered sacred in the Hindu religion, the first ritual after death is to put some leaves of basil (*tulsī*) (if not done at the time of dying) and a few drops of sacred water in the mouth of deceased person. The body is then placed on the ground which has been disinfected and sanctified by applying the cowdung (cow dung is considered pure and sacred in Hindusim). The old clothes are taken off and lifeless body washed with sanctified water. The body is thereafter wrapped in a new, unwashed, uncut piece of cloth (*kafana*). This is followed by laying the body on a bier (*nanami*) made up of bamboo canes tied with jute strings.

> "Everything the person calls his own will remain here—wealth will remain in locker; cattle will be remain under fences; wife will accompany him till the doorway; friends can be there with him till the cremation ground; and his body will be there with him till the funeral pyre; but finally the *jīvātamā* (with his actions) travels alone on the journey to the next world".

The body is then taken to the cineration fire by the family members reciting the Lord's name: *Rāma bolo bhāi Rāma/Rāma nāma satya hai* is the most frequently used phrase. In many places it is *hari bola, hari bola.*

The body is then laid on the funeral pyre, ghee is put over it and the fire ignited by the closest family member. Sometimes sesame seeds are also put into fire as the part of the ritual. The above-mentioned steps do not take place in the electric crematorium. Traditionally the fire ignited in the marriage function was later carried down to the groom's home and remained ignited in an altar all through the life. This symbolised that the institution of marriage was to be sustained through life's ups and downs, together. If one of the marriage partners expired, the *agni* (fire) was carried in a container to the funeral ground, where it was used to light the pyre. This signified the culmination of marriage and the onset of *agni* (*antyeṣṭi*) *saṁskāra*. The rituals, customs and observances which are thereafter followed differ in subsequent societies and regions of India. By burning the body, the body's five elementary constituents—known as *pañcha-bhūtas*—*pṛthvī* (earth), *teja* (fire), *jala* (water), *vāyua* (wind) and *ākāś* (space) are given back to the nature, thus sustaining the cosmic balance.

Though all the *saṁskāras*/rites have spiritual elements, some have direct relevance for the physical environment in one way or another. Scientists and researchers in the past few decades have started to recognise this. For example, they have found out that burning the dead body is the optimum, most efficient and pro-environment mechanism for disposing of the dead body. It has been observed that as compared to cremation, burial of the dead create difficulties related to space and groundwater contamination. It is recognised that corpses which have been infected with plague and slow virus diseases infect vectors which depend on them for food. This through a chain finally impacts human beings.

Asthi Sañcayana: Involves collecting the ashes and left over bones (*asthi*) in pitcher like container after cremation. It is customary to wash them with sanctified water and milk in some communities. The urn is thereafter carried off to any of the sacred rivers such as Gaṅgā, Narmadā or to the sacred confluence of the three rivers Gaṅgā, Yamunā and Sarasvatī, known as the Triveṇī Saṅgam, in Allahabad. During the custom a Brāhmaṇa priest chants Vedic *mantras* and conducts the last rites and rituals for the liberation of the soul of the deceased. The ashes are then dispersed into the river.

Days of Mourning: As death is a time of mourning the loss and involves considerable emotional trauma, the *ṛṣis* in the Hindu tradition have suggested a time period of 10 to 30 days for mourning and grieving recognising time to be the great healer. The duration of the grieving period differs from one community to another, however what is pertinent is that one's emotions are given a channel, crying-mourning is acceptable and encouraged. According to the sacred texts of Hindus the period of grief varies for different social classes—it lasts for 10 days for Brāhmaṇas and 40 days for non-Brāhmaṇas. The rationale given is that Brāhmaṇas are expected to be more inclined towards spirituality and more detached—having the knowledge of the cycle of death and rebirth—thus need a comparatively lesser period of time to come over their grief. In case an individual is unable to take out

10 days off from professional duties then it is recommended to take minimum of three days leave and follow the conventions of grieving which are:

1. Sleeping on the floor.
2. Refraining from sexual intercourse or any kind of recreational activity.
3. Refrain from cooking food, and eating only vegetarian diet.
4. Not leaving home for meeting or socialisation with guests.
5. Not shaving and cutting/trimming hair and nails.

The family is also free from the responsibilities of all religious activities and rituals other than those carried out for the posthumous rites. The reason behind this is to give family members enough time to saturate their thoughts of the dead person, to provide them enough time and scope to successfully come over all their inarticulate, implicit and inherent doubts, fears, conflicts, and emotions.

Sūtaka (Aśauca): This is also a period of ten to thirteen days during which the closest family members and relatives are exempted from performing their day-to-day religious rituals like *pūjā*, *ārati* and idol worship. People other than the immediate family members, friends or neighbours are assigned to do *pūjā* in place of them. However, the members can go to the temple for *darśana*. It is prescribed during this period to recite texts from scriptures and sing devotional songs to help the deceased in the attainment of *mokṣa*. It is also advisable to consume simple, non-oily vegetarian diet for a specific number of days as a part of *sūtaka* rituals. As per the custom, either on the eleventh, twelfth or thirteenth day, the family members offer *thāla* (food) to the God/deity in the nearby temple to repay *pitṛṇa* (ancestral debt). It is believed in Hinduism that after death, the soul pulls out and break away from the body and it embraces a new body whose limbs develop day by day. This "interim" body grows completely on the tenth day after death. In general, the eldest son of the dead person offers the *piṇḍa*s—food balls made from wheat flour and water—to the growing limbs, either daily for ten days or all ten together on the tenth day. This ritual is based on the belief that, till this day, the deceased person still carries on his connection with this world. For this reason the deceased is called *preta*, meaning one who has physically left the body, but has not disconnected from this world and not yet reached the other world. On the eleventh day, the *trimūrtis*—Brahmā, Viṣṇu, Rudra and God of death—Yama are invoked, with Lord Viṣṇu as the distinguished witness. In the presence of these gods the deceased is offered *piṇḍas*. On the twelfth day the soul of the deceased is transmitted away to the other world, where he then rests with his forefathers. The deceased is released from his *preta* body at the time as he reaches the other world. The family members are then freed from the *sutaka* and can carry on with their life duties and functions in a normal fashion. One of the other specific rites after the funeral ceremony, commonly witnessed in the Indian subcontinent, is shaving of hair by one or more male members of the family of the deceased. This is not very commonly followed by Hindus living outside India.

Sajjā: In many parts of India the relatives perform the *sajjā* ritual. As a part of this custom, they give a cow, a bed, utensils, eatables, clothing and footwear and other things that the deceased utilised to a Brāhmaṇa. The Brāhmaṇa performs a *pūjā* and accepts the items symbolically to transmit them to the soul of the deceased to be used by him in the next world.

Śrāddha Ceremony

Śrāddha is a religious ceremony performed by the Hindus annually, for appeasement and satisfaction of their departed ancestors who are traditionally known as *pitṛs*. According to Sage Pulastya, the word *śrāddha*, has its origin in: *śrāddhyā dīyate yasmat*, that is, that which is performed with great faith. The faith which is talked about here is the conviction in the Vedas, whose injunctions are seen as unchangeable and which calls upon performing *śrāddha* as a duty. Some of the essential elements of *śrāddha* are the *arghya* (water libation); *havana* (offering to the fire), feeding the Brāhmaṇas, *piṇḍa-dāna*, *vikira*, *dakṣiṇā* (offering to Brāhmaṇas) and *tarpaṇa*. Brāhmaṇa priests conduct *pūjā* to invoke the souls of the departed ancestors of three generations identified with Vasu, Rudra and Āditya on the paternal or maternal side, as the case may be and pray for their propitiation. On the occasion Brāhmaṇas considered to be holy and godlike are fed in a worshipful manner. During the ceremony, the *pitṛ*s, who live in *pitṛ-loka* in the form of Spirits, are called upon and fetched into the *śrāddha* venue by the viśvedevas or the universal soul.

Rationale for Śrāddha

A frequently asked question related to *Śrāddha* ceremony is: How does serving and feeding meal to some Brāhmaṇas in this world at a given moment leads to feeding and gratifying one's predecessors and forefathers who have died long back, and presumably, according to the kārmic theory of rebirth may be existing in different forms and regions.

The answer to this query is given in the *Matsya Purāṇa*: Through *śrāddha* one tries to invoke the souls of the deceased predecessors on the holy priests called for *pūjā*, and the former are guided to the place of *śrāddha* by Viśvedevas or the universal spirit. Thereby for practical purposes, the spirit of our forefathers, identified with Vasu, Rudra and Ādityas, the *śrāddha* deities, is there, and is worshipped by us. According to the Hindu ideology, the food consumed by the Brahmaṇas and the oblations that are transformed by the power of *mantra* and faith into the food items that are desired and befitting for the present bodies of the ancestors. This food is taken to them by celestial messenger, Agni, the God of fire, or the Vasus, Rudras, etc. who have presence everywhere and satisfy the *pitṛ*s. For instance, if the ancestor had taken birth as an Angel, the oblations goes to him as nectar; if he is born as herbivorous animal, it is received by him in the form of grass; or if born as human, it is delivered to him as food items like cereals, etc. Just like a calf is able to find its own mother from the herd of cows grazing, in the same manner the *mantra*s chanted in the *śrāddha* ceremony transport the food to the corresponding ancestors.

As per the theory of *śrāddha*, if the *pitṛdevatā*s, are satisfied by the worship, after the *śrāddha* ceremony, they give blessings to the performer and bestow him with good health, wealth, progeny and prosperity before departing to their abode. Many Smṛti writers have indicated and expressed that failure or inability on the part of the deceased to perform the *śrāddha* rite is bound to lead to the wrath of the departed souls. Irrespective of the religious benefits of *śrāddha* ceremony, it has psychological and emotional merits as it helps the descendants to remember with affection and gratitude their predecessors, which is a rewarding and satisfying feeling.

Other than the regular death rituals there are separate rituals for unnatural deaths, small children, and pregnant woman. In cases of violent or unnatural deaths such as accidents, murders, suicides, or death from a disease involving much pain and despair like cancer or AIDS a special rite known as Narayana Bali is carried out instead of the regular rituals, wherein prayers are offered and donations are given for charity on their behalf for the comfortable release of their souls which become imprisoned in the traumatic experiences of the unnatural death. In the case of children below aged 24 months the body is buried in the day time instead of cremation. The cremation rituals also vary for married, widowed, unmarried females and with old age person.

Conclusively it can be seen that these two *saṁskāra*s can govern the strength and continuation of Hindu practices and rich cultural tradition in any part of the world, if carried out with sincerity with its pure and glorious sentiments. The marriage and death *saṁskāra*s, with their sacred elements, holistically saṁmskārise (edify) all facets of a person's life. In addition to the religious benefits, the *saṁskāra*s assist in bringing family members, close relatives, and friends together, thereby strengthening the connectedness of the family unit. This further integrates and empowers the societal framework. This result in a strong and a cohesive social structure with a powerful sociocultural identity which smoothly refines, bolsters, and maintains its traditions, beliefs, practices, ethics, morals and cultural values.

The declaration of the indispensable divinity of an individual relates to the core of Hinduism. Thus, life is essentially a divine worship. The great truth and basic premise of Hinduism is the immortality of the soul as well as the extension of life after passing away. The superlative of the societal beliefs of the *Bhagavad Gītā* is *loka-saṁgraha*, the well-being as well as harmony of the sphere. This is carried approximately by every person by means of the presentation of *svadharma* in the essence which involves the ideology of not getting attached as well as giving way of the self as well as with the understanding of the immutable nature of the *ātman*. The *Gītā*, at the precise inception, speak out that the *ātman* could not be demolished.

> "One needs to understand to be enduring by which all this is permeated. Nobody can cause the devastation of that, the imperishable. He is not born, nor does He ever die; subsequently having been, He again terminates not to be; unborn, eternal, everlasting as well as ancient, He is not slaughtered when the body is killed" (II.17, 20).

The *Gītā* is gospel which talks about not getting attached, immortality of the soul as well as the conclusive freedom of the Self in the totality. It is the revered lessons which focuses on the total comprehensive inwardness of the spirit. The indispensability of non-attachment follows from the fact of the oneness of existence.

The Hindu scriptures recognise the changeable variations amidst persons as well as the resulting organisation of duties suited to their evolutionary stages which regulate their *guna* in addition to *karma*. The stages of life differ in different persons and their *dharma*s or duties in life are based on these phases of distinct growth. *Svadharma* is the duty prescribed to a person in accordance with the stage of life in which he is placed, not by any other person or persons, but by his own inner characteristics which he manifests in his daily behaviour and actions. *Dharma* which is the ethical value governing the individual exalts him to *mokṣa* which is the Infinite Value and the Goal of Life. Everyone is expected to conform to *dharma* which supports life and which shall protect him who protects it through dispassionate practice. The fourfold social cataloguing is done in order to make sure a contented as well as loving blending and fellowship among every individual, who, due to their intrinsic inclinations display their fitness for varying events in life and not a general equality in thought as well as deed.

The knowledge about Hindu practices, beliefs, philosophy can be summarised in the words of a foreign thinker, "Hinduism is almost not a doctrine on the other hand it is a functioning hypothesis of human conduct revised to diverse phases of psychic progress as well as different conditions of life." All beliefs, rites, practices are formulated to help the individual move towards one's true nature or Self.

Historically, Hinduism has incorporated equally conviction as well as ethos, and the sorting out of one from the other is rather challenging. It is significant that there is no Sanskrit equivalent for the word religion, and the term *dharma*, sometimes equated with religion, is far more inclusive. The unity of religion and culture in India obviated the need for special agencies for the transmission of the Hindu tradition. It was correctly assumed that a child would receive the necessary religious exposure by the mere fact of growing up in particular community. The conditions of life in modern Western societies, however, invalidate such an assumption. The unity of religion and culture is being severed, and the traditionally pervasive influence of Hindu beliefs, practices, philosophy is relegated to fewer areas of life. One of the reasons for this trend is the increasing disconnect of rituals and practices with their symbolic meaning leading to dogmatic and ritualistic behaviours without awareness of the higher spiritual or developmental purpose behind these traditions. Priests and teachers who serve in temples and who teach in communities are unable to help young men and women interpret their tradition in a relevant way to their particular circumstances. The other significant reason in the contemporary period is the race towards economic development, materialism and hedonism where religion, spirituality and all other existential questions do not have any place of relevance.

Hinduism in the next millennium will be challenged to define itself with precision in relation to a variety of competing choices. Its primary rivals today are those alternative world views that deny a transcendent character to human existence and those value systems that glorify greed and the economic systems based on it. Successful strategies and agencies need to be developed to ensure transmission from one generation to another. There is a need for committed teachers who have a background in the intellectual disciplines and critical methods of East and West and who can bring these to bear creatively in their reflection on the Hindu tradition. Communities, parents, and educational institutions will have to encourage and support young men and women who evince interest and aptitude for the study and teaching of respective religions and its relevance to how a life is lived. This is an effort in this direction so that knowledge attained from concept of *karma*, non-attachment to the fruits of action, *dharma*, reincarnation, *Brahman-Ātman* can be applied for the betterment of one's own life and those of others in the world.

Experiential Learning

Based on knowledge gained from Hindu practices and Eastern perspectives on Self.

Since students learn best when they are applying material to life and learning by experiencing, you can try this exercise to explore more about yourself and your peers:

"Hindu" is a word that comes from the name of the Indus River, which also gives the name of the modern state of India. Most Hindu people of the world have roots in the region.

ONE : Supreme Soul
TWO : *Puruṣa* and *Prakṛti*; *Para-Apara Vidyā*
THREE : *Triguṇa*s (*satva-rajas-tamsas*), *Trimūrti* (*Brahmā, Viṣṇu, Maheś*)
FOUR : *Puruṣārtha*s (*dharma, artha, kāma, mokṣa*); *varṇa*s (*Brāhmaṇa, Kṣatriya, Vaiśya, Śūdra*); *āśrama*s (*brahmacarya*, *gṛhastha*, *vānaprastha*, *saṁnyāsa*); *yuga*s (Satya, Tretā, Dvāpara, Kali).
FIVE : Pañca-koña (*annamaya, prāṇamaya, manomaya, vijñānamaya, ānandamaya*)
SIX : Philosophical schools (Sāṁkhya, Yoga, Nyāya, Vaiśeṣika, Mīmāṁsā, Vedānta)

Whereas Hindus believe in reincarnation, Catholics believe in resurrection. To believe in resurrection means to hold that people die only once, but that one day they will be raised from the dead with their own bodies by the power of God's Spirit, just like Jesus at Easter. Hindus believe that whatever they did in this life—the good and the bad—they bring with them into the next life.

Taking into account the concept of *dharma* in Hindu tradition, think about and discuss in group your roles in society and corresponding *dharma* (duty) for each role.

In a group, create a timeline showing Hinduism's life stages and some milestones. What are the accompanying rituals at each milestone? How do these stages and milestones reflect Hindu beliefs and values?

(i) Individually or in group, make notes and discuss about what characters and situations from epics of *Rāmāyaṇa* and *Mahābhārata* you can identify with most and least and why.

(ii) Share your learning's from watching or reading these historical stories.

God is considered both male and female, or as the one who has no sex or both. Hinduism has many deities, and its male deities often have female partners. Without the feminine side, these deities are seen as incomplete. All the female deities embody a strong, cosmic, feminine energy known as Śakti. Many Hindu women offer devotion to this feminine force.

There are five forms of formal traditional greeting enjoined in the *Śāstras* of which *namaskāram* or *namaste* is one. The two palms placed together in front of the chest and the head bows whilst saying the word *namaste*. The spiritual meaning of *namsate* is deeper. The Life Force, the Divinity, the Self or the Lord in me is the same in all. Recognising this oneness with the meeting of the palms, we salute with head bowed to the Divinity in the person we meet. Can you think of other Hindu rituals and practices where the belief of oneness with *Brahman* is indicated?

What does *pradakṣiṇā* (circumambulate) symbolise?

We cannot draw a circle without a centre point. The Lord is the centre, source, and essence of our lives. Recognising Him as the focal point in our lives, we go about doing our daily chores. This is the significance of *pradakṣiṇā*.

Also every point on the circumference of a circle is equidistant from the centre. This means that wherever or whoever we may be, we are equally close to the Lord.

Source: sanskritdocuments.org/articles/Hindu_Rituals.pdf

www.dpcdsb.org/nr/rdonlyres/3350557f.../wr_sb_ch_07_drna2.pdf.

References

Dasgupta, S.N. (1975). *A History of Indian Philosophy* (Indian edn., Vols. 1-5). Delhi: Motilal Banarsidass. (Originally published in 1922).

Davis, Richard (1988). "Cremation and Liberation: The Revision of a Hindu Ritual." *History of Religions*, *27*(1): 37-53.

Dṛgdṛśya Viveka (1931). (Ed. and Trans. S. Nikhilananda). Mysore, India: Sri Ramakrishna Asrama. (The date of the original work unknown).

Eliade, M. (1969). *Yoga Immortality and Freedom.* Princeton, NJ: Princeton University Press.

Filippi, Gian (1996). *MRTYU: Concept of Death in Indian Traditions.* New Delhi: D.K. Printwood (P) Ltd.

Fowler, Jeaneane (1997). *Hinduism: Beliefs and Practices.* Brighton: Sussex Academic Press.

Gandhi, M.K. (1996). *The Essence of Hinduism.* Ahmedabad: Navajiwan Publishing House.

Gesler, Wilbert M. and Pierce Margaret (2000). "Hindu Varanasi". *Geographical Review, 90*(2): 222.

Gnaneshwardas, Sadhu (1993). *Dharmik Vidhano ane Bhavana.* Amdavad: Swaminarayan Aksharpith, (Translated as *Hindu Rites and Rituals*).

Harman, William P. (1989). *Sacred Marriage of a Hindu Goddess.* Bloomington and Indianapolis: Indiana University Press.

Hindu Antyeshti Samskara (2008). Hindu Mandir Executives Conference, An initiative of Vishwa Hindu Parishad (World Hindu Council) of Americas Inc.

"Hindu Sastras and Samskara." Excerpts from V.A.K. Ayer's *Hindu Sastras and Samskaras.* Compilation by: SAVECA Canada.

James, W.T. (1975). *A History of Western Philosophy* (2nd and Rev. edn., Vol. 1-5). New York: Harcourt, Brace and World.

Justice, Christopher. (1997). *Dying the Good Death.* Albany, N.Y.: State University of New York Press.

Krishnamurthy, V. (1989). *Essentials of Hinduism.* Narosa Publishing House.

Kumar, P. (2014). *Model for Modern Youth.* Yuva Shakthi Publishers.

Kuppuswamy, B. (1985). *Elements of Ancient Indian Psychology.* Delhi: Konark.

Manu (1971). *The Laws of Manu* (Trans. G Bühler). Delhi: Motilal Banarsidass. (Translation first published in 1886; date of original work *Manu Smṛti* unknown).

Monier-Williams, Monier (1899). *A Sanskrit-English Dictionary.* Delhi. Motilal Banarsidass.

Mitchell, Katherine (2008). *Vivaha Samskara: The Marriage Rite.* http://www.mahavidya.ca/wp-content/uploads/2008/06/mitchell-katherine-vivaha.pdf

Pandey, R.B. (1962, reprint 2003). "The Hindu Sacraments (Saṁskāra)". In S. Radhakrishnan (ed.), *The Cultural Heritage of India*, Vol. II, pp. 391-92, Kolkata: The Ramakrishna Mission Institute of Culture.

Pandey, Rajbali (1969, reprint 2006). *Hindu Samskaras: Socio-religious Study of the Hindu Sacraments.* Delhi: Motilal Banarsidass.

Pandey, Rajbali (1993).*The Sixteen Saṁskāras*. New Delhi: Motilal Banarsidass. Production Board of Gujarat.

Paranjpe, A.C. (1998). *Self and Identity in Modern Psychology and Indian Thought.* New York: Plenum.

Paranjpe, A.C. (2008). "Sri Ramana Maharshi: A Case Study in Self-realisation". In K. Ramakrishna Rao, A.C. Paranjpe, and A. K. Dalal (Eds.), *Handbook of Indian Psychology,* pp. 564-76, New Delhi: Cambridge University Press, India.

Paranjpe, A.C. (2010). "Theories of Self and Cognition: Indian Psychological Perspectives". *Psychology of Developing Societies, 22*(5).

Radha Swami (1978). *Kundalini: Yoga for the West.* Spokane. WA: Timeless Books.

Ramaswami Aiyer, C.P. (1969). *The Cultural Heritage of India,* Vol. II, Calcutta: The Ramakrishna Mission Institute.

Rodrigues, H.P. (2006). *Introducing Hinduism*. New York: Routledge.

Roeser, R.W. (2005). "An Introduction to Hindu India's Contemplative Psychological Perspectives on Motivation, Self, and Development". In M.L. Maehr and S. Karabenick (Eds.), *Advances in Motivation and Achievement*, Vol. 14: *Religion and and Motivation*, pp. 297-345, Amsterdam: Elseveir.

Sharma, Arvind (1985). "Marriage in the Hindu Religious Tradition". *Journal of Ecumencial Studies*, *22*(1): 69-80.

Shelat, B.K. (1993). *Bharatiya samskaro*. Amdavad: University Book.

Sinha, J. (1961). *Indian Psychology,* Vol. 2: *Emotions and Will.* Delhi : Motilal Banarsidass.

Swami Sivananda. (1997). *All About Hinduism*. A Divine Life Society Publication.

Vivekpriyadas, Sadhu (1998). *Apano Samskrutik Varaso*, Part 2. Amdavad: Swaminarayan Aksharpith.

Yogananda, P. (1972). *The Autobiography of a Yogi*. Los Angeles: Self-realisation Fellowship.

7

The Impermanence of Our "Being"

The Buddhist Approach

Gautam Buddha says,

> "Birth is suffering, ageing is suffering, illness is suffering, death is suffering; union with what is displeasing is suffering; separation from what is pleasing is suffering; not to get one wants is suffering; in brief, the five aggregates subject to clinging are *dukkha* (suffering)." (Bodhi, 2000 as cited in Dhar, 2011)

The doctrine of Buddhism lays on the ideas of impermanence of all things, the absence of a separate self, and the facts of sorrow and suffering. Humans suffer because of desire, because they tend to live in live in a deluded view of the self, trying to attain something that will ultimately cease to exist. The Buddha did not only give us a diagnosis of the problem, but also its cure. He claimed that the cure is to realise a higher state of being wherein self-knowledge has eliminated the sense of a separate self, delusion, attachment, and desire (Ramaswami and Sheikh, 1989, p. 120).

Buddhism does not dictate any final doctrine or philosophy because it believes that there is no absolute truth, even an absolute

Buddha, in this world of impermanence. Buddhist tradition inclines with human realities. They emphasise upon eradicating the feelings of discontent and inadequacy which are the products of a finite, selfish ego (Frager and Fadiman, 2013).

History: The Life of Buddha

The school of Buddhism originated from the teachings of Siddhārtha Gautam, the Buddha. The term *buddha* is an honorary title, not a name. It means "the one who is awake" or "the one who has accomplished complete *humanness*".

According to Buddhist philosophy, there have been many other Buddhas before Gautama, and there will be many more after him. Gautama Buddha never claimed to be more than a mere human soul, and his accomplishments were the result of his solely human capacities. The fundamental basis of the Buddhist doctrine is that every human being possesses this Buddha nature, the ability to develop into the full potential of a human being and thus, becoming a Buddha. Buddhism was widespread in India and Asia before finally dying out as a result of resurgence of Hinduism, persecution by Mughal rulers, and the growing weakness of Indian Buddhism itself. Once again, Buddhism is expanding in India today.

Buddhism currently has two major traditions: The Theravāda or Hīnayāna tradition and the Mahāyāna tradition. The Theravāda tradition is more popular in the southeast Asia, in Sri Lanka, Burma, and Thailand. The Mahāyāna tradition, on the other hand, is primarily found in Tibet, China, Korea, and Japan. The Mahāyāna tradition which originated as a result of a liberal movement within the Theravāda tradition, is less strict in the interpretation of the traditional monastic disciplinary rules, more inclusive with regards to householders, and more inclined towards adopting later additions to the Buddhist scriptures. Theravāda's emphasis is more on self-discipline as compared to the Mahāyānists who place more value on compassion. Zen Buddhism is a major school of the Mahāyāna tradition. A new third tradition has been becoming popular in the West, Tibetan Vajrayāna Buddhism (Frager and Fadiman, 2013).

Major Concepts in Buddhism

Gautam Buddha says, "No one saves us but ourselves. No one can and no one may. We ourselves must walk the path".

The Buddha observed that we call as "I" or a "being" is nothing but a series of the five impermanent aggregates, viz., the bodily form, consciousness, perception, feelings, and volitional mental formations, whose functions are interdependent on each other, changing every moment in agreement with the law of cause and effect; there does not exist an immutable entity called "me" (Dhar, 2011).

What these aggregates are and how these are of the nature of *dukkha*, we can understand from a *sutta* (Bodhi, 2000a):

> "The four great elements and the form derived from the four great elements: this is called form. ... And why, *bhikkhu*s, do you call it form? "It is deformed" *bhikkhu*s, therefore it is called form. Deformed by what? Deformed by cold, deformed by heat, deformed by hunger, deformed by thirst, deformed by contact with flies, mosquitoes, wind, sun and serpents.
>
> And what, *bhikkhu*s, is feeling? There are these six classes of feeling: feeling born of eye-contact, feeling born of ear-contact, feeling born of nose-contact, feeling born of tongue-contact, feeling born of body contact, feeling born of mind-contact. This is called feeling. And *bhikkhu*s, why do you call it feeling? "It feels", *bhikkhu*s, therefore it is called feeling. And what does it feel? It feels pleasure, it feels pain, it feels neither pain nor pleasure.
>
> And what, *bhikkhu*s, is perception? There are these six classes of perception: perception of forms, perception of sounds, perception of odours, perception of tastes, perception of tactile objects, perception of mental phenomena. This is called perception. With the arising of contact there is the arising of perception. ... And why, *bhikkhu*s, do you

call it perception? "It perceives", *bhikkhus*, therefore it is called perception. And what does it perceive? It perceives blue, it perceives yellow, it perceives red, it perceives white....

And what, *bhikkhus*, are volitional formations? There are the six classes of volition: volition regarding forms, volition regarding sounds, volition regarding odours, volition regarding tastes, volition regarding tactile objects, volition regarding mental phenomena.

With the arising of contact there is the arising of volitional formations. And why, *bhikkhus*, do you call them volitional formations? "They construct the conditioned", *bhikkhus*, therefore they are called volitional formations.

And what, *bhikkhus*, is consciousness? There are the six classes of consciousness: eye-consciousness, ear-consciousness, nose-consciousness, tongue-consciousness, body-consciousness, mind-consciousness. With the arising of name and form there is the arising of consciousness. And why, *bhikkhus*, do you call it consciousness? "It cognizes", *bhikkhus*, therefore it is called consciousness. And what does it cognize? It cognizes sour, it cognizes bitter, it cognizes pungent, it cognizes sweet, it cognizes sharp, it cognizes mild, it cognizes salty, it cognizes bland....

... And, *bhikkhus*, from what are sorrow, lamentation, pain, displeasure, and despair born? How are they produced? Here, *bhikkhus*, the uninstructed worldling ... regards form as self, or self as possessing form, or form as in self, or self as in form. That form of his changes and alters. With change and alteration of form, there arise in him sorrow, lamentation, pain, displeasure, and despair.

He regards feeling as self ... perception as self ... volitional formations as self ... consciousness

> as self, or self as possessing consciousness, or consciousness as in self, or self as in consciousness. That consciousness of his changes and alters. With the change and alteration of consciousness, there arise in him sorrow lamentation, pain displeasure and despair."

In another *sutta* we find a clear enunciation of how the notion of "I" arises due to clinging to these five aggregates (Bodhi, 2000b):

> "It is by clinging, Ananda, that the notion of "I am" occurs, not without clinging. And by clinging to what does "I am" occur...? It is by clinging to form that "I am" occurs, not without clinging. It is by clinging to feeling ... to perception ... to volitional formations ... to consciousness that "I am" occurs, not without clinging. Suppose, friend Ananda, a young woman—or a man youthful and fond of ornaments would examine her own facial image in a mirror ... she would look at it."

As it can be seen from the above *sutta*, it is evident why these aggregates are the root cause of *dukkha* (suffering). These aggregates are inherently conditioned to change. Every person experiences these changes and because we perceive them as happening to "me", be it a change in the physical body due to illness or age, or changes in the mental capacities as a result of our interaction with the world; one tends to suffer. The basic reason for this suffering can be attributed to the attachment to any or all of these aggregates. This creates the entites of me and mine *vs.* thee and thine, and from these concepts arise the whole egocentric world which we relate to with a "self-centred" perspective, with cravings (*rāga*) and aversions (*doṣa*), with likes and dislikes, the very cause of all suffering (Dhar, 2011).

Gautam Buddha provided elaborate instructions on how to practically train the mind to achieve this "abandonment" of desire. It is clear that it cannot be done by merely exerting will power and subduing the desire as and when it arises; because it itself stems from the desire to eliminate the desire. The only way to do it is through non-judgemental acceptance of the reality of the desire, sans any reaction (aversion), waiting patiently for it to extinguish on its own. Since all conditioned phenomena are perishable, natural extinction of whatever arises in the mind is inevitable; all we need to do is not let our instinctive tendencies to indulge with it, and patiently notice its rise and passing away. Therefore, in essence, the path to the abandonment of desire involves systematised development of the mindfulness of the five aggregates explicitly imbibing their characteristics of impermanence, suffering, and no self (Dhar, 2011).

The delusion of the view that self is an imperishable entity, the notion of "me" or "I" as a separate person with an immortal identity, a unique image, which needs to be conserved, is the root cause of all *dukkha*. This is because from the notion of "I" arises mine, and from that emerge "thee" and "thine". We view this world from an egocentric perspective: those who help fulfil our dreams and desires are seen as friends, whom we like and appreciate; and those who seem to hinder our path, are treated as our rivals, whom we dislike and criticise. Consequently, our responses to the sensations and feelings as a result of the interactions with the world—are determined by cravings and aversions. Over time, these take the place of our deeply-seated habitual patterns making us act like an automata. Individually, we become never at peace, and neither the ones who interact with us; thus, leading to the viruses of mental degradation such as pride, dissatisfaction, anxiety, fear, ill-will, hatred which are manifested in the form of strife, crimes, and violence in the society. And unless these habits and their underlying tendencies are eliminated, the suffering would not subside (Nanamoli & Bodhi, 1995).

The Buddha had recognised this causal connection quite early in his spiritual journey. He ascertained that *sakkayadithi*—the mistaken belief that a unique person exists to whom the five aggregates belong—and the defilements of the mind, form a vicious circle strengthening each other. It is because of *sakkayadithi* that the mental defilements originate and they further strengthen *sakkayadithi*. The correct practice of the eightfold path that the Buddha discovered, gradually reduces the mental defilements and consequently the ego. As the shackles of self-view come to dissipate, the pure and pristine characteristics of the mind, which otherwise rest deep inside, hiding behind the impurieties of the mind, begin to manifest. The gradual manifestation of these characteristics, namely, loving kindness (*maitrī*), compassion (*karuṇā*), altruistic joy (*mudita*), and equanimity (*upekkhā*), ultimately lead to natural cessation of *dukkha* (Dhar, 2011).

At the centre of the Buddhist doctrine are three major characteristics of human existence: impermanence, absence of an immortal Self or soul, and dissatisfaction as a significant attribute of this world. From these three characteristics arise the basic principles of Buddhism—the Four Noble Truths and the Eightfold Path (Frager & Fadiman, 2013):

Impermanence: According to this Buddhist principle, nothing is permanent. Everything is constantly changing. Impermanence characterises all things—be it physical entities like trees, mountains, river, sun, moon, stars or be it mental properties like thoughts and ideas—all have a limited existence, a finiteness to them. Furthermore, all are in flux at any given point in time. The notion of impermanence implicates that there is no absolute authority or permanent truth, only a level of understanding appropriate for a particular place and time. For the conditions around us are never constant, what seems to be true at one particular time may become unsuitable or false at some other point in time. Therefore, Buddhism cannot be said to have a fixed set of beliefs. To comprehend the idea of impermanence is to realise that nothing ever truly and completely becomes Buddha and that even truth is subject to change and progress. To put it differently, everything around us is an ever-changing manifestation of the same reality that is also Buddha. The fundamental feature of the universe is change; however, we humans have a tendency of perceiving things around us as static. In reality, we are surrounded by things, objects, and processes are interdependent and ever-changing.

Selflessness: Whilst various other religions have also taught that the Self, or soul, is immutable or immortal; however, according to Buddhism, the concept of impermanence applies to our innermost self as well. The characteristic of selflessness holds that there does not exist a self or a soul in any individual. An individual is a collection of elements, all of which are prone to constant change and impermanence. According to the Buddha, the individual is made up of five basic factors: body, perception, sensation, consciousness, and mental activities (that is, thoughts, ideas, intentions, etc.). The term "I" is simply an effective linguistic tool to refer to an ever-changing combination of traits. In other words, our bodies and personalities are nothing but an impermanent pattern formed by the momentary interactions of its component processes. When these parts perish, the individual ceases to exist.

No part of our being or existence can live forever, although the consequences of our thoughts and actions may do. And this goes for all the other things—not only humans—everything lacks a separate, undying self, including trees, mountains, plants, and animals.

Dissatisfaction: Dissatisfaction is the third characteristic of existence. The notion of dissatisfaction encompasses birth, death, decay, sorrow, pain, and existence itself. According to Buddhist teachings, suffering comes from ourselves, not from the world around us. It rests in the finite ego—the relative consciousness—of every individual. The Buddhist doctrine offers us help to transcend our limited sense of self. It is only through self-transformation can we experience real satisfaction with ourselves and with the world around us.

The principle of dissatisfaction has been misinterpreted to mean that suffering is an inevitable part of our existence. The Buddha claimed that the root of the suffering lies within an individual and optimistically concluded that there is a way out of it. Gautam Buddha looked for a way to overcome the pain and suffering that he saw as an inescapable part of human life. According to Mosig (1990), Buddha probably made the most substantial psychological discovery of all time when he realised the universality of suffering, its cause, cure, and the path to liberation. Buddha gave his diagnosis in the form of the Four Noble Truths.

The Four Noble Truths

The Existence of Dissatisfaction: The first truth is the existence of dissatisfaction. In an average individual, dissatisfaction, or suffering is certain and unavoidable. The Buddha proposed understanding dissatisfaction as a way to liberate oneself from the shackles of pain and suffering. When we realise our own suffering, or dissatisfaction, the Buddha nature in us looks at it, finds its cause, and formulates a course of action that can transform it into peace, joy, and liberation (Hanh, 1998).

Craving as the Root of Dissatisfaction: The second truth is the result of the craving or desire. Craving is desire plus attachment, a feeling that "I must have this", which is even stronger than just possessing desire. Majority of the individuals are attached to anything that is positive and provides pleasure, and repel anything that is negative and painful. Craving creates a state of instability in which the present always tends to be unsatisfactory. If our desires remain unmet, we are driven to change the present. If satisfied, we fear change, which in turn births frustration and dissatisfaction. For all things eventually pass, the momentary pleasure of the fulfilled desires is weakened by the realisation that it is only temporary and that it will pass. Therefore, we are always caught up in wishing things to be different than they actually are. So, the stronger the craving, greater is the dissatisfaction because we know that that fulfilment will not last long.

Elimination of Craving: The third truth is the elimination of craving which points out to the cessation of suffering. According to Buddhist thought, it is possible to learn to accept the world without having to experience dissatisfaction. To eradicate craving does not mean to give up all the desires. Healthy desires—like those for food and sleep—are necessary for survival. Desires also help enhance our awareness. If all our wants are immediately satisfied, we can easily go into an inactive, unthinking state of contentment. Acceptance refers to an equable attitude of enjoying fulfilled desires without attaching oneself to the outcomes. Thus, one can enjoy the successes of their desires without dwelling on the unavoidable parts of our dreams that do not come true. Dissatisfaction will cease to exist if we learn to enjoy the priceless possessions we have—hearing, sight, health, and life itself (Hanh, 1998).

The Eightfold Path

The fourth truth comprises of the path to the eradicate craving and dissatisfaction: the Eightfold Path, or the Middle Way. More often than not, people seek the greatest possible degree of sense gratification, while others tend towards leading a life with subdued desires. The ideal case in Buddhism states moderation.

Buddhism proposes to take the middle path between the two extremes. It advises to avoid, on one hand, the path which involves low, crass, thoughtless indulgence in passion and grandeur; and on the other hand, the useless practice of self-torture and mortification. The Middle Path, as suggested by Buddha, leads to peace, wisdom and enlightenment (Lal, 1967: 22).

The Eightfold Path is comprised of right speech, right action, right livelihood, right effort, right mindfulness, right concentration, right thought, and right understanding. The basic premise is to avoid thinking and behaving in ways that can prove harmful to others as well as to oneself. The Eightfold Path has been further divided into three categories—ethical conduct, mental discipline, and wisdom.

(1) The first category of ethical conduct rests on the very basic Buddhist teachings of universal love and compassion for all. This category includes right speech, right action, and right livelihood.—*Right speech* includes abstaining from lies; gossip, slur, or any speech that may lead to disruption of unity and harmony; rude, unkind, abusive language; and pathetic and incompetent chatter and gossip. One should instead speak the truth and use language that is friendly, pleasant, kind, and useful. One should not speak recklessly; one should utter words considering the place and time. Lastly, if one cannot say anything useful, the ideal situation would be to keep "noble silence". —*Right action* means ethical, respectable, and peace-binding conduct. In order to attain this, one should restrain from destruction of life; stealing; dishonest actions; illegitimate sexual intercourse; and drugs or alcohol. Finally, one should help others live a peaceful and an honourable life.

—*Right livelihood* can be achieved if one abstains from living a life that causes harm to others, such as dealing in weapons, intoxicating drinks, drugs, or poisons; killing animals; or cheating. Right livelihood means to make a living that is respectable and does not cause any harm to anyone.

(2) The second category is of mental discipline. It comprises of right effort, right mindfulness, and right concentration.
—*Right effort* is using our will to (1) avoid unpleasant state of mind form arising; (2) getting rid of such states if they do arise; (3) working towards creating positive and wholesome states of mind; and (4) bringing perfection to the good states that are already present.
—*Right mindfulness* means to be aware of and observant of (1) the functions of the body; (2) sensations or feelings; (3) the activities of the mind; and (4) certain ideas, thoughts, and conceptions. A variety of meditative practices are present in different schools of Buddhism that focus on breathing, sensations, and on mental activities; to promote right mindfulness.
—*Right concentration* involves developing mental focus to help attain other aspects of the path.

(3) Wisdom is made up of right thought and right understanding.
—*Right thought* comprises of detachment, love, and non-violence.
—*Right understanding* is the understanding of the things as they are, without judgement.

It can be only accomplished by working deeply with the Four Noble Truths. In Buddhist psychology, there are two levels of understanding—first, which is the complete knowledge, memory, and cognitive grasp of the subject matter and the second, is the deep understanding of things without any names and labels. This type of understanding is only possible when the mind is free from its defilements and is developed through meditation (Frager & Fadiman, 2013).

Self to Non-self in Buddhism

Based on the teachings of Buddhism, one should develop a nonself-cultivating process that aims to extinguish desires and eradicate the self, leading to egolessness or selflessness (Shiah, 2016).

The self-comprises of perceptions, desires, needs, and psychological functions such as, conation, motivation, attention, cognition, emotion, and behaviour of the physical organism (Dalai Lama, 1995a; Dambrun and Ricard, 2011; Shiah and Yit, 2012). The biological body initially gives the individual a personal identity or uniqueness, a sense of control over the different phenomena in the mind, body, and the outside world (Albahari, 2006). This feeling of possessing a self is the result of a hedonic principle and the result of a deep-rooted erroneous belief (Albahari, 2014). The hedonic principle organises a very desire-driven approach to looking at objects, events, situations, the body, and at life itself (Leifer, 1999).

The universal Mandala Model of Self (MMS) was created to characterise the healthy self across cultural boundaries. Real and lasting happiness is the ultimate aim of the self. The MMS is appropriate for building the NT since the nonself is regarded as a functional self. The four MMS concepts—biology, ideal person, knowledge/wisdom, and action—are used to compare the ego and nonself components of psychological self-functioning and their underlying processes. Using the hedonic principle of pursuing pleasure driven by desire, the ego engages in psychological behaviours aimed at strengthening the self. On the contrary, a nonself approach entails putting the self-cultivation principle into practise in three ways: by letting go of cravings, by showing compassion, by engageing in meditation, and by trying to comprehend Buddhist wisdom. The purpose of these three approaches is to penetrate and transcend the illusion of the self in order to accomplish a profound metamorphosis that is inextricably linked to the experience of doing away with the sense of self and its psychological frameworks. Furthermore, the NT offers a thorough structure (Shiah, 2016).

For almost two millennia, Buddhists in the East have embraced a unique perspective on the self (Kelly, 2008).

According to Wallace and Shapiro (2006) and Shonin *et al.* (2014), Buddhism is typically defined as comprising Theravāda Buddhism of Southeast Asia, East Asian Mahāyāna Buddhism, Indo-Tibetan Mahāyāna, and Vajrayāna Buddhism. Overcoming the suffering and emotional disruptions brought on by life's obstacles, challenges, and stressors is these institutions' ultimate goal (Shiah and Yit, 2012). The goal of the Buddha's teachings is to cultivate a shift from the self-state to the nonself state in order to achieve a true, long-lasting bliss (Dalai Lama, 1995a, 2005). Buddhism maintains that the idea of a personal identity is illusory (Giles, 1993) and that everyone believes they are a self that ultimately does not exist. The main source of suffering is clinging to or becoming fixated on the illusory self (Dalai Lama, 1995a). *Nirvāṇa*, a state of nonself that entails a process of renunciating worldly things, especially those for which attractiveness springs from egoism and desires, while maintaining or elevating the self, or *ātma-graha*, is the eternal goal of Buddhists, in contrast to the concept of the self (Dalai Lama, 2005) and (Hwang and Chang, 2009; MacKenzie, 2010). *Nirvāṇa*, also known as the state of nonself and complete liberation, is the result of this process (Tsong-Kha-Pa, 2000; Shonin *et al.*, 2014). Nonetheless, the Buddhist concept of the total liberation state is multifaceted and goes beyond psychology (Tsong-Kha-Pa, 2000). However, the nonself state has psychological ramifications, including genuine and long-lasting happiness (Dambrun and Ricard, 2011).

The self and the nonself are the two types of self that are suggested by the current theoretical model. These two types of self are emphasised by two main dimensions: egoism and no self. These two types of self, in my opinion, are extremes on a continuum. Everybody on this continuum has a specific place where they fall. To me, egoism is a self-perceived identity based on desires (Albahari, 2014). We are all instances of egoism as long as we think we own a self (Dalai Lama, 1995a). Characteristics of egoism's psychological operation include biased self-interest, self-centredness, and egocentrism (Dambrun and Ricard, 2011). Therefore, egoism is taken to be the primary frame of reference for psychological activities, adhering to the hedonic principle of seeking pleasure triggered by stimuli (Shiah, 2016).

Conversely, as previously mentioned, a state of nonself entails giving up worldly possessions, especially those that appeal to egoism and desires. According to Giles (1993) and Joshanloo (2014), personal identity or the self is illusory; it is believed that such a self does not genuinely exist or is not stable (Dalai Lama, 1995b). According to the Dalai Lama (2005), realising that the self, or the I, is not intrinsically existing is what is meant to be understood by the term nonself.

The Buddha claims that the theory of an immutable entity called self or soul or *ātman* has been proposed only to diminish the instinctive fear in human beings of annihilation at death. All our experiences are nothing but the psychosomatic phenomena associated with the five aggregates. Since we strongly identify with them, we interpret them as happening to "me" or "I". According to Buddhist thought, these aggregates are finely interconnected and are constantly changing, thus making the existence of a permanent ontological entity called "me" or "I" implausible. Keeping the aggregates aside, there is no distinct "being"—the feeler, the thinker, the doer; like there is no river apart from the water flowing between the two shores (Dhar, 2011).

The apparent continuity of identity, its perseverance despite the obvious change in the aggregates, is the product of the illusion created by our memory, and the progressive nature of the change, particularly in the physical body and in the intellect that primarily govern our perceptions. These changes are so steady and gradual that we tend to not notice that they are continually changing, and we misperceive them as "continuity" of identity. When there takes place a substantial change, does one become conscious of the changes to one's "stable" identity, however, even then due to our conditioning, we see those changes as unpleasant events happening to "I" (Dhar, 2011).

This concept of "sel-ing" is also verified by recent development in scientific research studies. For instance, in studies by Damasio on neurobiology of emotions and feelings have found that the sense of self arises not just because we are able to think, but from the brain's ability to sense somatic sensations and associated feelings. But since these sensations and feelings are continuously changing, the sense of self also emerges from moment to moment (Damasio, 1994).

Zen Buddhism

Zen is a major school of the Mahāyāna tradition. Zen Buddhism was brought to China in the sixth century AD by Bodhidharma, and Indian Buddhist monk, who proposed the significance of contemplation and self-discipline over religious customs. With time, under the mastery of great Chinese monks, Zen eventually developed as an independent school of Buddhism with its own monasteries, monastic rules, and organisation. By 1000 AD, Zen had become the second most popular school of Buddhism in China (Frager & Fadiman, 2013).

The word *zen* is derived from the Sanskrit word for meditation, *dhyāna* (which is called *ch'an* in Chinese and *zen* in Japanese). Meditation is a central practice in Zen. There are two major schools of Zen meditation, or *zazen* (literally meaning "seated zen")—one involves simply sitting with awareness, and the other involves focusing on a koan (Frager & Fadiman, 2013).

Meditation on a koan. A *koan* is a question or an activity that is impossible to solve by using mere logic. *Koan*s are used in the Rinzai school of zen to evaluate students and to make them deeper into and beyond mere logical thinking into the enlightened mind. These koans are either found in the dialogues between the *zen* student and master, or in the questions asked by the *zen* masters to arouse students" understanding. The *koan*s distinctly display the *zen* master's deep understanding of Buddhism. They seem puzzling and above logic, compelling the questioner to go into the deeper recesses of mind, surpassing the inherent boundations of his/her familiar categories of experience.

Just sitting. When it comes to meditation, the Soto school's method can be described as "just sitting", devoid of any kind of mental exercise or *koan*. The goal of meditation is to sustain a focused awareness state in which the practitioner is completely awake but not tense or relaxed. It's like someone sitting by the side of the road and observing traffic. The meditator watches the passing thoughts without becoming sucked into them and losing sight of the need to be an attentive observer. *Zazen* is a way of showing one's faith. No matter how much they are taught, people without faith will not accept *zazen*. How can you trust yourself if you cannot trust the silence and the immensity of existence, if you do not immerse yourself in this world? (Katagiri, 1988: 43). When practised correctly, *zazen* should prevent visions and related experiences. These experiences usually stem from tensions built-up from sitting incorrectly during meditation or from dream-like states that appear during a particular stage of the practice. These delusions are thought to be useless for personal development. At best, they serve as diversion; at worst, they can be a source of conceit, egotism, and illusion.

Meditation is an efficient practice for developing inner peace and calm and for increasing concentration and maintaining balance of mind. Carrying out the work in *zazen* is like taking a bath. Just like a bath is required to cleanse the body, *zazen* helps in cleansing the mind regularly. In Buddhist tradition, the ultimate goal is not to seek the final enlightenment, rather it is to practise so that every moment that we live becomes our true life.

> "And, therefore, when we meditate, we sit for sitting; we don't sit for something else. If we sit for twenty minutes, these twenty minutes should bring us joy, life." (Hanh, 1988: 53)

According to the Soto School of zen, students are taught to learn to manage their own personal *koan*, their personal riddle of daily life, as it presents itself to the experiencer. There is not one ultimate solution to the *koan*, everyone has to find their own way which can only be done by changing one's viewpoint and personality. The problem remains the same, how one looks at it and how they cope with it can and do change. The individual never solves the *koan* but eventually learns to deal with it from a higher level. For example, Siddhārtha Gautam began his spiritual journey to solve the *koan* of life-sickness, old age, and death. Even after he became the Buddha, the problems did not disappear or got solved. He did not become immortal or imperishable, but his new wisdom transcended his previous understanding and concerns. Some people's *koan* is the feeling of inadequacy, feeling of not being enough, not being good enough, not knowing enough, or not being able to accomplish enough.

The practice of meditation is not just a technique to attain something, rather it is an end in itself.

Mindfulness

Zen master Thich Nhat Hanh has described the practice of meditation in the following way:

> "You've got to practice meditation when you walk, stand, lie down, sit, and work, while washing your hands, washing the dishes, sweeping the floor, drinking tea, talking to friends, or whatever you are doing: While washing the dishes, you might be thinking about the tea afterwards, and so try to get them out of the way as quickly as possible in order to sit and drink tea. But that means that you are incapable of living during the time you are washing the dishes. When you are washing the dishes, washing the dishes must be the most important thing in your life....
>
> While washing the dishes one should only be washing the dishes, which means that while washing the dishes one should be completely aware of the fact that one is washing the dishes. At first glance, that might seem a little silly: why put so much stress on a simple thing? But that's precisely the point. The fact that I am standing there and washing these bowls is a wondrous reality. I'm being completely myself, following my breath, conscious of my presence, and conscious of my thoughts and actions. There's no way I can be tossed around mindlessly like a bottle slapped here and there on the waves." (1976: 3-4, 23-24 as cited in Frager & Fadiman, 2013)

Meditation and mindfulness go hand in hand. On one hand, meditation brings a level of inner peace and calm and increased awareness into our lives, on the other hand, mindfulness helps us to sit with a calm awareness.

Enlightenment

The term "enlightenment" itself seems misleading because it appears to be implying a state that one can achieve permanently, thus violating the concept of impermanence in Buddhism (Frager & Fadiman, 2013).

A Buddhist concept related to enlightenment is *nirvāṇa*. *Nirvāṇa* is a state of mind in which all urges and desires have been destroyed. This state if mind is achieved through self-discipline, meditation, and understanding the notions of impermanence and selflessness. *Nirvāṇa* also means annihilation—of all concepts, ideas, and notions. Our concepts limit a deeper understanding of the world. Meditations helps us with removing these concepts (Hanh, 1998).

The experience is not static—it is sequential, dynamic, constantly changing state of being, like Maslow's concept of self-actualisation. An American Zen Master, Joh Daido Loori (2002) provided the story of the ugly duckling from the Hans Christian Andersen tale which is a good example of *kensho* (literally meaning "to see into one's own nature"). The ugly duckling suffered because he was different from the other ducklings. When he came to realise that he was a beautiful swan, he became overwhelmed with joy. In reality, nothing has actually changed. He just had realised his potential as a perfect, beautiful swan. He merely realised his true nature and became free from the delusion of imperfection. Realising the perfection of our Buddha nature is also the same. Enlightenment of perfect peace and harmony: no more, no less (Katagiri, 1988: 128).

Arhat and Bodhisattva

The Theravāda and Mahāyāna schools of Buddhist tradition have different ideologies about the nature of an ideal human being. According to the Theravāda tradition, the ideal human is *arhat*, the one who has completely cut off from all the worldly attachments to family, materialistic possessions, and comfort to become liberated of this world. The word *arhat* literally means "one who has slain the enemy", the one who has risen above all the humanly pleasures and passions as a result of their spiritual practice. The *arhat*, simply has achieved emancipation from pride, selfishness, hate, and greed, has attained wisdom and compassion (Frager & Fadiman, 2013).

One Buddhist text describes the *arhat*:

> "He exerted himself, he strove and struggled, and thus he realized that this circle of 'Birth-and-Death' ... is in constant flux. He rejected all the conditions of existence which are brought about by a compound of conditions, since it is their nature to decay and crumble away, to change and to be destroyed. He abandoned all the 'defilements' and won *arhat*ship ... Gold and a clod of earth were the same to him. The sky and the palm of his hand to his mind the same." (Conze, 1959a: 94)

The *arhat* strives for *nirvāṇa*, which is the cessation of craving and thus freedom from suffering. The person who undergoes such a transformation perceives *nirvāṇa* as the ultimate reality or absolute truth, a state outside of this world of ever-changing phenomena. According to the Mahāyāna tradition, the ideal human is *bodhisattva*, literally meaning "enlightenment-being". The *bodhisattva* is a highly compassionate being, who has promised to stay on the planet until all other beings have been freed from suffering (Frager and Fadiman, 2013).

The *bodhisattva* understands that he or she is a part of every other sentient being and that they will never fully achieve liberation until all beings are set free from suffering. The *bodhisattva* makes a vow not to pass into *nirvāṇa* until all sentient beings including grass blades—have attained enlightenment.

> "As many beings as there are in the universe of beings... egg-born, born from a womb, moisture-born, or miraculously born; with or without form; with perception, without perception, or with neither perception nor no-perception as far as any conceivable form of beings is conceived; all these I must lead to *Nirvāṇa*." (*Diamond Sutra* in Conze, 1959b: 164 as cited in Frager and Fadiman, 2013).

The ultimate virtue of a *bodhisattva* is compassion, which arises from genuinely experiencing every other person's suffering as one's own. According to the Mahāyāna perspective, this outlook represents enlightenment. The selfish ego is transcended during the enlightenment experience, not the outside world.

The path to achieving *bodhisattva* is to release oneself from attachment to the world, without letting go of its beings. The *arhat* path places less emphasis on service and more on the pursuit of inner perfection and world abandonment. The *arhat* philosophy is to better oneself before assisting others. The development of oneself must come before helping or instructing others, as someone who is lost in delusion is ineffective in these roles. Rather than being incompatible, these two ideals can be considered complementary. Both the *arhat* model and the *bodhisattva* ideal stress the importance of self-discipline and service to others, which are crucial components of inner development (Frager and Fadiman, 2013).

Recent Developments in Zen Buddhism

Buddhism's philosophy has greatly influenced many branches of psychology. There are a number of advantages of psychotherapy that may be obtained through meditation. Psychoanalysis and meditation techniques have been found to work well together (Carrington & Ephron, 1975; Engler, 1986, 1993). According to Erich Fromm (1970), *zen* and psychoanalysis share similar objectives, for example, knowledge of reality, freedom from the oppressive influence of the unconscious, and self-awareness are a few of these. According to Fromm, the idea that knowledge brings about transformation is also shared by psychoanalysis and *zen*. According to several studies (Boorstein, 1988; Claxton, 1986; Fuld, 1991; Kornfield, 1988 as cited in Frager & Fadiman, 2013), Zen meditation can be a beneficial addition to therapy. Additionally, Eastern psychotherapy influenced by *zen* has become more and more well-liked in the West (Reynolds, 1980, 1984, 1993). Despite the fact that psychedelics and other drugs are prohibited in Buddhism, Stolaroff (1999) contended that when used appropriately, psychedelics can be an effective tool for speeding and deepening Buddhist meditation practice. The psychology of transformation in *zen* has been thoroughly studied by Benoit (1990) and Manne-Lewis (1986). Buddhist texts have been interpreted in light of contemporary quantum physics by Soeng (1991). Basic principles of Buddhism and Gestalt therapy are also shared. Both emphasise how crucial it is to live in the moment with mindfulness. One of the main tools for change for both is awareness. Perls (1969) contended that the conscious mind is the enemy, not the unconscious. In a similar vein, the Buddha made note of how the conscious mind clings to desires and the unfounded notion of a distinct self. The insights of cognitive psychology and meditation have started to be combined by psychologists (Brown & Engler, 1986; Goleman, 1988; Shapiro, 1980; Shapiro & Walsh, 1984). Significant neurological and physiological effects of *zen* meditation have been shown by empirical research (Fromm, 1992; Hirai, 1989; Murphy & Donovan, 1988). Better health and the capacity to manage stress and tension have been linked to *zazen* and other Eastern meditation practices (Claxton, 1986; Dalai Lama *et al.*, 1991; Kabat-Zinn, 1990, 1994; Sheng-Yen, 1987).

The English literature on Zen Buddhism has ever been expanding. The works of Thich Nhat Hanh (1976, 1987, 1988, 1992, 1993, 1996, 1998, 2001, 2010), Katagiri (1988), Deshimaru (1985, 1987, 1991), Loori (2004, 2008, 2009), and Shunryu Suzuki (1997, 2002) have all had a significant impact. Zen and the Brain (1998), written by American neurology professor James Austin, is a thorough analysis of the *zen* meditation experience and the neurological mechanisms underlying spiritual states of awareness. Additionally, he is the author of two sequels: Selfless Insight (2009) and Zen-Brain Reflections (2006).

Obstacles to Growth

In Buddhism, the main hurdles in the path of growth are fundamentally psychological. All of us possess three propensities that act as major roadblocks in growth—greed, hate, and delusion. Another important roadblock is pride (Frager and Fadiman, 2013).

The three "fires" of Buddhism are greed, hate, and delusion. Any person has a combination of the three qualities, with usually one dominating over the other two. The balance among the qualities may change, depending upon the situation. In certain cases, one's greed may arise while in others, anger or delusional tendencies may take over.

Greed: It is the main problem for most of the people. We always have the urge to want more than we have—more money, more food, more pleasure. Normally, children are the most evidently greedy. It is often not possible to satisfy their wants, one piece of sweet only kindles desire for one more. The Buddhist scriptures have defined such people as been submitted to pride, conceit, discontent, love of luxury, food, and expensive clothes (Conze 1959b).

Hate: People who are controlled by hate have short tempers and are quick to aggressive response. For such people, life is all about fighting with their adversaries, taking revenge for their real or imagined injuries, and defending themselves against a potential ambush. These people tend to hold grudges, demean others, and themselves suffer from arrogance, jealousy, and parsimony (Conze, 1959b).

Delusion: It is defined as a generalised state of perplexity, lack of awareness, and uncertainty. People who are dominated by delusion find it hard to commit to something. They are always in a state of confusion and hesitation, they tend to do things clumsily and absent-mindedly. Such people's behaviours are characterised by laziness, obstinacy, confusion, worry, and volatility (Conze, 1959b). These urges can also develop into either neurosis or psychosis. Nonetheless, even psychosis is viewed as a temporary state which is nothing but an intensification of one of such tendencies.

Buddhism and Mainstream Psychology

According to the Buddhist philosophy, everyone suffers as the normal condition of (unenlightened) existence; this is the starting point, and is the central tenet of Buddhism to positively impact one's condition. Buddhist teachings offer not for those who are "unwell", but also for those who are "well" (Cassaniti, 2014).

According to a Thai scholar-monk, Buddhadāsa, one of the main characteristics of existence is that everyone suffers, and can decrease this suffering. As mentioned earlier in the chapter, Buddhism provides us with the first step out of suffering. Though it points out to the presence of dissatisfaction and suffering in everyone's life, Buddhism, in essence, is positive in its approach to life and living. It offers us the path to decrease our suffering and increase positive well-being. In fact, many Buddhist teachings can be linked to positive psychology. For example, the ideas expressed by the Four Noble Truths have been found to be associated with positivity so much so that they have been called the "precursors for the new positive psychology; and Buddha, the father of this evolving new science" (Pearsall, 2003: 58). The Four Noble Truths inform us how to live our lives up to our maximum potential (Cassaniti, 2014).

In Western psychology, the self is formulated in a variety of ways, and a large number of these are based on the idea that there is a distinct "I" entity (Shonin *et al.*, 2014). Numerous subject-hyphen-predicate relations, such as self-affirmation, self-awareness, self-comparison, self-concept, self-consistent, self-control, self-efficacy, self-esteem, self-fulfilment, self-handicapping, self-image, self-identity, self-perception, self-regulation, and self-reference, have henceforth been found to give psychology a significant role for the "self" (Klein, 2014). Early Christianity is where the idea of the individualistic view of the self first emerged (Shiah, 2016).

The influence of Buddhism on Positive Psychology can also be seen in one of its founding concepts, that is, the concept of flow. The psychological theory of flow, developed by Csikszentmihalyi (1990), draws from the teachings of Buddhism. Flow is defined as the state of being in which a person is completely immersed in an activity for its own sake. Research on the concept has shown that happiness arises from deep attention and engagement in an activity (Csikszentmihalyi, 1990, C.C. Wallace and Shapiro, 2006: 696).

Practices in Buddhist school seem to affect processes of self-construct and self-reference. Meditation tends to impact not only how the awareness and attention to the bodies and minds but also how we relate this awareness to the "self". Research shows that people who meditate display more "self-detached" processing as compared to the control group, showing more objective analyses of sensory occurrences, not strongly associated with self-constructs (Cassaniti, 2014).

Research in different fields of psychology has shown that there are different concepts of self across cultures (Markus & Kitayama, 1991; Mageo, 2002; Shweder & Bourne, 1984).

Buddhist perspectives on self, regard that there is no permanent entity called "self" (Collins, 1982) because everything is subject to change, and therefore nothing is permanent. Thus, according to Buddhist thought, detachment from what seems to create this temporary sense of self leads to positive outcomes. An important root cause of *dukkha* is looking at the world from this lens of a self. Instead of creating more and more layers to go deeper to understand one's self, Buddhism suggests letting go of what any attachments to this idea of having a self. However, amidst the psychological discourses of self-enhancement and self-growth in the Western psychology, it is difficult to grasp and accept the concept of nonself and detachment in the traditional models of self. As a result, this idea is either ignored or reinterpreted in the Western thought, for example in contemporary theories of mindfulness and meditation therapies (Cassaniti, 2014).

Buddhist Psychology

Buddhist psychology is both a psychology of transformation and a theory of cognition. As a psychology of transformation, it aims to develop the innate psychic potential of every being to its perfection. The ordinary state of being is "flawed" or pathological in the sense that one works with limited perceptions of the world and undergoes cycles of suffering and psychological tension in ceaseless attempts to cope with and respond to the world. These attempts fail to produce ever-lasting happiness because the perceptions about oneself and the world, which one formulates as the basis for action, are discordant with one's true nature. Buddhist psychology aims to transcend this entrapment. It begins the endeavour by analysing the root cause behind this pathology. In the absence of such an understanding, one might go after an enlightenment ideal with the same pathological tendencies that tie one to the miseries of ordinary being; and thus remain contented with an intermediate state of blissful experience, where the tendencies leading to future suffering may still be dormant.

The goal of the Buddhist psychology of transformation can be viewed as triple-fold, corresponding to the three scopes of motivation on the Buddhist path.The lower goal is about coping with the ordinary state of being while minimising suffering.

The middle goal is the everlasting liberation (*vimukti*) from suffering by eliminating afflictive tendencies. The higher goal is to achieve complete and perfect awakening (*sambodhi*). The process of awakening involves the attainment of total perfection in all dimensions of being, with their transformation into pristine wisdom (*jñāna*). The ultimate spiritual attainment on the Buddhist path, as described in the Great Perfection (*mahā-sandhi-yoga*, Tibetan: *rdzogs chen*) teachings, is to realise the primordial purity and spontaneous perfection of all appearances. This realisation is inseparably coalesced (*yuganaddha*) with a display of unceasing compassion. This is a state completely transcending ordinary psyche, without grounding in or clinging to its distorted projections and being able to appreciate the truth "as it is".

Buddhist psychology is also a theory of cognition. This is an inevitable part of Buddhist exploration since the higher goal of Buddhist training is the attainment of *sambodhi* that eliminates all cognitive "errors". The view of cognition that evolves through Buddhist psychology is that of the co-emergence of the person and the world. The distinction between inner and outer vanishes on deep analysis of the process of experiencing. Thus the scope of "personality" in Buddhist studies includes the entire sphere of experience covering not only the person, but also the world as perceived by the person. The study of the dynamics of this co-emergence equips Buddhist psychology with ways of altering the person and the world thus brought forth. This knowledge is applied in eliminating the cognitive "errors" of the ordinary state of being, and thus in relating to appearances in a whole new way as the person progresses on the path to omniscience.

An important theme running throughout Buddhist psychology is the five dimensions of underlying capabilities in which various aspects of personality and the awakened state are understood. At the mundane level, the manifestation of these capabilities in its distorted forms appears as the five aggregates (*skandha*) of personality. The aggravation of these distortions leads to five afflictions (*kleśa*), and to various psychological realms of experience. Through perfect awakening, clarified aspects of these capabilities manifest as the five aspects of the fully awakened omniscient wisdom (*buddha-jñāna*). These five clarified aspects are:

1. Seeing reality "as it is",
2. Unperturbed clarity in knowing all phenomena,
3. Perfect distinction of all details of phenomena,
4. Sensing the happiness and suffering of all beings with the experience of one—taste, transcending ordinary pleasure and pain, and
5. The creativity of spontaneously—accomplishing actions.

Buddhist psychology has formulated various ways of analysing personality. These could be termed as "the models of personality". These psychological models are valuable in studying a variety of experiences like the conventional experience of ordinary beings, of those in the stages of the path to awakening, and the qualities of the fully awakened state. These models are also useful in analysing experiences related to sleep, dream, death, after-death state, etc.

The Psychology of Transformation

The psychology of transformation includes distinctions between the subtler experiential states of *samādhi*, liberation (*vimukti*), stages on the path to full awakening (*sambodhi*), etc. Buddhism does not consider *samādhi* states as liberation from suffering, because these do not result in the irreversible transformation of the basis of suffering. Such a transformation is possible only through cultivating insight (*prajñā*) about the actual mode of existence of a person.

A person accesses the states of meditative absorption (*samādhi*) through subduing the five afflictions and cultivating the mental episodes of one-pointed concentration (*ekāgratā*). Eight major levels of *samādhi* states are identified, of which the first four are categorised as form-realm and the remaining as formless-realm. The *Suraṅgama-samādhisūtra* is one of the sources with detailed descriptions of these realms and their sub-realms (*Suraṅgama-samādhisūtra*, 2003).

One who is liberated from suffering is called an *arhat*. One progresses to the state of *arhat* through the union of insight meditation (*vipaśyanā*) and calm-abiding (*samatā*), by cultivating wisdom regarding the true nature of a person—*anātma*.

A person (*bodhisattva*) on the path to complete awakening (*sambodhi*) needs to remove the veil of knowable in addition to veil of afflictions. Removal of all the stains of *vāsanā* is essential for this. This can be achieved only through working with the projections of functional consciousness to actively modify *vāsanā*. Thus the path of progress of a *bodhisattva* is different from that of an *arhat*. It requires compassionate engagement (*upāya*) with the world along with insight (*prajñā*) into the true nature of all phenomena. These two necessarily need to go hand-in-hand, since the realisation of subtler levels of interdependence and enriched levels of compassion through post-meditational periods, and the realisation of deeper levels of emptiness through meditation, support each other. Through gradual coalescing of meditative and post-meditative experiences, one completely wipes out stains of *vāsanā*. This results in the irreversible abandonment of *ālaya* that structures experiences through past habits, and in a direct experience of truth "as it is". Then there is wisdom co-emergent with every sprout of experience. The eightfold collection of the ordinary personality transforms into the pristine wisdom that is ever-fresh.

Every human being, at some point in his life, does realise the reality of one's perishability, and is then forced to ask that big question: what is life? Most of us, unaware of the answer, suppress the question itself by keeping ourselves occupied in the different pursuits in life, distracting ourselves from the truths of our existence (Dhar, 2011).

According to Loy (2008), the never-ending sense of disease that humans suffer from with the suppression of not just the fear of extinction of oneself at death, but with the "uncomfortable sense of unreality at our core". This repression then manifests as something that is lacking or missing in life—be it money, power, authority, belongingness, enjoyment, fame, or love—it seems to give us a sense of something lacking for which we make intense efforts to fill in the gaps. The Buddha offers a way out of the anxiety occurring as a result of the missing things in life, that is, to confront it. Facing the reality of the unrealness of the self is the way out of suffering from anxiety. Practically, this is done by merely observing the interplay of the body and the mind, the five aggregates, without any craving or aversion. The repeated act of confronting our habitual patterns of thinking, feeling, and acting, ultimately begins to break down the instinctive entity we call "I". Hence, we begin to free ourselves from the tentacles of living in the illusion created by the false "self" (Dhar, 2011).

Jātaka Tales and Other Buddhist Stories

In 300 BC, the Jātaka tales were written for the mankind to gain knowledge and morality. Ever since, Jātaka tales have become story books that are both enjoyable as well as knowledgeable. Originally written in Pāli language Jātaka Buddhist tales have been translated in different languages around the world.

The luminous fables of Jātaka are intended to impart values of self-sacrifice, morality, honesty and other informative values to people. No less than 547 in number, Jātaka tales are an important part of Buddhist literature.

The word jātaka (pronounced *Jah-ta-ka*) means birth. The Jātaka tales are of over 500 stories said to have been told by the Buddha to his followers to illustrate his teachings. They are stories about his former lives, sometimes as an animal, for example, The Hare's Sacrifice, Banyan the Deer or The Monkey King.

They are a useful way to introduce Buddhist ethics and have been retold through the ages. Each story emphasises a particular moral point using the six perfections: generosity, patience, moral discipline, enthusiasm or determination, concentration and wisdom. All the stories illustrate the key Buddhist teaching that "Actions have Consequences".

Jātaka stories represent former incarnations of Buddha, at times like an animal, a bird and sometimes like a human being, the future Siddhārtha Gautam. The setting of the stories is made in or near Beneras (Varanasi), which is a holy city in north central India. Some of the popular story/tale from Jātaka collection are provided here.

An excellent collection of Jātaka tales which could be used as a basis for telling the stories is:

The Hungry Tigress
Siddhārtha and the Swan
The Monkey King

The Lion and the Jackal
The King and the Goat and many more.

Here we would be discussing about The Monkey King.

The Monkey King and the Mangoes:

Once upon a time, the Buddha came into the world as a Monkey King and ruled over 80,000 monkeys. In his kingdom on the banks of the Ganges River, there was a mango tree. The 80,000 monkeys jumped from branch to branch chattering and eating the fruit that was big and sweet. Sometimes a ripe mango fell into the river.

One day, the Monkey King strolled downstream and came upon a river palace where a human king lived. "Soon danger will come if the mangoes float downstream", he told the monkeys. "Pick all the mangoes and flowers on the trees and take them deep into the forest."

But one mango, hidden by a bird's nest, was left unseen by the 80,000 monkeys. When it was large and ripe, it fell into the river and floated downstream where the human king was bathing. The human king was very curious and tasted the mango. "This is delicious!" he exclaimed. "I must have more servants, find all the mangoes and bring them to me at once!"

Deep in the forest, the servants found hundreds of mango trees. In the trees were the 80,000 monkeys. When the human king heard about this he was angry, "The monkeys are eating my mangoes. Kill them all!" he ordered his archers. The archers chased the monkeys to the edge of the forest where they came to a deep cliff. There was no way for the monkeys to escape. Shivering with fright, they ran to the Monkey King and asked, "What shall we do?"

"Don't be afraid. I will save you", said their king. Quickly, he stretched his huge body as far as possible and made a bridge over the cliff to a bamboo grove on the other side. "Come monkeys, run across my back to the bamboo grove", he called and that is how he helped 80,000 monkeys to escape.

Forgetting about the mangoes, the human king went back to his palace by the river and ruled kindly and wisely for the rest of his life the Buddha was a great storyteller and often told stories to get his message across. Stories were also told about the Buddha by his followers both to explain and understand the *dharma*.

Source: http://hmindia.blogspot.in/2008/07/ack-012-013jataka-tales-monkey-stories 3808.html

Buddhism.....Meditation

Learning Outcomes

Readers will be introduced to the skill of meditation.

Explain to the readers that we mainly use our left brain to comprehend things. Today we will learn to use our right brain, our intuitive side. For Buddhists activity isn't everything—action needs to be balanced with times of inactivity, that being still is as significant as "doing". Buddhists believe that developing positive thoughts, concentration and kind wishes is extremely powerful.

Explain that the main skill a Buddhist tries to learn is control of the mind through meditation:

Meditation means "making the mind familiar". The purpose of meditation is mental development—to remove unhelpful states of mind (anger, greed, hatred) and to cultivate wholesome states of mind. When the mind is concentrated, like a mental laser, it can be focused directly onto the nature of things.

One should sit crosslegged on the floor or upright in a chair—relaxed but alert with straight backs, eyes slightly open, and quietly concentrating on their breath to calm down.

Guide them through a simple breath awareness meditation by focusing on the "in" and "out" of breathing:

Your posture should be alert, relaxed, comfortable. Close your eyes.

Focus on your breathing, follow your breath going in and your breath going out.

Feel your breath going in and out of your nostrils.

Guide them through a simple breath awareness meditation by focusing on the "in and out" of breathing

Your posture should be alert, relaxed, comfortable. Close your eyes.

Focus on your breathing, follow your breath going in and your breath going out.

Feel your breath going in and out of your nostrils.

Notice the cold air as you breathe in and the warm air as you breathe out.

Focus on your breath entering and leaving your body. When thoughts come, return the focus to your breath. Extend the length of your out breath.

Count your breaths as you breathe out. Count to 3 breaths and then start at one again.

As you breathe out imagine exhaling anxiety, tension, negativity, obstacles, distractions in the form of black smoke.

As you breathe in, imagine inhaling goodness, energy, warmth, comfort, peace, strength in the form of pure white light.

As you breathe out—breath out all the obstacles to getting what you hope for and as you breathe in breath in all you hope for in life.

We are now going to finish this meditation.

Wriggle your toes and fingers and feel yourself back in the room.

Eventually use a loving kindness meditation such as:

Your posture should be alert, relaxed, comfortable. Close your eyes.

Focus on your breathing, follow your breath going "in" and "out".

Notice cold air as you breathe in and warm air as you breathe out.

Focus on your breath entering and leaving your body. When thoughts come, return the focus to your breath.

Imagine a warm glow of loving kindness like a sun at your heart.

Feel this warm, friendly feeling towards yourself, accepting yourself, and make wishes for yourself. May I be well, may I be happy, may things go well for me.

Extend the feelings and wishes to a close friend.

Imagine the friend, imagine the warm glow reaching out to them.

May they be well, may they be happy, may things go well for them.

Extend the feelings and wishes to a stranger, someone you neither like nor dislike.

Imagine the stranger, imagine the warm glow reaching out to them.

May they be well, may they be happy, may things go well for them.

Extend the feelings and wishes to someone you do not get on with, someone who annoys or upsets you. Imagine this person you dislike, imagine the warm glow reaching out to them.

May they be well, may they be happy, may things go well for them.

Imagine the warm glow reaching out to all directions so it fills the room, building, neighborhood, country and universe. May all beings be happy.

After meditation debrief by asking:

What was the experience like for you?

Was your level of awareness any different from normal?

Were there any tensions in your body? Did they increase or decrease?

Did you find it difficult or easy to keep your mind following the instructions?

Did any thing in particular strike your attention?

How do you feel now? What do you think about when you are quiet?

What is there about this exercise that makes it of value for religious people?

References

Albahari, M. (2006). *Analytical Buddhism: The Two-tiered Illusion of Self.* Palgrave.

Albahari, M. (2014). "Insight Knowledge of no Self in Buddhism: An Epistemic Analysis." *Philosophers' Imprint, 14*: 1-30.

Austin, J.H. (1998). *Zen and the Brain.* Cambridge, MA: The MIT Press.

________ (2006). *Zen-brain Reflections.* The MIT Press.

________ (2009). *Selfless Insight.* The MIT Press.

Benoit, H. (1990). *Zen and the Psychology of Transformation.* Inner Traditions.

Bodhi, B. (2000a). *The Connected Discourses of the Buddha* (A Translation of the Saṁyutta Nikāya). Wisdom Publications.

— (2000b). *The Connected Discourses of the Buddha* (A Translation of the Saṁyutta Nikāya). Wisdom Publications.

Brown, D.P. and J. Engler (1986). "The Stages of Mindfulness Meditation". In K. Wilber, J. Engler and D. Brown (Eds.), *Transformations of Consciousness*. Shambhala.

Carrington, P. and H. Ephron (1975). "Meditation and Psychoanalysis". *Journal of the American Academy of Psychoanalysis, 3:* 43-57.

Cassaniti, J.L. (2014). *Buddhism and Positive Psychology*, pp. 101-24. https://doi.org/10.1007/978-94-017-8950-9_6

Claxton, G. (Ed.). (1986). *Beyond Therapy: The Impact of Eastern Religion on Psychological Theory and Practice.* Wisdom Publications.

Collins, S. (1982). *Selfless Persons: Imagery and Thought in Theravāda Buddhism.* Cambridge University Press.

Conze, E. (1959a). *Buddhism: Its Essence and Development.* Harper & Row.

— (1959b). *Buddhist Scriptures* (Trans.). Penguin Books.

Csikszentmihalyi, M. (1990). *Flow: The Psychology of Optimal Experience.* Harper and Row.

Dalai Lama (1995a). *The Path to Enlightenment.* Snow Lion.

________ (1995b). *The Power of Compassion.* Thorsons.

________ (2005). *The Many Ways to Nirvana.* Mobius.

________ *et al.* (1991). *Mind Science.* Boston: Wisdom.

Damasio, A. (1994). Descartes' Error: Emotion, Reason and the Human Brain. Avon Books.

Dambrun, M. and M. Ricard (2011). "Self-centeredness and Selflessness: A Theory of Self-based Psychological Functioning and Its Consequences for Happiness. *Review of General Psychology, 15*: 138-57. https://doi:10.1037/a0023059

Deshimaru, T. (1985). *Questions to a Zen Master.* Dutton.

— (1987). *The Ring of the Way: Testament of a Zen Master.* Dutton.

— (1991). *The Zen Way to Martial Arts.* Arcana.

Dhar, P.L. (2011). "No I, No Problems: The Quintessence of Buddhist Psychology of Awakening". *Psychological Studies, 56*(4): 398-403. https://doi.org/10.1007/s 12646-011-0111-0

Engler, J. (1986). "Therapeutic Aims in Psychotherapy and Meditation". In K. Wilber, J. Engler & D. Brown (Eds.), *Transformations of Consciousness*. Shambhala.

— (1993). "Becoming Somebody and Nobody: Psychoanalysis and Buddhism". In R. Walsh & F. Vaughan (Eds.), *Paths Beyond Ego.* Tarcher.

Frager, R., and J. Fadiman (2013). "Zen and Buddhist Tradition". In F. Robert, & F. James (Eds.), *Personality and Personal Growth.* (7th edn., pp. 354-381). Pearson.

Fromm, E. (1970). "Psychoanalysis and Zen Buddhism". In D.T. Suzuki, E. Fromm, & R. de Marino (Eds.), *Zen Buddhism and Psychoanalysis.* New York: Harper & Row.

— (1992). "Neurophysiological Speculations on Zen Enlightenment". *Journal of Mind and Behavior, 13:* 163-70.

Giles, J. (1993). "The No-self Theory, Hume, Buddism and Personal Identity". *Philosophy East and West, 43*: 175-200. https://doi:10.2307/1399612

Goleman, D. (1988). *The Meditative Mind.* Tarcher.

Hanh, T.N. (1976). *The Miracle of Mindfulness.* Beacon Press.

________ (1987). *Being Peace.* Parallax Press.

________ (1988). *The Heart of Understanding.* Parallax Press.

________ (1992). *Touching Peace.* Berkeley, CA: Parallax Press.

________ (1993). *The Blossoming of a Lotus.* Beacon Press.

________ (1996). *Cultivating the Mind of Love.* Parallax Press.

________ (1998). *The Heart of the Buddha's Teaching.* Parallax Press.

________ (2001[0]). *Essential Writings,* Robert Ellsberg (Ed.). Orbis Books

Hwang, K.K. and J. Chang (2009). "Self-cultivation Culturally Sensitive Psychotherapies in Confucian Societies". *Counselling Psychology, 37*: 1010-32. https://doi:10.1177/0011000009339976

Joshanloo, M. (2014). "Eastern Conceptualizations of Happiness: Fundamental Differences with Western Views". *Journal of Happiness Studies, 15*: 475-93. https://doi:10.1007/s10902-013-9431-1

Kabat-Zinn, J. (1990). *Full Catastrophe Living.* New York: Delacorte.

________ (1994). *Wherever You Go, There You Are.* New York: Hyperion.

Katagiri, D. (1988). *Returning to Silence: Zen Practice in Daily Life.* Shambhala.

Kelly, B.D. (2008). "Buddhist Psychology, Psychotherapy and the Brain: A Critical Introduction". *Transculural Psychiatry, 45*: 5-30. https://doi:10.1177/1363461 507087996

Klein, S.B. (2014). "Sameness and the Self: Philosophical and Psychological Considerations". *Frontiers in Psychology, 5*(29). https://doi:10.3389/fpsyg. 2014. 00029

Lal, P. (1967). *The Dhammapada* (Trans.). Farrar, Straus & Giroux.

Loori, J. D. (2002). *The Art of Just Sitting: Essential Writings on the Zen Practice of Shikentanza.* Wisdom Publishing.

Loy, D.R. (2008). *Money, Sex, War, Karma: Notes for a Buddhist Revolution.* Wisdom Publications.

MacKenzie, M. (2010). "Enacting the Self: Buddhist and Enactivist Approaches to the Emergence of the Self". *Phenomenology and the Cognitive Sciences, 9*: 75-99. https://doi:10.1007/s11097-009-9132-8

Mageo, J. (Ed.) (2002). *Power and the Self.* Cambridge University Press.

Manne-Lewis, J. (1986). "Buddhist Psychology: A Paradigm for the Psychology of Enlightenment". In G. Claxton (Ed.), *Beyond Therapy.* Wisdom.

Markus, H. & S. Kitayama (1991). "Culture and the Self". *Psychological Review, 98*(2): 224.

Mosig, Y. (1990, Spring). "Wisdom and Compassion: What the Buddha Taught". *Platte Valley Review,* 51-62.

Murphy, M. & S. Donovan (1988). *The Physical and Psychological Effects of Meditation.* San Rafael, CA: Esalen Institute.

Nanamoli, B. & B. Bodhi (1995). *The Middle Length Discourses of the Buddha* (A Translation of the *Majjhima Nikaya*). Wisdom Publications.

Pearsall, P. (2003). *The Beethoven Factor: The New Positive Psychology of Hardiness, Happiness, Healing and Hope.* Hampton Roads Publishing.

Perls, F. (1969). *Gestalt Therapy Verbatim.* Real People Press.

Ramaswami, S. & A. Sheikh (1989). "Buddhist Psychology: Implications for Healing". In A. Sheikh & K. Sheikh (Eds.), *Eastern and Western Approaches to Healing.* Wiley.

Reynolds, D. (1980). *The Quiet Therapies.* University of Hawaii.

________ (1984). *Playing Ball on Running Water.* Morrow.

________ (1993). *Plunging Through the Clouds.* State University of New York.

Shiah, Y.J. (2016). "From Self to Nonself: The Nonself Theory". *Frontiers in Psychology*, *7*: 112. https://doi.org/10.3389/fpsyg.2016.00124

Shiah, Y.J. and K.T. Yit (2012). "Adopting the Buddhist Concept of Nature of Death and Life Impermanence in Investigating the Death Terror". *Indigenous Psychological Research Journal of China, 36*: 167-89. https://doi:10.6254/2012.38.167

Shonin, E., W. Van Gordon and M.D. Griffiths (2014). "The Emerging Role of Buddhism in Clinical Psychology: Toward Effective Integration". *Psychology of Religion and Spirituality*, *6*: 123-37. https://doi:10.1037/a0035859

Soeng, M. (1991). *Heart Sutra: Ancient Buddhist Wisdom in the Light of Quantum Reality*. Primary Point.

Shapiro, D. (1980). *Meditation: Self-regulation Strategy and Altered States of Consciousness.* Aldine.

Shapiro, D. & R. Walsh (Eds.). (1984). *Meditation: Classic and Contemporary Perspectives.* Aldine.

Sheng-yen (1987). *The Advantages One May Derive from Zen Meditation.* Dharma Drum.

Shweder, R.A. and E.J. Bourne (1984). "Does the Concept of the Person Vary Cross-culturally?" In R.A. Shweder & R.A. LeVine (Eds.), *Culture Theory: Essays on Mind, Self, and Emotion,* pp. 158-99, Cambridge University Press.

Stolaroff, M.J. (1999). "Are Psychedelics Useful in the Practice of Buddhism?", *Journal of Humanistic Psychology* , *39*(1): 60-80.

Suraṅgama-samādhisūtra (2003). (Trans. E. Lamotte & S. Boin–Webb) *Suraṅgamasamādhisūtra: The Concentration of Heroic Progress.* New Delhi: Motilal Banarsidass (Date of original text uncertain).

Suzuki, S. (1997). *Branching Streams Flow in the Darkness: Zen Talks on the Sandokai.* University of California Press.

Suzuki, S. (2002). *Not Always So: Practicing the True Spirit of Zen.* HarperCollins.

Tsong-Kha-Pa (2000). *The Great Treatise on the Stages of the Path to Enlightenment* (Trans. T. Lamrin Chenmo Translation Committee). Snow Lion Publications.

Wallace, B.A. and S.L. Shapiro (2006). "Mental Balance and Well-being: Building Bridges between Buddhism and Western Psychology". *American Psychology*, *61*: 690-701. https://doi: 10.1037/0003-066x.61.7.690

8

The Islamic Way of Life and Sufism

The word "Islam" is an Arabic word which means "submission to the will of God". This word comes from the same root as the Arabic word *salām* which means "peace". Islam is seen as a natural religion in all its true senses. It is the message to which the entire community of God's Prophets and messengers has been exposed. Pure Monotheism is the message brought by all the God's Prophet like Jesus, Noah, Muhammad, Abraham, and Moses. People many a times believe that Prophet Muhammad was the founder of Islam but that is not true, he was the final prophet of Islam. Abraham was one of the earliest and the greatest of Prophets in Islam. God made his convention with Abraham, which he fulfilled years later by revealing his final message to Muhammad. This was the everlasting, ceaseless and a universal message for all of humanity.

Abraham's life and he himself could be seen as a soaring example of someone who submitted himself to God fully and submerged in Him totally without any expectations. Scholars believe that the path of Islam is same as the way of living of Prophet Abraham as the portrayal of Abraham by Quran and Bible is that of a believer, follower, and the biggest devotee. Islam is a very vast religion and limiting it in few teachings and beliefs is next to impossible, nevertheless, most of the religious beliefs and teachings of Islam were recognised and identified by Prophet Muhammad himself.

In short, Islam (an Arabic word meaning "peace and submission") is the name given by God Almighty (Allah) to the religion revealed by Him to the Holy Prophet Muhammad (peace and blessings of Allah be on him) through the Holy Quran. It means the attainment of peace through the surrender of one's will to the Will of Allah. One who so submits and follows the laws of Islam is called a Muslim.

Al-Quran/The Quran

The Arabic word "Al-Quran" literally means "the recitation". When this word is been used in Islam, the word means the final message of God to Prophet Muhammad, which is also called the final message for humankind. Quran in literal sense is the word of God itself. Quran is the words coming out of God and these words have a meaning, which shows the path of right living to all humankind. Quran has been conserved in terms of the spoken words and in terms of the living beings. In Arabic language, Quran is also seen as an alive wonder. Quran is incomparable to any of the sacred scriptures in terms of its form and spiritual impact. The final message of God to Prophet Muhammad was revealed in a long period of 23 years.

Many other religious books or sacred writings are been propagated by a religious group and even after many years it is seen as been written by religious cults. For Quran this has never been true and for the followers and believers of Quran it has always been seen as the Word of God.

Quran was not been revealed in close doors and in absence of people. It was completed and recited publicly and the public comprised of both Muslims and non-Muslims. The entire Quran was even written completely in the life course of Prophet Muhammad. The companions of Prophet Muhammad remembered and memorised the Quran word by word when it was being revealed. Quran is not like other scriptures; Quran has always been with people and in the hands of common believers. As Quran was been highly memorised by many, hence its conservation and preservation was perfectly done.

Unlike other sacred teachings of other religions, Quran is a scripture, which is addressed to all of humanity, for every human. It has not been related or recited to only few chosen people. The message, which Quran floats in not new, it is the message, which has long been taught to humankind, and this is to submit to one master fully and adhere only to that Almighty. The basic motto of God while revealing Quran was to teach all of humankind about the oneness within and the oneness of God. God wanted to organise the life of his children with peace and unity. Quran even contains the stories of the lives of previous prophets as well as commands and restrictions laid by God. Whenever a person gets confused, falls in the trap of doubts, he can found the solutions in Quran. The modern world fills the hearts of humans with bareness and havoc; this turmoil could be reduced by finding solutions given in Quran. Hence, it could be said that Quran is not only a book; it is the path of guidance, providing ways to deal with all the negative happening in one's life.

The Prophet Muhammad

Islam has had many founders but the final Prophet of Islam is a figure who lived his life as a historical figure and his full life and its minute details are been documented. Muslims do not only have the last message in the form of God's words but they also have conserved the sayings of Prophet Muhammad and his teachings, which is called "hadeeth" literature. Muslims never believed Prophet Muhammad to be as God, he was been seen as a man who is the chosen one by God and God chose him to provide his message to humankind. As Prophet, Muhammad never wanted Muslims to mistakenly take him as God hence he taught Muslims to refer to him as God's Slave or just his messenger. The goal of the last Prophet, which was Muhammad, was to impart the true knowledge to humans and this true knowledge was that there is nothing divine except God, so only that almighty should be worshipped. In short, God sent the disclosure to Muhammad, who in turn taught it, preached it, and put it into practice.

Prophet Muhammad was more than just a Prophet. He was a man who lived his life in the purest form, he established and showed a path of total submission to God. He not only concentrated in setting the way to almighty but he also showed how to fulfil all the duties and responsibilities of the relationships a person has in his life. He taught people what it means to be a good teacher, ruler, husband, warrior, etc. Hence, Muslims never see him as an end but a light, which leads to the end and this end, is the beginning of pure humanity. For this reason, Muslims follow him not for his own sake, but because he is seen as a human adhering to all roles given to him by God. Hence, it is easy to relate to a person following and fulfilling all his duties and roles and with that surrendering himself to God.

As other Prophets, even Prophet Muhammad faced a high degree of resistance, opposition and hounding during his mission. Nevertheless, he was a generous, wise man who never even ill-treated his enemies. He started his mission in the most remote places of the world but it spread to different places. The success of his mission could be seen from the spread of Islam from Spain to China within a hundred years of the death of Muhammad. Prophet Muhammad was the greatest of all the God's Prophet, not because he showed a different way or path of reaching to God but only because he was the last Prophet who was chosen by God and gave him message which was the golden way of living for all humanity. The way suitable for all era, all the time, places, and people. It is eternal and never ending until the Last Day.

Prophet Muhammad left two beautiful reserves for humankind: One being Holy Quran, which shows the teachings, beliefs and Islamic way of life and another his own life, which shows a person what all is to be done to become closer to one's master or originator.

He established the various stages of a person's life in the most wonderful manner: a phase of young, adult and old, for friends, family, parent, child, husband, ruler, saint, and the chief. The other Prophets in other religions, and the followers of other Prophet proclaimed them to be model for other men but only Prophet Muhammad claimed himself to be a model for all humankind.

Even Allah says in Holy Quran:

> "We have sent Prophet Muhammad as
> the messenger for all humanity.

He is the controller and chief who shows
the right path of living to people."

(a) *Core Teachings of Prophet Muhammad*

The known scholars of Islam have packed the teachings of Prophet Muhammad into few lines. These condensed statements are about every aspect of a person's life.

Some of these statements are:

1. Any action conducted is been judged by the intention and objective behind that act.
2. God in its true form is serene and pure and hence can only accept only those whose hearts and souls are unadulterated. God has given commands to his followers, those that he gave to his Prophets.
3. An observation of Islam by a true person leads to setting aside what actually concerns that person.
4. An advocate or believer becomes a true one only when he loves and wants exactly same for his brothers and sisters, what he desires for himself.
5. A person should not think of harming himself or others consciously.
6. Never focus on attaining the worldly pleasures and a person should not be concerned with what others have, then only he could be loved by God.

The Prophets have delivered the message and given right direction to humankind but Quran has also focused on the role of an Imam—a spiritual leader and a moral chief. Imams help people to maintain justice and equality in their deeds. These Imams lead their life's basing it on the teachings of Prophet. There are 12 Imams. The first after Prophet Mohammad was Imam Ali and the 12th and the last one is Imam al-Mahdi, who continuously helps his community and people to live a balanced and moral life, and brings them closer to the Almighty.

According to Quran, God teaches humankind that all people were created so that they could worship God. A true worshipper is one who longs for God consciousness. The teachings of Islam incorporate all the aspects of ethical life hence God consciousness is the ultimate aim, which is to be achieved by all humans. Islam suggested that all acts of worship should be directed to only Almighty and these acts should be done in accordance to the Islamic Laws. In Islam, worshipping is not only limited to the religious rituals, it encompasses much more.

The core beliefs of Islam and its teachings have the power of healing and curing one's soul and heart. The qualities like tranquillity, endurance, authenticity, charity, and sympathy are encouraged in a person. With it, Islam also condemns arrogance and superiority as Islam says that only Almighty could govern and judge the human acts.

Islam has never seen humans as born sinful. It sees man as having ability of doing both good and bad, being evil and saint.

(b) *Islam for a Better Life*

It should be seen that Islam like Buddhism, spoke about getting free from all desires and opting a path of morality and happiness. A person in Islam is seen to be developed to transcend his consciousness, as self-control and purity is a way for reaching a wholesome life which is attained by transcending the consciousness and becoming one with the Almighty.

Islam directs the life of its followers by emphasising on three important areas:

(a) Usul al-Din (it is also known as Religious Beliefs)
(b) Furu al-Din (it is also known as Religious Practice)
(c) Akhlaq and Adab (it is also known as Religious Ethics)

The two most respected sources of Islamic teachings in these three areas are Holy Quran, which for Muslims is the Book of God, which consists of God's message to his people. The message which brings all together and unites everyone. The other one is Sunna, the exemplary conduct of the Prophet and his virtuous successors to the prophetic mission. Quran provides the way of living and Sunna elaborates on the revelations provided in Quran.

Sunna provides details of every deed and actions performed by Prophet Muhammad and the Prophets who lived before him. The life's of these Prophets and the way they lived their lives teaches a whole lot to the followers. The narratives, stories helps the follower to lead life as it is meant to be lived and help the person to achieve a spiritual and morally well balanced life. The narratives, which carried these elaborations and information are designated as Hadith. Many Muslim Scholars in the nineteenth century developed an intricate and detailed system of classification of these Hadith. This was been done to maintain and enhance the reliability and validity of these information and also to extract from them the practices, actions, beliefs, duties, rights, and ethics to maintain a healthy and well-balanced community consisting of reasonable and impartial beings.

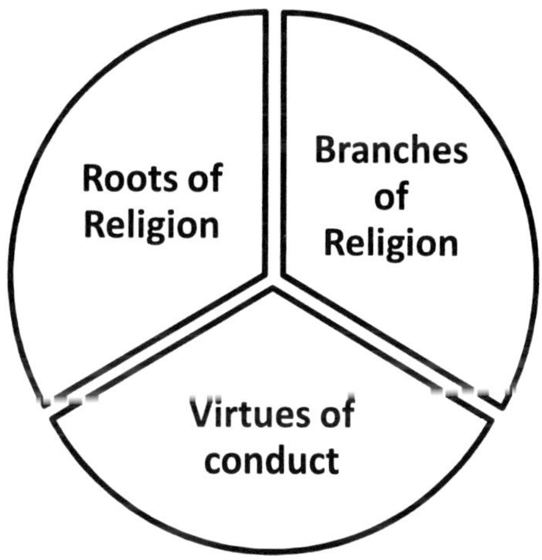

Fig. 8.1: Direction given by Islam to its followers

Beliefs, Practices, and Teachings of Islam

It is difficult to limit all of Islam into a few core values. Nevertheless, the most important beliefs and religious practices were identified by Prophet Muhammad himself. Thus, there is general agreement on them among all Muslims.

Additionally, Muslim scholars, past and present, have also identified and in certain cases agreed on the core teachings of the Quran, of Prophet Muhammad, and the “essentials” of Islamic Law (Shariah).

(a) *Core Islamic Beliefs: Six Articles of Faith*

More than a billion Muslims share a common set of fundamental beliefs that are described as "Articles of Faith". These articles of faith form the foundation of Islamic belief system and make the base of a person's life, his *mantra* for living, his perceptions about himself and his understanding about others around:

- **(i)** *Belief in One God (Tawhid):* Affirming belief in Divine Unity—the oneness of God. Islam teaches that only God should be worshipped and no other being should be kept at the place of God. If other beings are worshipped then it is a sinful act.
- **(ii)** *Belief in Angels:* God created unseen beings called angels who has a positivity attached to them. They are created with a purpose to manage and keep a check on the kingdom of everyone's ruler, which is Almighty. These angels are always present around us. They record our deeds and actions.
- **(iii)** *Belief in Prophets of God (Nubuwwah):* Belief in the necessity of prophets to guide humanity. Islam teaches that God could not be present everywhere so he gave the task of communicating his message to his people through Prophets. These Prophets are many like Abraham, Jesus, etc. and the last one was Prophet Muhammad. He all proposed that there is only one God, which is to be devoted and worshipped by all.
- **(iv)** *Belief in Revealed Books of God (Imamah):* Belief in the continuation of guidance through the line of Imams as rightly guided successors of the Prophet. Muslims believe that God's wisdom is collected in form of his words and these words are the teachings and beliefs, which God wanted his followers to understand and follow. For Muslim's Quran is the God's final revelation to Prophet Muhammad and it has been fully conserved.
- **(v)** *Belief in Day of Judgment (Maad):* Belief in resurrection to account for one's deeds on the Day of Judgement. God has set a particular day where everything would come to an end. Everyone would face death on that day. On this

day, every person would be evaluated for his actions. Those people who do good actions are evaluated in a positive light and the wrongdoers would be punished by God. One who is good is rewarded by heaven and the wrongdoers get hell.

(vi) *Belief in Destiny and Divine Decree (Adl):* Belief in the Divine Justice—the attribute that guarantees that all humans will be treated equally as God's creatures, and that all humans are endowed with the conscience to distinguish the right from the wrong.

Muslims believe that since God is the Sustainer of all life, nothing happens except by His Will and with His full knowledge. This belief does not contradict the idea of free will. God does not force anyone, the choices of each person are known to God beforehand because His knowledge is complete. This recognition helps the believer through difficulties and hardships.

The core beliefs make it clear that the oneness of God, believe in the Last Day, where everything would smash away and being in control of God's will leads the development of one's self in Islam.

Everything happens in the background and Allah is all around so to achieve a pure soul or to understand and develop one self, it is important to understand the importance of pure divine, the morality, happiness, and purity in heart which could be spread out to others.

(b) *The "Pillars" of Islam*

In Islam, worship is part of daily life and is not limited to mere rituals. The formal acts of worship are known as the five "pillars" of Islam. There are five simple but essential observances that all practising Muslims should accept and follow according to Islam. These "Pillars of Islam" represent the core that unites all Muslims.

(i) *The Declaration of Faith (Shahadah)*

The "Declaration of Faith" is the statement, *la ilaha illa allah wa muhammad rasul-ullah*, meaning "There is no deity worthy of being worship except God (Allah), and Muhammad is the Messenger (Prophet) of God". This declaration is known as the *shahadah* (witness, testimony). Allah is the Arabic name for God. By making this simple proclamation, one becomes a Muslim.

This above declaration shows Islam's wholesome belief in the oneness of God. He is the only one who is to be worshipped. Nothing else is comparable to God and if it is been done than that act would be sinful.

Quran says in this regard:

> "Almighty never forgives any person who relates something or someone with God.
> Anyone who provides partner to God has done wrongful act. This act or action leads to punishment from the side of God."

The second part of the testimony of faith states that Muhammad is a Prophet of God like Jesus, Abraham, etc. Muhammad is the most important among all of them. He brought the final revelation to the people. He brought the message of God to humankind. With it Muhammad's life served as a role model for all of humanity. A believer, who follows Muhammad's example of living life, shows the prominence of Islam on good action and practices.

(ii) *The Prayer (Salah)*

In the scenario of the continuous stress of world, family and surrounding, the believer can keep one's mind calm only by worshipping five times a day: at daybreak, noon, mid-afternoon, sunset and evening. It helps in concentrating on the spiritual path and dependency on Almighty. The prayers consist of standing, bowing, kneeling, putting the forehead on the ground, and sitting. The prayer acts as a means to connect the follower with his creator. The prayer includes passages from Quran, prayers for mercy. The prayer is also the expression of humility, submission, and admiration for God. The prayer should be conducted in a clean place, at mosque or home, indoors or outdoors. When done together the prayer portrays unity, togetherness, brotherhood, and equality. As Muslims pray, they pray by facing Mecca, the holy city centered around the Kaaba—Home of Allah build by Abraham. These prayers help Muslims in being united with that

Almighty and in peace with oneself morally and spiritually.

Prayers have a therapeutic effect on Muslims. For them prayers remove illness or psychological problems like fear, depression, anxiety, pain, etc. Therefore, prayer helps to restore the positive energy and serenity of heart, soul, and mind.

(iii) *The Compulsory Charity (Zakah)*

Islam believes that God owns everything. This is only God's Grace that He has trust in people and provides wealth to them. *Zakah* is a form of thanksgiving to God where a person supports and helps the poor ones. It is been believed that wealth if shared then it becomes purified. A person is required to contribute 2.5 per cent of one's money and assets to others. Therefore, *zakah* is an obligation on those who have wealth. It is for poor and the needy ones use it. Hence, in Islam, it is the duty of the wealthy to help the poor and needy.

It is very important to understand that for Muslims, charity or giving away a portion of their money to the needy forms a very important part of their living. It is their belief in the just world, where all are equal, which makes them.

(iv) *The Fast of Ramadan (Sawm)*

During the period of Ramadan, which is, the ninth month of the Islamic lunar calendar is spend in fasting. For Muslims this period of fasting is sacred and pure. In this period Muslims, from dawn to sunset do not eat, drink and indulge in sexual activity. This fasting helps Muslims to develop calmness and spiritual connection between God and oneself. During this period families rise before dawn to take their meal. This period shows the level of self-control and hence helps in building control over the urges and pleasures. This period makes the Muslims learn about the sympathetic behaviour towards others and value those who have little to eat. The month of Ramadan ends with one of the two major Islamic celebrations, the Feast of the Breaking of the Fast, called Eid-al-Fitr, which is a joyful festival where people wear new clothes, visit others, and exchange gifts with others.

(v) *The Fifth Pillar is the Pilgrimage (Hajj to Mecca)*

A Muslim who is fit physically and has enough money and time is required to leave the comforts of his life to go to the Hajj pilgrimage. This trip means surrendering oneself totally in the service of God. This is the wish of every Muslim to make a trip to the Pilgrimage at least once. This scared site is situated in Saudi Arabia. For a Muslim this is the spiritual journey, which conjoins the soul of a person with that Almighty.

Every year over two million believers from a diversity of cultures and languages travel from all over the world to the sacred city of Mecca to respond to God's call.

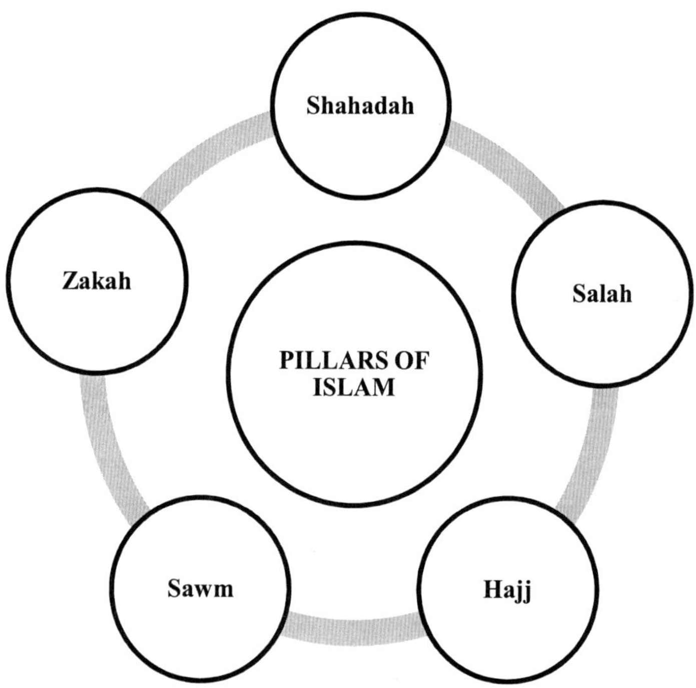

Fig. 8.2: Five Pillars of Islam

(c) *Surah-al-Fatihah: Core of the Quran*

The first chapter of Quran which is Surah Al-Fatihah, is been seen as the core of Quran by many scholars. Whenever a formal prayer is conducted, it is recited in the Arabic language. Its translation is as follows:

"A person always begins with the name of the God,
My Lord is the Most Generous.
His name benefits all of us.
The praises and gratitude is only for that Almighty.
He is the Lord for everyone and everything in the world.
He is the most lenient and forgiving.
He is the only one whom we all worship
And upon Him lays the task of saving
us and hence we ask for His help
whenever we come across a fix.
You Almighty be our torchbearer, You take us to
the path of unity, the path of Islam.
Bless us all as You have done before.
Show us the path You have shown to Your blessed ones
and not of those who You have moved away from
Yourself."

(d) *Core of Islamic Law or Shariah*

The human race deals with continuous inner pressure, conflicts, tension, and stresses, which are led due to refutation of reality (*kufr*) and destruction of moral being and its consciousness. Human beings do not understand their own inner potentials. To make them realise and understand about their actual strengths, God sends Prophets, to make human remind of their convention with God. From the beginning of the history, nearly 124,000 Prophets were born and sent by God. Out of these five are regarded as the messengers of God. These are Jesus, Moses, Noah, Muhammad, and Abraham. They were been send on earth to collect the people and bind them into one force by providing them the path of guidance which is revealed by God. As the Prophets show the right path and right direction, hence they become the role models for their followers. They assist their followers to build an ethical society and live in peace with all. This practical assistance takes the form of Religious Laws, the Shariah, which is been evaluated and continuously expanded to make it relevant and match in all times.

The Islamic Law believes in conservation and protection of:

(a) Family,
(b) Wealth,
(c) Religion,
(d) Life,
(e) Mind,
(f) Justice or Liberty.

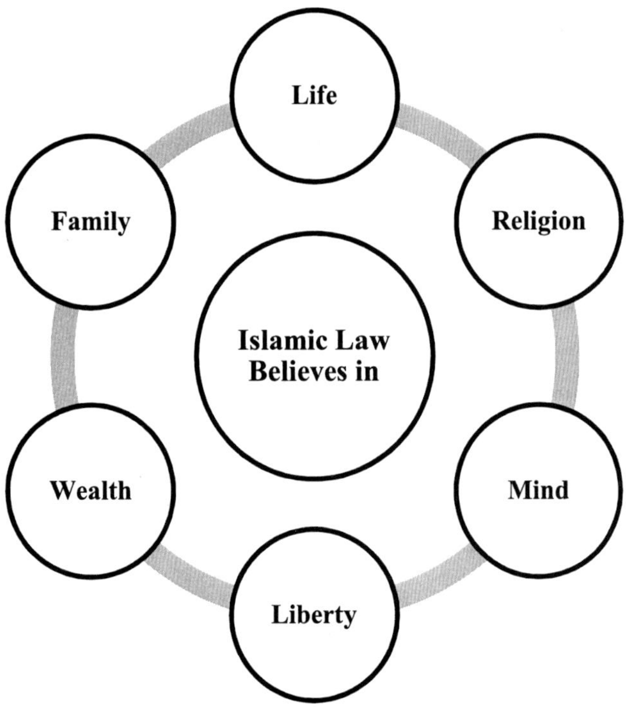

Fig. 8.3: Islamic Law

Islam values the life given by God, the Family and the mind, which leads to a positive path of life. For any person, the growth and development depends on the perception and treatment of people who are important to him, this is, the family. Hence being or become someone depends on how important others value you and how that value affects your own belief system about yourself.

Family, religion, mind, justice, and wealth are the forms which make the category of "essentials" according to Islam, as they are necessary for the welfare of the human community as a whole. So, the core of Islam in the smallest line could be explained as "Islam, the word itself has many meanings embedded in it: to be close, give out, devote, and submit to God his life forever".

Self, Spirit, and Soul: Perspectives of Islam and Sufism

The word "self" forms an important part of postmodern scholarly discourse in literature, religion, and space. Seemingly unambiguous, though, it is difficult to define. When juxtaposing the self and/or selfhood with Islam we encounter uncertainty with what the relationship is between the self and Islam. In the mystical traditions, reference to the self can signal the worldly desire against which the mystic-in-training must discipline him or herself to achieve a higher state of devotion to the Divine.

The term "self" is in closer correspondence with the Quranic term *nafs*. The Quran has used this word many times and in many forms (255 times)—*nafsun* and in other forms like *anfusakum*, *nafsene* and *nafasun*. It has numerous meanings. Tajul Uroos, a Sufi scholar, writes that this word is used normally to denote the total personality of a person. It also means intellect, knowledge, and mind. (Taj and Lis' anul Arab). It is also used in the meaning of blood, *nifasn* which pours out after the birth of a child (*taj*). *Nafasun* also means, "breath" and its plural is *anfasun*, Ibn-i-Faris says that its basic meanings are light and soft air. It also means a nice thing, which attracts a person.

In easy language *nafs* can be understood as "self", "soul" or "being". It is the essence of being human.

Connectedness Between Mind, Self, Soul, Spirit

The concepts of mind, self, soul, spirit, and happiness are closely related in the Holy Quran. They are interconnected, in the sense that understanding them individually cannot be complete without understanding how they are related to each other.

As human beings, we are elated over a lot of God's creations because of our ability to collect, process, and use data in a good way, by choice.

The human body is just an instrument that incubates and sustains the brain, which houses the human mind, from which the self develops and evolves throughout a person's lifetime on earth.

God Almighty started the process when He installed an essential part from His spirit in the human brain. This is what allows and enables the human self to start a life-long process of data collection, processing, and decision making while having the ability to differentiate between good and evil.

When the body dies, when it is no longer capable of sustaining the self, whether by old age, sickness, or accidental injury, then records of the human self are completed by angels.

In the hereafter, the self is going to be judged on the basis of its performance on earth. If it is obedient to God in its behaviour, it will be living in happiness in this life and in the hereafter. But, if the human self is disobedient to God, it suffers in its earthen life and in the hereafter.

To sum up, goodness is obedience to God and evil is disobedience to Him. Success or failure, in the Islamic sense, is in how you conduct yourself during the process.

Translators of the Holy Quran generally use the word "*soul*" as a translation for the Arabic word *nafs!* Sociologists use another term, "*self*", to refer to the body of knowledge, which is selected from the mind in a developmental process to form a unique identity for a living person.

For many religious scholars, the word "soul" has been used to explain a person's left over uniqueness after his death rather than his existence during his living. Hence, when we are alive our self-handles our performance on the Mother Earth whereas after dying, the soul which is the self existent after death takes care of the performances after death. The outcome, which this self after death (soul) faces in the form of rewards or punishments, is based on the conduction of self during its earthen performance.

Quran mentions self or *nafs* in different colours. Some portray self during its life and others after life.

A specific term has also been related to this word by Quran, which is "Human Personality". The Quranic concept of life relates to this term quite often. Deen-ul-Islam has this term at its very base. It sees *nafs* as not been extinct as the person dies. It is born with the person, prosper as the person lives his life, and stay alive after death. Therefore, it needs to be nourished to enable it to develop according to the evolutionary process. There are many laws and rules mentioned in Quran, according to which this whole process of nourishment should be enabled.

Many different characteristics of self are been mentioned in Quran. These could help in development of a complete picture of self, highlighting its capacity, capability, and its nature. Some of these are:

1. The self-moves to different phases and is influenced by the liabilities to which it is been uncovered, changes does occur but the total transformation of it to something else never happens. It starts its journey from a state of non-development or underdevelopment but with immense power, energy, and potentialities. It should not be perceived as a static material, which is affected and shaped by external factors, instead it is dynamic and active in nature. In highest sense, its activity is called *dini* activity, which means transformation and actualisation of its basic characteristics and transformation leads it much closer to the Most Perfect Self, that is, God. Through this development the humans self tastes the bliss and connectivity with God. Death should not be seen as a phase in this course and it does not terminate the activity of self.
2. In Quran, the self is seen as free. Freedom is a property, which is embedded in self. Although the surroundings and nature helps in its formulation, still it has potentialities to flow its own activities from within and not totally controlled by the external forces. Because the self is free, hence it acts as an agent which controls the morality. For a being, obligations and duties does have a meaning, it is already determined. As self is free that is why it is sensitive to all the demands, which are, ought

to be fulfilled. This responsibility comes from the sense of freedom. Self is capable of leading a moral life only because it is free. This shows that self has a real choice of freedom. Self could choose from many different ways and outlooks to fulfil its responsibilities and duties. But that does not mean that self enjoys an unlimited power and freedom. Its freedom is grown in the conditions around which its development occurs. The world around it keeps constraints and continuous check on different levels and degrees. The self chokes under these constraints. It can only develop in an environment of freedom. In a closely controlled society, self and its actions move on the route of contraction. Such restricted society curtails the self-expression and reduces the liberty to act in accordance to the will. Such conditions lead to decay and sufferings to self. Self can get its strength only by recapturing its freedom. The self can grow, build, and blossom in terms of thoughtful actions and deeds only in a free environment. Freedom is the essence of self and cannot be extinguished under external compulsion. The self is often choked in a strictly controlled society.

3. According to Quran, the self is never static. It has the capability to enhance, develop, and grow. With the endless power possessed by self based on its values, it continuously moves towards higher platforms of existence and being. The self works according to what it is destined to do. It develops, grows, and eventually actualises its full potential.

> Death never leads to end of existence, it only means going to higher and more powerful level of existence. According to Quran, the way to life or *din* is the path to reach higher level of living. When a person reaches the higher level of being, he feels as if the path of heaven is right in front of him. On the other hand, when a person falls to lower levels he gets the feeling that the hell is calling him and he is moving towards it.

The Quran provides a magical basket showing different levels of existence and leads to knowledge towards development of a person. A person's destiny is already been set and has been written in terms of symbols and to understand these symbols a person needs to have full understanding of his being. Whenever a person reaches to the higher level of being, these symbols unfold them in the mystical ways. If the Quran is been read and understood in depth then these symbols are unfolded and their true meanings are known.

4. Self has the competence for valuing the experience. Self is perceptive to the higher order qualities, the beautiful experiences, and values these experiences. When the self is emerged and understands its real potentials then only it is able to value experience. The value put to the experience could be at higher or lower levels. When the experience is on the higher side, it is more fulfilling and gratifying. When the self has got an understanding of itself, it starts craving for the higher order value experiences and the experiences which were rewarding till now, does no longer hold to the same level of contentment. It happens the other way round too, as the higher value experiences increases it lifts the self.
5. Self mainly grows because of its own will power, efforts and deeds. The actions self indulges in decides about its fall or rise. If the actions are immoral then falls in the outcome and if they are moral then it leads to rise. Quran Says:

   Self or *nafs* gets only what it achieves and earns and it moves to light or darkness in accordance to what it does to itself. Self gets what it gives. God never thinks of doing anything wrong with the self. It is not the God who manipulates self, it is the self, which works and the type and kind of actions it indulges into decides for the degradation or upliftment of it. External forces cannot affect self, until self itself wants to get affected, neither God does any injustice to self. So, the self is affected only by its own unjust or justified acts.

6. The self understands reality and comprehends the Divine attributes. It is been said that self should build on the qualities itself which reflects the attributes of the Divine. By building on these qualities, self becomes closer to itself and the Divine. Whenever self indulges into wrongdoing, it moves farther away from God and whenever right deeds are done self jumps one stage closer to God. Quran propagates that self becomes pure when it reaches God and this purity could only be achieved by taking the route of good actions. The Divine attributes are the end and means at the same time.

Sufism: Islam's Great Mystical Movement

Sufism is born from Islam but that does not mean that the perception of God and the way to achieve God is same for both. Sufism is a mystical movement developed out of the branches of Islam. *Suf* actually means "wool" and this is because many Sufis wore woollen garments. For Islam, God is the supreme power who controls, judges, builds, and break like a king. He is one who knows everything and is much above human thinking. Whereas for Sufism, God is everywhere, He is the beloved and to relate to Him or to reach Him, one has to be absorbed in Him. He is all and everything.

(a) *Origin of Sufism*

In its earliest form, Sufi teachings stressed that an individual should give more emphasis to the spiritual aspects of Islam, a result of many losing sight of this lofty goal of Islam. After a period of time, however, infamous Sufi elders introduced practices foreign to Islam which were welcomed by its followers. Practices introduced included dancing, playing music, and even consuming *hashish*.

The scholar Ibn al-Jawzi, wrote in his book *Talbis Iblis* about the origin of the name used by this group, saying: "They are called by this name in relation to the first person who dedicated his life to worship around the Ka'bah, whose name was Sufah." According to this, those who wanted to emulate him called themselves "Sufis". Ibn al-Jawzi also mentions another reason, he said: "they would wear woollen clothes". Wool in Arabic is called *soof* and woolen clothes were the sign of an ascetic during those times, since wool was the cheapest form of clothing and was very rough on the skin; in short it was a symbol of asceticism. In any case, the word Sufi was not present at the time of Prophet Muhammad and his companions. Instead it first appeared at about 200 Hijrah (200 years after the migration of the Prophet from Makkah to Madinah. The well-known scholar Ibn Taymiyyah), mentions that the first appearance of Sufism was in Basrah, Iraq, when same people went to extremes in worship and in avoiding the worldly life.

(b) *What Exactly is Sufism?*

Sufism is a series of concepts and practices that range from poverty, seclusion, deception, depriving the soul, singing, and dancing; and is based on a mix of many different religions and philosophies such as Greek philosophies, Zoroastrianism, Buddhism, Hinduism, as well as Islam. It has taken bits and pieces from different religions but it has born from Islam. That is why Sufis refer to them as "Islamic mysticism".

(i) *Meaning of Sufism*—The word "Sufism" is variously traced to an Arabic source (*saaf*) which means "purity" or to the Greek *sophos*, meaning wisdom. Inayat Khan, bringer of Sufism to the West in 1910, describes Sufism as a path of the heart, a path of love, and a path of oneness. Although of ancient origins, pre-dating Islam, Sufism is also an active, contemporary path. *Ruh* is spirit or breath of God, thus this a path of remembering God with every breath.

It was the mystical poet, Kabīr, who said, "Kabīr talks only about what he has lived through. If you have not lived through something, it is not true." Sufism is not a path of a book and is primarily an oral tradition, "based on experiences not premises" (Al-Ghazali— the writings of Abu Hamid Muhammad Ibn Muhammad). It is more about a way of living, a way of being in the world but not of it.

(ii) *Principles of Sufism*—"Willful and total submission to the Sheikh", is probably the motto of Sufism. From a glance, it is clear that a special and complete bond is formed between the head of the Sufi order (the "Sheikh/Teacher") and the *mureed* (follower); understanding the principles of Sufism lies in understanding its basic structure. So what is it all about? Basically, the follower takes a pledge of allegiance, whereby he pledges to obey the Sheikh, and in turn the Sheikh promises to deliver the follower from every problem or calamity that may befall him. The Sheikh also offers the sincere follower lucrative fringe benefits. Once a follower agrees, he is blessed and assigned a set of *dhikr* (chants). The follower is also to carry on with his life in a manner that is laid out by the Sufi order. If a conflict arises between his duties within the order and outside duties, the follower is to act upon the instructions of the Sheikh. In this manner, the Sheikh's hold over the follower becomes absolute. In addition, the Sheikh leads the follower towards the path of tranquillity, peace, and oneness.

The essence of Sufism consists of uplifting our spiritual dimension to a certain degree of maturity and making it receptive to the knowledge and love of the Lord, and thereby imparting onto it that certain blend required for reuniting with the Real.

The Sheikh or the chief has been given the utmost importance in Sufism, as he is the one who shows the path of liberation to a follower.

(iii) *Need of a Guide*—The guide or teacher is a very important person in Sufism. The teacher and the teachings hold an imperative bond. This learner must have total faith in the teaching and teacher per se. For a learner, it is important to understand and believe in the power of respect, surrender, will, truthfulness, forgiveness, etc. The teacher through his knowledge unchains the searcher and presents the truth in front of him. He is sometimes called Sheikh, Murshid, or Pir. There are many names attached but the work is that of bringing the learner closer to his real self.

(iv) *The path of Sufism*—God shows different ways to a man to break his worldly dreams and come closer to Him. When people get up they become a searcher, a searcher who is moving on the path of truth and Divinity. A searcher whose journey has started and this journey would lead him to the end, where the Divine is waiting. His behaviours, actions, thinking, and even emotions change. This change builds them and they begin to realise the difference between what they always felt as real and what real actually is. They start to understand the real meaning of life and for what purpose they are born on this earth. The core becomes stronger and stronger day by day and they are feeling the real depth. They could use any path but these paths lead to one end, only one reality, that is, Divinity.

To become a true traveller, it is important to break the chains of external unreality. It is the time to become the slave and surrender oneself to the Almighty.

(v) *The aim of Sufism*—The aim of the Sufi way is to impart the zest of morality onto the heart of a believer; a zest for mercy, affection, generosity, forgiveness, and gratitude.

Sufism typifies the highest aim of humankind; the objective to free each and every human being from moral defects and endow them with the attributes or moral traits of the Lord and His Messenger—upon him blessings and peace—and thereby enable them to attain to the pleasure of the Almighty. This entails that the ego be subjected to the authority of religion and attuned to offering deeds of worship with sincerity, as befits the notion of *ihsan*.

This purifies the heart and steers it in the direction of spiritual realities, and ultimately, to the pleasure of Allah, glory unto Him. Insofar as his original essence is concerned, man has been created as the best of all creation and "in the best nature" (at—Tin,4); yet, on the other hand, with an ever-looming potential to alienate itself from his original reason of existence, man has a tendency to defy and corrupt its otherwise incorrupt nature and become even more bewildered than animals. Therefore, the only criterion to determine the honour and value of man is faith (*iman*) and afterwards, good morality (*akhlaq*). Likewise, the aim of the Sufi way is to save people from tyranny, against both themselves and others, and ignorance and equip them with the characteristics of perfection. The antonym of tyranny (*zulm*) is justice (*adl*), which refers to the validity and balance of the deeds offered by a servant. While the antonym of ignorance (*jahl*), on the other hand, is knowledge (*ilm*), in order to become a truly knowledgeable person, one needs to absorb both exoteric and esoteric sciences.

In this context Ghazzali says, "The heirs to Prophets are those who possess a combined knowledge of both exoteric and esoteric sciences". The salvation of humans depends on purging the bad characteristics existent in the ego and on performing deeds in accordance with the criteria laid down for valid righteous deeds (*amal salih*), and no less, on putting knowledge into practice, exclusively through which one becomes a better human being.

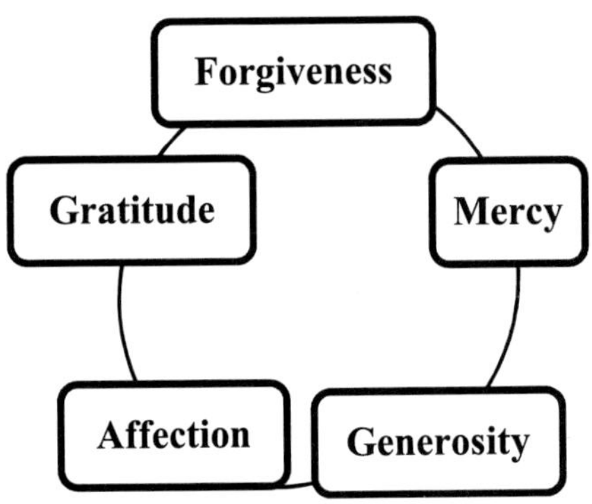

Fig. 8.4: Aims of Sufism

In Sufi terminology, then implies transforming ordinary knowledge into irfan, that is, gnosis or wisdom. In the final analysis, Sufism deals with theoretical and practical instructions to bring this project to life.

Interpretation of the Quran: Through the Eyes of Sufis

Sufis claim that most verses of the Quran have an outward

meaning and an inward meaning. Solely the Sufi elders understand the inward meaning. On account of this, Sufis have introduced concepts and words that are totally foreign to the teachings of Islam. In the Quran God, Almighty encourages a person to properly understand His words.

God tells us:

> "(This is) a Scripture that We have revealed unto you, full of blessing,
> That they may ponder its revelations,
> and that men of understanding may reflect."
> (Quran 38: 29)

Whereas, the Sufi way is about purifying the heart and the soul. Since man has come to this world for trial, he is afflicted, until death, with the presence of the ego or the lower self (*nafs*), which contains innumerable negative aspects. Even if one reaches the highest point of sainthood, he always remains face to face and under the threat of three main obstacles: "the temporal world, ego, and *satan*". He is always vulnerable to the deceiving tricks, whispers and traps set by these three elements. The merit of servanthood starts the moment a believer turns his heart to the Lord, and by eliminating the dangers caused by the three aforementioned elements, thereby saves him from the deceptive glitters of worldly pleasures.

The purification of the heart and soul is an essential undertaking in rectifying the evil inclinations existent in human nature and subsequently planting the seeds of piety (*taqwa*) therein. For this reason, every human being is responsible for acquiring knowledge of the Almighty, in proportion to his personal capacity. This responsibility also includes moving a step beyond the conventional knowledge of the Almighty to attain the real knowledge of Him, and to complement this with righteous deeds. Such is the meaning of "servanthood" in the truest sense.

Actualising this kind of servanthood requires one to embark upon purifying the heart and soul; and this entails a bypassing or a purging of the obstacles set by the ego and turning all desires to the eternal. Such is the only way to reach the Lord both here and in the Hereafter.

The innate nature of the heart is that it is the precinct of the Divine Gaze; in other words, it is the point on which the Sight of the Lord is fixed. As such, the heart is open and receptive to Divine inspiration on the condition that it is cleansed of every kind of worldly desires and selfish concerns. A heart dominated by these meagre desires is spiritually impure and therefore unreceptive to the inspirations and disclosures coming from the way of the Lord. Living up to this principle does not necessarily require that one loves no person other than the Lord, though having said that, those triumphant in attaining a heart of purity at the end of this road have developed an immunity against the love of anything else other than the Lord (*masiwa*). Given that common human beings, however, cannot entirely erase their love for "things" of the world from their hearts, it is hoped that they will in fact benefit from these metaphorical loves, as long as they do not allow them to weigh heavier than their love for the Real. Recalling the function and status of the heart, both spiritual and material, will help us better appreciate the vitality of purifying it.

The Prophet states,

> "There is a piece of flesh in human body…
> if good then so is the whole body;
> and if bad, so the entire body becomes bad. Beware…
> that this (piece of flesh) is the heart."
> (Bukhari, Imam, 39)

A well-known Sufi mystic and poet, Rumi gives a symbolic explanation of the same reality and states that when a person tries to fill an empty sack, he needs to make sure that the sack does not have any holes, otherwise, his efforts are useless.

Likewise, Rumi continues, human deeds become meaningful and lead to eternal salvation only if performed with a purified heart, for the rewards of deeds depends on the intention, and the intention itself is a deed exclusive to the heart. In light of this strong connection, one needs to correct his intention and adorn it by means of sincerity, but this is not a simple undertakings.

Only qualified masters can guide one in the process of purifying the heart, at the end of which one can attain the desired spiritual state. Saints train their disciples in educating the heart, helping them reach the spiritual perfection of *ihsan*, where they acquire a spiritually innervated heart that feels the presence of the Lord at all times. Reaching this said level of spiritual perfection requires the purification of the heart from all desires and objects other than the Almighty. A heart endowed with such quality starts perceiving subtle and deep realities and becomes the locale for the manifestation of Divine Names and spiritual secrets, the depth of which depend on the depth of spiritual maturity the heart has acquired. Knowledge of the Divine (*marifatullah*), which is to know the Lord in and through the heart, appears inside a heart of such calibre, and this appearance signals the beginning of the transformation of ordinary knowledge (*ilm*) into real knowledge or wisdom (*irfan*).

For Sufis—He who knows his soul knows his Lord.

Sufism has been described as a way of knowledge and also as a way of love. Similar to the goal of other spiritual traditions, Sufism helps in making us experience a deeper reality beyond our limited waking state. This experience leads to knowing and direct contact with truth. Different stages of Sufi practices and understanding of self from the eyes of Sufism could lead to in-depth understanding of self as seen and stated by this mystical path.

Stages of Sufi Practice

There are four stages of Sufi practice: *shariat* (religious law), *tariqat* (spiritual path), *haqiqat* (truth/Divine reality) and *marifat* (gnosis or certain knowledge of God). These could be explained as:

(i) *Shariat*

It forms the basis for the other three stages, and deals with teaching of right and wrong and the proper way to live in the world. *shariat* is the Divine and sacred law of Islam. It makes one distinguish between right and wrong, between forbidden and permissible actions. Just as a house cannot be built without a foundation, Sufism cannot be practised without first following the *shariat*, which in Arabic mean “road”. It is not possible to develop spiritually without following the moral rules of right conduct.

All the rules, ethical principles, and beliefs revealed to the Prophet, are collectively called the *shariat*. The scholars of *tawhid*, *fiqh* and *tasawwuf* did the crucial labour of deriving, extracting, and compiling the *shariat* from its twin sources the Quran and Sunnah.

The practice of the *shariat* and carrying out the commands of the *shariat* to the best of one's ability, is referred to as the *tariqat*. The word *tariqat* which means "road" or "method" is the practice of the *shariat*.

(ii) *Tariqat*

It refers to actual Sufi practice leading to the spiritual or inner path to truth. This path is not marked in a clear and precise manner. *Tariqat* is the beautification of the *shariat* whereby whatever one has understood in *shariat* is made firm in one's heart under strict spiritual discipline. In this stage one has to have complete trust in God and also have lots of patience in whatever condition God keeps him in. This is the stage where one's soul is cleansed to receive God's Divine attributes.

The inner practice of Sufism has to be approached with the help of a guide or teacher who is familiar with the path. This teacher is called Sheikh. The *shariat* helps in making the external clean and ordered, and the *tariqat* makes us clean and pure from inside.

(iii) *Haqiqat*

It means truth. This is concerned with the true understanding, without which one will only blindly copy the teachers who have attained *haqiqat* or truth. In the first two stages, there is only imitation of those who know, but in this stage the practice of the earlier stages becomes a truth and is internalised.

The third aspect, referred to as the *haqiqat*, is the fruit of knowledge and its continuous practice. The *haqiqat* is the fruit of the *shariat* and the *tariqat*. As the Prophet is reported to have said, "He who practices what he knows, Allah will teach him what he doesn't know."

The *haqiqat* in itself involves three important phases of development:

- The lifting or thinning of the veil between the seeker and what he believes in of the Divine Essence and His Attributes, His Majesty and Beauty, and His Nearness to us. As a result of these realisations and this deeper and more direct heart knowledge the seeker gains access to the secrets of the *tariqat* and the lights and insights of the *haqiqat*.
- The *nafs* is cleansed of all the lower qualities and rebuilt with the praiseworthy qualities. For instance his patience, repentance, *taqwa*, *istiqamah* (regular worship), reliability and *tawakkul* (trust in Allah) are deep rooted and genuine
- His chest has now finally opened to the nur of Islam. *Ibadah* and good deeds comes to him without any effort. He has reached the stage of *al-nafs al-mutmainnah* (the peaceful self) and reached a state of complete acceptance at every level of his being.

(iv) *Marifat*

It is the goal to recognise the creator (God), or to become God-conscious in every state and action. In this state, there is no "time-space". Here only purity exists and only the pure can come close to God. In this state, the seeker does not forget that he (or she) is still a servant and no matter how high he may progress spiritually he still remains the created and God the Creator. This state cannot be expressed through the very limited human faculties.

It is gnosis, which is a deep realisation or an inner knowing. This is knowledge of the true reality which only very few people attain, such as the Prophets and Messengers of God, and great sages.

So to summarise it can be said that the *shariat* is the boat humans have to sail on, the *tariqat* is the sea, and the *haqiqat* is the jewels and pearls we extract from the sea; or the *shariat* is the tree, the *tariqat* are the branches and the *haqiqat* is the fruit we enjoy. *Marifat* is always the goal (which could be the shore and could be the pleasure attained after enjoying the fruit).

Sharia

- **Religious Law**

Tariqa

- **Spiritual Path**

Haqiqat

- **Divine Reality**

Marifa

- **Gnosis**

Fig. 8.5: Stages of Sufi Practice

The Reality of the Nafs

As, discussed earlier, being the pearl of all creation, man possesses an inborn capacity towards good and evil, and thus his high or low position among creation depends on the way he uses his will. The success of humans in this undertaking is proportional to his personal success in enhancing his good qualities and, at the same time, curbing his evil aspects. The merit of a human being becomes evident in this battle ground where the good and evil features stake conflicting claims over the control of the person. According to Sufis, the negative and positive inclinations that exist in human have two locale or focal points in "the animal soul" and "the lordly soul". The animal soul is a subtle faculty that enables man to stay alive in this world and to keep his biological existence under control. It is also called "life" or "self".

Since the animal soul keeps running its basic operations in the human body even while a person is asleep, most of the biological functions in the body are involuntarily carried on during sleep. However, the lordly soul leaves the body during sleep, to return to it once again the moment a person wakes up.

The animal soul sets the body in motion, makes it speak, and enables it to operate all the other basic bodily functions. The animal soul leaves the body on death. Its location is between the brain and the heart, from where it spreads out to the whole body and undertakes its main operations through the circulating blood. This soul is related to "the temporal and created world (*alamu'l-khalq*)" and constitutes the starting point of human actions. If untrained, this soul may exercise negative influences over a human being.

The lordly soul refers to the human soul which the Almighty had breathed of His spirit. This quality differentiates a human being from the rest of creation. The lordly soul belongs to "the world of unconditioned existence (*alamu'l-amr*)" and accompanies the human body so that humans may perform good deeds. With the help of this soul, humans lead a decent and observant lifestyle in servanthood and obedience. The lordly soul does not perish or disappear with the death of the body, though by death the effect of the lordly soul over the body comes to an end.

Human beings give directions to their life depending on the exact nature of the battle taking place in her/his inner dimension between the animal and lordly souls. When the lordly soul wins the battle, humans become inclined towards good deeds and morality. But when the animal soul takes the control, humans become inclined towards all kinds of sin and immorality. Humans responsibility for her/his actions is based on her/his preferences and decisions between good and evil deeds.

Since man is given a capacity to perform his actions in accordance with his free will, and thereby, take his animal soul under control to a certain extent, he is liable for what he does and eligible for both reward and punishment. The human ego constitutes one of the biggest obstacles that stand in front of man in this world of tests and trial. For this reason, in general, we think of the human self, or *nafs*, as a negative concept. In reality, however, the self has positive qualities embedded in its essence. To make this essence appear in all its glory, human beings must instead polish the *nafs* from all kinds of dirt through spiritual purification.

Man should continually keep himself busy with striving for good causes in this world so that he could reach a blissful life in the world to come, as every man shapes his own eternal life in this world and reaps whatever he sows. Depending on the quality of his deeds, each person will attain a pleasant or an unpleasant life in the hereafter.

One of the essential conditions of eternal happiness and salvation for human beings is to mature the lower self or the ego to a proper degree of ripeness, so as to accustom it to offering good deeds.

An untamed and uncontrolled self cannot take its possessor to the sublime and celestial aims of life. In fact, the self, or *nafs*, functions as a two-dimensional vehicle. While it has a potential to elevate man's value to the peaks of maturity and make him the pearl of all creation, it might also degrade his value to the lowest of the low.

The self, therefore, has a potential to head towards both directions, like a two-edged knife. When properly trained it heads towards the good, though if not, it recklessly heads towards evil. Every human soul that remains deprived of spiritual guidance and control, functions like a dark curtain of ignorance that covers the surface of realities. But as mentioned above, despite the obstacle of the ego, if a person purifies himself by salvaging his soul from the hands of immoral characteristics, he can reach advanced points even higher than that of angels. For the merit of every end is proportionate to the level of difficulty experienced and of the obstacles overcome for the sake of reaching this end. Immoral characteristics in the soul interfere with the communication between the Almighty and the servant.

Only through the practice of the required spiritual methods can one remain firm against these relentless interferences, and this means an equally relentless struggle against the ego's lowly temptations and desires. Such a course of action requires a persistent and determined toil.

Although the struggle against the lower self, or the ego, does not kill it, it nonetheless takes it under control. In fact, Sufism does not so much aim at utterly destroying the self, as withholding it from transgressing and immunising it against lowly desires and inclinations. The Sufi way undertakes this operation in accordance with Divine instructions.

In this regard, Ghazzali compares human's position with a rider and says,

> "The *nafs* is the spirit's saddled beast. If a person lets go of the bridles of the *nafs* and follows its direction, his destruction becomes unavoidable. If he tries to destroy the self (as it is in the case of certain Hindu

> religions and mystical philosophies), then he is bound to remain behind on the path of reality, without any saddled beast. Better you hold on tight to the bridles of the beast and make use of it."

Following this course of action in dealing with the self is a requirement, and moreover, an essential part of the prophetic method in human education. The course of action leads to different states through which self flourishes.

The States of the Self

Nafs represent an ascension of the soul to the highest possible level, peace with God. The soul is meant to transform through the stages. At the lowest level, the *nafs* has overcome the person. At the highest level, the person overcomes the *nafs*. Through ritual, contemplation, spiritual practices, ethical imperatives, and religious teachings the soul can ascend to the highest level of being.

In Islam, body and spirit are directly opposed, as spirit is Divine and body is of earth. The *nafs* is the mediator of these two parts where the Divine and the worldly come together. The *nafs* has different levels (the first three comprises of the basic levels) that humans can attain, from the most base to the most Divine.

According to a classification well-known to Sufi circles, in the process of spiritual training and perfection, the human *nafs* may assume seven types of states. These are:

(i) *The Evil-Commanding Self* (*Nafs al-ammara*)

The first level of *nafs* is the *nafs al-ammara*, the commanding soul. The soul at this level is driven by desires, impulses, fears, appetites, and egos. Islam teaches that most humans exist at this level. The soul at this level seeks to protect its self-interest, which is the basis for habitual and addictive behaviours. The soul will seek out satisfaction and justify its actions to satiate base desires. The self-controlled by moods and impulses will even distort reality to ensure the body responds to its demands. This is the lowest level of the soul.

Nafs al-ammara (imperative, impassioned, or instinctual soul), a source of unbridled motivations or even unrestrained sensuality that vigorously attack reason, the intellect—that is, the criterion for the good, this impels man toward evil, that is, toward a set of morally forbidden intentions, attitudes, and behaviour. In many verses of the Quran, the impulsive function of the *nafs al-ammara* could be grasped. For example:

> "I no longer call myself completely innocent: the passionate Soul leads to evil." (Quran 12/53)

This is the lowest and most disobedient state of the human self. It removes a servant from his Lord and incites him to engage in evil activities. The word *ammara* means overly commanding. A *nafs* stuck in this state insatiably follows carnal and sensual desires. This is a self under the yoke of lust and a friend of *satan*, it has a strong penchant for following its selfish desires and committing sin. The mark of a person in the state of the evil-commanding self is that he inconsiderately follows the selfish and carnal desires of his ego, without showing the least resistance.

In Sufi terminology, the evil-commanding self is symbolised by the image of a poisonous serpent. Through this symbolisation, Sufi calls careful attention to the venom of this self.

Poet Nevizade Atai uses this image in his poetry when he says,

> "Each immoral character trait resembles a serpent;
> and the serpent king is the evil-commanding self."

For this reason, every believer of right mind must be engaged in a continuous combat against the evil-commanding self. Human reason and personal will are the two essential weapons to help the believer in this combat.

Through strengthening the feelings of Divine fear, a person could resist the strong temptations of the evil-commanding self. It is only the heart that can decisively reject the deceptive charms of the world and seek refuge in the Almighty. The Holy Quran states that the strongest weapon to protect a believer against the disaster wrought by the evil-commanding self is the embodiment of Divine fear.

The evil-commanding self causes man to undervalue his original merit, making him plummet down from the highest degrees of Paradise to the lowest ditches of Hell. A person dominated by the evil-commanding self is stubborn and conceited, even when meeting the means that might take him to his own eternal happiness and salvation. In a way, he finds pleasure in looking down upon people around him, lying, backbiting, and keeping himself busy with cheap and useless things. He cannot safeguard himself from impurity. The number of people dominated by this malicious *nafs* is quite large. They act heedlessly and ignorantly, preferring the fleeting tastes of the world to the everlasting joys of Paradise and to the indescribable delight of witnessing the Lord's Beauty in the world to come. When dominated by the evil-commanding self, the rational soul becomes enslaved to the animal soul, and humanly qualities disappear from the scene to leave the stage to animal characteristics.

A believer with an evil-commanding self is similar to a sick person who needs treatment. The most basic spiritual measure he is expected to take is to call his self to account continually, so that he might promote his position from the evil-commanding self towards the self-blaming *nafs* (*nafs al-lawwama*).

(ii) *The Self-Blaming Self* (*Nafs al-lawwama*)

The next stage of being is *nafs al-lawwama*, the blaming soul. At this intermediate stage, the soul experiences inner *jihad* or struggle. Recognising a higher reality, the soul seeks to control its impulses and centre its consciousness to manage the self. The person can experience inner and active *jihad* to fulfil the covenant made with God. The self becomes aware of its own imperfections and seeks to improve them to be brought before Allah.

The Arabic word *lawm* means "to blame" or "to reproach". Accordingly the expression *nafs al-lawwama* refers to the *nafs* which blames and reproaches itself over its wrongdoings and shortcomings. This type of self is aware of the fact that it does not diligently follow Divine instructions, for which he blames himself remorsefully. A person with the self-blaming *nafs* has effectively repented and protected himself from some of the negativities peculiar to the evil-commanding self. This means that his heedlessness and desire for committing sins are less in comparison with the evil-commanding self. But still, since his level of spiritual maturity is not yet perfected, he remains vulnerable to the lure of sins.

Nafs al-lawwamu is the critical soul that disapproves the projects of the *nafs al-ammara* and reproaches man for his subjection to it. Indeed the *nafs al-lawwama* constitutes the moral order; it is a version of the Divine Law that man must constantly take into consideration and to which order and human law must be identified. The guardian soul is always present in the heart of the faithful, in his conscience. In addition, this presence is evident. Transgression of the law of the guardian soul signifies regression to the impulsive state, the sinking of moral conscience into denial.

In the state of the self-blaming *nafs*, the rational soul is not enslaved unconditionally to the animal soul. Each time he commits a sin, he is overcome by remorse. Laying the blame on himself, he asks the Almighty's forgiveness. But he cannot keep a secure and stable position in his repentance, as he has not yet overcome his lower self. Even though his conscience disapproves of misdeeds, he cannot completely protect himself from committing them and as is open to the negative external influences like peer pressure.

Generally stated, a person who possesses a self-blaming *nafs* is happy with his good deeds and sad with his bad deeds. He strives to protect himself from sensual desires and puts up a resistance. He is more strongly inclined to repentance. His heart has been enlightened by a little ray of spiritual light and his mind has been awakened, to a certain degree, against heedlessness. He has a more increased sense of observing Divine commands and offering righteous deeds, which are mostly for the sake of the Almighty. But since he is yet to receive the peace and tranquillity supplied through Divine inspirations, he also carries a desire to make his deeds visible to others. This means that the evil-commanding self is somewhat still in action, though the servant does eventually blame himself over this weakness too.

A person whose *nafs* is of a self-blaming nature may protect himself from misconducts, only under a spiritual guidance and environment. Although under normal conditions he would not go back to making his previous mistakes, some immoralities like hatred, jealousy, and self-conceit still lie dormant in the heart, and this keeps the risk ever alive. Under this spiritual guidance, a servant proceeds forth from the self-blaming *nafs* to the inspired self (*nafs al-mulhimah*), through *rabitah*, an important method in spiritual training. Here, one always remembers his promise to his master to stay away from unlawful things and to observe religious commands. This promise enables him to imagine the spiritual presence of his master at all times, which acts as a medium for him to keep his act together. Constantly calling his self to account, he must remain fixed on his resolution to leave his immoral characteristics and act in repentance. He should then strive to replace these negative character traits with positive ones; for instance, he should replace self-conceit and jealousy with humbleness and non-envious friendship. He must not seek to single out the mistakes he sees in his friends and instead keep himself occupied with his own faults. He should remember that a believer is a mirror to his fellow-believer, thus should he look at him through an evil eye, he will of course see nothing but evil. But looking at him with a good eye, he will see only good qualities. Persistence in remembering the Lord and keeping away from sins are also essential in this state, in order to enlighten the heart with the light of Divine love.

(iii) *The Inspired Self* (*Nafs al-mulhimah*)

By advancing through the evil-commanding self and the self-blaming *nafs* one reaches the inspired self, primarily through repentance, asking the Almighty's forgiveness, staying away from sins and implementing the practices necessitated by spiritual guidance.

Nafs al-mulhimah (calm and balanced soul or ego) is a state of certitude, a state of being without crisis and without worry. This implies realisation of the higher stage during the euphemic evolution of inner life. The balanced Ego comes into action when the passionate Ego, under the careful watch of the blaming Ego, has been subjected to the principle of reason (*aql*). The *nafs al-mulhimah* is thus the highest human potentiality in the hierarchy of the trilogy of the soul. This ego incarnates the subtle organ of the heart (*qalb*, a psychic heart synonymous with intellects, the faculty for knowing the transcendent). This heart is receptive to Divine Truth.

The people at this level have gone beyond the stage of the epiphany of the attributes and have arrived at the stage of direct contemplation (*mushahada*). At this level of elevation, the human and the Divine each become the mirror of the other, the sublime place of encounter where they interpenetrate one another while reflecting themselves in one another.

Nur Ali-Shah (eighteenth century) famous Sufi, designates this soul-spirit as the universal soul that is the sovereign of the corporal territory. This soul, which sanctions the spirit (*roh*), is a luminous spiritual essence. The heart, located at the boundary of the unknown of the suprasensible, becomes the transcendent centre, the seat of the soul-spirit, the spirit radiating through the openings of this heart.

According to Nur Ali-Shah, this heart is both the mirror that reflects the world and a sea of light, at the very depths of which the Face of the Beloved appears. This soul-heart receptive to the infinite is thus the supreme stage of human evolution in which arises the mystic superconsciousness. On the other hand, if the ego with possessive instincts dominates man's internal space, he suffers from deep sadness of heart, from which arises the impotence of the conscious or critical ego and the impossibility of achieving a state of balance. This inner blinding could be seen as psychological alienation.

(iv) *The Tranquil Self* (*Nafs al-mutmainnah*)

The tranquil self is the type of *nafs* that has been saved from inner afflictions. This spiritual safety is brought about by an assiduous observing of Divine commands and prohibitions. This self has thereby reached a real and steadfast faith, which results in genuine happiness, peace, and tranquillity. Through a persistent remembrance of the Lord, the heart has been purified from doubts and uncertainties, it is at ease in a sincere feeling of gratitude for and praise of the Lord. A servant with a tranquil self has effectively replaced his immoralities with positive moral characteristics, having willfully followed Prophet Muhammad's exemplary character traits. His heart is now filled with patience, contentment, and trust in the Almighty.

The tranquil self belongs to people of piety, who have acquired certain knowledge of the Almighty. Their hearts continually busy with Divine remembrance. They have, furthermore, gained a profound comprehension of the inner meanings of religious instructions.

The tranquil self is a highly advanced level of spiritual maturity; a precious gift but an enormous responsibility at the same time. To draw a comparison, those whose rational faculty have not come of age cannot be held responsible for fulfilling religious duties, insofar as responsibility is dependent upon possessing the faculty of reason. In a similar fashion, a wayfarer (*musafir*) newly initiated into a Sufi order is regarded as an innocent child with respect to the greater responsibilities of Sufism. Until he covers a certain distance in his spiritual training, his faults are treated with tolerance; since in Sufism, spiritual maturity only comes with progress. But after having received a certain level of training, he is considered responsible for things that are not duties ordinary believers need to fulfil. Until he steps inside the door of the tranquil self, the wayfarer is not responsible for things that are regarded as shortcomings. This responsibility begins only after the point when the wayfarer assumes the tranquil self, since it is here that he attains the maturity.

The tranquil self is the self which has reached reality (*haqiqat*), peacefulness (*sakinah*), and certainty (*yaqin*). It has become protected from worldly grieves and concerns and, in addition, it has received certain spiritual unveilings and inspirations. In the state of the tranquil self, the veils of heedlessness and ignorance over the heart are lifted. At the level of *ayn-al-yaqin*, the heart beholds realities beyond appearances. Furthermore, the heart has been made secure from doubts and uncertainties. It has attained a tranquillity and peacefulness through a complete submission to the Almighty.

It has been seen that the states of the *nafs* prior to that of the tranquil self do not receive a Divine addressing. Only the tranquil self and the states beyond are privileged with this merit. In order for a person to be worthy of this receipt, he needs to genuinely struggle to rein in his ego. The distinguished servants who enjoy the state of the tranquil self then gradually begin to move forward towards the three higher spiritual states in line; namely, the satisfied self (*nafs al-radiyah*) the satisfying self (*nafs al-mardiyyah*), and the perfect self (*nafs al-kamila*) respectively. The more successful a servant is in this progress, the closer he gets to his Lord.

(v) *The Satisfied Self* (*Nafs al–radiyah*)

This is the *nafs* that has persistently kept its focus on the Almighty, and by continually considering itself to be in Divine presence of The Almighty, it has embodied a highly advanced level of piety. The satisfied self is now content and satisfied with his Lord. Not only has it left his personal will aside, it has further annihilated it within Divine Will.

The tests and afflictions a satisfied self undergoes are much more difficult to endure than those of the previous spiritual states, for the higher the self ascends, the thornier the path becomes. Only after having overcome the obstacle of the lower self can man reach a level of spiritual maturity that enables him to meet tribulations with endurance and rest content with Him. As great a reward this spiritual maturity is, it only comes at the end of an enormous show of patience and endurance.

In the eyes of a believer with a satisfied self, everything in the world deserves the same treatment, regardless of whether it causes joy or grief. Since his heart is detached from the world, worldly pleasure, temporal and pain are on level par to him. With a full-fledged insight into the fact that everything really comes from the Almighty, he is content with everything, both good and evil.

In the spiritual state of the satisfied self, the servant begins to have an insight into Divine Secrets. He comprehends the meaning of Divine Oneness and spiritual realities become unfolded in front of his eyes. He is given the honour of receiving the special disclosures of Divine Names and Attributes. His character becomes an overflowing spring of goodness, beauty, and truth. He is a welcoming observant of Divine commands and prohibitions.

The ultimate objective is the Almighty alone.

(vi) *The Satisfying Self* (*Nafs al-mardiyyah*)

The satisfied self is in need of a further spiritual perfection. To receive and fully benefit from all the Divine disclosures shone upon its heart, the satisfied self must at the same time seek to become "satisfying" for the Almighty as well. In other words, being satisfied with the Lord does not suffice, also expected, in return, is the Lord's satisfaction. The satisfaction must not be one-sided and should come from both directions, as it were.

Even though the attribute of "satisfying" refers to the Almighty, it is the servant who is in fact expected to make the effort to actualise this satisfaction. This nuance makes this quality attributable to the servant himself, and thus to his *nafs*. It could, therefore, be said that while the satisfied self refers to the spiritual state of those who are content with the Almighty, the satisfying self refers to the Almighty who, in turn, is content with them.

In the state of the satisfied self, immoral characteristics have by now disappeared, replaced instead by positive qualities. Those who have reached this spiritual state see all creation through the vantages of affection, mercy, love, generosity, and forgiveness. Since all creation is the artwork of the Almighty, wherever they look, they only see goodness. A servant in the state of the satisfying self calls himself to account in the most riveting correct manner and meditates on it. At every breath, he is mindful of the underlying reality of creation and the nature of his own self, with an unyielding awareness of its devilish whispers.

Also in this spiritual state, the servant also completely submits himself to his Lord under all circumstances. Whatever it be that comes from the Almighty, he welcomes it, knowing it is nothing but a Divine manifestation.

A servant who has attained such spiritual perfections sees everything from the vantage point of *haqq-al-yaqin*, of an assured knowledge based on personal spiritual experience. By the will of the Almighty, hc may even become acquainted with certain secrets of the unseen world. Because of his spiritual exertion, the Almighty, brings him closer to Him, to the point where He virtually becomes his eyes that see, ears that hear, tongue that speaks. The words and behaviour of such a person then begin to exercise a deep influence on persons around him. The spiritual manifestations he had previously witnessed as a satisfied self are now digested and internalised, becoming an integral part of his mindset. A relentless patience and trust in the Almighty have now become the dominant traits of his character.

According to the conventional Sufi classification, the levels of the human *nafs* throughout the spiritual path of purification are divided into these six categories. But some Sufi masters talk about an additional stage called the perfect self (*nafs-al-kamila*) or the pure *nafs* (*nafs-al-safiyayh*).

(vii) *The Perfect Self* (*Nafs al-kamila*)/*The Pure Self* (*Nafs al-Safiyyah*)

The perfect self is a type of soul that has become thoroughly purified by way of the spiritual process. It is a pure, mature, and sublime *nafs*. In this spiritual state, the *nafs* receives all kinds of heavenly secrets. This state is only a gift from the Almighty. Personal efforts cannot guarantee the attainment of the perfect self, it is a God-given spiritual quality, a mystery of Divine predestination.

The station of the perfect self is also called "the station of guidance", insofar as the Lord entrusts those, who have attained to this state, with the responsibility of guiding other people. Their words and actions are rendered influential, to facilitate the correction of the wrongdoings and faults of others. When a person with a perfect self meets a sinner, he instantly understands his condition, and through an exemplary conduct, informs him of the remedies he needs to save him from his inner and spiritual illnesses. Feeling remorseful over his ways, the sinner then comes around to himself, and leaves acting heedlessly, so long as his heart is not sealed or locked to spiritual realities.

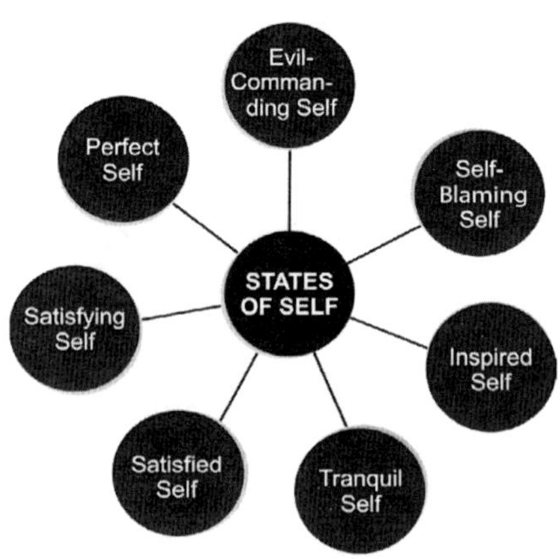

Fig. 8.6: Seven States of Self

Understanding of different states of *nafs* clearly shows the path of its purification and development.

The Purification of Lower Self/Nafs

Like the word *tazkiyah* means to cleanse and purify. It also denotes increasing, improving, and a blessing. From this semantic perspective, *tazkiyah* comprises the entire process of spiritual education. Purifying the *nafs* means is to cleanse it primarily from unbelief, ignorance, evil thoughts, false convictions, and immorality.

In other words, the purification of the self is an act of cleansing aimed at eliminating all kinds of theoretical and practical impurities. This process ends in filling the *nafs* with good religious and moral qualities, such as sound belief, knowledge, gnosis, wisdom, and spirituality. The Sufi purification concentrates on lessening the lowly desires of the *nafs*, breaking its authority over the body, and establishing the spirit's authority instead. This occurs only through practices of abstinence that strengthen the will-power against the lower self and this involves a strict self-discipline with regards to food, sleep, and speech.

Sufism thus outlines the methods of disciplining the soul through three interconnected concepts: little of food (*qillatu'l-taam*), little of sleep (*qillatu'l- manam*), and little of speech (*qillatu'l-kalam*). In establishing a spiritual authority over the *nafs*, these rules constitute the earliest steps. It should also be borne in mind that a wayfarer should not exaggerate the practice of these rules. Since the Almighty has entrusted one's body to the person, it has to be kept in mind the need to deal with it in moderation. In other words, during the process of purifying the lower self, a servant should kept himself away from excess in either direction. He should not overdo spiritual exercises in the name of taking the self undercomplete control; for Sufism commands moderation in all states and actions, and warns people against all kinds of exaggerative behaviour.

Furthermore, neither is it not possible to eliminate the self all together, nor is this required. Instead, a believer is expected to purify his self in the sense of bridling and training it in accordance with Divine instructions. The act of training and purifying the self is itself the most decisive factor in determining the nature of man's ultimate end, whether it will be one of destruction or happiness. To fulfil this process of purification, a servant should readily submit himself to Divine Will and resist against his lustful passions and indecent expectations. Every believer should be aware of his shortcomings, weaknesses, and ignorance. At the same time, he should truly comprehend the absolute glory and power of Allah, glory unto Him, and regulate his actions accordingly.

If the believer is successful in this undertaking, then his "evil commanding self" becomes purified from immorality and thus turns into a praiseworthy self.

On account of the immense level of difficulty involved, humans struggle for purifying his self is regarded as "the greater *jihad*", in the sense of being a *jihad* against the lower self.

The Noble Proph *et al.* so says,

> "A mindful person is he who takes his lower self under control,
> calls it to account, and performs good deeds for the world to come.
> A foolish person is the one who expects something good from the
> Almighty in vain, while following the desires of his lower self."
>
> —Tirmidhi, Qiyamah; Ibn Majah, Zuhd

Consequently, every believer should be mindful of the characteristics of his self and the responsibility he carries for its purification. He should take great care and use the appropriate methods, in order not to fall victim to the *nafs* in the process.

In other words, he who corrects his self will reach his destination safe and sound, while he who leaves his self to wallow in its excess and arrogance will face utter disappointment. This means that the *nafs* includes two functions, working in the opposite poles. If one follows it unconditionally, he would end up in an eternal loss. But if one trains the self and takes it under control, he could reach a spiritual level even higher than that of angels. The self is the unique means that can lead one to both directions. Although all good deeds come with an outward aspect, they always have an essential, inner dimension to be discerned. According to the Holy Quran, there are many verses in relation to purification of the soul. The term "purification" (*tazkiyah*) in these verses comprises three main aspects:

1. The Almighty's purification.
2. Prophet Muhammad's—upon his blessings and peace—purification.
3. A person's own purification of his *nafs*.

1. *Purification by the Almighty*

It has been seen and believed that purification belongs in reality to the Almighty—who, by way of His limitless favour and mercy, enables his servant to practice good deeds and guides him to the means of purification. The servant, therefore, should keep himself away from conceit and self-promotion, and instead hold the Almighty as the actual Purifier. The servant should be mindful of the fact that his entire personal efforts towards purification will be useless in the Hereafter, unless the Almighty purifies him.

This mindset provides the ultimate means to reach eternal salvation. Even though purification might be attributable to the servant with respect to personal will and effort, and to Prophets and spiritual masters with respect to providing guidance and teaching, in the final analysis, purification is attributable only to the Almighty, who creates the means of purification for His servant and enables him to find these means.

2. *Purification by the Messenger of Allah*

This fact indicates that those who possess unpurified *nafs* cannot attain the true knowledge of things from their masters. Their knowledge will not benefit them, even if they might possess some bits of it. Since knowledge and wisdom are of invaluable importance, they do not dwell in ordinary places. A heart set to become a dwelling place for knowledge and wisdom, is to be freed of all kinds of useless and dangerous grimes.

For this reason, Prophets and saints first conveyed the Divine signs, and then embark upon purifying the hearts of those to whom they have conveyed the signs. It is only at the end of this process that Prophets teach the Book and Wisdom to persons who have thus become spiritually purified. The secrets embedded in this universe open themselves gradually only to those who possess a heart purified. Those who possess such hearts may even become springs of wisdom in their own right.

3. *A Person's Own Purification of His Self*

The Sufi saints see this purification as the most important one. As purification of ones *nafs* is the end of the road as it reaches to the Truth or the Divine itself.

The command to purify is significant. The servant is expected to:

(a) First cleanse his heart, body, and possessions from all negativity and immorality; which
(b) Results in unveiling the curtains of ignorance that stand between the servant and the Almighty;
(c) After which, with a body nurtured by lawful food and a heart mindful of the Almighty, the servant enters into the realm of mature servanthood and spiritual enjoyment.

The believer is first expected to empty his heart and whole existence of all kinds of negative moral characteristics, which resemble minor deities. Then comes the confirmation, which is when the heart becomes ready to receive and to be filled with the Divine Light.

When a servant sets his heart only upon the Almighty, his reward becomes even greater, he becomes eligible, in the hereafter, to witness the manifestations of Divine beauty and perfection (*jamalullah*), which are beyond the limits of linguistic description in this world. Whoever willingly directs his attention to the Lord alone and takes his Lord to be his sole concern, becomes freed of all kinds of petty, temporal concerns. As for acquiring the knowledge of the Divine (*marifatullah*), it begins with purifying the self, which then leads to a real understanding of its nature.

The well-known Sufi phrase, "Whoever knows his *nafs*, knows his Lord" refers to this delicate relationship between the human *nafs* and the knowledge of the Divine.

In this day and age where human beings live under the yokes of materialism and self-centredness that darken their soul, there are innumerable obstacles that hinder one from the all-important task of directing his focus on the reality of the human soul and other spiritual matters. There is, therefore, a greater need today for spiritual masters to correct our misplaced direction.

In Sufi terminology, this conduct is referred to as an "inward investigation" (*al-tafahhusu'l-batini*). This cross-examination of the self, where all actions are re-evaluated, should take place at least once a day. When one becomes accustomed to it, he becomes less insistent on his habitual wrongdoings.

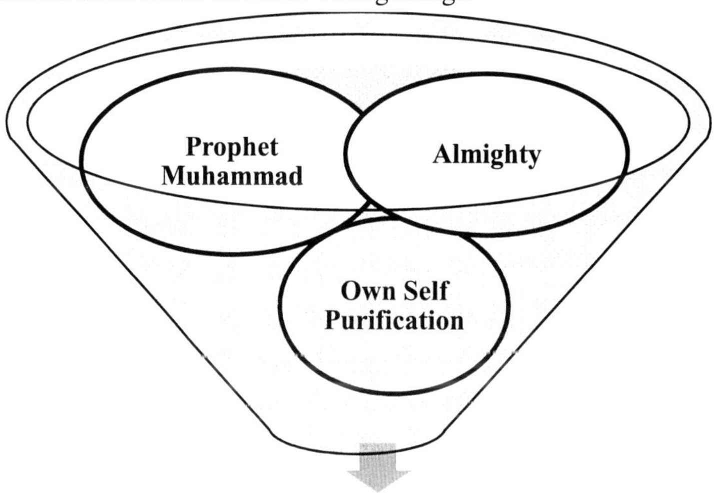

Three ways for Soul Purification

Fig. 8.7: Ways for purification of Soul

Ghazzali says in this context:

> "With the dawning of each day, a believer should sit together with his "self" right after his dawn prayer and reach certain agreements on the basis of certain conditions."

This act is similar to a merchant's agreement with his partner regarding their shareholdings, right before him submitting his capital to the partner. Meantime, the merchant does not neglect to give certain warnings to the partner.

Likewise, a person should give the following warnings and instructions to his self.

> "My whole capital is my lifetime. When I lose my life, my capital also comes to an end, and profit and loss do not mean anything to me anymore. But now a new day begins. The Almighty has given me this day as a great opportunity. If He had made me dead, I would give anything just to return to this life again, even for a single day, to perform only good deeds."

When he calls his self to account, he needs to make it sure that all of his deeds are performed uniquely for the sake of the Almighty, not for the sake of any other authority including his own self. As a result of the purification of the *nafs*, the heart acquires the quality of "soundness" (*salim*).

A believer with a sound heart embodies three characteristics:

1. He does not hurt anybody. This comes from a fear of the Almighty. The heart is protected from the evils of the ego, which brings exemplary character traits to the surface.
2. He is never hurt or offended by anybody. This comes from a profound feeling of love. He never pays attention to the praises or censures of ordinary people.
3. He always prioritises the pleasure of the Lord at all costs. On being compelled to make a choice between the worldly and the hereafter, they never hesitate in choosing the latter.

In short, the Almighty has made this life a platform of trials and has assigned humans to the task of returning to Him by overcoming the obstacle that is the soul; to transform its evil to good, the reward of which is incomparable to anything in this world.

A person with a purified soul represents a masterpiece of the Supreme Artist (the Almighty) as he has become a platform of the manifestations of Divine disclosures.

Transforming the Self

The goal of all mysticism is to cleanse the heart, to educate, or transform the self, and to find God. The lowest level of the self is dominated by pride, egotism, and totally self-centred greed and lust. This level is the part within each person that leads away from Truth. The highest level is the pure self, and at this level there is no duality, no separation from God.

A known Sufi poet once wrote:

Self or *nafs* is not bad in itself .
It is not to be charged.
The work of Sufism is not to provide a
certificate of good or bad. The work is improvement.
Moving from the lowest state of being
which is being captured by the desires.
The next come the fight with oneself to act in limits
of rationality and adhere or achieve higher ideals
and being able to condemn oneself when failure comes.
A much higher state is to be pleased and contented
with whatever God has given oneself,
whether it is actually gratifying the wishes, wants, and
desires of a person or not.

Love: The Beginning and the End in Itself

The foundation of Sufism is love (*mahabbah, hubb*). The Sufis even say of their teachings as of "hymn to the Divine Love" and call it *tassawuri* (love) vision. Love is considered in Sufism as the power, which strengthens one's feeling of being contained in God. This process results in understanding that in the world there is nothing but God, who is the Lover and the Beloved at the same time.

One of the tenets of Sufism is

ishq allah mabud allah (God is Lover and the Beloved).

A truly loving Sufi gradually submerges, sinks, and becomes dissolved in the Creator—in his or her beloved.

The principle of regarding God as the Beloved originated from the Sufi direct experience. The Sufis describe this in the following way:

Man chooses a certain path and this path leads him to love.
God help him at each step by bringing him
closer to himself and man starts
to undergo a heightened level
of love which is the Divine's or the God's love.

According to the great Sufi poet Rumi, the love leading humans to God develops:

1. Through the development of the emotional, cordial love for all the beautiful and harmonious in the world;
2. Through active, sacrificial love-service to people;
3. And then through extending this love to all manifestations of the world without discriminating between them;
4. Such developed love for all elements of the Creation is redirected then to the Creator—and man begins to see that, according to Rumi, "the Beloved is present in everything".

Understanding the nature of the *nafs* and the modifications it undergoes in the process of psychospiritual transformation into the cosmic self, is at the core of the teachings in the Sufi tradition. Sufi practice begins with the first stage of psychospiritual transformation, spiritual awakening. Once the first stage is perfected (as demonstrated by a lack of recourse to the previous tendencies of the *nafs*), *nafs al-ammara* undergoes a gradual process of transformation known as *fana,* which means ego-annihilation or loss of self-centred personality characteristics.

As *nafs al-ammara* becomes modified and transformed, a new self is experienced. This is called *nafs al-lawwama.* The term *lawwama* literally means "blaming" or "accusing". *Nafs al-lawwama* is perhaps best described (in functional terms) as self-in-transition, or regretful self. Regret is the result of the new consciousness, which reveals the imperfections of the *nafs* and the futility of its unconscious ways of being in the world. Many refined and mature human beings, whether Sufis or not, manifest the characteristics of *nafs al-lawwama,* both in their inner life and outward behaviour. Such persons are decreasingly influenced by the tendencies of *nafs al-ammara,* and increasingly show the signs of higher emotions and subtler behaviours. A Sufi practitioner in the second stage, characterised by "abstinence", actively avoids all forms of inferior impulses and tendencies by observing the ethical codes of the discipline (*adab*) until eventually the third stage, or "non-attachment" is mastered.

It is crucial to distinguish abstinence (detachment) from non-attachment. While abstinence is required as an initial step, it does not automatically lead to non-attachment as the roots of craving still persist. Overemphasis on abstinence may result in lopsided development, extreme asceticism and the development a pious self which becomes judgemental and critical of others, which further separates one from the others. Sufism prescribes modesty in abstinence only with the goal of de-conditioning the *nafs* from its original habits and addictions.

By means of successive passages into the next two stages, "spiritual poverty" during which the heart is perfectly purified and "patience", longing for Divine grace, the practitioner attains the sixth stage, referred to as "self-surrender", or "reliance on God", through completion of which all tendencies of *nafs al-ammara* are eradicated at the root. Completion of the sixth stage also marks the cessation of all effort on the part of the individual. Beyond this point experiences of cosmic self and universal consciousness occur spontaneously, or by Divine grace. At the seventh and last stage, called contentment", the self takes on its final mode, *nafs al-motma'enna,* which is characterised by joyful satisfaction and removal of all doubts.

Fana, or ego-annihilation, is also described in terms of a parallel process for an initiated seeker-annihilation of the ego first in the *sheikh* or teacher, and then in the Prophet Mohammad, and eventually in God or cosmic consciousness. At first a disciple undergoes a process of loss of self-identity through identification with the qualities of his or her teacher. Sufi practice, like those of other traditions, is best mastered under the guidance of a teacher. Just as ordinarily a lover at first loses his or her identity in that of the beloved, a sincere disciple is so impressed by the love and characteristics of a teacher that through observation and identification with the *sheikh* he or she becomes immersed in the virtues of the teacher. The *sheikh,* in the beginning, acts as a mirror through which the disciple gains insight into his or her characteristics of personality. Slowly the disciple observes the many virtuous qualities of the teacher and cultivates them.

If the teacher happens to be a Perfect Master, then he or she reflects the ninety-nine attributes of the Prophet Mohammad, who is known to the Sufis as a perfected human being *(insan al-kamil).* The attributes of the Prophet are themselves nothing but the reflection of the ninety-nine attributes of Allah, or God. These ninety-nine perfections are the object of contemplation by Sufis at various stages of the practice. The practices of contemplation are generally called *zikr* (*dhikr*), and they take the form of chanting, movement or mediation exercises. Nurbakhsh (1990) summarised the relationship between *dhikr* and self-development in the following way:

> ...*dhikr* is considered to be like a torrent which in addition to eliminating the undesirable qualities of the disciple and substituting Divine Attributes for them, in the final analysis effaces the individual ego in such a way that not a trace of the "I" remains. This is the end of the *tariqa* and the beginning of the sea of annihilation or *fana.*

According to Nurbakhsh (1990),

> "...the goal of Sufism is knowledge of absolute reality, not as learned men explain it to us through logic and demonstrations but as it is in itself. This knowledge can be attained only by the "eye of the heart", that is, by means of illumination and contemplation". Contemplation on Divine attributes is the final means of self-purification. From the Sufi point of view a perfected individual is one who has escaped the domination of *nafs al-ammara.*

As one approaches perfection, the *nafs* makes its final attempts to take control of the psyche. These reappearances, despite their decreasing frequency, may be immensely difficult to withstand. That is why, until the final illumination, a certain degree of doubt as to the full annihilation of *nafs al-ammara* remains in the mind of the (by now) saint undergoing final transformation.

With the eventual disappearance of doubt the sixth stage of Sufi practice (self-surrender) is completed, and the last stage (contentment/joy) is attained. At this point the individual free-will is replaced by Divine Will. As mentioned earlier, the process of annihilation of the ego is known as *fana.* It takes place through successive stages of annihilation of the ego in the teacher (*fana-fe'sheikh*), in the Prophet (*fana-fe'-rasul*), and in God (*fana-fe'-llah*). However, *fana* has another process complementary to it, *baqa.* As Nurbakhsh (1990) explained:

> *Baqa* consists of subsistence in God and is realised when God gives a new will to the disciple directly from himself, in order to replace that which had become annihilated in the course of the path.... At this very advanced stage God docs not veil the world from the Sufi, nor does the world veil God; no sort of separation exists any longer and duality is transformed into Unity.

Concepts of the Self in Islamic Tradition and Western Psychology: A Comparative Analysis.

For understanding self in a better manner, it is important to comprehend the spiritual map of self and its perceptiveness in the holistic manner. This map is the way to acknowledge self fully. The parts of self are conjoined with different areas and parts of the map.

Islam views the self in its real form, so the reality of soul is addressed as *nafs*. In Arabic language, *nafs* and *ruh* are two words which are been used interchangeably. *Nafs*, which is soul, and *ruh*, which is spirit, many a times, give the impression of oneness. However, in Quran there are many other meanings attached to the word *nafs*, it has not only related to soul but also to self or even functions of self.

By understanding the different meanings of *nafs* in accordance to Quran, the different elements of *nafs* could be perceived in the form of constitution of a man's soul map. The first branch of this map is:

(i) *Nafsi Ammara* (*Source of Evil, Evil Commanding*)

Nafsi ammara relates to the body and its nature, it concentrates on a person's bodily pleasures and desires of a person. According to the Islamic scholars, it puts a person down to the base level. It channelises the energy towards the bad things and deeds.

Like in Western psychology, especially in Freudian Models of Personality, *nafsi ammara* is close to the concept of Id. It is closely related to the functions and aspects of Id. Many different psychologists while explaining similarities between *nafsi ammara* and Id explains:

Id is an instinctual element; it is animalistic and is unorganised. The Id forms the major part of the unconscious. The logic does not apply for Id and it functions in leading a Life of pleasure and with pleasure. It is amoral aspect of unconscious mind and it pulls a person down leading him to only concentrate on the unmet passions and desires. It is the powerhouse for the unconscious but this powerhouse only supplies energy to fulfil instincts and wishes Id always wants an immediate gratification and it is demanding without having sense of reality Id contains the repressed ideas and needs but not everything is repressed in Id.

Nafsi ammara also leads a man to the downfall as it only concentrates on fulfilling the bodily needs and desires. In Quran it is seen as having an evil nature. The difference in case of *nafsi ammara* is that in Quran, *nafsi ammara* has two functions, which leads it to different directions. The first one where the *nafs* is active is called as *nafs hawa*, in other words passions. The second one where the *nafs* is passive and is in control of *satan* or evil spirits.

(a) *Hawai Nafs* (*Passions*): *Hawa* is that part of *nafs* which has a negative influence on soul. *Hawa* has both positive and negative connotation attached. *Hawa* leads a person to move towards all sensual impulses and lust and also it is an impulse, which weakens a person mentally, and he just let go of himself to immoral desires and wants. Islamic scholars define *hawa* as an evil, which leads the mind to only those needs, which the Islamic disapproves of. *Hawa* could also be seen as dependency.

Dependency on ones wishes, pleasures, lustful desires; all pulls a person to his knees, meaning that he is not been able/to stretch himself and gear to reach to the heights of liberty and wholeness. *Hawa* has to be controlled by the self-consciously as it makes a person move on the path of wrongdoing and leads him to perform actions, which are not right according to the religion. Quranic language, a straying from the right path is called *dalal.*

An Islamic scholar once said that:

> "*Hawa* is the most imperative cause of *dalal.*
> The person who works according to the wishes
> of *hawa* moves to a wrong path
> and those who follow such a person
> would eventually move away from that almighty.
> *Hawa* itself means an unorganised, immoral, and
> means leaning of a person's soul towards the
> lustful instincts and wishes. *Hawa* misleads
> a person and takes him away from his rightful actions."

(b) *Satan/Devil*: *Satan* is that spiritual evil which manipulates a person's consciousness and makes him unaware of his right will. It is an invisible power that controls person's consciousness and eventually leads him towards hell. As blood moves in the body of a person, similarly *satan* moves like blood in the mind of the person.

According to Quran, *satan* has different ways to weaken a person. *Satan* can make use of feelings and could break a person emotionally. It could also make use of different images, which reduces a person's will power and reduces his self-esteem.

Quran uses the expression of *vasvasa* and this is been explained with the help of "AT". This expression of *Al* shows that the role of *satan* and its sole goal is compunction, scrupling and misgiving.

So, while talking about the passions, its effect is on channelising the impulses in the direction where the fulfilment of the desire and wishes of a person takes place whereas *satan* controls consciousness, it reduces the control of the mental set of person. It hampers the will power and intellectual ability of a person and then *satan* presents all the bad things in a beautiful package, this package attracts the person and forces him to attain or gain those things.

Quran specifies that the *satan* can only control a person, if he does not listen and understand the guidance being provided to him by God. However, those who surrender themselves, their consciousness relates to that Almighty and His presence, do not have to worry about the *satan* and his evil effects. The supreme presence of God protects his children from the satanic energy and protects his followers.

The understanding of *satan* in Western psychology also exists. In this regard, Sir Muhammad Iqbal says:

> "The followers of Freud have done an unexplainable task by eliminating the *satan* from the Divinity."

The theory could be explained as follows: While growing up, a person has to adjust to the kind and type of environment he is placed into. He is exposed to different kinds of stimuli. With more and more experiences with the stimuli, a person starts to organise them in a fixed system. This system is not permanent but it grows as and when new stimuli occur. The impulses, which fit in the system, are made used of and retained whereas others, which are not fitted, are rejected. These rejected impulses move to the closest called the "unconscious region" of the mind. These rejected ones do not keep silent they wait for the right opportunity when they can come on the surface. As they are revengeful and repressed they may disturb a person's normal plans of action, can find ways in our dreams, distort our mental balance and even moves us back to our primitive stages which our evolutionary process has left far behind.

The same point as explained by Muhammad Iqbal, is been spoken by Jung. Jung termed it as complexes. These complexes have the power to disturb a person's thinking process and affect his behaviour or actions.

Jung has often spoken about the shadow as an archetype. This shadow is seen as the source of the satanic energy. The complexes he explained as the impulses, which have demonic strength or influence, and is struggling against and trying to move towards the higher will. This struggle can itself leads a person closer to that Divine power.

Jung saw shadow as an unacceptable, immoral, uncontrolled part of the self. It could also be seen as the animal part of the self, which could only think about fulfilling one's own unacceptable desires. The images of devil, which are spoken about, are seen as the part of shadow. Shadow is that part of the being which is inferior in nature. It is that part which forces or lures a person to do everything which he does not want to do. It is everything that we are not.

Jung perceives a person as innately having positive psychic energy. For Jung, shadow is a metaphysical concept, which explains the loss of connection with the universal positive psychic processes. Once the metaphysical concept looses it capabilities to recall the original experiences, they become worthless and even comes across as a dirty stone on the clean road of higher development. It has to regain its true meaning by bringing changes in its physical being.

As an angel has a positive connotation attached to itself, similarly shadow is a negative aspect, which exists in the psyche of every being. It stores all the negative energy, ruthless power, spontaneity, and vitality. Hence, it could also be seen as the stored energy for creativity. The shadow has its roots in the collective unconscious; individual could be allowed an access to it. The valuable part which is been rejected by ego could also be regained by it.

Shadow's structure is formed by the emotionally arousing themes. These themes are aspects of self from which a person has dissociated either consciously or unconsciously. The defence mechanisms are the ways to deal with these unpleasant, threatening emotionally arousing themes. Either one's own self reflects these themes or it is done by the relationships one has.

These themes are developed and shaped during the early childhood experiences, traumatic events, role expectations, identification with parental figures, etc. Painful, rejected, feared, and aggressive ideas and images about oneself are excluded from the conscious identity because of the pain it inflicts. When the persona becomes distrustful and difficult to handle then the shadow splits and becomes unapproachable to the ordinary awareness. Then this persona is developed into false self, which eventually leads shadow out of the awareness.

Freud gave two aspects. One Eros which is also, called Life Instinct and the other one is Thanatos which is also, called Death

Instinct. Freud saw Thanatos as having the satanic effect, which continuously battles with the life instinct, to dominate it.

Rollo May also introduced the concept of devil called demonic. It is the traditional symbol of cosmic evil. This demonic could work in both good and evil. A person could not disown it or live without it. According to Rollo May, a person has the potential to realise that he has both positive and negative side. The achievements of a person are bound by the conflicts, which the demonic instincts put on it.

Beck brings out a comparison between demonic evil and human evil. According to him, Human Evil is a specific form of mental illness. This illness is chronic in nature. Beck believed that Demonic Evil is an outcome of the custody and possession by minor demons or by *satan*, for whose treatment exorcism is needed.

All the above explanations given by different psychologists and scholars make it apparent that the soul of human beings has a power that imposes evil and negativity. It is in the hands of a person what he chooses and what he rejects.

(ii) *Nafs/Self* (*Ego*)

The second element of the map is *nafs* as the quintessence of a person. It is also called *zat*. It is the essence of self. In Islam, *nafs* is also used as a synonym to self-consciousness. Self does not develop aloof; it is in constant contact with the body, intellect, heart, and *satan*. Therefore, both evil and angel surround self.

Islamic scholars believe that self and the spiritual form of self could be formed even in emptiness and closet. It is connected to the parts of the body and is departed by the bodily parts. It has the ability to discriminate between the "I" and the world. This self-filled with consciousness is only existent in humans; this consciousness of self has not been created in animals. Hence, animals cannot distinguish between themselves and the external world. Only man has the power to understand the distinction between the environment and oneself and hence can internalise the understanding and move towards the higher level of consciousness.

Al-Ghazali uses the term *anniya* meaning heart or *sirru'l-kalb* meaning secret of heart. He describes it in this way,

> "The Lord commands the man and
> Allah ignites the light from His own light.
> This light is reflected in all the truths
> shown and given by God."

Many scholars like Ibn Arabi and Ibn Rushd that any bodily action without the existence of the self is impossible. Self makes a connection between desires, wishes, requirements, and the physical acts performed with the body. Hence, self and body is inseparable. Islamic scholars do not differentiate between self and ego, for them self is psychological and a spiritual reality. Here, ego could be related to lung's self-concept and his theory of collective unconscious. Freud in his theory showed ego as not synonym to consciousness. For Freud much of the part of ego is unconscious or preconscious but for lung this was never the case, for him ego is the focal for consciousness and is the centre for total psyche, including both unconscious and conscious. Lung never viewed these two aspects as separate entities. He saw them as two sides of same coin.

Taking into consideration the classical Western psychology, the word ego is been used as a system which is rational, realistic part of person. It channels the right cognitive and perceptual processes.

As Ibn Sina described in his theory the words like *mudrike* (Perceiver) and *muharrike* (Mover). He explained the power of ego to perceive the internal meanings and then relate it to the external environment. Hence, ego could make a balance between what is needed and what really exist in the environment. Ibn Sina's theoretical point of view moves in the direction of Freud's work, where he explained ego as a rope, at one side of the rope exists Id impulses which are moulded in accordance to the rules of reasons and on the other side exists the external viewpoint, according to which the impulses are to be expressed.

However, Ibn Sina did not perceive ego as free as Freud did. For him, ego did not have the power to be a mover whereas Freud saw ego as having the power of manipulation and expression keeping in mind the reality.

In addition, many Islamic scholars were on agreement that there are different actions been performed by the person but these different elements does not need different powers. Just one power can change its forms and lead to different deeds. This aspect was same as that of Freud. Freud's central theme was that instinct of lust is the bases of human behaviour. However, Islamic scholars were on the same lines as Freud was but in Islam lust is not perceived as sexuality, it is only seen as a desire.

For the excessive emphasis on the concept of sexuality, Freud has many critics from his own followers like Adler, Horney, and lung. The opposition of Freud's concept by his own people shows that the approach of Islam is much better in dealing with sexuality and lust.

Jung was on the same platform as Islam for explaining this concept. Lung also considered it as the energy of life. This energy is much needed for the proper and balanced functioning of a person both physically and mentally.

Quran supports it and explains that self-indulgence to the worldly objects is described as lust. As earlier explained that *nafsi ammara* the stage where self is at the level of Id. Self is not been developed in the early phase of life. However, with the developmental levels, the self also improves its skills and functioning and now the ego takes control of the Id or *nafsi ammara*. It is this time that the ego starts keeping an eye on the wishes of *nafsi ammara* and opposes it. Ego begins to discipline Id according to certain rules and concepts laid by religion, morality, and surroundings.

According to Quran, after this point superego shapes but for shaping of superego, it is important that *nafsi lawama* (superego) dominate *nafs*.

(iii) *Nafsi Lawama/Superego*

The third building block of this map is *nafsi lawama* (superego) which also means Blaming Evil. Here the *nafs* keeps away from all the malevolence and evil, also, it tries to remove these evils. It is called *nafsi lawama* as the *nafs* blames itself if the wrongdoings are not been controlled.

According to Quran and Islam, *nafsi lawama* is that essence which glows with the light of heart. This light warns oneself and other of the wrong deeds and shows them the path of correctness. This part is always alert and vigilant. It juggles between the natural doings and Divinity. When a person began to involve himself in actions for gratification of worldly desires, immediately *nafsi lawama* gives the person a Divine warning and ceases his action. Eventually, person returns to the original self, which is pure and is much closer to God. Sufism perceives *nafsi lawama* as auto correction software, which controls and eradicates the wishfully actions and deeds performed by *nafsi lawama. Nafsi lawama* is similar to the concept of Western psychology of Superego. It acts as a judge for the actions and thoughts of Ego and Id. It has inbuilt code which consist of norms and code of conduct, all moral codes and different standards of conduct are imbedded in it. These codes and standards act as inhibitions for the person's behaviour and actions.

Nafsi lawama restricts, moderates, evaluates, and controls the activities of ego but it does it both consciously and unconsciously. According to Freud's theory, superego is formulated by the parental instructions. However, for other theorists like Murray, the discipline and instructions from the side of the parents are not enough. For formulation of superego society, friends, groups, surroundings are needed.

For the believers and followers of Islam, religious faith and constructs help in formulation and development of superego. The promise made to that Almighty and the punishment for the wrongdoings by God, helps in development of the qualities of Superego in the people's souls.

(iv) *Nafsi Mutmainah* (*Possessor of Serenity and Tranquillity*)

The fourth element of this map is *nafsi mutmainah*. It has the qualities of calmness, serenity, and tranquility. According to Islam, these qualities in self are formulated from faith and the religious life.

According to Islamic scholars *nafsi mutmainah* is a kind of *nafs*, which admires righteousness, goodness, and worships with the pure heart. It hates the aspects of bad actions and disowns them. An Islamic scholar, Ibn Taymiyyah says that whatever is been prohibited by the religion is to be hated by the follower, as he moves away from such behaviour, he moves towards the natural faith. These are facets and dimensions of *nafsi mutmainah.*

It is important for a person to avoid the forbidden behaviours; once such behaviours are prohibited, they do not attract or tempt the mind and feelings of a person anymore.

Harmful impulses are reduced in *nafsi mutmainah.* Calm and peace dominates it and *satan* or evil has no effect on it. *Nafsi mutmainah*, helps keeping away anxiety, depression, and maintains physical and psychological health. Here, exists a connection with God, which is Divine and pure. A person who has surrendered oneself for the serving of God could only reach *nafsi mutmainah* and their primary aim is to reach to this level.

Sufi tradition sees other divisions of *nafs*, which are beyond *nafsi mutmainah*. These are: *nafsi mulhimah*, *radiyah, mardiyyah* and *safiyyah* (or *kamila*). At every dimension of *nafs*, follower receives certain in-depth perceptions from the Divine and it leads to opening of new views of the world. By indulging into religious rituals, *dhikr*, person can open his eyes and mind fully.

Many scholars believe that modern Western psychology has not even touched upon the periphery of these religious life and is far from the valuable rich religious experience.

Modern Psychology has not really focused upon reaching to these higher spiritual goals but the motto of Islam is to reach the zenith. However, Maslow's and Kurt Goldstein's self-actualisation and self-transcendence is partially similar to these dimensions of *nafs*.

Goldstein sees it as one of the motives and Maslow perceives it as a level of development. They view humans as having a need to realise all their potentials. According to Goldstein, it is a master motive, much above all motives, and it is in a sense the only true motive a person possesses. Maslow feels that self-actualisation is the need, which makes a person fresh, lively, natural, calm, and serene. They are not bothered by the man-made concepts, abstractions, expectations, stereotypes, etc. They live more in the real world of nature.

It could be concluded from the above discussion that in Qurari Self formulates the spiritual core. It has the capability and capacity to improve, grow, and progress. All religious facets are related to self or its parts. However, for Western psychology, the aspects of the higher levels of self are been discussed about. There are both overlaps and contradictions in the idea of self but the Divinity is still out of reach for the system under Western psychology.

Sufism: A Futuristic Approach

Soul, spirit, and self—have been seen as conjoined terms in Sufism. Sufi tradition sees seven facets of the soul. Each soul is represented at a different juncture of evolution and development. These could be divided into the mineral soul after which comes the vegetable soul then the animal soul, the personal soul, the human soul, the secret souls and at last the secret of secrets.

Sufi does not view the model of souls in a hierarchy, where growth of one means growth of all the preceding souls and movement of growth in progression. For Sufism, a balanced view of these souls is necessary. Each soul has something important to give and for a real spiritual expansion to occur, a balanced development of the individual, as a whole is needed, which comprises of growth of his body, mind, spirit, and soul.

In modern times many systems and disciplines have come up which focus on spiritual healing of mind or of body. They stress on different spiritual beliefs, values; philosophies, and techniques. Sufism perceives the whole life of a person as a spiritual practice. It places attention on the importance of family, work, leisure, and relationship in providing enough opportunities for spiritual development as done by prayers or reflections.

The Arabic word *ruh*, which is used for soul, has other meanings too like "spirit" and "breath". The sparkling of God's spirit is called the secret of secrets and it is placed at the highest level of the souls.

Each component of the soul has its own strengths, needs, and desires. According to the time a person is in, different souls become dominant. For a Sufi teacher, it is important to know when a particular soul is active and when it is passive. For example, a dream coming from a particular soul would be analysed differently than dream from another soul.

Different souls cater to different needs of humans. These needs could be bodily, mental, or spiritual. Concern about one soul and ignoring others could lead to imbalance. These imbalances are dangerous for the human species as it leads to fulfilment of only one particular kind of need. Balance of all seven souls brings about balanced health and enlargement of a prosperous and fuller life.

(i) *The Mineral Soul*

The mineral soul is also called the *ruh madeni.* It is located in the skeletal system. It is that part of soul, which does not revolt against Almighty's Will. It is as a rock, which is placed once, would never move from there until the time an external force compels for it to move.

The mineral soul can be compared to the skeleton. Just as skeleton is hidden inside the body of a person, similarly the inner structure of soul is *ruh madeni.* As when there is certain imbalance in skeleton, it could lead to higher flexibility or total rigidity. Similarly, mineral soul is one, which is not independent in its own movement. If the mineral soul is affected by the external manipulations a lot then it does not have the independence of its own movement but if the person is emotionally, physically, and mentally strong then it can hold on to places, people, positions, and himself. Like a boneless jellyfish who survives only at the mercy of the tides. Similarly, mineral soul survives only at the mercy of that Almighty.

(ii) *The Vegetable Soul*

The vegetable soul is located in the liver and is related to the digestive system. It is also called the *ruh nabati.* The vegetable soul regulates enlargement and incorporation of nutrients. It is that kind of soul as God gave to plants. Its functions are new in comparison to the mineral soul, as mineral soul has no need of nourishment.

As plants gets energy by transforming the light and oxygen and this energy helps them to grow. Similarly, when we are in the womb, vegetable soul mainly functions. In the womb, we are rooted to the mother's uterus by the umbilical cord through which the nourishment is passed on. We grow and develop through the help of this nourishment. It has immense intelligence. The intelligence of vegetable soul has been overlooked since ever as the importance to the abstract learning related to the head. It should not be forgotten that all the physical functions are been carried out by the vegetable soul.

(iii) *The Animal Soul*

The animal soul is located in the heart and is connected to the circulatory system. It is also called *ruh haywani*. This soul includes our fears, angers, passions, and desires. All organisms move towards what is rewarding and moves away from whatever is punishing.

These rewarding and pushing principles work on the universal principle of attraction and repulsion. These two basic instincts have got a lot of attention in psychological studies and researches.

As been clearly put by many psychologists that to live it is important to preserve oneself, sense danger, and avoid it. These instincts are needed for species preservation. Rewards help to learn the fruitful actions and punishment helps to reduce the dangerous acts. In comparison to animals, the instincts to reproduce and survive are limited. Animals are far more flexible and responsive to their surroundings.

Animal soul roots its passion in the reproductive instinct. It not only concentrates on sexual process but the love, affection, and nurturance.

According to Sufism, all the souls should be in balance to each other. In a balanced state, animal soul acts as a precious asset to the happiness, well being, and health.

(iv) *The Personal Soul*

The personal soul is located in the brain and relates to the nervous system. It is also called *ruh nafsani*. The animals are distinguished on the levels of development of heart and circulatory system from the plants. Similarly, humans differ from animals in the development of a complex nervous system. This complex system brings the ability of greater memory, decision making, planning, rationality, and thinking. The personal soul has the intelligence which allows humans to understand their surrounding in a holistic manner in comparison to intellectual abilities of mineral, vegetable, and animal souls.

Personal soul helps a person to respond to the environmental aspects in a better manner. A person can plan what he wishes to do and a mental model could be prepared for the outcome of the actions, which have already taken place and would eventually take place.

The ego also found its place in the personal soul. A person has both negative and positive egos in him. The positive ego helps a person to organise his memory and intellect and gives a sense of self. It gives vigour and strength to aspects like accountability, reliability, integrity, and self-respect. On the other hand, the negative ego is the force which triggers arrogance, egotism, self-centredness and sense of separation from the Divinity. The positive ego acts as a friend which helps in building inner stability during the thick and thin of life whereas negative ego acts as an enemy. It distorts the perception of the external world and colors the relationship between people and surroundings.

One major distinction between negative and positive ego is that negative ego always tries to become the master of the being whereas positive ego acts as a servant.

(v) *The Human Soul*

The human soul is located in the galb, the spiritual heart. It is also called *ruh insani*. It is more refined than the personal soul. It is the centre of reliance, empathy, and originality. It is the place where the person's spiritual standards, values, and experiences exist.

Creativity first occurs at the level of the soul. The brain, which develops in the personal soul, works like a computer where all the information is stored, manipulated, and retrieved. However, the inventiveness only happens at the heart.

The real imagination comes from the heart. However, it is unfortunate that focal point for all educational system is the expansion of intellect and little attention is paid to the development of the heart. Heart is centre for arts, love, empathy, and service to others. Hence, it is important to grow the intelligence of Heart.

The heart intelligence of the human soul and the abstract intelligence, both complement each other. Cognitive aspects relate to logic, rationality and heart adds faith and consideration to it.

Combination of these two kinds of intelligence leads to a better judgement. It is always said that the heart knows what is right; the head knows what is most effective but the effectiveness not always leads to the right path.

The conscious use of reasons is nourished by the faith and trust in God or in the larger reality. It develops through self-observation, arbitration, meditation, compassion, inner awareness, and delightfulness for the nature, animals, and people.

(vi) *The Secret Soul*

This secret soul is that part of human's that remembers Almighty. It is that inner consciousness which is located in the inner heart. It is also called *ruh sirr*. This soul has a full understanding of its birth and culmination. It knows where it came from and where it would be heading.

A known Sufi teacher once wrote,

> "The inner most consciousness is that
> part of consciousness, which God
> purposefully hid as He Himself,
> observes and keeps a check over it."

Another Scholar adds to it,

> "The body is like a dark room and
> its lighting lamp is the inner
> consciousness. If one has no inner
> consciousness, he would forever suffer
> from darkness and aloofness."

When the souls were incarnated, The Almighty asked them a question, "Am I your Lord?" and the souls replied, "Yes, indeed". The soul who responded to the question was the secret soul. It knew who it was and still knows who it is. This secret soul breathes in the shadow of God's presence. The loss of connection with the Almighty only happens when it is reincarnated in this materialistic universe.

(vii) *The Secret of Secrets*

The supreme transcendent, beyond time and space, is included in *sirr-ul-asrar*. This is that pure soul (*ruh*) which Allah breathed into humankind. It is the core of the soul. It is also called the soul. It is that pure part which has Divinity attached to it and it sparkles like gold. Humans have to understand that we are not only what we have, we are not only our personalities or thinking our feelings. We are much more and more above then all this. We are the Divine enclosed within our bodies. Human's competence and ability for spiritual intensification and indulgence is virtually unlimited.

All the kinds and types of soul have a place to reside in the body, which helps to understand the functions each one performs. The balance between all these souls reaches a healthy and peaceful end.

Sufism and Consciousness

The traveller on the path to truth must have intelligence, understanding, and insight. These are his prerequisites.

The consciousness of Sufism is a science of consciousness that holds the reality that knowledge comes through experience. Therefore, the true study of Sufism leads not only to greater understanding, but also to increased awareness and consciousness. Different levels of consciousness could be distinguished.

Richard M. Bucke delineates three levels of evolution and proposes that the human mind progresses through these levels of evolution, summarised as follows:

1. Simple Consciousness—ability for sensory stimulation and perception.
2. Self-Consciousness—The development of the ability to conceptualise, use language, and are conscious of the self.
3. Cosmic Consciousness—humanity's cumulative experiences bring ever increasing information and knowledge.

On the path of Sufism, the quest for knowledge is equated with the attainment of knowledge through experience. There is no distinction between studying consciousness and increasing consciousness; they are one in the same. Consciousness comes through experience of the complete system of Unity. The philosophy or psychology of Sufi consciousness is not a subject of mental inquiry but rather a direct inquiry from within the longing of the Sufi's heart as he or she seeks to understand the Wisdom of Divine intellect.

Therefore, to explain something or to have veritable knowledge or science of it means to be able to relate it to Being itself, to relate all of the properties and qualities of that particular being to its ontological status. What is found by means of observation and logical inferences from it does not lead to the "metaphysical secrets" of things but rather to the discovery of certain aspects of their outward manifestation or to the relation of phenomena. True science is to relate these phenomena to their inner aspect, which are the essence and the centre relating them to Pure Being.

The concept of existing on more than one level is an important aspect of Sufism. The levels of "simple", "self", and "cosmic consciousness" are not separate or distinct. Sufism is a path that leads toward agreement of intention, thought, and action.

The Heart of Consciousness

In Sufism, the heart is considered to be the centre of the intellect and the conscious centre of Being. Many individuals may strive for the knowledge of unity, the vision of Universal Reality, yet few achieve this knowledge in a lifetime. Those who do achieve this level are called Sufis.

One phrase that is used in Sufism to describe the realm of multiplicity is that the heart is veiled in ignorance, which indicates a state of less than full consciousness. This state is also defined as living in darkness or searching for light. The light can be considered a metaphor for ultimate or cosmic consciousness. In Sufism, it is understood that wisdom, light, and a complete system of existence exists, yet they are often hidden from view.

Once the Sufi practitioner knows where to look, then comes the understanding of the process of uncovering and seeing the light and moving away from ignorance and darkness. Whatever is seen in the darkness is a limited view with hidden angles. From this limited view we remain in the realm of multiplicity, which is the term used for anything less than knowledge and experience of unity.

The Consciousness of Unity

In Sufism, as has been stated, the goal for life is to become conscious in every moment. As in some other disciplines or on other spiritual paths, attachment to the goal may be a distraction from full awareness. However, in Sufism, it is clear from the beginning what the goal is. In this way, there is a standard by which to live and a way to determine, by the knowledge of a teacher, if one is moving toward the intended goal. This goal of consciousness includes awareness in every movement and every breath. The awareness is transcendent and beyond any imitation or separation. The limitations are also referred to as illusions in Sufism. Seeing a part of something is an illusion in contrast to seeing the whole. Attraction to or the distraction of the physical realm and its possessions is one of the limitations of human nature. However, because of the rule of balance, the Sufi does not practise extended seclusion or mortification. These practices may be considered distractions or limitations at the other extreme rather than attraction to the world.

The journey of Sufism is a return to the origin. A return to the level of knowledge that existed before physical form was manifested and still exists beyond the physical realms. The practice on this path includes focusing all the scattered energy within one point, within the heart. Through this concentration and awareness, one may remember the source of creation within the centre of being.

Advanced Stages of Consciousness

According to Sufism, there are two advanced stages of consciousness. It could be seen as the stages of perfect spiritual obedience: *fana* (annihilation) and *baqa* (continuance/return).

The Quran uses *fana* and *baqa* paradigms to state that everything in the physical universe will perish except the face of God.

Fana is the Sufi term for extinction. It means to annihilate the self, while remaining physically alive. Persons having entered this state are said to have no existence outside of, and be in complete unity with Allah. *Fana* may be attained by constant meditation and by contemplation on the attributes of God, coupled with the denunciation of human attributes. It is a sort of mental, yet real, death. It liberates man from all contingency outside of his spiritual quest; his ultimate aim is the Truth. Three degrees of *fana* could be distinguished: *fana* of acts, attributes, and essence.

The Sufi *fana* in its triple manifestation does not have an exclusively negative effect or action; it is the annihilation of everything contingent, whether this be in the form of action, attribute, or essence; more precisely, it is the annihilation of everything that is not God, and God is the supreme object of all good, all beauty.

Fana thus conceived is an internal state, which requires from the Sufi a sustained and permanent effort of concentration to break his fetters and take on the demands and calls of truth, by his acts, his moral virtues, his whole being. That implies perfect control of himself: in words, deeds, and thoughts. It is at this price that he attains an interior spiritual state where he becomes the pure and clear mirror in which the lights of Truth are reflected in their entire splendour.

Sufism has explained many gradations of submission and surrender to that Almighty (*fana*).

These are:

(a) Submission to the personal guide (*fana-fi-sheikh*)
(b) Submission to the teacher who has passed on from one to another (*fana-fi-pir*)
(c) Surrender to the divine messenger or prophet (*fana-fi-rasul*)
(d) Effacement of the being in Oneness (*fana-fi-lillah*)
(e) Effacement in revivification into one's own true nature (*fana-i-baka*)

The second aspect is a state of return, or persistence, or continuance—*baqa*—in which one is part of the world but not concerned about one's worldly position or rewards. This is the stage when a person, after a complete negation of the self, begins to act under Divine motivation and instigation, and after the cessation of all baser movements is set into motion under Divine inspiration. The individual is in the world but not separate from anything in it.

In one sense, Sufism is essentially a path of self-transformation ending in *fana* and *baqa*. Arasteh and Sheikh (1989) describe the states of *fana* and *baqa* in psychological terms. *Fana* is the disintegration of one's narrow self-concept, social self, and limited intellect. *Baqa* is the reintegration as the universal self, or the activation of one's totality.

Sufism and Humanity's Future

With the changing times and the era of globalisation and industrialisation, many discoveries have increased human knowledge and understanding of the universe. The knowledge has given new perspectives and newfound capabilities to the human beings but instead of being grateful for these gifts, humans have exploited them for their own selfish needs and desires. As a result of this, the lives of humans are devoid of peace, tranquillity, and serenity. The greed and higher levels of materialism has lead to increasing number of unresolved problems for all humankind. Ravenousness and scepticism is flourishing day by day. Increasing conflicts among different classes, creed, religion, interests among the inhabitants of the planet is leading all the species on a path of self-destruction and aloofness.

Human race was once a child who was restless, inquisitive, and naive. This child was not supervised and hence through its own guidance and supervision it had made this progress. The result of this kind of extreme control on its own behaviour has lead to confusion, helplessness, and is perplexed. In this mechanistic world, this child has lost its purity in the endless race of excitement and terror of failure. There was once a stage when these technologies made people comfortable and secure but that stage of comfort has long been left behind.

The biggest mistake of today's time is the focus of almost everyone on the external reality. This focus leads to a temporary blindness. This blindness leads a person to give more importance to only rationality and sensory information. He fails to realise the hidden treasure of knowledge in the heart of every being. The transcended modes of awareness and knowledge remain unexploited. The alienation this human race is facing and the kind of problems, which are left unresolved, could only be resolved with multi-dimensional understanding of the universe rather than an imperfect perspective.

It has to be understood that the remedy of all the problems exists in the humans itself. One has to reach to one's potential to remove all these troubles and for doing so, it is necessary to concentrate on the internal reality rather than external one. Complete knowledge could only be attained through the help of indulging in the inner pool of strength within a person. This does not mean that external reality is futile; it only means that inner knowledge is much more valuable to reach the zenith of humanity and Divinity.

The religious groups and spiritual traditions have always stressed upon the fundamental reality. Each has laid down certain guidelines, which could enhance the potentialities and capabilities existing inside a person. These practical guidelines change according to the era they fall in but the teachings are same and lead to the lightened path of wisdom. A person's mind has to be continuously in motion so that one could attach one's interpretations to the teachings. Rigidity and fixation cannot work as the time, era, and circumstances keep on changing. It is very important to have a match between the needs and requirements of an era and the given teachings.

The Sufi order matches both the requirement of the surrounding and the inner need, both wisdom of past and future considerations, both the person concerns and the global problems. Its teachings emphasise that as a single atom consist of endless energy similarly the most evolved matter which is human body has a pool of inner strengths and potentialities.

The follower or the student moving on the path of Sufism searches for this reservoir by applying scientific and experimental approach. S/he tries to understand the basic and pure nature of human being, humanity, universe and the relationship of universe with humanity in the ways which are pertinent to present and future.

These discoveries by the followers lead to finding solutions to all the human beings problems whether collectivist or individualistic. The materialistic discoveries would continue to serve humanity but Sufism has a broader aim of uncovering the capabilities within the human self. So that these potentialities could be utilised for the benefits of all establishments.

The hidden treasure, which Sufism seeks to utilise, is love. It is this power of love which breaks the chains of narrow-mindedness, materialism, selfishness, and greediness. It is love which gives use to sympathy, sacrifice, surrender, empathy, forgiveness, patience, and generosity. Love motivates a person to do good deeds. It inspires a person to be courageous and helpful. It challenges a person to move beyond one's own past performance an eventually it satisfies one's own need of being loved.

God could only unfold the future. Nevertheless, humanity can evolve from generation to generation, understanding the inner self, one's attitudes, feelings and thinking. The higher knowledge could enable humans to relate to the needs of all the species, planet, and universe. It could bring about the understanding of interrelatedness of humanity with Divinity and the Creator. Through this awareness, an era of boundless and limitless love could be shaped and lived in.

This chapter was an attempt to provide a brief overview of Islam and its mystical dimension, Sufism. Emphasis was given to the psychological aspects of the process of spiritual transformation and the associated processes and stages of self-transformation merely in an outline fashion. There is much more that can be said about all the issues that were raised in this limited space. It is important to remember, however, that all that can be said in this manner makes only a map; the territory is the actual experience of the seeker and is always a unique process that cannot be molded into any model or description however sophisticated. It is hoped that the map will simply provide an inspiration for the seeker of God.

Exercise 1: For Self-understanding

Imagine that you are facing a gate. On your side of the gate is the infinitely large and complex world of phenomena—the grasses in the prairies, the teeming cities, the clouds over the ocean, babies crying, wars being fought, suffering, love making, your thoughts, everyone's thoughts, the stars sprinkled in the heaven, every single appearance everywhere, everything, every self. On the other side of the gate is non-dual reality, selflessness, enlightenment, the absolute, God. The gate is the gate of awakening. This gate of awaking could only be opened by first understanding the one who wants to go onto the other side that, is you-your own self.

Understanding self is a difficult area to conquer but the starting point could be to first understand the external realities and which part of that reality brings what all emotions are inside you. The emotions could be of joy, anger, sadness or jealousy, disgust, etc.

The exercise starts by finding a soothing place where you could be surrounded by the natural beauty, then feeling and writing about all the experiences of happiness and sadness of that day.

Making a diary of the experiences for a month and then reflecting upon it. By understanding the joyous moments, and the reason behind them, could open the whole spectrum of sheer pleasure and happiness.

Exercise 2: For Realising the Inner States

Inner states, thoughts, feelings, and emotions can be understood more by reflecting upon them, by looking back at what they have done to you and your life, by examining their repercussions and how they make you think, feel, and act.

By looking back over time, you can see the different inner states that have arisen or you can follow a single one, seeing the events they have been part of.

To do this exercise, sit or lie down, and relax the body totally, then become aware of your present inner state and watch the different thoughts and emotions as they arise. Concentrate the mind with a practice specifically for that, or pronounce a *mantra* or rhythm or a soothing song to silence the mind, and then remember the inner state.

You can look back over the day's events to see what inner states (egos) manifested and what they made you do, or you can go into a specific inner state in more depth by looking back over it, seeing how it has worked throughout your life, and then analysing it.

Remember the past as though you are looking at a movie in a detached way, getting information about your inner states and their related events in your life and reflecting upon them.

Exercise 3: For Understanding the Process of Spiritual Realisation

Imagine the sky on a clear spring morning—utterly transparent, empty, and vividly fresh. It is alive, though there is nothing there. This experience of the sky's emptiness and at the same time its living presence is often pointed out as analogous to the experience of spiritual awakening. The sky is perceived simultaneously as both a presence and an absence. The same paradox becomes apparent in the instant of spiritual realisation. There is an unexplainable sense of absence and presence, of emptiness and fullness. Yet the analogy with the sky is not perfect, because the sky is usually perceived as something "out there", separate from the perceiver.

The simultaneous realisation of emptiness and living presence that occurs with spiritual awakening is not limited by this kind of subject-object relation.

The first process of this awakening is attainment of selflessness.

This nature of awareness is attained by first the process of selflessness. To be selfless is a difficult process. One can start by taking a task of performing one selfless behaviour each every day, so that the happiness and joy of that act could be developed and tested by the person for long.

Exercise 4: Exercise for Understanding of Silence

Music is divine. It gives pleasure and calmness. To understand music it is also important to realise the silence before it or the silence as music itself. Before a melody or rhythm begins, there is silence. Then the first sound appears. We may notice how the first sound, and the second, and the third, and so on, are each given freely into the moment. They appear out of silence, out of not being. We may also notice how the note that will be played in a few moments does not yet exist ... and suddenly it is here! What gives it existence?

We can only say it is born from the infinite potential of the void. Then, what happens? It vanishes! Where does it go? It returns into the emptiness of silence, into not being.

Yes, it may linger a moment or two in memory as its fleeting presence touches the fleeting presence of the sounds that flows, but silence precedes it and silence finishes it.

This birth from emptiness and dying in the same gives way to understand the essence of being. Try to find a place where a clam music, which ignites your heart, could be played. Listen to all the tones, pitches and rhythms. Now imaging a tone to be equal to your own emotion. Differences in tones show different emotions of your life. The task is to analyse each emotion and then build on the one which is most soothing, that is, happiness and joy.

Exercise 5: For Knowing and Improving Human Relations

You need Drawing sheets and Colours for this exercise.

Draw a picture of your home as you currently picturise it in terms of human relationships and how are people related to each other in your home, what all distorted relationship exists, how many lovely relationship and strong bonds exist.

Then make another drawing showing what actually you want the relationship in your family to be. The ideal human connection in the house. Make a contrast between the two drawings and find the missing proportions. Now sit and analyse why these missing portions exist, what are the reasons for it, how it has developed and the last task is to find ways to improve or make the relationship between people in your family better. Same exercise could be taken up for the world around, and then the ways could be found out to change it. A change from one person matters a lot, it could lead to the chain of changes.

The Islanders—A Fable

Once upon a time there lived an ideal community in a far-off land. Its members had no fears as we now know them. Instead of uncertainty and vacillation, they had a purposefulness and a fuller means of expressing themselves.

Although there were none of its stresses and tensions which mankind now considers essential to its progress, their lives were richer, because other, better elements replaced these things.

Theirs, therefore, was a slightly different mode of existence. We could almost say that our present perceptions are a crude, makeshift version of the real ones that this community possessed.

They had real lives, not semi-lives.

They had a leader, who discovered that their country was to become uninhabitable for a period of, shall we say, 20,000 years. He planned their escape, realising that their descendants would be able to return home successfully, only after many trials.

He found for them a place of refuge, an island whose features were only roughly similar to those of the original homeland.

Because of the difference in climate and situation, the immigrants had to undergo a transformation.

This made them more physically and mentally adapted to the new circumstances: coarse perceptions, for instance, were substituted for finer ones, as when the manual labourer becomes toughened in response to the needs of his calling.

In order to reduce the pain which a comparison between the old and new states would bring, they were made to forget the past almost entirely.

Only the most shadowy recollection of it remained, yet it was sufficient to be awakened when the time came.

The system was very complicated, but well arranged. The organs by means of which the people survived on the island were also made the organs of enjoyment, physical and mental. The organs which were really constructive in the old homeland were placed in a special form of abeyance, and linked with the shadowy memory, in preparation for its eventual activation.

Slowly and painfully the immigrants settled down, adjusting themselves to the local conditions. The resources of the island were such that, coupled with effort and a certain form of guidance, people would be able to escape to a further island on the way back to their original home. This was the first of a succession of islands upon which gradual acclimatisation took place.

The responsibility of this "evolution" was vested in those individuals who could sustain it. These were necessarily only a few, because for the mass of the people the effort of keeping both sets of knowledge in their consciousness was virtually impossible. One of them seemed to conflict with the other. Certain specialists guarded the "special science".

This "secret", the method of effecting the transition, was nothing more or less than the knowledge of maritime skills and their application. The escape needed an instructor, raw materials, people, effort and understanding. Given these, people could learn to swim, and also to build ships.

The people who were originally in charge of the escape operation made it clear to everyone that a certain preparation was necessary before anyone could learn to swim or even take part in building a ship. For a time the process continued satisfactorily.

Then a man who had been found, for the time being, lacking in the necessary qualities rebelled against this order and managed to develop a masterly idea. He had observed that the effort to escape placed a heavy and often seemingly unwelcome burden upon the people. At the same time they were disposed to believe things which they were told about the escape operation. He realised that he could acquire power, and also revenge himself upon those who had undervalued him, as he though, by a simple exploitation of these two sets of facts.

He would merely offer to take away the burden, by affirming that there was no burden.

He made his announcement:

> "There is no need for man to integrate his mind and train it in the way which has been described to you. The human mind is already a stable and continuous, consistent thing. You have been told that you have to become a craftsman in order to build a ship. I say, not only do you not need to be a craftsman—you do not need a ship at all!
>
> "An islander needs only to observe a few simple rules to survive and remain integrated into society. By the exercise of common sense, born into everyone, he can attain anything upon this island, our home, the common property and heritage of all."

The tonguester, having gained a great deal of interest among the people, now proved his message by saying: "If there is any reality in ships and swimming, show us ships which have made the journey, and swimmers who have come back!"

This was a challenge to the instructors which they could not meet. It was based upon an assumption of which the bemused herd could not now see the fallacy. You see, ships never returned from the other land. Swimmers, when they did come back, had undergone a fresh adaptation which made them invisible to the crowd.

The mob pressed for demonstrative proof.

"Shipbuilding," said the escapers, in an attempt to reason with the revolt, "is an art and a craft. The learning and the exercise of this lore depends upon special techniques. These together make up a total activity, which cannot be examined piecemeal, as you demand. This activity has an impalpable element, called "baraka", from which the work "barque"—a ship—is derived. This word means "the Subtlety", and cannot be shown to you."

"Art, craft, total, baraka, nonsense!" shouted the revolutionaries.

And so they hanged as many shipbuilding craftsmen as they could find.

The new gospel was welcomed on all sides as one of liberation. Man had discovered that he was already mature! He felt, for the time at least, as if he had been released from responsibility.

Most other ways of thinking were soon swamped by the simplicity and comfort of the revolutionary concept. Soon it was considered to be a basic fact, which had never been challenged by any rational person. Rational, of course, meant anyone who harmonised with the general theory itself, upon which society was now based.

Ideas which opposed the new one were easily called irrational. Anything irrational was bad. Thereafter, even if he had doubts, the individual had to suppress them or divert them, because he must at all costs be thought rational.

It was not very difficult to be rational. One had only to adhere to the values of society. Further, evidence of the truth of rationality abounded—providing that one did not think beyond the life of the island.

Society had now temporarily equilibrated itself within the island, and seemed to provide a plausible completeness, if viewed by means of itself. It was based upon reason plus emotion, making both seem plausible. Cannibalism, for instance, was permitted on rational grounds. The human body was found to be edible. Edibility was a characteristic of food. Therefore the human body was food.

In order to compensate for the shortcomings of this reasoning, a makeshift was arranged. Cannibalism was controlled, in the interests of society. Compromise was the trademark of temporary balance. Every now and again someone pointed out a new compromise, and the struggle between reason, ambition, and community produced some fresh social norm.

Since the skills of boatbuilding had no obvious application within this society, the effort could easily be considered absurd. Boats were not needed—there was nowhere to go. The consequences of certain assumptions can be made to "prove" those assumptions. This is what is called a pseudocertainty, the substitute for real certainty. It is what we deal in every day, when we assume that we will live another day. But our islanders applied it to everything.

The words "displeasing" and "unpleasant" were used on the island to indicate anything which conflicted with the new gospel, which was itself known as "Please". The idea behind this was that people would now please themselves, within the general need to please the state. The state was taken to mean all the people.

It is hardly surprising that from quite early times the very thought of leaving the island filled most people with terror. Similarly, very real fear is to be seen in long-term prisoners who are about to be released. "Outside" the place of captivity is a vague, unknown, threatening world.

The island was not a prison. But it was a cage with invisible bars, more effective than obvious ones ever could be.

The insular society became more and more complex, and we can look at only a few of its outstanding features. Its literature was a rich one. In addition to cultural compositions, there were numerous books which explained the values and achievements of the nation. There was also a system of allegorical fiction, which portrayed how terrible life might have been, had society not arranged itself in the present reassuring pattern.

From time to time instructors tried to help the whole community to escape. Captains sacrificed themselves for the reestablishment of a climate in which the now concealed shipbuilders could continue their work. All these efforts were interpreted by historians and sociologists with reference to conditions on the island, without thought for any contact outside this closed society.

Plausible explanations of almost anything were comparatively easy to produce. No principle of ethics was involved, because scholars continued to study with genuine dedication what seemed to be true. "What more can we do?" they asked, implying by the word "more" that the alternative might be an effort of quantity.

Or they asked each other, "What else can we do?" assuming that the answer might be "else"—something different. Their real problem was that they assumed themselves able to formulate the questions, and ignored the fact that the questions were every bit as important as the answers.

Of course, the islanders had plenty of scope for thought and action within their own small domain. The variations of ideas and differences of opinion gave the impression of freedom of thought. Thought was encouraged, providing that it was not "absurd".

Freedom of speech was allowed. It was of little use without the development of understanding, which was not pursued.

The work and the emphasis of the navigators had to take on different aspects in accordance with the changes in the community. This made their reality even more baffling to the students who tried to follow them from the island point of view.

Amid all the confusion, even the capacity to remember the possibility of escape could at times become an obstacle.

The stirring consciousness of escape potential was not very discriminating.

More often than not the eager would-be escapers settled for any kind of substitute.

A vague concept of navigation cannot become useful without orientation. Even the most eager potential shipbuilders had been trained to believe that they already had that orientation. They were already mature. They hated anyone who pointed out that they might need a preparation.

Bizarre versions of swimming or shipbuilding often crowded out possibilities of real progress. Very much to blame were the advocates of pseudoswimming or allegorical ships, mere hucksters, who offered lessons to those as yet too weak to swim, or passages on ships which they could not build.

The needs of the society had originally made necessary certain forms of efficiency and thinking which developed into what was known as science. This admirable approach, so essential in the fields where it had application, finally outran its real meaning. The approach called "scientific", soon after the "Please" revolution, became stretched until it covered all manner of ideas.

Eventually things which could not be brought within its bounds became known as "unscientific", another convenient synonym for "bad". Words were unknowingly taken prisoner and then automatically enslaved.

In the absence of a suitable attitude, like people who, thrown upon their own resources in a waiting room, feverishly read magazines, the islanders absorbed themselves in finding substitutes for the fulfilment which was the original (and indeed the final) purpose of this community's exile.

Some were able to diver their attention more or less successfully into mainly emotional commitments. There were different ranges of emotion, but no adequate scale for measuring them. All emotion was considered to be "deep" or "profound"—at any rate more profound than non-emotion. Emotion, which was seen to move people to the most extreme physical and mental acts known, was automatically termed "deep".

The majority of people set themselves targets, or allowed others to set them for them. They might pursue one cult after another, or money, or social prominence. Some worshipped some things and felt themselves superior to all the rest. Some, by repudiating what thcy thought worship was, thought that they had no idols, and could therefore safely sneer at all the rest.

As the centuries passed, the island was littered with the debris of these cults. Worse than ordinary debris, it was self-perpetuating. Well-meaning and other people combined the cults and recombined them, and they spread anew. For the amateur and intellectual, this constituted a mine of academic or "initiatory" material, giving a comforting sense of variety.

Magnificent facilities for the indulging of limited "satisfactions" proliferated. Palaces and monuments, museums and universities, institutes of learning, theatre and sports stadiums almost filled the island. The people naturally prided themselves on these endowments, many of which they considered to be linked in a general way with ultimate truth, though exactly how this was so escaped almost all of them.

Shipbuilding was connected with some dimensions of this activity, but in a way unknown to almost everyone.

Clandestinely the ships raised their sails, the swimmers continued to teach swimming....

The conditions on the island did not entirely fill these dedicated people with dismay. After all, they too had originated in the very same community, and had indissoluble bonds with it, and with its destiny.

But they very often had to preserve themselves from the attentions of their fellow citizens. Some "normal" islanders tried to save them from themselves. Others tried to kill them, for an equally sublime reason. Some even sought their help eagerly, but could not find them.

All these reactions to the existence of the swimmers were the result of the same cause, filtered through different kinds of minds. This cause was that hardly anyone now knew what a swimmer really was, what he was doing, or where he could be found.

As the life of the island became more and more civilized, a strange but logical industry grew up. It was devoted to ascribing doubts to the validity of the system under which the society lived. It succeeded in absorbing doubts about social values by laughing at them or satirising them. The activity could wear a sad or happy face, but it really became a repetitious ritual. A potentially valuable industry, it was often prevented from exercising its really creative function.

People felt that, having allowed their doubts to have temporary expression, they would in some way assuage them, exorcise them, and almost propitiate them. Satire passed for meaningful allegory; allegory was accepted but not digested. Plays, books, films, poems, lampoons were the usual media for this development, though there was a strong section of it in more academic fields.

For many islanders it seemed more emancipated, more modern or progressive, to follow this cult rather than the older ones.

Here and there a candidate still represented himself to a swimming instructor, to make his bargain. Usually what amounted to a stereotyped conversation took place.

"I want to learn to swim."

"Do you want to make a bargain about it?"

"No. I only have to take my ton of cabbage."

"What cabbage?"

"The food which I will need on the other island."

"There is better food there."

"I don't know what you mean. I cannot be sure. I must take my cabbage."

"You cannot swim, for one thing, with a ton of cabbage."

"Then I cannot go. You call it a load. I call it my essential nutrition."

"Suppose, as an allegory, we say not 'cabbage' but 'assumptions' or 'destructive ideas'?"

"I am going to take my cabbage to some instructor who understands my needs".

Source: The Islanders: A Fable, from book *The Sufis*, by Idries Shah.

References

Ansari, Z.A. (1992). *Quranic Concepts of Human Psyche.* Islamabad: International Institute of Islamic Thought (IIIT).

Baba, M. (1967). *Listen Humanity*. New York: Dodd, Mead.

Bakhtiar, L. (1987). *Sufi: Expressions of the Mystic Quest.* New York: Avon.

Beg, M.A. (1970). "A Note on the Concept of Self, and the Theory, and Practice of Psychological Help in the Sufi Tradition." *Interpersonal Development, 1.*

Chand, T. I. (1979). *Thought and the Sufis-in-the World of the Sufi.* UK: The Octagon Press Ltd.

Choueiri (Ed.), Y.M. (1997). *Islamic Fundamentalism.* London: Pinter.

Dawood, N.J. (1968). *The Koran.* Baltimore: Penguin Books.

Erikson, E. (1964). *Insight and Responsibility*. New York: Norton

Erikson, H.E. (1978). *Identity Youth and Crisis.* New York, London: Norton and Company.

Fadiman, J. and R. Frager, (1999). *Essential Sufism.* New York, USA: Harper Collins Publishers Inc.

Fadiman, J. and R. Frager (1999). *Heart, Self and Soul: The Sufi Psychology of Growth, Balance and Harmony.* Wheaton, IL: Quest Books.

Foster, W. (1968). *Sufi Studies Today.* London: Octagon.
Frager, R. and J. Fadiman (1998). *Personality and Personal Growth*, 4th Edn., United States: Longman.
Gregory, B. (1991). *Sacred Unity: Further Steps to an Ecology of Mind.* New York: Harper Collins.
Guillaume, A. (1956). *Islam.* New York: Penguin.
Haeri, F. (1989). *The Journey of the Self.* Dorset, England: Element Books.
Harre, R. and R. Lamb (1986). *The Dictionary of Personality and Social Psychology.* Cambridge: The MIT Press.
Izutsu, T. (1983). *Sufism and Taoism.* Berkeley, CA: University of California Press.
Jonathan, B. (2013). *Encyclopedia of Islam and the Muslim World.* Boston: Leiden.
Jung, C.G. (1933). *Modern Man in Search of a Soul.* New York: A Harvest Book. Press.
Khan, H.I. (1962). *The Sufi Message*, Vol. 5: *Metaphysics.* Katwijk, Holland: Service Publishers.
Khan, P.V. (1974). *Toward the One.* New York: Harper and Row.
Kung, H. (2007). *Islam: Past, Present, and Future.* USA: Oneworld Publication.
Margaret, M. (1997). *Sigmund Freud Explorer of the Unconscious.* Oxford University Press.
Maududi, A.A. (1990). *Towards Understanding Islam.* New York: ICNA Book,
Mijares, S.G. (2002). *Modern Psychology and Ancient Wisdom: An Anthology of Healing Practices from the World's Religious Traditions.* New York: Haworth Press.
Nasr, S. (1987). *Islamic Spirituality: Foundations.* New York: Crossroads.
Nurbakhsh, J. (1990). "Sufism and Psychoanalysis". *Sufi*, *5*: 5-10.
Perry, W.N. (1971). *A Treasury of Traditional Wisdom.* New York: Simon & Schuster.
Polly, Y.E. and J. Hall (1991). *Jung's Self-psychology, a Constructivists' Perspective.* New York: The Guilford Publications.
Qayyum, A. (1976). *Letters of Al-Ghazali.* Lahore, Pakistan: Islamic Publication.
Rahman, F. (1982). *Islam and Modernity: Transformation of an Intellectual Tradition.* University of Chicago Press.
Rushbrook Williams, L.F. (1974). *Sufi Studies: East and West.* UK: Tonbridge Printers Ltd.
Saikal, A. (1990). "Islam Resistance and Reassertion in the World Today". In G.W. Choudhary (Ed.), *Islam and the Contemporary World.* London: Indus Thames Publisher Limited.
Schimmel, A. (1975). *Mystical Dimensions of Islam.* Chapel Hill: University of North Carolina Press.

Shaffi, M. (1985). *Freedom from the Self.* USA: Human Sciences Press Inc.
Shah, I. (1980). *The Way of the Sufi.* UK: The Octagon Press Ltd.
Shah, S. (1933). *Islamic Sufism.* London : Rider
Starrett, G. (1998). *Putting Islam to Work: Education, Politics, and Religious Transformation in Egypt.* Berkeley: University of California Press.
Stoddart, W. (1981). *Sufism: The Mystical Doctrines and Methods of Islam.* Lahore: Suhail Academy.
Trimingham, J.S. (1973). *The Sufi Orders in Islam.* Oxford Publishing House.
Watt, W.M. (1963). *The Faith and Practice of Al-Ghazali.* USA: Oneworld Publication.

9

Convergence of the East and the West

During the past few years there has been growing interest in psychological concepts and phenomena such as *samādhi*, satori, meditation, *gurus*, and others which originated in such Eastern traditions as *Yoga* and Zen Buddhism. In the West, *Yoga* is no longer restricted to exercises at the Y.M.C.A., to such popular movements as Transcendental Meditation, or to a few secluded *āśrama*s run by *guru*s imported from the East. Interest in psychological concepts of Eastern origin is spreading among university students and teachers. Systematic theoretical and experimental work is being published in psychological and medical journals ranging from the *Journal of Humanistic Psychology* to *E.E.G. and Clinical Neurophysiology.* Charles Tart's book, *Altered States of Consciousness* (1969/1972), which includes several papers on meditation and yogic states, has become popular among students of psychology.

Another volume edited by Tart (1975), called *Transpersonal Psychologies*, which brings together contributions on the psychologies of Yoga, Buddhism, and Sufism. Robert Ornstein's *Psychology of Consciousness* (1972) represents a serious attempt to integrate concepts from the East into the mainstream of modern psychology. Recent publications attempting to link Eastern and Western approaches to psychological issues are too many. This healthy trend in publication deserves a warm welcome.

For a world that is shrinking in its dimensions due to faster means of communication, such a trend is, in fact, overdue. There is no reason why anyone should deprive himself/herself of knowledge or techniques on the basis of their time and place of origin. During the long history of the Indian continent, many men have asked themselves the same types of questions that have intrigued their Western counterparts. Sometimes thinkers separated by time and place have arrived independently at similar answers to the same questions. Sometimes those in the East have arrived at solutions that have eluded Westerners, sometimes the reverse. For want of better communication and comparative study we may unnecessarily tread paths proven fruitless elsewhere, or keep asking questions which have already been satisfactorily answered. A preliminary acquaintance with the histories of Eastern and Western thought indicates that psychological insights of *Yoga* have much to contribute to the understanding of the higher reaches of human experience and potential. These contributions may prove to be a valuable complement to the excellence of Western psychologies in analytical rigor, measurement, experimentation, and technology. An integration of the right aspects of both traditions should give us a broader and more comprehensive view of humans, and more viable psychology. In this chapter I propose to present a modest attempt at converging Indian and Western thinking on a few issues in psychology.

An attempt to integrate two different traditions requires a systematic comparison of the contributions of both to some common issues. Such a comparison has more to it than simply retrieving valuable insights attained in the past that might otherwise be lost. An attempt to compare two different systems necessitates "stepping out" of both systems now and then, since this enables us to assess each of them as a whole. Temporary distancing from a system of ideas enables us to stop and question whether things which we have taken for granted are indeed unconditionally true. Thus, our implicit assumptions become explicit in the process of comparison. A continual comparison of diverse systems usually accentuates the differences between them. Problems which are brushed aside as unimportant in one system are sometimes found to be legitimate and important issues in the other system. A "blind spot" in one tradition turns out to be one which is illuminated in the other system. We tend to exaggerate our strengths and discount our weaknesses when working within only one system, while a comparative perspective enables us to see the strengths and weaknesses of our own as well as other systems in their real proportions.

Before starting on a comparative study, one may wish to know briefly what the Indian tradition may have to offer. Certainly it has much more to offer than the little that psychologists in India or elsewhere have been able to translate into modern terminology. First, there is a vast literature on various systems of philosophy that involves critical thinking concerning the mind. Second, there is a centuries-old, living tradition that has transmitted techniques such as meditation and breathing exercises which can help one reach higher states of consciousness. This means that there are persons living today who have acquired traditional techniques through apprenticeship or other forms of learning. Such persons can demonstrate that what is written in books is not merely words or hollow ideals, but something that is actually practised. Third, in India today there are social institutions using highly developed methods of counselling to help individuals toward personality growth. These methods could be developed into techniques which would be useful in psychological counselling throughout the modern world.

In other words, the Indian tradition has the following main ingredients that are required to make a comprehensive system of psychology: an elaborate conceptual framework comprising a world view, a theoretical analysis of the structures and processes relating to human personality, a normative account defining the nature of higher and lower levels of the functioning of personality, a set of techniques designed to help the not-so-well-developed individual reach more desirable levels of development, and a set of social institutions within which growth of personality can be facilitated.

A statement like the one above, asserting the existence of a system of psychology of Indian origin, is bound to raise doubts and questions, not only outside India but also among psychologists at the universities of India itself. If India has had a psychology of its own, how is it that even the Indian universities do not teach courses based on it? The answer to this question is simple. In India, as in many other countries, separate departments devoted to teaching and research in psychology were started in opposition to philosophy, the "mother discipline" of psychology. In the process of growing up, psychology has often taken a rebellious stand against mother philosophy, and many psychologists have neglected the historical roots of their thinking. In many Indian universities, the new departments were staffed by scholars trained in England or the United States, and American textbooks have long dominated the psychology curricula. As a result, most of the psychology taught in India today is another edition of Western psychology. Durganand Sinha, a senior Indian psychologist, has castigated his compatriots for turning their backs on their own rich tradition. He has rightly ascribed the neglect of their own cultural roots to bedazzlement by the scientific psychology of the West and to the anti-philosophical stance of psychology in general (see Sinha, 1965). A mature approach to psychology, however, cannot afford to neglect the philosophical underpinnings of contemporary theories, nor their historical roots.

It must be granted that a separate, independent academic discipline called psychology is not very old, either in the East or in the West. Only recently have there been books labelled "textbook of psychology" or a community of people who call themselves psychologists. Psychology, as a formal, independent academic discipline, is a relatively recent phenomenon. Patañjali did not call himself a psychologist, nor did he label his *Yogasutra* a textbook of a psychology. But the absence of a label does not alter the content, which is obviously psychological. A common belief among psychologists is that psychology was born in Germany with the founding of Wundt's laboratory between 1875 and 1879. What began with Wundt, however, was not psychology itself, but the application to psychology of the method of experiment developed by the natural sciences. It is, of course, not necessary to be labour this point, since many historians of Western psychology, such as Brett (1912/1962), the Murphys (1968), and Watson (1978) begin their accounts of psychological thought with such ancient Greek philosophers as Aristotle.

The historical roots of Indian psychological thought can be traced back to the Upaniṣads, the mystical and philosophical discourses which were composed from approximately the eighth century B.C. onward. The most important source of the psychological concepts of India is Pantaṣjali's well known text of aphorisms on *yoga*. Dating such texts from the Indian tradition is a historian's nightmare since historical record-keeping was one of the neglected aspects of Indian culture. There are differences of opinion among scholars about the date and author of the full text, but Patañjali's text seems to have been completed no later than the fifth century A.D. Philosophically, Patañjali's *yoga* is closest to the Sāṁkhya system, a dualistic philosophy that is one of the oldest known. But the Advaita, or non-dualistic system, particularly as interpreted by Śaṅkara (788-820 A.D.), is the most dominant school of Indian philosophy. However the Advaita conception of the psychic apparatus, as noted by Hiriyanna, the well-known historian of Indian philosophy, closely resembles that of Pantaṣjali (Hiriyanna, 1932).

There are six major and several minor systems of Hindu philosophy besides the separate and well-developed systems of Jainism and Buddhism. Each of these schools has contributed in its own way, to a greater or lesser extent, to thinking about perception, the nature of self, and other psychological issues. Psychologically significant material can also be found in the numerous texts written by religious communities that are known by the name "Tantra", a word that means, literally, "a device or technique", and often refers to their spiritual practices. There are also several texts describing elaborate techniques of breathing and bodily posture in the tradition set forth by Patañjali's old text. There are treatises that describe in detail the nature of gains resulting from the practice of breathing exercises. Some texts speculate on the physiological underpinnings of the yogic techniques. It must also be noted that India's indigenous system of medicine, called Āyurveda, deals with various forms of psychopathology and suggests ways of treating them. Taken together, these sources represent a vast field that is worth exploring for phenomena, concepts, and techniques relevant to psychology.

The initial development of psychological thought in the West occurred in the context of philosophical speculation, and the same is true in the case of Indian thought. Modern Western psychology developed under the influence of the natural sciences, mainly biology and physiology, in the university setting. A second source of influence was medicine (as in the case of Freud who developed psychoanalysis in the therapeutic context). In India however, psychology developed primarily (although not exclusively) in the context of what is called *ādhyātma*, a Sanskrit word meaning "pertaining to the *ātman*" or the self. The word *ātman* is alternatively translated as "soul". As in the West, the Indian quest for the nature of the soul has been associated with humans search for immortality and existence after death. The attempt to liberate the soul from the continuous cycle of birth, death, and rebirth has been the preoccupation of Indian religions.

But here the similarity between the Western and Indian traditions ends. In the West, especially under the influence of the Roman Catholic Church during the medieval period, organised religion claimed authority over everyone's soul, and theologians monopolised the quest for the nature of the individual self. In India, however, the clergy could not claim such monopoly. The sphere of *ādhyātma*, the domain of man's quest for the nature of his self and his effort to attain whatever heights he is capable of attaining, developed autonomously, free from the influence of priests, deities, and rituals. As an example, we may refer to the concept of a *guru*, which, despite its apparently religious character, has social and psychological significance in the sphere of *ādhyātma*, and not in the domain conventionally associated with priesthood. Thus, a *guru* is not a priest, but a spiritual guide who facilitates the disciple's spiritual development. Any person who aspires to enlightenment and spiritual progress may seek guidance from the *guru* who seems most suitable to his idiosyncratic needs without obstacles arising from differences in social background between himself and the *guru*. Discrepancies in age, sex, wealth, status, and even caste do not pose a barrier between the aspirant and his *guru*, although such differences prove to be formidable barriers in almost all other types of social relationships. The *guru* is not an agent of an organised religion guaranteeing a place in heaven for the follower after his death, but a person, who, somewhat like a modern therapist, provides personal counselling.

The context of *ādhyātma* has influenced the development of Indian psychology in a way that stands in sharp contrast to the continual conflict between science and religion in the development of psychological thought in the West. The nature of the influence on Western psychology of this long and bitter conflict is an important issue, so far as the comparison of Indian and Western psychologies is concerned.

As a consequence of the opposition between organised religion and science in the history of Europe, many students of Western psychology tend to avoid anything that seems associated with religion—whether it is the concept of a soul or spiritual progress, meditation, or *yoga*. This being the case, it might be useful to point out that we are not concerned here with yoga or Vedānta as religious doctrines, but as philosophical viewpoints involving a "theory of personality". Besides the association of yoga with religion, there is another aspect of yoga that has negative connotations for many psychologists today. This concerns Patañjali's reference to such phenomena as extrasensory perception, clairvoyance, and telepathy, considered taboo in modern psychology. Certainly, Patañjali's indicates the powers that can be attained through the practice of *yoga*, and it is true that many people are attracted to *yoga* as a tool in their pursuit of power. Patañjali's 3.37, however, has clearly stated that these powers are but obstacles in the way of the attainment of the desirable state of *samādhi*. This is an important point because the de-emphasis on power, wealth, and control is a value of the Indian tradition which contrasts sharply with the dominant Western values. It is important to note this contrast in values because it has led to the growth of divergent psychological thought. Whether or not the claims to extrasensory powers of perception are valid is a separate issue, with which I shall not deal in the present work. The emphasis here, as suggested earlier, is on the system of psychology implicit in the yoga and Vedānta traditions.

It has been fashionable in recent psychological writings to refer to Eastern psychologies as esoteric. The dictionary meaning of the word esoteric is "designed for or understood by the specially initiated alone", or "relating to knowledge that is restricted to a small group". In addition, the image of yoga as a secret doctrine is associated with magic. Since many self-proclaimed *yogīs* are found demonstrating their extraordinary powers and performing magical feats, yoga appears mysterious and even dangerous. The English expression "mystical experience", often associated with descriptions of yogic and other "religious" pursuits, refers to a psychological phenomenon, such as a highly pleasurable experience, that is considered beyond description. But the word "mystic" has other connotations, including "occult", "mysterious", "obscure", or "having magical properties". This is an unfortunate situation, and un-necessarily adds to suspicion and fear. It must be noted that, so far as psychological theories such as Patañjali's are concerned, nothing is secret or inaccessible: the original texts and their numerous commentaries and translations are available on book stands all across the globe. One is extremely unjustified in calling such publicly available theories esoteric, and the English expression "mystical experience", as we have seen, lumps together a broad range of phenomena which have been assigned distinct terms in Sanskrit. As we begin to explore the terrain charted by students of yoga, we will begin to adopt the existing labels from Sanskrit (just as we use the German term "Gestalt" for want of an English equivalent), or perhaps coin new words. Once this is done, we need not be trapped by the incidental connotations of the word "mystic". A proper understanding of the goals of yoga will enable us to assign to the yogic "feats" their legitimate place, which is one of minimal importance.

The Western world is influenced by religious creeds that seek converts and even proselytise. Those exposed to such creeds may find it hard to appreciate the fact that there are religions that do not seek converts. Although yoga is associated with Hinduism and is theistic, it is a system of philosophy in its own right. It need not arouse suspicion as a religious creed in disguise any more than do the philosophies of Descartes, Kant, and Kierkegaard, all of whom believed in the existence of God. It is also necessary to note that when a *yogī* concentrates on the image of a deity or God, the implicit meaning and function of this variety of theism is radically different from that in the West. Geraldine Coster (1934, 1972) has put it well:

> "Here again we have a reversal of values between East and West. The Western mystic sets high value on one-pointedness because it leads the soul to God; the Eastern *yogī* sets high value on the conception of God because it leads to one-pointedness".

One-pointedness here implies extreme concentration of attention, which is considered a necessary step in controlling psychological processes such as ideation and thinking so as to enable the individual to attain states considered superior to normal. The image of God is often used as an object upon which attention is concentrated and, as such, serves as a means to an end-self-realisation.

There is a sphere of life in which psychology, religion, and philosophy overlap: call it the search for happiness, fulfilment, growth of personality, self-actualisation, self-realisation, understanding the meaning of life, or what you will. Certainly, most modern psychologists tend not to focus on this common sphere, or to consider the field of psychology a science independent of religion and morals. Some may even consider psychology and religion to be opposed in many respects. The anti-religious stance of psychologists and their scientists is partly a product of the legitimate disillusionment of modern man regarding churchmen who have spread wars in the name of universal brotherhood. Notwithstanding the context of antagonism between the Church and science within which modern psychology was born, a continual interaction between psychology and the Judeo-Christian tradition has been maintained. Despite Freud's anti-religious views, for instance, the father of psychoanalysis transformed several aspects of the Jewish mystical tradition into a secular, "scientific" format (see Bakan, 1958). The similarity between the cathartic effect of the Catholic confession and psychoanalytic free association is well known. Pastoral counselling overlaps with secular psychological counselling in many ways: both try to allay the anxiety, fear, and guilt of their clients, and both types of counsellors have borrowed directly and indirectly from each other. A clear example of the mutual influence of psychology and religion in more recent times is the development and widespread use of T-groups, sensitivity training and other such techniques in secular as well as religious settings in the West. It has been pointed out, for instance, that the technique of using "negative feedback" from peers to recognise the hidden aspects of one's social image in order to improve one's understanding of oneself is borrowed by psychologists from the ritualistic method of open mutual criticism of members of a congregation used by certain church groups. The technique of negative feedback has now become part of the standard package used by group leaders in psychological laboratories that train T-group leaders. Certain church organisations have been sponsors and users of T-group methods. It is not an accident that Carl Rogers, a renowned psychologist and a leader of the encounter group movement, happened to be a student of theology before he turned to psychology. Whether the fields of psychology and religion should encroach upon one another is a matter of opinion; that the two overlap is a matter of fact.

With reference to Indian psychological concepts that are couched in old, religion philosophical contexts, some readers may ask: In what ways are such concepts relevant to modern, scientific, and secular interests? The answer is that they are relevant in several ways. First, the concept of self is as relevant and central to psychology today as it has always been. The Indian approach to this concept is different than the approaches of most modern schools of psychology. Being different, it avoids the danger of pursuing just one more version of the existing Western models. Moreover, the Indian view of the self promises to be a valuable complement to Western views. Second, the Indian tradition has much to contribute to the study of states of consciousness, a topic to which many psychologists have returned with a revitalised interest in the past few years. Third, ideas concerning the philosophy of the mind directly influence the nature of psychological theory, and the Indian thought has much to offer in this area. Fourth, the Yogic methods of controlling the body and the mind involve voluntary control of functions normally considered to be under the influence of the autonomic nervous system, and such control has already become an object of study by physiological psychologists and medical professionals. Fifth, finding ways to improve the human condition is a perennial theme for psychologists and philosophers, ancient as well as modern. The traditional and contemporary interests converge on this common focus. There are other questions which some readers may ask. Is an attempt to compare and integrate Indian and Western systems of psychology particularly relevant now? Has it not already been done? If some work has already been done, is it inadequate? If it is adequate, why has it been neglected for so long? These are relevant questions and they can be reasonably answered.

The exposure of Western audiences to Indian thought is certainly not new. British officers and missionaries in India began to translate important philosophical and religious texts into English during the early days of British influence on the Indian continent. The Indian spiritual leader and missionary, Vivekananda, introduced yogic and Vedāntic concepts to the United States in the 1890s. The theosophical movement involved Europeans and Americans interested in the study of the "occult" phenomena associated with yogic practices. It helped promote the dissipation and integration of ideas across the continents. In the year 1926, Radhakrishnan, an Indian philosopher, was invited to deliver the Upton Lectures at Oxford University (published as *The Hindu View of Life*), an indication of early recognition of Indian philosophy in Western academic circles. In fact, certain German, British, and American universities had much earlier started publication of standard translations of basic philosophical texts of India in comprehensive series. The Harvard Oriental Series, for instance, published James Woods's translation of Patañjali's aphorisms as early as 1914. It has certainly been a long time, however, since translations of the basic sources of Indian psychological thought have been available in English, French, and German.

It is important to note that in the West, acquaintance with Indian thought was initially limited to indologists and philologists, and later spread to the field of philosophy. James Woods, the translator of Patañjali, was a philologist, not a psychologist. Since the subject matter of the text is basically psychological in nature, someone trained in psychology and Sanskrit could have produced a better translation. It is also important to remember that in 1914 when Woods's translation was published at Harvard, psychology was a brand new discipline trying to establish its independent existence as a university department. The writing of William James, the father of American psychology, shows the transition of psychological thought from its philosophical roots to the modern scientific format. Thus, James in his long chapter on the self (Principles, 1890), reviews the most important contributions of Western philosophy, from Locke through Kant and J.S. Mill. Here he indicates no familiarity with Indian philosophy, although in his *Varieties of Religious Experience* (1902) he once makes reference to Vivekananda, the Indian missionary who had lectured at Harvard in 1896. In the same book there are also a few references to Ramakrishna, the great mystic saint, and spiritual guide (*guru*) of Vivekananda. These references show James's awareness and appreciation of Indian thought.

A disciple of Vivekananda, Swami Akhilananda, stayed in the United States for a length of time on behalf of the Ramakrishna Vedānta Society and wrote two books attempting to integrate Indian and Western views on a few topics in psychology and mental health (Akhilananda, 1948, 1952). Without trying to review these works at length, it may be noted that the author was well versed in Indian thought but was handicapped by a lack of formal training in Western psychology. Also, whatever their merit, these works did not seem to reach a broad audience in psychology, and are quite outdated in view of developments in Western psychology. More recently, Gardner and Lois B. Murphy edited a volume called *Asian Psychology* (1968) in which they excerpted translations of selected passages from the Indian texts of the ancient *Ṛgveda*, through the Upaniṣads to Patañjali. These selections offer a glimpse into the typical Indian way of thinking regarding psychological issues, but they do little in the way of concentration on specific topics of common interest, or of a systematic integration of Indian and Western ideas.

Like William James, Sigmund Freud also seems to have been aware of *Yoga* and of certain concepts of Indian origin, as stray references in his writings indicate. But some of the references suggest that he was neither very much interested nor, perhaps, much impressed by what he had heard (see, for example, Freud, 1930, 1961). Jung, however, was very much interested in Eastern philosophy, had read several works in this field, and had even journeyed to India. To some readers in the West he may appear to be the only well-known psychologist to have attempted an integration of psychological concepts of Eastern and Western origin. Undoubtedly he may be credited with popularising terms such as *maṇḍala* and arousing curiosity about Eastern concepts among readers. Many of Jung's readers who have good acquaintance with Indian literature, however, question the quality of Jung's work. It is small wonder that he evaluates psychological concepts of *yoga* from his own psychoanalytical point of view. Thus, in a paper on the "Tibetan Book of the Great Liberation", he admits that consciousness is inconceivable without the ego. He says, "I do not doubt the existence of mental states transcending consciousness", but concludes that consciousness that transcends the ego must only be "unconscious" (Jung, 1939, 1958). One can understand the difficulties in trying to interpret higher states of consciousness without extending the psychoanalytical framework. However, when Jung goes on to suggest that "to the West ... *samādhi* is nothing but a meaningless dream state" (p. 492), he shows that he has misunderstood and misinterpreted some very basic concepts of Yoga. The problem with Jung does not end with such misconceptions. Note, for instance, the following statement from this presumed integrator of Eastern and Western psychologies: "You cannot mix fire and water. The Eastern attitude stultifies the Western, and viceversa" (p. 483). Now take another statement of his: "Critical philosophy, the mother of modern psychology, is foreign to the East as to medieval Europe". These very brief quotations should indicate Jung's typical bias.

Luckily, the Jungian type of bias is not commonly found in the published literature. More common, of course, is lack of interest in, and information about, the older systems. This is true in India as well as elsewhere. Part of the problem is language. The original sources of the Indian systems are in Sanskrit, a language which is as difficult and unknown to many modern Indians as are Greek and Latin to most Euro-Americans. Those, like Geraldine Coster (1934, 1972), who rely on consultants to translate original works for them, may find the help unreliable. But language need no longer be a major obstacle, as many more original works are now translated than were available in Coster's time, and some of the translations are better than the previous ones. Yet, translations do not always prove adequate. Although the study of Sanskrit appears to be declining, scholars well trained in Sanskrit texts are still not rare. In fact, dependable Sanskritists are now available not only in India but also in many North American universities.

There is another field of study related to Indian psychology which does not depend on the interpretation of old texts since it focuses on such phenomena as breathing exercises and their directly observable physiological effects. Interest in the study of physiological aspects of yoga goes back to the early days of the British rule in India, when British doctors came across *yogīs* who claimed to bury themselves alive in pits for long periods of time, voluntarily control their breathing, or perform similar feats that seemed humanly and medically impossible. Serious experimental testing of such claims and recording of physiological phenomena associated with yogic states, however, did not begin until the early 1930s. One of the pioneers in this field was K.T. Behanan, an Indian student pursuing graduate studies in psychology at Yale University, who in 1931 obtained a fellowship to study Yoga in a modern institute of *yoga* near Bombay. As part of his doctoral work he studied the physiological aspects of breathing exercises, such as the rate of oxygen consumption, and, on the experiential side, reported a condition of "extreme pleasantness" as a result of the exercises. His experimental observations and impressions about certain yogic practices were later published in the form of a book entitled *Yoga: A Scientific Evaluation* (Behanan, 1937/1964).

Around 1935, Therese Brosse, a French cardiologist, visited India to study certain physiological aspects of *yoga*. In a paper published in English in 1946, Brosse reported a *yogī* who, while under medical observation, buried himself for a period of ten hours. She conducted several studies using electrocardiographic and anemographic recording of *yogīs* and reported finding them to be "incontestable masters" of bodily functions such as blood circulation and rate of metabolism. She remarked that a *yogī* could voluntarily put his body "in a state of slowed-up life comparable to that of hibernating animals" (Brosse, 1946). In the mid-1950s, Wenger, a physiological psychologist from the University of California at Los Angeles, conducted electroencephalographic studies of yogic states at Kaivalyadhama (the yoga institute where Behanan and Brosse had experimented) and at other places in India. One of his studies concerned voluntary control of the heart and pulse, as did Brosse's earlier study (Wenger, Bagchi and Anand, 1971). Another study dealt with the electrical activity of the brain during certain yogic exercises (Bagchi and Wenger, 1957, 1971). A similar study by Anand, Chhina and Singh (1961) reports that when a *yogī* reached the ecstatic state of consciousness called *samādhi*, his brain produced alpha waves (electrical waves of a frequency ranging from about 8 to 12 cycles per second) persistently and with greater strength (increased amplitude). In Japan, Kasamatsu and Hirai (1972) reported similar findings (along with some other observations) with practitioners of Zen meditation.

The claim of the electrophysiological studies of Anand, Kasamatsu, and others that meditative states are associated with high alpha activity of the brain has attracted the attention of a great number of people. Anyone who has heard of the fabulous "high" the *yogī*s are said to reach would be attracted to studies of the *samādhi* states. Since these studies found something "concrete"—curves inscribed by a machine—that could be associated with ecstatic states heretofore described in the most abstract and obtuse terms, they have appeared as a significant landmark in the understanding of complex psychological phenomena. Further, Joe Kamiya's experiments in Chicago and San Francisco demonstrated that subjects could easily be trained to voluntarily produce high alpha activity of the brain (Kamiya, 1972). In this technique, called biofeedback training, a subject hears a beep produced by electronic equipment as soon as a scanning mechanism identifies wave forms within the alpha range of frequency produced by the electrical activity of the subject's brain. Most subjects readily learn to get the instruments to react with a beep by increasing the alpha output of their brains, although most cannot say how they accomplish this task. Since the state of the subject when he produces high alpha waves is considered to be one of pleasant relaxation, biofeedback has attracted many psychologists interested in a technique by which to help subjects relax, reduce tension and acquire a state of well-being. Biofeedback has appealed to some psychologists as a breakthrough in methodology, opening new avenues in brain-behaviour research. To many people biofeedback is a quick road to "instant *samādhi*", a short-cut to the fabled goal of Yoga. Notwithstanding the cheap popularisation of biofeedback and the faddishness of its fans, it is true that electrophysiological studies of *Yoga* and Zen meditation have led to a new field of collaborative psychological research in the United States, India and Japan.

"Maharishi" Mahesh Yogi's "Transcendental Meditation (TM)" is a popular movement that has induced some psychophysiological research related to the "TM" brand of meditation techniques. A typical piece of research of this type is R.K. Wallace's doctoral study in physiology at the University of California at Los Angeles. Wallace studied various physiological effects of the practice of TM over long and short periods of time. He found that TM produces a rapid decrease in oxygen consumption, decreases heart rate, cardiac output, and acidity of the blood, and increases the intensity of alpha waves produced by the brain. After comparing the physiological correlates of the meditative states of TM practitioners with normal characteristics of wakefulness, deep sleep, and dreaming, Wallace concluded that "transcendental meditation produces a fourth major state which is physiologically and biochemically unique" (Wallace, 1970).

The Wallace study illustrates an expanding trend in the researchstarted by Behanan and Brosse which conjoins Western techniques and Eastern concepts. While such convergence is welcome as a sign of East-West cooperation, decreasing prejudices, and expanding frontiers of psychological research, the findings of this research must be examined with care. It is dangerous to assume, for instance, that Wallace's study helps explain the "Fourth State" (*turīya avasthā*) about which the *yogīs* have spoken. First, there is no specific claim by Wallace that he is referring to anything like the *samādhi* experience, although the fourfold classification used closely resembles the traditional Indian view. Second, he says little about the nature of the experience of the meditators during the experiments, although a pleasant character is alluded to by the description of the TM technique as being "easy and enjoyable". Third, given the fact that many of Wallace's subjects had practised meditation for very short periods, it is difficult to believe that they have attained the Fourth State of Consciousness described by Vedānta (see Wallace, 1970 for data on duration of practice among Wallace's subjects). The convention suggests that the pathway to such "superior" states of consciousness is a difficult path on which aspirants make very slow progress. Fourth, and the most important reason for caution in evaluating the merit of the psychophysiological studies of Wallace and others, is their common explicit or implicit assumption that all states of consciousness, including the higher states described by Yoga, have a definite biochemical base. Such studies are based on the implicit assumption that there are two independent worlds of reality, mind and matter, so that the experiences of the mind have definite correspondence with states of the material body. The assumption that every experiential state can be reduced to an electrochemical state of the brain is an axiomatic principle or an untested (and perhaps untestable) assumption derived from an ontological theory in the Cartesian tradition. The Vedāntic concept of the Fourth State of Consciousness is not based upon such a Western theory of reality. To say the least, it is essential that the fundamental assumptions on which Western methods are based must be examined carefully before they are used in interpreting concepts based on different and perhaps contradictory assumptions about reality.

For many people the convergence of East and West in psychology means the application of the techniques of modern science to the study of phenomena described by yoga or Zen Buddhism. In 1948, Gordon W. Allport sounded a note of caution about such applications. In his brief introduction to Swami Akhilananda's book, *Hindu Psychology*, Allport says that he is convinced that American psychology would improve in richness and wisdom if it took into account the phenomena related to meditation. But he says he is not sure about the more "occult" manifestations of mental powers associated with Hindu psychology.

> "Whether the occult in Hindu psychology stems from its relative lack of acquaintance with what we in the West call 'scientific method' or whether this Western 'scientific method' is nothing but a narrow cult that blinds itself to uncongenial phenomena, I am not at this moment prepared to say. Perhaps concessions are needed to both sides" (Akhilananda, 1948).

Allport's words of caution are well taken. About three decades have passed since he expressed his doubts about the use of scientific method. We are now in a better position to understand the nature of this issue in light of the problems in cross-cultural understanding, which have been discussed from a variety of angles over the past several decades. The cultural limitations of psychological knowledge have been recognised. It has long been recognised, for instance, that Freud's views of the role of guilt in neurosis were partly a result of the "Victorian morals" of the patients he observed in his clinic. A large number of cross-cultural studies have been conducted wherein Western psychological concepts and techniques have been carried across the world; and while examining their observations and comparing them across cultures, many psychologists have become aware of the limitations on the cross-cultural applicability of psychological models (Berry, 1969; Paranjpe, 1975). Sociologists like Mannheim and others have pointed out that the pursuit of scientific knowledge is a social undertaking that is usually guided and sometimes constrained by the needs, goals, and ideologies of the scientists' communities. The historian of science, Thomas Kuhn (1970), has suggested that communities of scientists share sets of assumptions, values, model methods or exemplars, or frameworks of ideas (usually called paradigms) to which they are committed as a group. Such commitments are not universal and everlasting, but vary across groups and cultures, and are revisable from time to time. Further, Alan Buss (1975) has suggested that a new field of study he calls "the sociology of psychological knowledge" is now emerging. What this means is that there is a growing concern about the social context of psychological theories and the nature of its influence on what we know about psychological phenomena.

All the developments referred to in the previous paragraph are of relatively recent origin. The recent awareness of the sociocultural context of psychological inquiry and of the restrictive influence of that context has led many students of Western psychology to be receptive to perspectives from distant places. Ornstein (1972) mentions the popularity in the United States of the "esoteric" disciplines of the East, such as Zen Buddhism, Tibetan Buddhism, Sufism, and Yoga, as one of the factors leading to an extension of the scope of psychology. He mentions the following aspects of the changing American culture as additional factors contributing to this extension: the emergence of a "counter cultural" community opposed to "science", which exhibits a distaste for rational thought and its products, such as machines, computers, and technology in general, a widespread interest in consciousness-altering or "psychedelic" drugs, and, at the same time, the development of research tools such as electroencephalography that have made it possible to study sleep, dreams, hypnosis, and other states of consciousness. Such states were formerly considered purely "private" phenomena, no aspect of which was accessible to recording and "scientific" study. Now that recordings of phenomena such as the rapid eye movements during dreams are possible, the scope of psychology has been extended to the study of dreams. In other words, a variety of events has induced an extension of conventional perspectives in Western psychology.

At the same time in India, too, the blinding influence of Western psychology in the universities, which had led Indian psychologists to turn their backs on their Indian heritage, is gradually receding. Several Indian psychologists are looking for psychological concepts rooted in their own native tradition. Indian books on Yoga, for instance, are no longer the monopoly of philosophers, philologists, or Hindu missionaries: psychologists trained in India are gradually turning their attention to this field which they had neglected for so long (Joshi, 1967; Kulkarni, 1972; Ramachandra Rao, 1962; and Safaya, 1976). Then again, outside the field of psychology there is a renewed interest in mystical experience, a topic that is of central importance in Indian psychology (Bharati, 1976; Scharfstein, 1973/1974; and

Staal, 1975). The study of mysticism has so far been largely influenced by students of religion, but some of them are now turning to psychology for help in understanding the nature of mystical experience. Frits Staal, a scholar of the Sanskrit language and Eastern religions has recently surveyed psychological and physiological studies of mysticism. Although he concludes that psychological studies are unsatisfactory and that they reveal the limitations of present-day psychology, he thinks that the future outlook for the psychological study of mysticism is not bleak, but "very promising". Staal stresses, however, that the prospects for such study will be bright if "psychology would be deepened and widened so as to be in a position to take account of these particular aspects of the mind" (Staal, 1975). Widening the scope of modern Western psychology to enable us to account for such phenomena as mystical experience can be meaningfully done by incorporating into its mainstream perspectives from Indian psychology which have been well developed.

From the paragraphs it is clear that the time is now right for extending the scope of psychology by integrating ideas from the Indian and Western traditions.

References

Akhilananda, S. (1948). *Hindu Psychology*. London: George Allen & Unwin.

Akhilananda, S. (1952.) *Mental Health and Hindu Psychology*. London: George Allen & Unwin.

Anand, B.K., G.S. Chhina and B. Singh (1961). "Some Aspects of Electroencephalographic Studies in Yogis". *EEG and Clinical Neurophysiology, 13*: 452-56.

Bagchi, B.K. and M.A. Wenger (1971). "Electro-physiological Correlates of Some Yogi Exercises". In J. Kamiya, N.E. Miller, D. Shapiro and J. Stoyva (Eds.), *Biofeedback and Self-control: An Aldine Reader on the Regulation of Bodily Processes and Consciousness*. Chicago: Aldine/Atherton. (Reprinted from *EEG and Neurophysiology*,1957, Supplement).

Behanan, K.T. (1964). *Yoga: A Scientific Evaluation*. New York: Dover. (Originally published, 1937).

Berry, J.W. (1969). "On Cross-cultural Comparability". *International Journal of Psychology, 4:* 119-28.

Bharati, A. (1976). *The Light at the Center: Context and Pretext of Modern Mysticism*. Santa Barbara: Ross-Erikson.

Brett, G.S. (1962). *Brett's History of Psychology.* (Abridged and rev. edn.) (ed. R.S. Peters). Cambridge, Mass.: M.I.T. Press. (Originally published, 1912).

Brosse, T. (1946). "A Psychophysiological Study". *Main Currents in Modern Thought 4:* 77-84.

Buss, A.R. (1975). "The Emerging Field of the Sociology of Psychological Knowledge". *American Psychologist, 30*: 988-1002.

Coster, G. (1972). *Yoga and Western Psychology: A Comparison.* New York: Harper and Row (Originally published, 1934).

Freud, S. (1961). "Civilization and its discontents", In J. Strachey (Ed.), *The Standard Edition of the Complete Psychological Works of Sigmund Freud* (Vol. 21). London: Hogarth. (Originally published, 1930).

Hiriyanna, M. (1932). *Outlines of Indian Philosophy.* London: George Allen and Unwin.

James, W. (1950). *The Principles of Psychology* (2 vols.). New York: Dover. (Originally published, 1890).

James, W. (1958). *Varieties of Religious Experience.* New York: New American Library. (Originally published, 1902).

Jung, C.G. (1958). "Psychological Commentary on the 'Tibetan Book of the Great Liberation'." In H. Read & M. Fordham (Eds.), *The Collected Works of C.G. Jung* (Bollingen Series, Vol. 11). New York: Pantheon. (Original in English, 1939).

Kamiya, J. (1972). "Operant Control of EEG Alpha Rhythm and Some of Its Reported Effects on Consciousness. In C.T. Tart (Ed.), *Altered States of Consciousness* (2nd edn.). Garden City, New York: Doubleday.

Kasamatsu, A. and T. Hirai (1972). "An Electroencephalographic Study of Zen Mediation (Zazen)". In C.T. Tart (Ed.) *Altered States of Consciousness* (2nd edn.). Garden City, N.Y.: Doubleday.

Kuhn, T.S. (1970). *The Structure of Scientific Revolutions* (2nd edn.). Chicago: University of Chicago Press.

Kulkarni, T.R. (1972). *Upanishads and Yoga: An Empirical Approach to the Understanding.* Bombay: Bharatiya Vidya Bhavan.

Murphy, G. and Murphy, L.B. (Eds.) (1968). *Asian Psychology.* New York: Basic Books.

Ornstein, R.E. (1972). *The Psychology of Consciousness.* San Francisco: W.H. Freeman.

Paranjpe, A.C. (1975). *In Search of Identity.* New York: Halsted Press/Wiley.

Ramachandra Rao, S.K. (1962). *Development of Psychological Thought in India.* Mysore: Kavyalaya Publishers.

Safaya, R. (1976) *Indian Psychology: A Critical and Historical Analysis of the Psychological Speculations in Indian Philosophical Literature.* New Delhi: Munshiram Manoharlal.

Scharfstein, B.A. (1974). *Mystical Experience.* Baltimore: Penguin. (Originally published, 1973).

Sinha, D. (1965). "Integration of Modern Psychology with Indian Thought". *Journal of Humanistic Psychology, 5*: 6-17.

Staal, F. (1975). *Exploring Mysticism.* Harmondsworth: Penguin.

Tart, C. (1972). *Altered States of Consciousness* (2nd edn.) Garden City, N.Y.: Doubleday/Anchor Books. (First edition, 1969).

Tart, C. (1975). *Transpersonal Psychologies.* New York: Harper and Row.

Wallace, R.K. (1970). *The Physiological Effects of Transcendental Meditation.* Los Angeles: Students International Meditation Society.

Watson, R.I. (1978). *The Great Psychologists* (4th edn.). Philadelphia: Lippincott.

Wenger, M.A., B.K. Bagchi and B.K. Anand (1971). "Experiments in India on "Voluntary" Control of Heart and Pulse". In J. Kamiya, N.E. Miller, D. Shapiro, and J. Stoyva (Eds.), *Biofeedback and Self-control: An Aldine Reader on the Regulation of Bodily Processes and Consciousness.* Chicago: Aldine/Atherton. (Reprinted from *Circulation,* 1961, 24).

Bibliography

Ajaya, Swami (1983). *Psychotherapy East and West: A Unifying Paradigm*. Honesdale, PA: Himalayan Institute.

Akhilananda, S. (1948). *Hindu Psychology*. London: George Allen & Unwin.

Akhilananda, S. (1952.) *Mental Health and Hindu Psychology*. London: George Allen & Unwin.

Albahari, M. (2006). *Analytical Buddhism: The Two-tiered Illusion of Self*. Palgrave.

Albahari, M. (2014). "Insight Knowledge of No Self in Buddhism: An Epistemic Analysis." *Philosophers' Imprint*, *14*: 1-30.

Anand, B.K., G.S. Chhina and B. Singh (1961). "Some Aspects of Electroencephalographic Studies in Yogis". *EEG and Clinical Neurophysiology, 13*: 452-56.

Anand, K.C. (2000). *What is Consciousness?: Know Thyself Series*-3. All India Magazine Booklet, Sri Aurobindo Society, Pondicherry, India.

Ansari, Z.A. (1992). *Quranic Concepts of Human Psyche*. Islamabad: International Institute of Islamic Thought (IIIT).

Apte, V.S. (1988). *The Student's Sanskrit English Dictionary*. Delhi: Motilal Banarasidass.

Au, T.K. (1983). "Chinese and English Counterfactuals: The Sapir-Whorf Hypothesis Revisited". *Cognition*, *15*: 162-63.

Au, T.K. (1984). "Counterfactuals: In Reply to Alfred Bloom". *Cognition*, *17*: 289-302.

Aurobindo, Sri (1914/1998). *The Secret of the Veda*. Pondicherry: Sri Aurobindo Ashram Publication Department.

Austin, J.H. (1998). *Zen and the Brain.* Cambridge, MA: The MIT Press.

Austin, J.H. (2006). *Zen-brain Reflections.* The MIT Press.

Austin, J.H. (2009). *Selfless insight.* The MIT Press.

Baba, M. (1967). *Listen Humanity.* New York: Dodd, Mead.

Bagchi, B.K. and M.A. Wenger (1971). "Electro-Physiological Correlates of Some Yogi Exercises". In J. Kamiya, N.E. Miller, D. Shapiro and J. Stoyva (Eds.), *Biofeedback and Self-control: An Aldine Reader on the Regulation of Bodily Processes and Consciousness.* Chicago: Aldine/Atherton. (Reprinted from *EEG and Neurophysiology,*1957, Supplement).

Bakhtiar, L. (1987). *Sufi: Expressions of the Mystic Quest.* New York: Avon.

Beg, M.A. (1970). "A Note on the Concept of Self, and the Theory, and Practice of Psychological Help in the Sufi Tradition." *Interpersonal Development, 1.*

Behanan, K.T. (1964). *Yoga: A Scientific Evaluation,* New York: Dover. (Originally published, 1937).

Belenky, M.F., Clinchy, B.M., Goldberger, N.R. and J.M. Tarule (1986). *Women's Ways of Knowing: The Development of Self, Voice, and Mind.* New York: Basic Books.

Benoit, H. (1990). *Zen and the Psychology of Transformation.* Inner Traditions.

Berry, J.W. (1969). "On Cross-cultural Comparability". *International Journal of Psychology, 4:* 119-28.

Berry, J.W., Y.H. Poortinga, M. Segal, and P.R. Dasen (1992). *Cross-cultural Psychology: Research and Applications.* Cambridge, UK: Cambridge University Press.

Bhaktivedanta, A.C.S. Prabhupada. *Bhagavad Gita* as It Is. Bombay: The Bhaktivedanta Book Trust.

Bharati, A. (1976). *The Light at the Center: Context and Pretext of Modern Mysticism.* Santa Barbara: Ross-Erikson.

Bhawuk, D.P.S. (2008). "Anchoring Cognition, Emotion, and Behaviour in Desire: A Model from the Bhagavad-Gita". In K.R. Rao, A.C. Paranjpe, and A.K. Dalal (Eds), *Handbook of Indian Psychology* (pp. 390-413). New Delhi, India: Cambridge University Press.

Bloom, A. (1981). *The Linguistic Shaping of Thought.* Hillsdale, NJ: Erlbaum.

Bloom, A. (1984). "Caution: The Worlds You Use may Effect What You Say: A Response to Au". *Cognition, 17*: 281.

Bodhi, B. (2000a). *The Connected Discourses of the Buddha (A Translation of the Samyutta Nikaya)*. Wisdom Publications.

Bodhi, B. (2000b). *The Connected Discourses of the Buddha (A Translation of the Samyutta Nikaya)*. Wisdom Publications.

Bond, M.H. (1986). *The Psychology of the Chinese People*. New York: Oxford University Press.

Brett, G.S. (1962). *Brett's History of Psychology*. (Abridged and rev. edn.) (ed. R.S. Peters). Cambridge, Mass.: M.I.T. Press. (Originally published, 1912).

Briggs, J. (1970). *Never in Anger*. Cambridge, MA: Harvard University Press.

Brosse, T. (1946). "A Psychophysiological Study". *Main Currents in Modern Thought 4:* 77-84.

Brown, D.P. and J. Engler (1986). "The Stages of Mindfulness Meditation". In K. Wilber, J. Engler and D. Brown (Eds.), *Transformations of Consciousness*. Shambhala.

Bruner, J. (1986). *Actual Minds, Possible Worlds*. New York: Plenum Press.

Buck, R. (1988). *Human Motivation and Emotion* (2 edn.) New York: Wiley.

Bühler, G. (Trans.) (1886). *Sacred Books of the East: The Laws of Manu* (Vol. XXV). Oxford. Available online as The Laws of Manu.

Buss, A.R. (1975). "The Emerging Field of the Sociology of Psychological Knowledge". *American Psychologist, 30*: 988-1002. Cambrige: The MIT Press.

Carrington, P. and H. Ephron (1975). "Meditation and Psychoanalysis". *Journal of the American Academy of Psychoanalysis, 3:* 43-57.

Cassaniti, J.L. (2014). *Buddhism and Positive Psychology*, (pp. 101-24). https://doi.org/10.1007/978-94-017-8950-9_6

Chand, T. I. (1979). *Thought and the Sufis-in-the World of the Sufi*. UK: The Octagon Press Ltd.

Chao, R.K. (1995). "Chinese and European American Cultural Models of the Self-reflected in Mother's Child-rearing Beliefs". *Ethos, 23*: 328-54.

Chiu, L.H. (1972). "A Cross-cultural Comparison of Cognitive Styles in Chinese and American Children." *International Journal of Psychology*, *7*: 235-42.

Chodorow, N. (1978). *The Reproduction of Mothering: Psychoanalysis and the Sociology of Gender*. Berkeley, CA: University of California Press.

Choueiri (Ed.), Y.M. (1997). *Islamic Fundamentalism*. London: Pinter.

Claxton, G. (Ed.). (1986). *Beyond Therapy: The Impact of Eastern Religion on Psychological Theory and Practice*. Wisdom Publications.

Collins, S. (1982). *Selfless Persons: Imagery and Thought in Theravāda Buddhism*. Cambridge University Press.

Conze, E. (1959a). *Buddhism: Its Essence and Development*. Harper & Row.

Conze, E. (1959b). *Buddhist Scriptures* (Trans.). Penguin Books.

Cornelissen, M. (2001). *Cornelissen, Mconsciousness and Its Transformation: Papers presented at the Second International Conference on Integral Psychology*. Sri Aurobindo International Centre of Education, Sri Aurobindo Ashram, Pondicherry, India.

Cortright, B. (1997). *Psychotherapy and Spirit: Theory and Practice in Transpersonal Psychotherapy*. Albany, NY: State University of New York Press.

Coster, G. (1972). *Yoga and Western Psychology: A Comparison*. New York: Harper and Row (Originally published, 1934).

Cousins, S. (1989). "Culture and Selfhood in Japan and the US." *Journal of Personality and Social Psychology*, *56*: 124-31.

Csikszentmihalyi, M. (1990). *Flow: The Psychology of Optimal Experience*. Harper and Row.

D'Andrade, R. (1981). "The Cultural Part of Cognition." *Cognitive Science*, *5*: 179-85.

Dalai Lama (1995a). *The Path to Enlightenment*. Snow Lion.

Dalai Lama (1995b). *The Power of Compassion*. Thorsons.

Dalai Lama (2005). *The Many Ways to Nirvana*. Mobius.

Dalai Lama *et al.* (1991). *Mind Science*. Boston: Wisdom.

Dalal, A.K., R. Sharma and S. Bisht (1983). "Causal Attributions of Ex-criminal Tribal and Urban Children in India". *Journal of Social Psychology*, *119*: 163-71.

Dalal, A.S. (1987). *Living Within: The Yoga Approach to Psychological Growth and Health.* Pondicherry: Sri Aurobindo Ashram, India.

Dalal, A.S. (1990). *Growing Within: The Psychology of Inner Development.* Sri Aurobindo Ashram, Pondicherry, India.

Dalal, A.S. (1990). *The Hidden Forces of Life.* Pondicherry: Sri Aurobindo Ashram, India.

Dalal, A.S. (1998). *Power Within.* Pondicherry: Sri Aurobindo Ashram, India.

Dalal, A.S. (2001). *A Greater Psychology: An Introduction to the Psychological Thought of Sri Aurobindo.* Sri Aurobindo International Centre for Education, Sri Aurobindo Ashram, Pondicherry, India.

Damasio, A. (1994). *Descartes' Error: Emotion, Reason and the Human Brain.* Avon Books.

Dambrun, M. and M. Ricard (2011). "Self-centeredness and Selflessness: A Theory of Self-based Psychological Functioning and Its Consequences for Happiness." *Review of General Psychology*, *15*: 138-57. https://doi:10.1037/a0023059

Darwin, C.R. (1896). *The Expression of Emotions in Man and Animals*. New York: Philosophical Library.

Dasgupta, S.N. (1975). *A History of Indian Philosophy* (Indian edn., Vols. 1-5). Delhi: Motilal Banarsidass. (Originally published in 1922).

Datta, D.M. (1972). *The Six Ways of Knowing: A Critical Study of the Advaita Theory of Knowledge*. Calcutta: University of Calcutta. (Original work published 1932).

Davis, M.H. and W.G. Stephen (1980). "Attributions for Exam Performance." *Journal of Applied Social Psychology*, *10*: 235-48.

Davis, Richard (1988). "Cremation and Liberation: The Revision of a Hindu Ritual." *History of Religions*, *27*(1): 37-53.

Dawood, N.J. (1968). *The Koran*. Baltimore: Penguin Books.

De Riviera, J. (1984). "The Structure of Emotional Relationships". In P. Shaver (Ed.), *Review of Personality and Social Psychology: Emotions, Relationships, and Health* (pp. 116-45). Beverly Hills, CA: Sage.

Deshimaru, T. (1985). *Questions to a Zen master*. Dutton.

Deshimaru, T. (1987). *The Ring of the Way: Testament of a Zen Master*. Dutton.

Deshimaru, T. (1991). *The Zen Way to Martial Arts*. Arcana.

Dhar, P.L. (2011). "No I, No Problems: The Quintessence of Buddhist Psychology of Awakening". *Psychological Studies*, *56*(4): 398-403. https://doi.org/10.1007/s 12646-011-0111-0

Dhawan, N., L.J. Roseman, R.K. Naidu, K. Thapa, and S.I. Rettek (1995). "Self-concepts Across Two Cultures: India and United States." *Journal of Cross Cultural Psychology*, *26*: 606-21.

Doi, L.T. (1973). *The Anatomy of Dependence*. Tokyo: Kodansha.

Doi, L.T. (1986). *The Anatomy of Self: The Individual vs. Society*. Tokyo: Kodansha.

Drgdrsya Viveka (1931). (Ed. and Trans. S. Nikhilananda). Mysore, India: Sri Ramakrishna Asrama. (The date of the original work unknown).

Ekman, P. (1972). "Universals and Cultural Differences in Facial Expression of Emotion." In J.K. Cole (Ed.), *Nebraska Symposium on Motivation* (pp. 207-83). Lincoln: University of Nebraska Press.

Eliade, M. (1969). *Yoga Immortality and Freedom*. Princeton, NJ: Princeton University Press.

Engler, J. (1986). "Therapeutic Aims in Psychotherapy and Meditation". In K. Wilber, J. Engler and D. Brown (Eds.), *Transformations of Consciousness*. Shambhala.

Engler, J. (1993). "Becoming Somebody and Nobody: Psychoanalysis and Buddhism". In R. Walsh and F. Vaughan (Eds.), *Paths Beyond Ego*. Tarcher.

Erikson, E. (1964). *Insight and Responsibility*. New York: Norton

Erikson, H.E. (1978). *Identity Youth and Crisis*. New York, London: Norton and Company.

Fadiman, J. and R. Frager (1999). *Essential Sufism*. New York, USA: Harper Collins Publishers Inc.

Fadiman, J. and R. Frager (1999). *Heart, Self and Soul: The Sufi Psychology of Growth, Balance and Harmony*. Wheaton, IL: Quest Books.

Festinger, L. and J.M. Carlsmith (1959). "Cognitive Consequences of Forced Compliance, *Journal of Abnormal and Social Psychology*, *58*: 203-10.

Fiedler, F.E. (1978). "Recent Development in Research on the Contingency Model." In L. Berkowitz (Ed.), *Group Processes* (pp. 209-25). New York: Academic Press.

Filippi, Gian (1996). *MRTYU: Concept of Death in Indian Traditions*. New Delhi: D.K. Printwood (P) Ltd.

Foster, W. (1968). *Sufi Studies Today.* London: Octagon.

Fowler, Jeaneane. (1997). *Hinduism: Beliefs and Practices.* Brighton: Sussex Academic Press.

Frager, R. and J. Fadiman (1998). *Personality and Personal Growth*, 4th Edn., United States: Longman.

Frager, R., and J. Fadiman (2013). "Zen and Buddhist Tradition". In F. Robert, and F. James (Eds.), *Personality and Personal Growth*. (7th edn., pp. 354-381). Pearson.

Freud, S. (1961). "Civilization and Its Discontents", In J. Strachey (Ed.), *The Standard Edition of the Complete Psychological Works of Sigmund Freud* (Vol.21). London: Hogarth. (Originally published, 1930).

Frijda, N.H., P. Kuipers and E. Schure (1989). "Relations Among Emotion Appraisal and Emotional Action Readiness." *Journal of Personality and Social Psychology*, *57*: 212-28.

Fromm, E. (1992). "Neurophysiological Speculations on Zen Enlightenment". *Journal of Mind and Behavior, 13,* 163-170.

Fromm, E. (1970). "Psychoanalysis and Zen Buddhism". In D.T. Suzuki, E. Fromm and R. de Marino (Eds.), *Zen Buddhism and Psychoanalysis*. New York: Harper & Row.

Fromm, E. (1976). *To Have or To Be*? New York: Harper and Row.

Gandhi, M.K. (1996). *The Essence of Hinduism.* Ahmedabad: Navajiwan Publishing House.

Gesler, Wilbert M. and Pierce Margaret (2000). "Hindu Varanasi". *Geographical Review, 90*(2): 222.

Giles, J. (1993). "The No-self Theory, Hume, Buddism and Personal Identity". *Philosophy East and West*, *43*: 175-200. https://doi:10.2307/1399612

Gilligan, C. (1982). *In a Different Voice: Psychology Theory and Women's Development*. Cambridge, MA: Harvard University Press.

Gilligan, C. (1986). "Remapping the Moral Domain: New Images of the Self in Relationship." In T.C. Heller, M. Sosna, and D.E. Wellbery (Eds.), *Reconstructing Individualism: Autonomy, Individuality, and the Self in Western Thought* (pp. 2237-52). Stanford, CA: Stanford University Press.

Gilmor, T.M. and D.W. Reid (1979). "Locus of Control and Causal Attribution for Positive and Negative Outcomes on University Examinations." *Journal of Research in Personality*, *13*: 154-60.

Gilovich, T. (1983). "Biased Evaluations and Persistence in Gambling." *Journal of Personality and Social Psychology*, *40*, 797-808.

Gnaneshwardas, Sadhu (1993). *Dharmik Vidhano ane Bhavana*. Amdavad: Swaminarayan Aksharpith, (Translated as *Hindu Rites and Rituals*).

Goethals, A. (1989, April). "Studies of False Uniqueness". Paper presented at the Research Centre for Group Dynamics Seminar, Institute for Social Research, University.

Goleman, D. (1988). *The Meditative Mind*. Tarcher.

Greenberg, J., T. Pyszczynski and S. Solomon (1982). "The Self-serving Attributional Bias: Beyond Self-presentation." *Journal of Experimental Social Psychology*, *18*: 56-67.

Greenwald, A.G. (1980). "The Totalitarian Ego: Fabrication and Revision of Personal History." *American Psychologist*, *35*: 603-18.

Greenwald, A.G., and A.R. Pratkanis (1984). "The Self." In R.S. Wyer and T.K. Shrull (Eds.), *Handbook of Social Cognition*, *3*: 129-78, Hillsdale, NJ: Erlbaum.

Gregory, B. (1991). *Sacred Unity: Further Steps to an Ecology of Mind*. New York: Harper Collins.

Guillaume, A. (1956). *Islam*. New York: Penguin.

Haeri, F. (1989). *The Journey of the Self*. Dorset, England: Element Books.

Hanh, T.N. (1976). *The Miracle of Mindfulness*. Beacon Press.

Hanh, T.N. (1987). *Being Peace*. Parallax Press.

Hanh, T.N. (1988). *The Heart of Understanding*. Parallax Press.

Hanh, T.N. (1992). *Touching Peace*. Berkeley, CA: Parallax Press.

Hanh, T.N. (1993). *The Blossoming of a Lotus*. Beacon Press.

Hanh, T.N. (1996). *Cultivating the Mind of Love*. Parallax Press.

Hanh, T.N. (1998). *The Heart of the Buddha's Teaching*. Parallax Press.

Hanh, T.N. (2001[0]). *Essential Writings*, (Ed.) Robert Ellsberg. Orbis Books

Harman, William P. (1989). *Sacred Marriage of a Hindu Goddess*. Bloomington and Indianapolis: Indiana University Press.

Harre, R. and Lamb, R. (1986). *The Dictionary of Personality and Social Psychology*. Cambridge: The MIT Press.

Harter, S. (1990). "Causes, Correlates and the Functional Role of Global Self-worth: A Lifespan Perspective." In R.J. Sternberg and J. Kolligian, Jr. (Eds.), *Competence Considered*, pp. 67-97. New Haven, CT: Yale University Press.

Hayashi, C. (1988). *National Character of the Japanese*. Tokyo: Statistical Bureau, Japan.

Hess, R., H. Azuma, K. Kashiwagi, W.P. Dickson, S. Nagano, S. Holloway, K. Miyake, G. Price, G. Hatano and T. McDevitt (1986). "Family Influences on School Readiness and Achievement in Japan and the United States: An Overview of a Longitudinal Study." In H. Stevenson, H. Azuma and K. Hakuta (Eds.), *Child Development and Education in Japan*, pp. 147-66. New York: Freeman.

Hilgard, E.R. (1987). *Psychology in America: A Historical Survey*. New York: Harcourt Brace Jovanovich.

Hindu Antyeshti Samskara (2008). Hindu Mandir Executives Conference, An initiative of Vishwa Hindu Parishad (World Hindu Council) of Americas Inc.

Hindu Sastras and Samskara. Excerpts from V.A.K. Ayer's *Hindu Sastras and Samskaras* Compilation by: SAVECA Canada.

Hiriyanna, M. (1932). *Outlines of Indian Philosophy*. London: George Allen and Unwin.

Hofstede, G. (1980). *Culture's Consequences: International Differences in Work-related Values*. Beverly Hills, CA: Sage.

Hollander, E.P. (1985). "Leadership and Power." In G. Lindzey and E. Aronson (Eds.). *Handbook of Social Psychology*, *2*: 485-537, New York: Random House.

Hwang, K.K. and J. Chang (2009). "Self-cultivation Culturally Sensitive Psychotherapies in Confucian Societies." *Counselling Psychology*, *37*: 1010-32. https://doi:10.1177/0011000009339976

Izutsu, T. (1983). *Sufism and Taoism*. Berkeley, CA: University of California Press.

James, W. (1890). *Principles of Psychology*. New York: Holt.

James, W. (1950). *The Principles of Psychology* (2 vols.). New York: Dover. (Originally published, 1890).

James, W. (1958). *Varieties of Religious Experience.* New York: New American Library. (Originally published, 1902).

James, W.T. (1975). *A History of Western Philosophy* (2nd and Rev. edn., Vol. 1-5). New York: Harcourt, Brace and World.

Johnson-Laird, P.N. (1983). *Mental Models: Towards a Cognitive Science of Language, Inference, and Consciousness.* Cambridge, MA: Harvard University Press.

Jonathan, B. (2013). *Encyclopedia of Islam and the Muslim World.* Boston: Leiden.

Jordan, J.V. and J.L. Surrey (1986). "The Self-in-relation: Empathy and the Mother-daughter Relationship." In T. Bernay and D.W. Cantor (Eds.), *The Psychology of Today's Women* (pp. 81-104). Cambridge, MA: Harvard University Press.

Joshanloo, M. (2014). "Eastern Conceptualizations of Happiness: Fundamental Differences with Western Views". *Journal of Happiness Studies*, *15*: 475-93. https://doi:10.1007/s10902-013-9431-1

Joshi, K. (2002, September 16). *Isha Upanishad: Super School—Auroville —Session 1: The West and the East; The Upanishadic Quest with Transcript.* [Speech audio recording]. Kireetjoshiarchives. https://www.kireetjoshiarchives.com/audio-video/session/144.html

Joshi, K. (2002, September 17). *Isha Upanishad: Super School — Auroville — Session 2: Three Characteristics; The Methods of Vedantic Knowledge with Transcript.* [Speech audio recording]. Kireetjoshiarchives. https://www.kireetjoshiarchives. com/audio-video/session/145.html

Joshi, K. (n.d.). *Vedic Knowledge and Supermind in the Light of Sri Aurobindo.* Kireetjoshiarchives.https://www.

kireetjoshiarchives.com/philosophy/philosophy-and-yoga-of-sri-aurobindo-and-other-essays/vedic-knowledge-and-supermind-in-the-light-of-sri-aurobindo/&page=43

Joshi, K. and M. Cornelissen (2004). *Consciousness, Indian Psychology and Yoga*, Vol. 11, Part-3. Project on History of Science, Philosophy, and Culture, New Delhi: Centre for Study in Civilisations.

Joshi, R.V. (1979). *Studies in Indian Logic and Metaphysics*. Delhi: Bharatiya Vidya Prakashan.

Jung, C.G. (1933). *Modern Man in Search of a Soul*. New York: A Harvest Book. Press.

Jung, C.G. (1958). "Psychological Commentary on the "Tibetan Book of the Great Liberation." In H. Read and M. Fordham (Eds.), *The Collected Works of C.G. Jung* (Bollingen Series, Vol. 11). New York: Pantheon. (Original in English, 1939).

Jung, C.G. (1963). *Memories, Dreams, Reflections*. New York: Random House, Vintage Books.

Jung, C.G. (1971). *The Portable Jung*. New York: The Viking Press (Penguin Paperback, 1977).

Justice, Christopher (1997). *Dying the Good Death*. Albany, N.Y.: State University of New York Press.

Kabat-Zinn, J. (1990). *Full Catastrophe Living*. New York: Delacorte.

Kabat-Zinn, J. (1994). *Wherever You Go, There You Are*. New York: Hyperion.

Kail, R. and J.C. Cavanaugh (2004). *Human Development: A Lifespan View* (3rd edn.). Belmont, CA: Wadsworth/Thomson Learning.

Kakar, S. (1978). *The Inner World: A Psychoanalytic Study of Childhood and Society in India*. Delhi, India: Oxford University Press.

Kamiya, J. (1972). "Operant Control of EEG Alpha Rhythm and Some of Its Reported Effects on Consciousness. In C.T. Tart (Ed.), *Altered states of Consciousness* (2nd ed.). Garden City, New York: Doubleday.

Kapur, P. and G. Misra (2005). "Image of Self in the Sikh Community: Continuity of the Core and Global Presence." *Psychology and Developing Societies, 15*: 103-16.

Kasamatsu, A. and T. Hirai (1972). "An Electro-encephalographic Study of Zen Mediation (Zazen)". In C.T. Tart (Ed.) *Altered States of Consciousness* (2nd edn.). Garden City, N.Y.: Doubleday.

Kashima, Y., U. Kim, M.J. Gelfand, S. Yamaguchi,, S. Choi and M. Yuki (1995). "Culture, Gender, and Self: A Perspective from Individualism Collectivism Research." *Journal of Personality and Social Psychology, 69*(5): 925-37.

Katagiri, D. (1988). *Returning to Silence: Zen Practice in Daily Life*. Shambhala.

Kelly, B.D. (2008). "Buddhist Psychology, Psychotherapy and the Brain: A Critical Introduction". *Transculural Psychiatry, 45*: 5-30. https://doi:10.1177/1363461 507087996

Khan, H.I. (1962). *The Sufi Message*, Vol. 5: *Metaphysics*. Katwijk, Holland: Service Publishers.

Khan, P.V. (1974). *Toward the One*. New York: Harper and Row.

Kim, U. and J.W. Berry (1993*). Indigenous Psychologies*. New Delhi: Sage.

Kitayama, S., and H. Markus (1990, August). Culture and Emotion: The Role of Other Focused Emotions. Paper presented at the 98th Annual Convention of the American Psychological Association, Boston.

Kitayama, S., H. Markus, P. Tummala, M. Kurokawa and K. Kato (1990). *Culture and Self-cognition.* Unpublished manuscript.

Klein, S.B. (2014). "Sameness and the Self: Philosophical and Psychological Considerations". *Frontiers in Psychology*, *5*(29). https://doi:10.3389/fpsyg. 2014. 00029

Krishnamurthy, V. (1989). *Essentials of Hinduism*. Narosa Publishing House.

Kuhn, T.S. (1970). *The Structure of Scientific Revolutions* (2nd edn.). Chicago: University of Chicago Press.

Kulkarni, T.R. (1972). *Upanishads and Yoga: An Empirical Approach to the Understanding*. Bombay: Bharatiya Vidya Bhavan.

Kumar, P. (2014). *Model for Modern Youth*. Yuva Shakthi Publishers.

Kung, H. (2007). *Islam: Past, Present, and Future*. USA: Oneworld Publication.

Kuppuswamy, B. (1985). *Elements of Ancient Indian Psychology*. Delhi: Konark.

Lal, P. (1967). *The Dhammapada* (Trans.). Farrar, Straus & Giroux.

Lalljee, M. and R. Angelova (1995). "Person Descriptions in India, Britain, and Bulgaria". *Journal of Cross Cultural Psychology, 26*: 645-57.

Lau, R.R. (1984). "Dynamics of the Attribution Process." *Journal of Personality and Social Psychology, 46*: 1017-28.

Lebra, T.S. (1976). *Japanese Patterns of Behaviour*. Honolulu: University of Hawaii Press.

LeDoux, J.E. (1987). "Emotion". In V. Mount Castle (Ed.), *Handbook of Physiology:* Vol. 1. *The Nervous System*, (pp. 419-59). Bethesda, MD: American Physiological Society.

Levy, R. (1973). *The Tahitians*. Chicago: University of Chicago Press.

Liu, I. (1986). "Chinese Cognition". In M.H. Bond (Ed.), *The Psychology of the Chinese People* (pp. 73-105). New York: Oxford University Press.

Liu, T.Y. and M. Hsu (1974). "Measuring Creative Thinking in Taiwan by the Torrance Test". *Testing and Guidance, 2*: 108-09.

Loori, J. D. (2002). *The Art of Just Sitting: Essential Writings on the Zen Practice of Shikentanza.* Wisdom Publishing.

Loy, D.R. (2008). *Money, Sex, War, Karma: Notes for a Buddhist Revolution*. Wisdom Publications.

Lutz, C. (1988). *Unnatural Emotions: Everyday Sentiments on a Micronesian Atoll and Their Challenge to Western Theory.* Chicago: University of Chicago Press.

MacKenzie, M. (2010). "Enacting the Self: Buddhist and Enactivist Approaches to the Emergence of the Self". *Phenomenology and the Cognitive Sciences, 9:* 75-99. https://doi:10.1007/s11097-009-9132-8

Mageo, J. (ed.) (2002). *Power and the Self.* Cambridge University Press.

Manne-Lewis, J. (1986). "Buddhist Psychology: A Paradigm for the Psychology of Enlightenment". In G. Claxton (Ed.), *Beyond Therapy*. Wisdom.

Manu (1971). *The Laws of Manu* (Trans. G Bühler). Delhi: Motilal Banarsidass. (Translation first published in 1886; date of original work Manu Smrti unknown).

Margaret, M. (1997). *Sigmund Freud Explorer of the Unconscious.* Oxford University Press.

Marks, G. (1984). "Thinking One's Abilities are Unique and One's Opinions are Common." *Personality and Social Psychology Bulletin, 10*: 203-08.

Markus, H. and S. Kitayama (1991). "Culture and the Self". *Psychological Review, 98*(2): 224.

Markus, H., and D. Oyserman (1988). "Gender and Thought: The Role of the Self-concept." In M. Crawford and M. Hamilton (Eds.), *Gender and Thought* (pp. 100-127). New York: Springer Verlag.

Markus, H.R. and S. Kitayama (1991). "Culture and the Self: Implications for Cognition, Emotion, and Motivation." *Psychological Review, 98*(2): 224-53.

Marriott, K. (1990). *India Thought Hindu Categories.* New Delhi: Sage.

Mascolo, A.H., G. Misra and C. Rapisardi (2004). "Individual and Relational Conceptions of Self in India and the United States." *Culture and Developing Selves: Beyond Dichotomization, 104*: 9-26.

Mascolo, M.F. and S. Bhatia (2002). "The Dynamic Construction of Culture, Self, and Social Relations." *Culture and Developing Societies, 14*: 55-92.

Maslow, A.H. (1954). *Motivation and Personality.* New York: Harper.

Maslow, A.H. (1971). *Farther Reaches of Human Nature.* New York: Penguin Books.

Masterton, R.B. (1980). "The Nervous System and Behaviour". In Gregory A. Kimble, Norman Garmezy, and Edward Zigler, *Principles of General Psychology.* (5th edn.), New York: Wiley and Sons.

Matsumoto, D. (1989). "Cultural Influences on the Perception of Emotion." *Journal of Cross Cultural Psychology, 20*: 92-105.

Matsumoto, D., T. Kudoh, K. Scherer and H. Wallbott (1988). "Antecedent of and Reactions to Emotions in the United

States and Japan." *Journal of Cross Cultural Psychology, 19*: 267-86.

Maududi, A.A. (1990). *Towards Understanding Islam.* New York: ICNA Book,

Merrell Wolff, F. (1973). *The Philosophy Through to Space: A Personal Record of Transformation in Consciousness.* New York: Julian Press.

Mijares, S.G. (2002). *Modern Psychology and Ancient Wisdom: An Anthology of Healing Practices from the World's Religious Traditions.* New York: Haworth Press.

Miller, J.B. (1986). *Toward a New Psychology of Women* (2nd edn.). Boston: Beacon Press.

Miller, J.G. (1984). "Culture and the Development of Everyday Social Explanation." *Journal of Personality and Social Psychology, 46*: 961-78.

Misra, G. (2001). "Culture and Self: Implications for Psychological Inquiry." *Journal of Indian Psychology, 19*: 1-20.

Misra, G. and R. Giri (1995). "Is Indian Self-predominantly Interdependent?" *Journal of Indian Psychology, 11*: 15-19.

Misumi, J. (1985). *The Behavioural Science of Leadership: An Interdisciplinary Japanese Research Programme.* Ann Arbor, MI: University of Michigan Press.

Mitchell, Katherine (2008). *Vivaha Samskara: The Marriage Rite.* http://www.mahavidya.ca/wp-content/uploads/2008/06/mitchell-katherine-vivaha.pdf

Monier-Williams, Monier (1899). *A Sanskrit-English Dictionary.* Delhi. Motilal Banarsidass.

Moser, D. (1989). If This Paper were in Chinese, would Chinese People Understand the Title? Unpublished manuscript, Indiana University.

Mosig, Y. (1990, Spring). "Wisdom and Compassion: What the Buddha Taught". *Platte Valley Review,* 51-62.

Much, N. (1995). "Cultural Psychology." In J.A. Smith, R. Harre, and L.V. Langenhove (Eds.), *Rethinking Psychology.* New Delhi: Sage.

Murphy, G. and L.B. Murphy (Eds.) (1968). *Asian Psychology.* New York: Basic Books.

Murphy, M. and S. Donovan (1988). *The Physical and Psychological Effects of Meditation*. San Rafael, CA: Esalen Institute.

Murray, H.A. (1938). *Explorations in Personality*. New York: Oxford University Press.

Myers, D. (1989). *Social Psychology* (3rd edn.). New York: McGraw Hill.

Nanamoli, B. and B. Bodhi (1995). *The Middle Length Discourses of the Buddha* (*A Translation of the Majjhima Nikaya*). Wisdom Publications.

Nasr, S. (1987). *Islamic Spirituality: Foundations*. New York: Crossroads.

Nurbakhsh, J. (1990). "Sufism and Psychoanalysis". *Sufi*, *5*: 5-10.

Ornstein, R.E. (1972). *The Psychology of Consciousness*. San Francisco: W.H. Freeman.

Pandey, R.B. (1962, reprint 2003). "The Hindu Sacraments (*Saṁskāra*)". In S. Radhakrishnan (ed.), *The cultural heritage of India*, Vol. II (pp. 391-92), Kolkata: The Ramakrishna Mission Institute of Culture.

Pandey, Rajbali (1969, reprint 2006). *Hindu Samskaras: Socio-religious Study of the Hindu Sacraments*. Delhi: Motilal Banarsidass.

Pandey, Rajbali (1993).*The Sixteen Saṁskāras*. New Delhi: Motilal Banarsidass. Production Board of Gujarat.

Paranjpe, A. (1998). *Self and Identity in Modern Psychology and Indian Thought*. New York: Plenum Press.

Paranjpe, A.C. (1975). *In Search of Identity*. New York: Halsted Press/Wiley.

Paranjpe, A.C. (2008). "Sri Ramana Maharshi: A case Study in Self-realisation". In K. Ramakrishna Rao, A.C. Paranjpe, and A.K. Dalal (Eds.), *Handbook of Indian Psychology* (pp. 564-76), New Delhi: Cambridge University Press, India.

Paranjpe, A.C. (2010). "Theories of Self and Cognition: Indian Psychological Perspectives". *Psychology of Developing Societies, 22*(5).

Pearsall, P. (2003). *The Beethoven Factor: The New Positive Psychology of Hardiness, Happiness, Healing and Hope*. Hampton Roads Publishing.

Pennebaker, J.W. (1982). *The Psychology of Physical Symptoms*. New York: Springer Verlag.

Perls, F. (1969). *Gestalt Therapy Verbatim*. Real People Press.

Perry, W.N. (1971). *A Treasury of Traditional Wisdom*. New York: Simon & Schuster.

Polly, Y.E. and Hall, J. (1991). *Jung's Self-psychology, a Constructivists' Perspective*. New York: The Guilford Publications.

Prabhavananda, S. and F. Manchester (1969). *The Upanishads: Breath of the Eternal*. New York: New American Library, Mentor Books.

Purani, A.B. (1963). *Studies in Vedic Interpretation*. Varanasi: Chowkambha Sanskrit Series.

Qayyum, A. (1976). *Letters of Al-Ghazali*. Lahore, Pakistan: Islamic Publication.

Radha Swami (1978). *Kundalini: Yoga for the West*. Spokane. WA: Timeless Books.

Rahman, F. (1982). *Islam and Modernity: Transformation of An Intellectual Tradition*. University of Chicago Press.

Rama, S. (1982). *Enlightenment Without God: Mandukya Upanishad*, Honesdale, PA: Himalayan Institute.

Rama, S. and S. Ajaya, (1976). *Emotion to Enlightenment*. Honesdale, PA: Himalayan Institute.

Rama, Swami., Ballentine, R. and Swami Ajaya (1976). *Yoga and Psychotherapy*. Honesdale, PA: Himalayan Institute.

Ramachandra Rao, S.K. (1962). *Development of Indian Psychological Thought*. Mysore, India: Kavyalaya Publishers.

Ramakrishna Rao, K.B. (1966). *Theism of Pre-classical Samkhya*. Mysore, India: Prasaranga, University of Mysore.

Ramanujan, A.K. (1990). "Is There an Indian Way of Thinking?: An Informal Essay." In M. Marriott (Ed.), *India Through Hindu Categories*. New Delhi: Sage.

Ramaswami Aiyer, C.P. (1969). *The Cultural Heritage of India*, Vol. II, Calcutta: The Ramakrishna Mission Institute.

Ramaswami, S. and A. Sheikh (1989). "Buddhist Psychology: Implications for Healing". In A. Sheikh and K. Sheikh (Eds.), *Eastern and Western Approaches to Healing*. Wiley.

Rao, K.R. and A.C. Paranjpe (2016). *Psychology in the Indian Tradition*. Springer.

Read, H., M. Fordham and G. Adler (1953-80). *The Collected Works of C.G. Jung* (Trans. by R.F.C. Hull). Bollingen Series, No. 20, 18 volumes. Princeton, N.J.: Princeton University Press; London: Routledge and Kegan Paul.

Reynolds, D. (1980). *The Quiet Therapies*. University of Hawaii.

Reynolds, D. (1984). *Playing Ball on Running Water*. Morrow.

Reynolds, D. (1993). *Plunging Through the Clouds*. State University of New York.

Rodrigues, H.P. (2006). *Introducing Hinduism*. New York: Routledge.

Roeser, R.W. (2005). "An Introduction to Hindu India's Contemplative Psychological Perspectives on Motivation, Self, and Development". In M.L. Maehr and S. Karabenick (Eds.), *Advances in Motivation and Achievement*, Vol. 14: *Religion and and Motivation* (pp. 297-345), Amsterdam: Elseveir.

Roland, A. (1988). *In Search of Self in India and Japan: Toward a Cross-cultural Psychology*. Princeton, NJ: Princeton University Press.

Rosaldo, M.Z. (1984). "Toward an Anthropology of Self and Feeling." In R.A. Shweder, and R.A. LeVine (Eds.), *Culture Theory: Essays on Mind, Self, and Emotion* (pp. 137-57). Cambridge University Press.

Roseman, I.J. (1984). "Cognitive Determinants of Emotion: A Structural Theory." In P. Shaver (Ed.), *Review of Personality in Social Psychology* (5: 11-36). Beverly Hills, CA: Sage.

Ross, M. and G.J.O. Fletcher (1985). "Attribution and Social Perception." In G. Lindzey, and E. Aronson (Eds.), *The Handbook of Social Psychology*, *2*(3): 73-122, New York: Random House.

Rushbrook Williams, L.F. (1974). *Sufi Studies: East and West*. UK: Tonbridge Printers Ltd.

Sachhidananda Saraswathi, Swami (1956). *Chhandogya Upanishad*. Kannada translation with commentary of Sri Śaṅkaracharya. Holenarshipura, Karnataka, India: Adhy*ātmā* Prakasha Karyalaya.

Safaya, R. (1976) *Indian Psychology: A Critical and Historical Analysis of the Psychological Speculations in Indian Philosophical Literature.* New Delhi: Munshiram Manoharlal.

Saikal, A. (1990). "'Islam Resistance and Reassertion' in the World Today". In G.W. Choudhary (Ed.), *Islam and the Contemporary World.* London: Indus Thames Publisher Limited.

Salagame , K.K.K. and A. Raj (1999). "Ahamkara and Ego Functions Among Meditators and Normals." *Journal of Indian Psychology, 17*(1): 46-55.

Salagame, K.K.K. (1988). "States of Consciousness: Perspectives from Modern Psychology." In M.A.S. Rajan (Ed.), *Consciousness: Proceedings of the Workshop.* Melkote, India: The Academy of Sanskrit Research.

Salagame, K.K.K. (2006). *Concepts of Self and Identity in Indian Thought and Their Implications for Mental Health Profession.* Psycho award oration delivered at the 32nd Annual Conference of the Indian Association of Clinical Psychologists, Jaipur.

Salagame, K.K.K., A. Raj, K.P. Murthy, N. Parimala, K. Rekha and S. Gaur (2005). "Concept Ahamkara: Theoretical and Empirical Analysis." In K.R. Rao (Ed.), *Towards a Spiritual Psychology: Essays in Indian Psychology.* New Delhi: Samveda Publishers.

Sampson, E.E. (1989). "The Challenge of Social Change for Psychology: Globalization and Psychology's Theory of the Person." *American Psychologist, 44*: 914-21.

Sarvananda, Swami (1976). *Mandukya Upanishad.* English translation with a summary of Gaudapada's Karika. Madras: Sri Ramakrishna Math.

Scharfstein, B.A. (1974). *Mystical Experience.* Baltimore: Penguin. (Originally published, 1973).

Scherer, K.R. (1984). "Emotions as a Multi-component Process: A Model and Some Cross Cultural Data." In P. Shaver (Ed.), *Review of Personality and Social Psychology: Emotions, Relationships, and Health* (pp. 37-63). Beverly Hills, CA: Sage.

Schimmel, A. (1975). *Mystical Dimensions of Islam.* Chapel Hill: University of North Carolina Press.

Schwartz, J.M. and W.P. Smith (1976). "Social Comparison and the Inference of Ability Difference." *Journal of Personality and Social Psychology, 34:* 1268-75.

Scotton, B.W., A.B. Chinen and J.R. Battista (1996). *Textbook of Transpersonal Psychiatry and Psychology*. New York: Basic books.

Sen, I. (1998). *Integral Psychology: The Psychological System of Sri Aurobindo*. Sri Aurobindo International Centre for Education, Pondicherry, India.

Shaffi, M. (1985). *Freedom from the Self.* USA: Human Sciences Press Inc.

Shah, I. (1980). *The Way of the Sufi.* UK: The Octagon Press Ltd.

Shah, S. (1933). *Islamic Sufism*. London : Rider

Shankara (1978). *Crest-jewel of Discrimination*. (Translated by Swami Prabhavananda and Christopher Isherwood). Hollywood, California: Vedanta Press.

Shapiro, D. and R. Walsh (Eds.). (1984). *Meditation: Classic and Contemporary Perspectives*. Aldine.

Shapiro, D. (1980). *Meditation: Self-regulation Strategy and Altered States of Consciousness.* Aldine.

Sharma, Arvind. (1985). "Marriage in the Hindu Religious Tradition". *Journal of Ecumencial Studies*, *22*(1): 69-80.

Sharma, Subramanya (1947). *Prasna Upanishad.* Kannada translation with commentary of Sri Saṅkaracharya. Holenarsipura, Karnataka, India: Adhyatma Prakasha Karyalaya.

Shaver, P., J. Schwartz, D. Kirson and C. O'Connor (1987). "Emotion Knowledge: Further Exploration of a Prototype Approach." *Journal of Personality and Social Psychology, 52*: 1061-86.

Shelat, B.K. (1993). *Bharatiya Samskaro*. Amdavad: University Book.

Sheng-yen (1987). *The Advantages one May Derive from Zen Meditation.* Dharma Drum.

Shiah, Y.J. (2016). "From Self to Nonself: The Nonself Theory". *Frontiers in Psychology*, *7*: 112. https://doi.org/10.3389/fpsyg.2016.00124

Shiah, Y.J. and K.T. Yit (2012). "Adopting the Buddhist Concept of Nature of Death and Life Impermanence in Investigating the Death Terror". *Indigenous Psychological Research Journal of China. 36*: 167-89. https://doi:10.6254/2012.38.167

Shikanai, K. (1978). "Effects of Self-esteem on Attribution of Success-failure." *Japanese Journal of Experimental Social Psychology, 18*: 47-55.

Shonin, E., W. Van Gordon and M.D. Griffiths (2014). "The Emerging Role of Buddhism in Clinical Psychology: Toward Effective Integration". *Psychology of Religion and Spirituality, 6*: 123-37. https://doi:10.1037/a0035859

Shrutiprakashdas, Shastri, Shastri Parmananad Dave, and Shastri Ghanshyam Shukla (1998). *Naimittikkarmaprakashaha.* Gandhinagar: AARSH, Akshardham.

Shweder, R.A. and E.J. Bourne (1984). "Does the Concept of the Person Vary Cross-culturally?" In R.A. Shweder and R.A. LeVine (Eds.), *Culture Theory: Essays on Mind, Self, and Emotion* (pp. 158-99), Cambridge University Press.

Shweder, R.A., N.C. Much, M. Mahapatra and L. Park (1997). "The Big Three of Morality (Autonomy, Community, Divinity) and the Big Three Explanations of Suffering." In A. Brandt and P. Rozin (Eds.), *Morality and Health.* New York: Routledge and Kegan Paul.

Singelis, T.M. and W.F. Sharkey (1995), "Culture, Self-construal, and Embarrassability." *Journal of Cross Cultural Psychology, 26*: 622-44.

Sinha, D. (1965). "Integration of Modern Psychology with Indian Thought. *Journal of Humanistic Psychology, 5*: 6-17.

Sinha, D. and R.C. Tripathi (1994). "Individualism in a Collectivist Culture: A Case of Co-existence of Opposites." In U. Kim, H.C. Triandis, C. Kagitcibasi, S. Choi, and G. Yoon (Eds.), *Individualism and Collectivism: Theory, Method, and Applications* (pp. 123-36). California: Sage Publication.

Sinha, J. (1961). *Indian Psychology,* Vol. 2: *Emotions and Will.* Delhi : Motilal Banarsidass.

Sinha, J.B.P. (1990). "The Salient Indian Values and Their Socio-ecological Roots. *Indian Journal of Social Sciences, 3*: 477-88.

Sinha, J.B.P. and R.N. Kanungo (1997). "Context Sensitivity and Balancing in Organisational Behaviour". *International Journal of Psychology, 32*: 93-105.

Sinha, J.B.P. and A. Pandey (2007). "Indian's Mindsets and the Conditions that Evoke Them." *Psychological Studies*, *52*: 1-11.

Sinha, J.B.P. and J. Verma (1987). "Structure of Collectivism." In C. Kagitcibasi (Ed.), *Growth and Progress in Cross-cultural Psychology* (pp. 123-29). Lisse: Swets and Zeitlinger.

Sinha, J.B.P., T.N. Sinha, J. Verma and R.B.N. Sinha (2001). "Collectivism Coexisting with Individualism: An Indian Scenario." *Asian Journal of Social Psychology*, *4*: 133-45.

Sinha, Jadunath (1961). *Indian Psychology* Vol. 2: *Emotions and Will*. Delhi: Motilal Banarsidass.

Smith, C. and Ellsworth, P.C. (1987). "Patterns of Appraisal and Emotion Related to Taking an Exam". *Journal of Personality and Social Psychology*, *52*: 475-88.

Soeng, M. (1991). *Heart sutra: Ancient Buddhist Wisdom in the Light of Quantum Reality*. Primary Point.

Solomon, R.C. (1984). "Getting Angry: The Jamesian Theory of Emotion in Anthropology." In R.A. Shweder and R.A. LeVine (Eds.), *Culture Theory: Essays on Mind, Self, and Emotion* (pp. 238-54). Cambridge, England: Cambridge University Press.

Sri Aurobindo (1994). *Essays Divine and Human*. Sri Aurobindo Ashram, Pondicherry, India.

Srimat Swami Saradanandaji Maharaj (1952). *Sri Ramakrishna: The Great Master*.

Srinivasan, G. (1967). *The Existential Concepts and the Hindu Philosophical Systems*. Allahabad, India: Udayana Publishing.

Srivastava, R. and G. Misra (1997). "Self-construal, Control and Eastern Orientation". Unpublished manuscript, Department of Psychology, University of Delhi: New Delhi.

Staal, F. (1975). *Exploring Mysticism*. Harmondsworth: Penguin.

Starrett, G. (1998). *Putting Islam to Work: Education, Politics, and Religious Transformation in Egypt*. Berkeley: University of California Press.

Steele, C. (1988). "The Psychology of Self-affirmation: Sustaining the Integrity of the Self." In L. Berkowitz (Ed.), *Advances in Experimental Social Psychology*, *21*: 181-227, SanDiago, CA: Academic Press.

Stevenson, H., H. Azuma and K. Hakuta (1986). *Child Development and Education in Japan*. New York: Freeman.

Stewart, A.J. and M.B. Lykes (Eds.) (1985). "Conceptualising Gender in Personality Theory and Research." *In Gender and Personality: Current Perspectives on Theory and Research* (pp. 2-13). Durham, NC: Duke University Press.

Stipek, D., B. Weiner and K. Li (1989). "Testing Some Attribution-emotion Relations in the People's Republic of China." *Journal of Personality and Social Psychology*, *56*: 109-16.

Stoddart, W. (1981). *Sufism: The Mystical Doctrines and Methods of Islam.* Lahore: Suhail Academy.

Stolaroff, M.J. (1999). "Are Psychedelics Useful in the Practice of Buddhism?" *Journal of Humanistic Psychology* , *39*(1): 60-80.

Suraṅgama-samādhisūtra (2003). (Trans. E. Lamotte and S. Boin–Webb) *Suraṅgama-samādhisūtra: The Concentration of Heroic Progress*. New Delhi: Motilal Banarsidass (Date of original text uncertain).

Sutich, A.J. (1969). "Some Considerations Regarding Transpersonal Psychology." *Journal of Transpersonal Psychology*, *1*(1): 15-16.

Suzuki, S. (1997). *Branching Streams Flow in the Darkness: Zen Talks on the Sandokai.* University of California Press.

Suzuki, S. (2002). *Not Always so: Practicing the True Spirit of Zen.* HarperCollins.

Swami Sivananda. (1997). *All About Hinduism.* A Divine Life Society Publication.

Swann, W.B. Jr. and S.J. Read (1981). "Self-verification Processes: How We Sustain Our Self-conceptions." *Journal of Experimental Social Psychology*, *17*: 351-72.

Swargiary, K. (2023, October 18). Sāṁkhya Philosophy. *Research Gate*. https://www. researchgate.net/publication/374582107

Takata, T. (1987). "Self-deprecative Tendencies in Self-evaluations Through Social Comparison." *Japanese Journal of Experimental Social Psychology*, *27*: 27-36.

Tart, C. (1972). *Altered States of Consciousness* (2nd edn.) Garden City, N.Y.: Doubleday/Anchor Books. (First edition, 1969).

Tart, C.T. (1969). *Altered States of Consciousness: Book of readings.* New York: John Wiley & Sons.

Tart, C.T. (1975). *Transpersonal Psychologies: Perspectives on the Mind from Seven Great Spiritual Traditions*. San Francisco: Harper Collins.

Tathagatananda, S. (n.d.). *Fundamental Principles of Vedānta.* Vedānta Society of New York. https://www.vedāntany.org/articles/blog-post-title-two-6txr3

Taylor, S.E. and J.D. Brown (1988). "Illusion and Well-being: A Social Psychological Perspective on Mental Health." *Psychological Bulletin, 103*: 193-210.

Tesser, A. (1986). "Some Effects of Self-evaluations Maintenance on Cognition and Action." In R.M. Sorrentino and E.T. Higgins (Eds.), *Handbook of Motivation and Cognition: Foundations of Social Behaviour* (pp. 435-64). New York: Guilford Press.

The Mother (1978/1999). *On Education.* Pondicherry: Sri Aurobindo Ashram Publication Department.

Triandis, H.C. (1989). "The Self and Social Behaviour in Differing Cultural Contexts." *Psychological Review, 96*: 506-20.

Trimingham, J.S. (1973). *The Sufi Orders in Islam.* Oxford Publishing House.

Tripathi, R.C. and U. Leviatan (2003). "Individualism and Collectivism: In Search of a Product or Process." *Culture and Psychology, 9*: 79-88.

Tsong-Kha-Pa (2000). *The Great Treatise on the Stages of the Path to Enlightenment* (Trans. T. Lamrin Chenmo Translation Committee). Snow Lion Publications.

Varma, P. K. (2004). *Being Indian: The Truth about Why the 21st Century will be India's.* New Delhi: Viking.

Vivekpriyadas, Sadhu (1998). *Apano Samskrutik Varaso*, Part 2. Amdavad: Swaminarayan Aksharpith.

Wada, M. (1988). "Information Seeking in Self-evaluations of Ability (Abstract)." *In Proceedings of Japanese Psychological Association Meeting, 52*: 222.

Wallace, B.A. and S.L. Shapiro (2006). "Mental Balance and Well-being: Building Bridges between Buddhism and Western Psychology". *American Psychology, 61*: 690-701. https://doi: 10.1037/0003-066x.61.7.690

Wallace, R.K. (1970). *The Physiological Effects of Transcendental Meditation.* Los Angeles: Students International Meditation Society.

Watson, R.I. (1978). *The Great Psychologists* (4th edn.). Philadelphia: Lippincott.

Watt, W.M. (1963). *The Faith and Practice of Al-Ghazali*. USA: Oneworld Publication.

Weiner, B. (1986). *An Attributional Theory of Emotion and Motivation*. New York: Springer Verlag.

Weisz, J.R., F.M. Rothbaum and T.C. Blackburn (1984). "Standing Out and Standing in: The Psychology of Control in America and Japan." *American Psychologist*, *39*: 955-69.

Wenger, M.A., B.K. Bagchi and B.K. Anand (1971). "Experiments in India on "Voluntary" Control of Heart and Pulse". In J. Kamiya, N.E. Miller, D. Shapiro and J. Stoyva (Eds.), *Biofeedback and Self-control: An Aldine Reader on the Regulation of Bodily Processes and Consciousness*. Chicago: Aldine/Atherton. (Reprinted from *Circulation,* 1961: 24).

Whitley, B.E., Jr. and Frieze, I.H. (1985). "Children's Causal Attributions for Success and Failure in Achievement Settings: A Meta-analysis." *Journal of Educational Psychology, 77*: 608-16.

Wylie, R.C. (1979). *The Self-concept,* Vol. 2: *Theory and Research on Selected Topics*. Lincoln: University of Nebraska Press.

Yang, K.S. (1982). "Causal Attributions of Academic Success and Failure and Their Affective Consequences." *Acta Psychologica Taiwanica*, *24*: 65-83 (From Psychological Abstracts, 1985: 72, Abstract No. 13126).

Yang, K.S. and W.H. Liang (1973). "Some Correlates of Achievement Motivation Among Chinese High School Boys" (In Chinese). *Acta Psychologica Taiwanica*, *15*: 59-67.

Yogananda, P. (1972). *The Autobiography of a Yogi*. Los Angeles: Self- realisation Fellowship.

Zuckerman, M. (1979). "Attribution of Success and Failure Revisited, or: The Motivational Bias is Alive and well in Attribution Theory." *Journal of Personality*, *47*: 245-87.

Index